FOOD AND THE MEMORY

PROCEEDINGS OF THE OXFORD SYMPOSIUM
ON FOOD AND COOKERY 2000

FOOD AND THE MEMORY

PROCEEDINGS OF THE OXFORD SYMPOSIUM
ON FOOD AND COOKERY 2000

EDITED
BY
HARLAN WALKER

PROSPECT BOOKS
2001

Published in 2001 by Prospect Books, Allaleigh House, Blackawton, Totnes, Devon TQ9 7DL, England

©2001 as a collection Prospect Books (but ©2001 in individual articles rests with the authors)

Designed and typeset by Jennifer Campbell and Tom Jaine.
Printed by the Cromwell Press, Trowbridge, Wiltshire.

ISBN 1 903018 16 1

The cover illustration, 'Anchovy and Cleopatra', is by Simon Drew.

Contents

Folk Tale Memories as Illustrated and Interpreted in the
Fairy Story of Hansel and Gretel 11
   Joan P. Alcock

Madeleines and Other Aides-mémoire: the Importance of
Food References in Proust's *Recherche* 22
   Rose Arnold

Omiyage: Constructed Memories and Reconstructed Travel in Japan 31
   Michael Ashkenazi

The Language of Flavour: Learning and Memory 39
   Anthony Blake

Amarcord: the Flavour of Buried Memories 49
   John F. Carafoli

Spice Memories 56
   Fred Czarra

Dining With the Caesars 62
   Andrew Dalby

Journeys through Smell and Taste: Home, Self, Identity 89
   Ferda Erdinç

Whisky Sours, Flapjacks and Woodsmoke: a Century
in the Life of an Adirondack Picnic 100
   Elizabeth Field

Memories of M.F.K. Fisher 107
   Geraldene Holt

Memory as a Culinary Skill and Necessity 115
   Philip Iddison

Remembrance of Meals Past: Cooking by Apicius' Book 123
   Cathy K. Kaufman

The Diet of the Greeks: 'Genetic' and Recent Memories 131
   Sotiris Kitrilakis and Lidia Kitrilakis

Food as a Vehicle for Remembering: the Case of the
Thessalonikan Jews 136
   Vasiliki Kravva

Notes on an Eighteenth-century Manuscript Recipe Book 145
   Janet Laurence

Food History and the Death of Memory 157
   Gerald Mars and Valerie Mars

The Digest of Memory: Food, Health and Upbringing in
Early Childhood 163
   Stephen Massil

Damra Bound: Indian Echoes in Guyanese Foodways 173
   Gaitri Pagrach-Chandra

A Scientific Approach to Flavours and Olfactory Memory 185
   Marcia Levin Pelchat and Fritz Blank

Learning by Mouth: Edible Aids to Literacy 192
   Gillian Riley

Food and Forgetfulness at Socratic Symposia 199
   Luciana Romeri

The Memory Factor in American Breakfast Joints 205
   Robert Rubright

Devouring the City 210
   Alice Wooledge Salmon

From Pharmacy to Fast Food: the Evolution of the Persian Kitchen 216
   Margaret Shaida

A Slice of the Moon 223
   Sue Shephard

The Bialy Eaters: the Story of a Bread and a Lost World 238
   Mimi Sheraton

Passionate for the Pasty: the Cornish Pasty in Michigan's
Upper Peninsula 245
   Leslie Cory Shoemaker

False Memories: the Invention of Culinary Fakelore and Food Fallacies . 254
   Andrew F. Smith

Memories of a Vanishing Eskimo Cuisine 261
   Zona Spray

Prisoners of the Rising Sun: Food Memories of American POWs
in the Far East During World War II 273
   Jan Thompson

Between Their Memories and Mine: Confit Revisited 287
   Renée Valeri

The Velveeta Chronicles: a Food Memoir 294
   Phyllis Weaver

Memories of a Time, Place and People where Food Nurtured
Intimate Social Community Values: Thai Street Vendors,
a Vanishing Human Connection 304
   Su-Mei Yu

Breakfast in Memory 308
   Sami Zubaida

Other Papers Given at the Symposium 313

List of Those Attending the Symposium 316

Introduction

This volume of papers presented at the Oxford Symposium on Food and Cookery follows the pattern of previous collections. The Symposium entitled *Food and the Memory* was held in September 2000 at Saint Antony's College, Oxford, under the joint chairmanship of Alan Davidson and Dr Theodore Zeldin.

Again, the success of the Symposium resulted in the number of papers being such that it has not been possible to publish them all. A list of the papers given in Oxford but which are not in this volume is given on pages x–y below.

We must also mention the talk by Daphne Derven about the American Center for Wine, Food and the Arts which will open in Napa, California, in November 2001. Its purpose will be to explore the distinctly American contribution to the character of wine and food in close association with the arts and humanities. She quoted Bran Ferren on the subject of museums and similar organizations connected with history as it is involved with physical activities: 'The ability to effectively establish and understand context, both sensory context as well as historical context…is what institutions do…people go there because they are taking something valuable away with them.' She hoped that many of the people who come to our Symposium may visit and perhaps take part in the activities of this new centre.

On Saturday evening we enjoyed a Roman banquet, devised and supervised by Sally Grainger. This was tremendous fun as well as surprising and delicious. Andrew Dalby selected and hand-delivered appropriate wines for this ancient feast. We are very grateful to them both as well as to the Oxford University Press for kindly hosting the dinner, with particular thanks to the organizers Graham Oulds, Karen Ohm, and Frank O'Hara the chef.

Our thanks go to St Antony's for hosting our Symposium once again: to Charles White in the conference office, Nigel Sherwood in the kitchen and in particular to the steward Tony Squirrell and all his staff who supported us through the weekend.

We would also like to thank the following for their help: Lidia and Sotiris Kitrilakis, who yet again provided one of the most delicious, fresh and simple Sunday lunches from Greece, assisted by Patricia Michelson; Alex Veness (our logo designer) and Ben Walker, who helped them bring it all together in time for lunch, besides helping with registration, problem solving and running repairs to faulty equipment; Patsy Iddison and Helen Saberi who ran the Bring & Buy with charm and efficiency, raising a record amount of money in the process; Dan Schickentanz, who yet again supplied all of our bread for the weekend, and devised for us a new range of Roman loaves.

And of course we must thank Jane Levi, who makes everything that we do actually happen and happen so agreeably and apparently easily. Few of us are aware of the endless effort and hard work that goes on throughout the year to give us all the pleasure that we have in this weekend in Oxford.

Harlan Walker
June 2001

Folk Tale Memories as Illustrated and Interpreted in the Fairy Story of Hansel and Gretel

Joan P. Alcock

The moral fairy story

Memories of food may be linked to memorable meals; childhood memories are often connected with hunger. When children live in poverty, food is linked to deprivation, both physical and mental, for they feel betrayed by the food providers. This theme is the basis of many fairy stories, part of a collective memory of fable and tradition handed down through generations, and particularly in the story of *Hansel and Gretel*. The folk tale, collected by the Brothers Grimm, was elaborated in editions, published between 1812 and 1858, moving from oral tradition (tales to be told) to *Buchmärchen* (books to be read). The twentieth century attributed to it political interpretations or saw it as a vehicle for black humour. The story was expanded when it inspired Humperdinck's opera in 1893. Visual interpretations of the opera, in two modern versions, produced respectively in 1987 and 1998, emphasized the links between poverty, plenty and childhood fantasies. With imagination and wit, both operas provided comprehension of a child's rite of passage through stages of hunger and gluttony. If *Hansel and Gretel* was initially a *Kinderstuben-weihfestspiel*, as the composer Humperdinck called it, then the operatic audience was to be disabused. The message was clear: childhood memories of food may be the stuff of nightmares.

The Brothers Grimm

The story of *Hansel and Gretel*, one of many collected by the Brothers Grimm, may be based on a Neapolitan story, *Nenello e Nennella*, first printed in a collection of stories *Lo Cunto de li Cunti* by Gianbattista Basile (1634). Jacob (1785–1863) and Wilhelm (1786–1859) Grimm (one might almost begin their life history by the words 'Once upon a time') collected folk tales mainly, as Jacob stated, because these were part of continuous oral tradition (Zipes 1988).

Both Jacob, who followed a political career, and Wilhelm, who was appointed to the Kassel Royal Library, steadily enhanced their collection, including stories from Austria, Bavaria, Bohemia, Hesse and Switzerland. Between 1830 and 1837 the brothers were professors at the University of Göttingen, but after the revocation of the Hanoverian Constitution by King Ernest August II in 1837, they accepted an invitation from Frederick William IV of Prussia to become professors at the University of Berlin. Jacob resigned in 1848 to become a representative to the newly formed parliament at Frankfurt, which was to create a constitution for a united Germany; he withdrew within a few months, disillusioned with the lack of liberal progress. After Wilhelm resigned his professorship, both brothers devoted themselves to research in literature, history, jurisprudence and collecting folk tales until Wilhelm's death in 1859 and Jacob's in 1863.

German folk tales
The manuscript edition of the folk tales dates from 1810. The Grimms were inspired to publish the stories because Achim von Arnim and Clemens Brentano had published a collection of folk tales, *Des Knaben Wunderhorn*, which drew on German oral tradition (Michaelis-Jena 1970, 47). The Grimms' first volume was published in 1812; seven more editions followed, the last in 1858. The brothers altered and refined the stories, adding details and indirect speech to create what Jacob referred to as 'everlasting food for the young and open-minded.'

There was more to it than this. The Brothers Grimm did not, as they implied, gather their stories from German peasants, but from the middle classes (Psaar and Klein 1976). Jacob stated in the preface to the first edition that several stories had come from Dorothea Viehmännin, a peasant woman telling tales known in the Hesse region. She, however, was of French origin, one of a large community of Huguenots settled in the region (Ellis 1985, 32) more familiar with the fairy stories of Charles Perrault and certainly not a transmitter of German fairy stories. In fact Henriette Dorothea Wild, a middle-class woman, whom Wilhelm later married, told many stories to the brothers. The Grimms' stories drew on folk memories but were designed to cultivate a bourgeois, historical tradition, linked to the cult of emerging German nationalism (Zipes 1983, 59).

In many tales a previous memory lingers. In *Snow White* the queen orders the huntsman to take Snow White into the forest and bring back lungs and liver as evidence that she has been killed. Lungs and liver were the humblest portions (the umbles) taken by the huntsman when the deer was killed; the gentry received the venison. The *Snow White* huntsman gave the umbles to the palace cook to be baked in a pie for the queen to eat.

The queen, however, is not merely eating food; in primitive folk memory, the eater acquires the power and characteristics of what is eaten. Thus the

queen hungers for the youth and beauty of Snow White (Bettelheim 1976, 207). The ogre stepmother, like the witch in *Hansel and Gretel*, is cannibalistic. Both long for human meat, raw in the case of the stepmother of Snow White and the mother-in-law in Charles Perrault's *Sleeping Beauty*. The latter story contains a neat twist. The dish is served in a piquant sauce; we are, after all, in France. An English translation in 1750 condescendingly provides the recipe as a French sauce made of onions, shredded and boiled tender in bouillon, to which are added vinegar, mustard, salt, pepper and a little wine.

Before Snow White meets the dwarfs she eats just a little from each of their plates and drinks a drop from each glass. This delicacy of tasting indicates her noble birth; Hansel and Gretel gorge themselves on the witch's house with the hunger of the peasant class, the same peasant hunger as when Goldilocks eats all the porridge in Perrault's story.

The apple in the story of *Snow White* stands for love and sex, for both of which she hungers. An apple has both benevolent and dangerous aspects. It is the memory of the apple given to Eve and the apple of Aphrodite, the cause of the Trojan Wars. The queen eats the whole apple, which is harmless; Snow

White eats only the red part, which is the dangerous part, for this is the end of innocence and the beginning of sexual knowledge.

In modern versions our memory of these stories is given a jolt. 'Once upon a time there was a prince who found a sleeping Snow White. And, since she lay there so beautiful and peaceful, he slit her throat, took her apple and ate it himself' (Schrauff 1982). Perhaps Heinz Langer's cartoon (1984) may be preferred; two dwarfs stand by a glass coffin in which Snow White lies with an apple core protruding from her mouth. The dwarfs are hitching a lift. Down the road appears a hearse. Thus are childhood memories destroyed.

Hansel and Gretel

Nowhere is the elaboration of the folk tales clearer than in *Hansel and Gretel*. In the 1810 manuscript the children are not named; they are called Little Brother and Little Sister. The mother is their real mother and not their stepmother. The children are abandoned in the forest because the household lacks food. They are given a piece of bread, the constant antidote to hunger. The first time they find their way home by following pebbles dropped by Hansel, a memory of being given stones for bread; the second time he drops breadcrumbs, which the birds eat. Once lost in the forest, they find a little house, bread walls, cake roof, sugar windows. In it is a little old woman. The boy is fattened on 'good food'; the girl is given crab shells to eat, 'because she is not to be fattened'. After the old woman is burned in the oven, the children steal her jewels and return home.

The children are given names in the first edition (1812). They are left in the forest because 'there was nothing to eat and scarcely daily bread'. They eat much of the house before the 'old woman who was a wicked witch' caught them. Descriptive detail includes the feeding of Hansel, the pushing of the witch into the oven and her screaming and wailing. The father greets the children joyfully on their return and the conflict between him and the children is played down.

In the second edition (1815) the witch serves them milk and pancakes with sugar, apples and nuts, simple food which the children remember from the past. She gazes at them and murmurs, 'that will be a nice morsel for me.' Details are given of the house, the making of dough, the oven and the escape. An older memory is linked to the rhyme which is introduced. When Gretel nibbles at the house a voice calls out:

Nibble, nibble, gnaw,
who is nibbling at my little house?

In the opera this is put more picturesquely:

Nibble, nibble mousekins, (*Knusper, knusper, knäuschen*)
Who's nibbling at my housekins? (*Wer knuspert mir am Häuschen?*)

The children pause, then say, reassured:

The wind, the wind, the heavenly child
(*Der Wind, der Wind, das himmlische Kind*)

Wilhelm Grimm in his preface to the 1812 edition refers to a saying, 'Flour for snow', and to an older story, not by the Grimm brothers, where a miller and a baker are fighting each other by throwing our. The proverb and the story link to an old custom in which people threw flour out of the window during a snow storm to feed and calm the greedy wind:

Calm down dear wind, (*Lege dich, lieber Wind*)
Bring this to your child. (*Bring dies deinem Kind*)

In the fourth edition (1840) the mother becomes a stepmother. Given the high mortality rate of women during childbearing years, the introduction of a stepmother into a household was probably a frequent occurrence (Weber 1981). The emphasis changes as she becomes a food-withholding person, centred firmly in the traditional childhood memory as a wicked stepmother. Everything has been eaten up, 'we don't have half a loaf of bread in the house.' Here the memory is of an old German proverb, 'Need was everywhere apparent in the house' (Mieder 1986), which refers to lack of food or the inability of the housewife to provide food. By the fifth edition (1843), the stepmother is saying that if they do not abandon the children, 'we shall all four die of hunger, you can just smooth the boards for the coffin.'

Through the story runs folk memory. In the seventeenth century the states of Germany suffered from brutal wars, the Thirty Years' War (1618–48) being one of the most destructive, when marauding armies fought their battles on German soil. In particular the Swedish invasion of 1630 created such devastation, especially as the troops brought plague with them, that whole areas suffered from famine. Children were orphaned and abandoned and travellers reported cases of cannibalism (Beneke 1978, 37; Robinson 1906, 207). For peasants, especially, the imaginative and magic elements of tales about houses of food and hidden treasure had specific attraction.

In the eighteenth century war still despoiled parts of Germany, particularly in Prussia during the reign of Frederick the Great (1740–86). The Napoleonic Wars were to bring more problems, including cases of infanticide and child abuse, and it was not until 1815 that Europe began to reverse the effects of hunger and famine. In fact, at the beginning of the story in the fifth edition,

Wilhelm Grimm introduces the theme of a devastating famine, indicating a social concern for the welfare of a country shattered by war.

An even more distant memory can be noted in the fact that Hansel is placed in a cage. Each day the witch checks him to see if he has become fatter; each day he pokes out a bone to deceive her. During the Reformation dissidents were placed in cages and left to starve. The most famous case was that of the Anabaptist revolt in Münster (1534–35), which resulted in the tortured bodies of the leaders being placed in cages, still to be seen on the cathedral steeple.

Witchcraft and witch-hunting were endemic in Europe, especially Southern Germany, until the seventeenth century. Witches, often lonely old women, were accused of stealing and eating children. The transmogrification of the old woman into a witch is therefore a logical step, as is the fact that she wanted to eat Hansel. She is seeking food in the midst of a forest, a desolate place. Here cannibalism is linked with the predatory role of the older female on the young male. It is the young female who saves her sibling. The witch is also a parasite symbolizing feudal greed and brutality. The children, acting as adults, justify her killing.

Modern versions
Modern versions bring in social and political nuances. In a neat reversal of the story (Lerche and Gmelin 1978), the witch is not a witch but an outcast who lives by her wits, gathering food where she can. She does not want to eat children, but to exploit them and place obstacles in their quest for food. Poor parents are not enemies of the children, rather poverty is the source of their troubles. The children wander in the forest and return with nothing. There is no house, there are no jewels. The authors emphasize co-operation to a left-wing readership. The children may be active in determining their own fate but have no memory of hunger because the state will provide.

During the 1930s folklore had been encouraged as emphasizing Germanic traditions, Nordic cultural heritage and the role of a folk community triumphing over difficulties, especially with the help of a strong leader (Zipes 1983). Both Hansel and Gretel play leadership roles in their story. In 1945, the occupying forces in Germany banned their publication arguing that interpretation along racist and elitist lines was partly responsible for the attitudes which had led to the acceptance of the Nazis (Kamenetsky 1972; Kamenetsky 1977). They gave children false impressions making them susceptible to lies and irrationality (Zipes 1993, 167).

Maar (1968) sympathizes with the witch who was a kind woman giving food and shelter to the children as she remembered being given these in her childhood. The ungrateful children murdered her. Their only concern is to fill their stomachs and steal her jewels. This underlined his point that modern children have no respect for old age and was an ironic comment on the materialistic, selfish well-being of West Germans in the 1950s.

Hans Traxler (1963) creates a brilliant satire on the earnest scholarly discussion then taking place on Germanic folklore. An amateur archaeologist investigates through recently discovered manuscripts, excavations, and photographic evidence a theory that Hansel and Gretel were bakers who wanted the recipe for the *Nürnberger Lebkuchen* from an old woman living alone in a wooded area of Hesse. The excavation is precisely located at a spot next to the autobahn linking Frankfurt to Würzburg. Excavation of an artificial mound uncovers the original gingerbread house and the ossified remains of *Lebkuchen* and other sweets. The report concludes that the child-bakers killed the witch and stole the recipe to make their fortune.

Black humour in America utilizes the premise that 'the gingerbread house is an image nobody forgets' (Bettelheim 1976, 161). Cartoons show houses containing 'glucose, dry skimmed milk, oil of peppermint, dextrose, etc' or labelled 'no saccharin' (*New Yorker Album of Drawings 1925–75*; *Ladies Home Journal*, November 1977). Hansel, sniffing at the chimney, eagerly says to Gretel, 'Let's go in. Someone's smoking pot' (*Playboy*, August 1969). The witch, driving down the road with a gingerbread house trailer, pulls up, 'Hi, Kids! Want a lift?' Adult humour plays on the memory of warning children about modern day perils (Mieder 1987, 31).

The health lobby is not forgotten. A Swiss cartoon has the children refusing to enter, '*Nein danke, wir essen nur Bro-Kost*' ('No thanks, we only eat health food') (Mieder 1987, 33). Equally sophisticated children remark to the witch, 'Gingerbread? Really? How did you get a mortgage?' (*Better Homes and Gardens*, March 1977). And the witch is a loser in a modern sense. An estate agent says to a smirking Hansel and Gretel, prospective buyers, 'We just listed it. Some punks vandalized the place and cooked the owner' (*San Francisco Chronicle*, 21 March 1980). Adult humour draws on childhood memories of bedtime tales.

The last word lies with Laurie Anderson (1990), who disillusioned children of their childhood memories:

> Hansel and Gretel are alive and well,
> And they're living in Berlin.
> She is a cocktail waitress;
> He has a part in a Fassbinder film,
> And they sit around at night now
> Drinking Schnapps and gin.

The opera

The composer Engelbert Humperdinck (1854–1921) was directed to the story by his sister, Adelheid Wette. She had devised a dramatic version giving to the parents the names Gertrud and Peter. They did not deliberately wish to get rid of the children. The accident of breaking the milk jug caused the mother to lose her temper and provoked the rash action. Adelheid added the characters of the Sandman, the Dew Fairy and choruses of echoes and angels. Humperdinck added the 'redeemed gingerbread children' (*Kinderkuchen*) saved by Hansel and Gretel from the witch's spell.

Humperdinck created a singspiel for Adelheid's play, later expanded into the full-length opera, to a libretto by his sister. This was first performed with great success at Weimar on 23 December 1893. Its Deutsche-Romantik success made it difficult for the composer to follow with a work of comparable stature. 'Everything is either bloody murder, rubbishy operetta or simpering fairy tales,' he exclaimed in 1895, referring to the many librettos offered to him. Eventually he composed his only other opera of note, *Königskinder* (Children of Kings), first performed in 1910 at the Metropolitan Opera, New York.

English National Opera

The usual versions of the opera pass over the theme of hunger, mostly emphasizing traditional German cultural aspects. The English National Opera highlighted hunger, particularly childhood memories of hunger, and a vision of life seen through the eyes of a child. The kitchen incorporated the flimsy utility furniture, china sink and geyser of the post-1945 kitchen, capturing the post-war nostalgia for a safe world, already being destroyed. The household is on the breadline. Father is drunk with a half bottle of gin in his pocket; mother wears shabby clothes, but transmogrifies into the witch so that the children's memories become a nightmare.

The wood becomes a park, haunted by tramps and flashers, but the children are protected by their memories. In a dazzling sequence their guardian angels in shining white clothes surround them – familiar figures from their ordinary lives – postman, policeman, milkman with his pint bottles, cinema salesgirl bearing a tray of Kia-Ora cartons (a neat period touch). Mother and father are a young newly-married couple presented by the baker with a wedding/birthday cake, lit with candles.

The children greedily attack the witch's house. It is, according to the witch, 'a place a child could go mad in. There are apple tarts and meringues like snow, chocolate mousse, Black Forest gateaux. There's buttermilk and cream that's so good in, your favourite, yes, I know, it's rice pudding.' Her kitchen is the same utility kitchen decked out with red checked gingham to hide its now evil aspect. The children's memories have added colour to it. The witch/mother tempts 'I love little children to have them for tea,' a sinister double meaning.

Once the witch is in the oven the house splits in two, revealing the gingerbread children who rise from their graves by the awakening touches of Hansel and Gretel. The witch, brought from the oven, is now a scarecrow, her head a loaf of bread, which the children tear apart. Their memory, on wakening, is for the staple food of life.

Welsh National Opera
In the Welsh National Opera production hunger is again dominant, as the front curtain, displaying an empty plate, establishes. Before the second act begins it appears again, smeared with blood, a knife and fork across it. What memory is this trying to awake?

In the bleak kitchen, sparsely furnished, the children dream of food; they are hungry and cold: 'For it is hunger which bites me.' Lack of food dominates, but once the children have been driven out, the father arrives with food and the mother cooks him bacon and eggs. Here is the desired food, which the children could not have.

In the forest, the children pick berries smearing themselves with juice as if bloodying themselves. But as they sleep, a masterly scene unfolds. Fourteen angel-winged, porcine creatures, precisely dressed as chefs, set a long table, supervised by a fish-headed, Magritte-like butler. The children sit, now in evening dress, driven by memories of adult behaviour at a banquet. The chefs place silver salvers on the table, then raise the covers to reveal delicacies, all the food for which the children have longed. It is a culinary choreographic ballet in masterly precision.

As the children wake a vast mouth appears. Through it comes a huge chocolate cake, five slices high, resting on a vivid red tongue. This symbolic witch's house is a child's vision of over-indulgence set between fearsome teeth. The kitchen is part catering establishment, part abattoir – steel walls, steel oven, steel table – with a battery of knives, saws and meat cleavers. Children's dreams have become nightmares, especially when a man portrays the witch. He/she places Hansel on a salver, trussed ready for roasting, hands, feet and head dressed with paper crowns. Memories of eating become one of being eaten and the cannibalistic witch is no longer the terror in dreams but an omnipresent reality.

Tossing ingredients into the food processor, the witch force-feeds Hansel like a Périgord goose, but Gretel manipulates the witch into the oven, now food to be cooked for eating. Then Hansel and Gretel indulge in a deranged dance amidst the food debris. The revitalized gingerbread children, freed from the spell, pull the charred body of the witch from the oven and tuck into it frenziedly. Memories flood in of horrifying scenes in concentration camps and famine regions where anything remotely edible is greedily eaten. This opera is a memory of a fundamental urge: our craving for food and what we will do to satisfy that urge.

Conclusion

Hansel and Gretel draws on children's memories and perceptions. Poverty and deprivation force the parents to discuss abandoning their children. Hansel and Gretel, lying awake with hunger, overhear this discussion. How often does a child, awakening hungry in the dark, feel rejected by the Mother who is the source of food? The Grimm brothers had felt the loss of their mother keenly. In a letter to Wilhelm on 10 September 1809, Jacob wrote, 'since her death, our house is uncomfortable .... and there is no longer any order at meal times' (Grimm, Hinrichs and Schoof 1963, 156). In both interpretations of the opera the children are driven out because they break the milk jug thus destroying the mother's food.

Their abandonment in the forest is the ultimate rejection. It is not surprising that they fantasize about food and out of this memory springs the house. It is a bread, cake and sugar house; only in the twentieth century does it become a gingerbread house. Bread is the staple food, cake the extravagance, the rich man's food, and sugar the craving for the sweets denied to them. This house they fall on and destroy. There is no thought that it could give them shelter and certainly not for any occupant. They think nothing of eating it because, according to Bettelheim (1976, 170), 'it symbolically stands for the bad mother, who has deserted them.' Memory is entirely linked to hunger. 'The house,' comments Bettelheim (1963, 161), 'stands for oral greediness and how attractive it is to give in to it,' a concept disconcertingly displayed in the Welsh National Opera cake set between gaping jaws.

But oral greediness can lead to destruction. In the case of *Hansel and Gretel* the agent is a cannibalistic witch. It is noticeable, however, both in later editions of the story and in the opera, that the stepmother/mother goes with the father to seek the children and joins in the general rejoicing at the end. Thus the mother becomes the food provider again. The lesson is learned both in reality and in the fairy story that uncontrolled voraciousness cannot be tolerated and the memory of that must be the controlling element. As the German poet, Schiller, wrote, 'deeper meaning resides in the fairy tales told to me in my childhood than in that taught to me in life.'

BIBLIOGRAPHY

Anderson, L. (1990) 'The Dream Before', in *Strange Angels*, Audio Tape, Warner Bros 1989, Collected Video, Warner Reprise Video, 1990.
Basile, Gianbattista. (1634-46) *Lo Cunto de li Cunti*, ed. Rak, M. (1987), Milan: Gazanti.
Beneke, G. (1978) *Germany in the Thirty Years' War*, London: Arnold.
Bettelheim, B. (1976) *The Uses of Enchantment. The Meaning and Importance of Fairy Tales*, London: Penguin.
Ellis, J.M. (1985) *One Fairy Tale Too Many. The Brothers Grimm and the Tales*, Chicago: Chicago University Press.
Grimm, H., Hinrichs, G., and Schoof, H. (eds.) (1963) *Briefwechsel zwischen Jacob und Wilhelm Grimm aus der Jungenzeit*, Weimar: Herman Böhlhaus.
Grimm, J. and Grimm, W. (1812 and 1815) *Kinder – und Hausmärchen, Gesammelt durch die Brüder Grimm*, 2 vols., Berlin. Subsequent editions 1819, 1837, 1840, 1843, 1850, 1858.
Hasse, D. (1993) *The Reception of Grimm's Fairy Stories*, Detroit: Wayne State University Press.
Kamenetsky, C. (1972) 'Folklore as a Political Tool in Nazi Germany', in *Journal of American Folklore*, 85, pp. 221–35.
——— (1977) 'Folklore and Ideology in the Third Reich', in *Journal of American Folklore*, 90, pp. 168–78.
Langer, H. (1984) *Grimmige Märchen*, Munich: Hugendubel.
Lerche, D. and Gmelin, O.F. (1978) *Märchen für Tapfere Mädchen*, Giessen: Schlot.
Maar, P. (1968) *Die Geschichte vom bösen Hänsel, der bösen Gretel und der Hexe*, Hamburg: Oetinger.
Michaelis-Jena, R. (1970) *The Brothers Grimm*, London: Routledge and Kegan Paul.
Mieder, W. (1986) 'Wilhelm Grimm's Proverbial Additions in the Fairy Tale', in *Proverbium*, 3, pp. 59–83.
——— (1987) *Tradition and Innovation in Folk Literature*, Hanover: University Press of New England.
New Yorker Album of Drawings 1925–75, (1975) New York: Viking Press.
Psaar, W. and Klein, M. (1976) *Wer hat Angst vor der bösen Geiss?*, Braunschwig: Westermann.
Perrault's Complete Fairy Tales, (1961) London: Penguin, Kestrel Books.
Robinson, J.H. (1906) *Readings in European History*, London: Ginn and Co.
Schrauff, C. (1986) *Der Wolf und seine Steine*, Hanover: SOAK.
Traxler, H. (1963) *Die Wahrheit über Hänsel und Gretel. Die Dokumentation der Märchens Brüder Grimm*, Frankfurt am Main: Bärmeier und Nikel.
Weber, E. (1981) 'Fairies and Hard Facts: the Reality of Folklore', in *Journal of the History of Ideas*, 42, pp. 93–113.
Williams, G.H. (1962) *The Radical Revolution*, Philadelphia: Westminster Press.
Zipes, J. (1983) *Fairy Tales and the Art of Subversion*, London: Heinemann.
——— (1988) *The Brothers Grimm. From the Enchanted Forest to the Modern World*, New York: Routledge.
——— (1993) 'The struggle for the Grimms' Throne. The Legacy of the Grimms' Tales in the FDR and the GDR since 1945' in Hasse, D. *The Reception of Grimm's Fairy Stories*, pp. 167–206.

Madeleines and Other Aides-mémoire: the Importance of Food References in Proust's *Recherche*

Rose Arnold

Tasting the novel

Proust's *A la recherche du temps perdu* is, arguably, the greatest novel of the twentieth century. An enormous, protean work, it was the fruit of a whole lifetime, unfinished at the time of the author's death in 1922. The three final volumes were still unpublished, and Proust was annotating the text; as with *Persuasion*, the reader can see and understand work in progress. Proust more than once evinces Michaelangelo's giants emerging from the rock, an appropriate analogy for the novel. So it is with considerable trepidation that I focus in this paper on the ways in which Proust makes use of food references in *A la recherche*. The novel is a web of psychological insights, philosophical exploration, social comedy and historical re-creation, centring on the attempt to recapture the past, to redeem 'lost time'. References to food – to flavour and scent, to the sight of spread tables and the sounds of dining – are only a small part of Proust's complexity. They may, however, both interest in their own right and provide ways of viewing the great novel as a whole.

In the novel, Proust seeks to investigate the springs of memory and to overcome the tyranny of the moment. The culmination of the opening section of the first part, *Combray*, has become recognized as the quintessence of such scenes. The narrator, who had concluded that the past was lost, irrecoverable, finds 'the immense edifice of memory' surge up out of the serendipitous putting to his mouth of a piece of madeleine dipped in tea:

> ...immediately the old grey house on the street...came like a theatrical backdrop...and with the house, the town, the Square where they sent me before lunch, the streets, from morning to night, and in all sorts of weather, where I used to run errands, the lanes along which we used to walk if it was fine. And – like that game in which the Japanese amuse

themselves, soaking in porcelain bowls little pieces of apparently shapeless paper which, no sooner immersed, unfold, twist, take colour, differentiate themselves, becoming flowers, houses, people, solid and recognizable – in just that way now all the flowers of our garden and those of M. Swann's park, and the waterlilies on the Vivonne, and the good people of the village and the church and all Combray and its surroundings, everything taking on form and solidity, emerged, town and gardens, from my cup of tea.[1]

Most novels aim to create the illusion of reality, and the evocation of the reader's sensory experience is an avenue by which this may be achieved. Like Coleridge building Kubla Khan's palace before us upon the intensity of remembered music, so Proust involves all our senses in his *recherche*. A disciple of Ruskin, he can make us see hawthorn blossom in Pre-Raphaelite detail; we listen as yearningly as Swann for the re-emergence of the 'little phrase' in Vinteuil's sonata; we feel the textures of materials and flesh; we smell the lilac. Often, though, it is on the sense of taste, and all its concomitant references to the preparation, serving, consumption and digestion of food that Proust relies. 'On y mange beaucoup, et partout.'

There is a second advantage to such heavy reliance upon evocation of food, however, beside that of tapping into our shared sensory experience. By referring to food, an author is able, for social and historical verisimilitude, to invoke customs and behaviour connected with it. Since Proust was a snob and a considerable gourmet, given to treating his friends at the Ritz, and since his subject-matter was on one level the social snobberies and glamour of the *belle époque*, it should not surprise us that his work has much exercised food historians of different kinds. The sumptuous *Proust: la cuisine retrouvé*[2] combines the knowledge of noted Proustian Anne Borrel with the practical gastronomic expertise of Alain Senderens and the photographic skill of J-B Naudin. The result is the most flamboyant display imaginable of what Roland Barthes identified as *cuisine ornementale*, food re-invented to appeal to a less earthy sense, that of sight.[3] We are in the *côté de Guermantes* of the novel, the glamorous, aristocratic world of fashion and breeding, the desirable, rarefied air of the Faubourg St Germain. And food is for show, for gazing at. One re-creation to be found in it is of the pineapple and truffle salad served as part of the great set-piece dinner given by the Narrator's parents for M. de Norpois near the start of *A l'ombre des jeunes filles en fleurs*.[4] The recipe could not be simpler: one slices a fresh pineapple and a fresh black truffle, interleaves the slices, and leaves the flavours to mingle. The photograph by itself is spectacular. As for the combination of aroma and taste – not having a fresh truffle to hand,

I am content to accept J-P. Richard's analysis of the reluctance of M. de Norpois to take a second helping of the dish:

> He undoubtedly objected to the excessive disparity of this food. Between the two terms of the combination, too great a gustative (if not geographical) distance declared itself too provocatively.[5]

The domestic, bourgeois, normal family aspect of the *côté de chez Swann* is well exemplified, and contrasted with the flash of Borrel/Naudin/Senderens, in the chapter on Proust in Jane Grigson's *Food with the Famous*.[6] The quiet supremacy here of the written word, the gentle erudition, the unostentatious familiarity with Proust's novel, are all typical of Grigson's writing, and tap into the values which in *A la recherche* are linked to the Narrator's family roots in Combray, and, through the figure of Françoise the cook, to the whole history and culture of France. To illustrate the difference: Grigson and Senderens both give recipes for the little madeleines which trigger the theme of the novel. Before giving her recipe, which includes orange-flower water, Grigson comments, 'I sometimes feel that the many brands of madeleines on sale in France in plastic bags – some of quite good quality – have been made from the easier pound-cake mixture (4oz each of butter, sugar, self-raising flour, eggs – i.e. 2 eggs).' Senderens' recipe specifies precisely this heavier two-egg mixture, and omits the orange-flower water. Of course, it is Françoise from Combray who also prepares the pineapple and truffle salad in Paris, and so the glamorous world and the world of solid values become linked, just as, in the final volume of the novel, the Narrator realizes that the divergent paths, the Guermantes Way and Swann's Way, really merge into a circle – if one goes just a little bit further. The two Ways are also synthesized by time with the introduction, at the very end of the novel, of the lovely Mlle de St Loup, granddaughter of Swann and great-niece of the Duchesse de Guermantes.

The beloved past: Combray

The early pages of *A la recherche* imagine the people of the dead past as imprisoned in everyday things, impotent to communicate with us unless we summon them, but ready to spring back into being under the spell of our love, our attention, and the magical power of our – all too occasional – escapes from habit and boredom. The eating of the madeleine dipped in tea is just such a summoning, a 'recognition' which allows the past back to life.

Proust's first loving restoration is of childhood summers spent in Illiers, a small town on the *petit* Loir, built round a church which resembles 'a great golden holy brioche'.[7] Marcel is an only child, cosseted and scolded in the midst of an extended family which has as its pivot the ambivalent figure of

Françoise the cook. She is seen as a sort of embodiment of the history of the French people, and is endued with virtues such as loyalty and endurance, but also with vices – cruelty, sentimentality, snobbery, hypocrisy: 'there was latent in her some past existence in the ancient history of France', colouring her notions and beliefs. To the family, Françoise is an utterly devoted retainer, providing comforts both physical and psychological. The child Marcel sees her on New Year's Day, 'framed in the small doorway of the corridor like the statue of a saint in its niche.' To her kitchen he goes in delighted anticipation of the pleasures of the table:

> ...the menu for dinner was of fresh interest to me daily, like the news in a paper, and excited me as might the programme of a coming festivity.[8]

Later, we see the adolescent Marcel showing a similar avid attention to theatre posters on a *colonne Morris* near his Parisian home, and there is an important analogy between the boy's two interests. Both food and theatre embody and carry forward a national culture, and so Françoise really does embody France – as surely as the diva Berma whose *Phèdre* the boy longs to see – though less consciously.

The early part of the novel re-creates a simple, bourgeois, rural life *chez tante Léonie*, whose *petit train-train* is as self-restricted as Proust's own later became, and as luxurious. May and June are characterized by after-dinner drinks in the garden, by leisurely evening strolls, by the heady scents of hawthorn and lilac. The season is dominated by asparagus:

> ...tinged with ultramarine and pink which shaded off from their heads, finely stippled in mauve and azure, through a series of infinite gradations to their white feet – still stained a little by the soil of their garden-bed – with an iridescence which is not of this world. I felt that these celestial hues indicated the presence of exquisite creatures who had been pleased to assume vegetable form and who, through the disguise of their firm, comestible flesh, allowed me to discern in the radiance of earliest dawn, these hinted rainbows, these blue evening shades, that precious quality which I should recognize again when, all night long after a dinner at which I had partaken of them, they played (lyrical and coarse in their jesting as the fairies in Shakespeare's *Dream*) at transforming my chamber pot into a vase of aromatic perfume.[9]

It emerges, and is part of the boy Marcel's growing understanding of human complexity, that Françoise, so benign to him, is putting asparagus on the menu almost every day in order to torment the pregnant kitchen-maid, nicknamed 'Giotto's *Charity*', who is allergic to the vegetable. The boy also witnesses

Françoise's cruel enjoyment of killing the chicken which later he enjoys eating, despite feeling that his enjoyment makes him complicit in her sadism. The overwhelming impression in *Combray*, however, is of the freshest and best local produce, exquisitely prepared by Françoise, consumed at leisure and as part of a gentle, pleasant routine:

> ...the chicken...was to furnish me, in place of the poetic pleasure of the walk, with the sensual pleasures of good feeding, warmth and rest.[10]

Social comedy: the Guermantes aspect of A la recherche

The Narrator of Proust's novel grows up obsessed by the Faubourg St Germain. He adores titles, high living, exquisite manners, social exclusivity and fashion. One of the fascinations of the novel is that one cannot quite dissociate Proust the author from the Marcel who narrates. Proust was himself a through-going snob, as the magnificent biography by George Painter[11] makes clear and we find ourselves, as we read, complicit in his snobbery. Part of his purpose was to hymn the *belle époque*, the world of beauty, style, decorum and tradition which vanished with the First World War. Another part, since Proust was a master ironist, was to satirize the denizens of this world, showing them as shallow, brittle, hypocritical and casually cruel. In this aspect of the novel, food historians find themselves focusing on meals and dining-rooms. These loci and events may be seen as metonyms, in that they form only a part of the fabric of realistic background which Proust weaves from references to theatre, to fashion, to politics (notably to the Dreyfus case and, in *Le Temps retrouvé*, the First World War). A dinner, especially in Paris, is an opportunity to impress, to give pleasure, and to influence the influential.

Proust's own habits, especially after the death of his mother in 1905, were neurotic and bizarre. Cocooned in his cork-lined room, he slept by day and woke to work, and to socialize, by night. He would occasionally entertain a single guest to a meal. He himself would consume nothing but hot milk, but the food for the guest would have been the subject of earnest discussion with his faithful Céleste, its components chosen with scrupulous care. At other times, Proust took guests to the Ritz, insisting on hosting dinner parties at extraordinary hours of the morning, and of course prepared to pay handsomely for his eccentricity. At these dinners, he ate nothing, but moved his seat so that he was near all his guests for some of the time. By this time, Proust's life – as well as his fiction – was composed of memory. Eating was not an active pleasure for him, but he observed that others took pleasure in food, and wished to provide that pleasure for them. His own interest lay in the *appearances* of luxury and munificence, his pleasure in the expressions of appreciation by others. There is an important sense in which this distancing, or dislocation, is also a facet of *A la recherche*. It is striking that, in a novel so full of loving references to the appearance, preparation, serving and consumption of food, Proust has almost nothing to say about either taste or texture. For him there was dissociation between the pleasure (social, aesthetic, perhaps snobbish) of giving a dinner, and the normal gustatory pleasure of the table. This dissociation (itself only one aspect of Proust's neurotic response to sensual pleasure in general) is evident in the novel. In a work which is rich in gastronomic *mise-en-scène*, and full of metaphoric food references, almost no words are used to define, describe or characterize actual tastes. There is, of course, one exception to that – Proust's madeleine, that most famous of all taste allusions. We shall come to the madeleine in due course.

The set-piece dinners of *A la recherche* are social and visual. Proust's evocations of setting are unforgettable: the cosy camaraderie of Doncières, the cool seaside breeze in the great dining-room of the hotel at Balbec, the warm dusk of the garden at Combray, the stresses of dinner with the Verdurins at la Raspalière with its spectacular marine views. Always there is a sense of that decorum which almost amounts to performance. Proust's characters are part of a drama which we watch through the eyes of the Narrator, sharing his appreciation and amusement, and also his self-consciousness.

Proust was a celebrated writer of literary pastiche, and perhaps the most spectacular account of a display dinner-party, at the Verdurins' in the time of Swann and Odette which forms a sort of parallel prehistory for the Narrator, is cast as an extract from an unpublished journal by the Goncourt brothers. The Verdurins are comic grotesques, patrons of the arts and eventual conquerors of the social scene. They are very rich, very hospitable, and very domineering. The pastiche builds up from a lyrical description of plates, precious and beautiful, 'an extraordinary cavalcade of plates which are nothing less than masterpieces of the porcelainist's art.' On these wonderful plates and dishes is served 'a meal most subtly concocted...'

> Even the foie gras bears no resemblance to the insipid mousse customarily served under that name; and I do not know of many places in which a simple potato salad is made as it is here with potatoes firm as Japanese ivory buttons and patina'd like those little ivory spoons with which Chinese women sprinkle water over their new-caught fish. Into the Venetian glass which I have before me is poured, like a rich cascade of red jewels, an extraordinary Léoville bought at M. Montalivet's sale, and it is a delight to the imagination of the eye...to see a brill placed before us...on a wonderful Ching Hon dish streaked with the purple rays of a sun setting above a sea upon which ludicrously sails a flotilla of large lobsters...[12]

The enthusiastic prose eventually disengages from the food (and the sentence), and moves to a more detailed and ironically pointed description of the personalities present and their conversation. What can be seen in the quotation just cited, though, is the way in which the decoration and the food become confused, so that it is not at first clear whether the lobsters are as corporeal and digestible as the brill, or part of the design on the plate, and so a feast for the eyes only. Food for display indeed!

Sometimes, particularly in the Guermantes parts of the novel, almost no reference is made to the food on the table: we concentrate upon the interaction of the guests, and may take for granted that their food is as luxurious and beautiful as their clothes. Particularly in the earlier volumes, however, where the settings are more likely to be in the Narrator's family home and therefore within the ambit of Françoise, the menus of meals are very lovingly detailed. Nowhere is this more true than in the meal already mentioned, given by the Narrator's parents for the grand and sententious M. de Norpois, at which the pineapple and truffle salad is served.

Food as metaphor

The main course of the dinner for M. de Norpois consists of *bœuf à la gelée*. This is also referred to as *une daube de bœuf* and as *le bœuf froid aux carottes*. Kilmartin for some reason refers to it as 'cold spiced beef'. Only at the end of *Le Temps retrouvé* is it finally – and properly – called *bœuf à la mode*. It is in its preparation that Françoise becomes 'the Michelangelo of our kitchen', and the meat is 'couched...upon enormous crystals of aspic, like transparent blocks of quartz.' Proust develops the analogy with Michaelangelo as he describes Françoise choosing the raw materials of the dish at Les Halles, as if she were at Carrara, choosing the very best of the *carrés de romsteck*, along with shin of beef and a calf's foot. This type of cuisine, which distils the essence from various ingredients, converting them into something refined, reduced, essential, lies of course at the heart of French cookery. It is also a metaphor, as Proust well knew, for the human memory – for the very core of the novel. Right at the end of the final volume, in pages which make explicit the Bergsonian philosophy which inspired him, Proust has his narrator plan to make his projected book from:

> numerous impressions derived from many girls, many churches, many sonatas and combined to form a single sonata, a single church, a single girl, so that I should be making my book in the same way that Françoise made that 'bœuf à la mode' which M. de Norpois found so delicious, just because she had enriched its jelly with so many carefully chosen pieces of meat.[13]

The limpid, delicious jelly surrounding the beef may be taken as a metaphor for the art of the writer, surrounding, sustaining and presenting his subject-matter. 'The meat fills and enriches the jelly, which in turn surrounds and supports the meat, and keeps it all of a piece.'[14]

But if Proust uses the image of a meat dish to explain the fullness of his revivification of the dead past, the spring from which the great novel grew in the first place was the remembered taste of the *petite madeleine* dipped in tea. (For some reason this tea has entered into folklore as lime-blossom tisane, *tilleul*. This is true even in Alan Davidson's wonderful *Oxford Companion to Food*, whose every entry is pure *bœuf à la mode*.) The Narrator remarks that he was unaccustomed to drinking tea, and so the invoking of an 'involuntary' memory became possible in the combination of its taste with that of the little cake. The madeleine is well known, a common, pleasant, ordinary commodity on supermarket shelves all over France. It has, however, a history. We know that the equivalent experience in real life for Proust involved eating a *biscotte* or a piece of toast dipped in tea. So why this transmutation?

The name of the cake goes back only to the mid-eighteenth century, all authorities agree. It is said to have been the invention of a cook named Madeleine Paulmier, and named after her. As is so often the case, the authorities trace back to a single source, in this case Grimod de la Reynière's *Almanach des gourmands* (1803–1812). Extensive hunting through this wonderful source-book, however, failed to turn up the reference. What I did find, though, in one of the dictionaries I consulted during the hunt, was a use of *des madeleines,* attributed to Colette, to mean what, I think, were called *goffering* irons in English: instruments for crimping ruffs and frills. There is a direct analogy here with the underneath of a madeleine, moulded in a fluted tin. The name for the iron itself may well have come from the pleated wimples of nuns, some orders of whom were called Madeleines. Françoise is described as having her face framed by 'the frills of a snowy bonnet as stiff and fragile as...spun sugar'[15] in the Narrator's earliest memory of her. But Proust is also evoking old memories in a way connected with the shape, rather than the name, of the cake. He describes the madeleine as a 'little scallop-shell...so richly sensual under its severe, religious folds.'[16] The cakes are moulded in tins which echo (though less precisely in the case of *véritables petites madeleines de Commercy*, which are longer and narrower) the scallop-shell badge of the pilgrim to St James of Compostella. One of the ancient roads to Santiago passed through Illiers-Combray, and its church is dedicated to that saint. So in the small crumb from which the enormous individual memory rises, the germ of the novel, we also have a distillation of all the cultural richness of collective memory.

Strawberry cream and orangeade

It has been calculated[17] that there are 142 references to food and drink in just the first volume of *A la recherche*, and that in the work as a whole 225 different edible or potable commodities are mentioned. This paper has really done little more than look at the most developed, for the novel is full of delightful details such as the comparison of pink hawthorn blossom to strawberries mashed into crème fraîche, the elegant sipping of orangeade at Guermantes' receptions (another memory trigger, this time in *Le Temps retrouvé*), or Albertine's enthusiastic enumeration of ice-cream flavours, to take a few examples.

Proust uses food references in order to give verisimilitude to his descriptions. The cultivated Swann, for example, is a source for recipes as well as an arbiter of fashion and an expert on art history. So gastronomy is part of the tissue of social display and, beyond that, of culture itself. And taste and food images throughout the novel enhance our understanding of the novel's philosophical and psychological bases. The sense of taste opens the novel, as the Narrator's route to the re-creation of the 'solid and recognizable' past. Gastronomic reference, to the *bœuf à la mode* which is Françoise's masterpiece, sums up, after 3,000 and more pages, the value of the memories evoked. And food and drink references, as both metonymy and metaphor, have been important ingredients in the miraculous spell by which Art can annihilate Time.

REFERENCES

Apart from titles, I have used the Scott-Moncrieff/Kilmartin translation published by Penguin under the title *Remembrance of Things Past* (1983). References, marked *RTP*, cite volumes in Roman numerals, pages in Arabic numbers.

[1] *RTP*, I, 51.
[2] 1991; as *Dining with Proust*, Ebury Press, 1992.
[3] R. Barthes, *Mythologies*, 1957.
[4] *RTP*, I, 465 ff.
[5] J-P Richard, op. cit.
[6] Penguin, 1981.
[7] Illiers, in Eure-et-Loir, is now renamed Illiers-Combray.
[8] *RTP*, I, 129.
[9] *RTP*, I, 131.
[10] *RTP*, I, 145.
[11] Chatto & Windus, 1959 (Penguin 1983).
[12] *RTP*, III, 731.
[13] *RTP*, III, 1091.
[14] J-P Richard, op. cit.
[15] *RTP*, I, 57.
[16] *RTP*, I, 50.
[17] Colette Cosnier, 'Gastronomie de Proust', in *Europe* (496–7).

Omiyage: Constructed Memories and Reconstructed Travel in Japan

Michael Ashkenazi

Introduction

Gift-giving, or 'prestation' as anthropologists would have it, is a universal human phenomenon. It is, as Mauss (1966) noted, a polysemic activity: in the guise of a disinterested sacrifice, we actually negotiate for and acquire prestige, social credit, and other non-material goods.

One of the most common forms of gift-giving is the presentation of food. Food forms such an important part of gift-giving for a number of reasons: food is an 'intimate' gift, implying comfort and closeness; food is a primary need for humans and offering it implies emotional support; and food is a gift which covers a wide range of prices, and can thus be made appropriate for almost any occasion.

Japanese gift-giving is an elaborate and important part of social interaction. As with many institutions in Japanese society, gift-exchanges are highly ritualized and elaborate forms of social interaction. There are specific and determinate rules for the types of gift, its wrapping (Hendry 1993) and the seasons it is to be offered (Moeran and Skov 1997). In many instances, gifts can be made of cash (Brumann 2000), more rarely of goods. The most common gifts, however, are gifts of food, which are accompanied by extensive and significant protocols.

Related to the issue of food is the issue of travel. The Japanese have been inveterate tourists since the seventeenth century. Tourist services, which started as services to pilgrims, had become a major economic sector by the eighteenth century. Today, Japanese tourists in various categories and guises trot the globe with their needs being catered to by a massive infrastructure within and outside Japan. Food is a major element in this industry. Several of my acquaintances have told me in the past that they never travelled without *furikake* (flaked seaweed and other condiments) to make their rice overseas more palatable.

The tourism and gift industries come together in the universal Japanese institution of *omiyage*. Literally 'earth [local] produce', *omiyage* are gifts brought by travellers to the stay-at-homes. In most cases, such gifts are gifts of food, and, supposedly, represent the *meibutsu*, the 'famous product' of the area or site visited. This demand, of course, produces a supply of goods and a dynamic of its own. In this paper I want to explore the phenomenon of *omiyage* in two ways: the kinds of *omiyage*, and the mechanisms by which they are created and disseminated on the one hand, and the sort of memory that they are intended to recall, and, more often, to create.

The omiyage *phenomenon*

Virtually every rural and urban tourist destination in Japan, and many metropolitan ones, have food items for sale. Many of these items are fascinating in themselves, sometimes similar to those on offer in other countries, sometimes radically different. These *omiyage* are prepacked and wrapped local produce intended as gifts. In the past two decades, the number of *omiyage* offered throughout the country has radically increased. This is directly related to the issue of modernization, and what DeWitt Smith calls the 'metropolitization' of Japanese society. Japan, like, for example, the UK, is a central-metropolis culture, in which most power and resources are controlled by and emanate from the central city, in this case, Tokyo. As the regions have become wealthy and successful, and as the strains of relations with metropolitan domination grow, so is there a perceived need for regions, towns, and villages to identify and enhance their differences. This is important for the retention of their own populace (which they have been losing at a frightening rate to the metropolitan areas) as well as to generate new incomes for themselves.

As a direct result, famous products and would-be famous products have captured a slice of the market. This slice, however, is limited in two ways: firstly, the market it is a part of is that associated with luxury goods, that is, for the average shopper, it is part of disposable, not dedicated, income. Secondly, as more and more areas climb on the bandwagon, the cake is sliced into smaller and smaller pieces.

What characterizes food *omiyage*, and to a lesser extent all *omiyage*, is the need on the one hand to appeal to commonly acceptable tastes while, at the same time, distinguishing the product from other similar products and identifying it with its place of origin. This in turn often implies either the existence, or no less often, the creation, of a 'traditional' provenance.

To take one example, a trout farm, in an area not known traditionally for its fish, now markets special *omiyage* of lightly salted trout *sushi*. These are wrapped, as tradition dictates, in bamboo leaves (said to preserve freshness), and much is made, on the wrapper, of the traditional freshness and goodness of the food. That the fishery has been in existence for not much more than twenty years is not noted anywhere.

Omiyage also need, of course, to stand out. They must be something that will be remembered and will remind the user of the place. In truth, although some *omiyage* do evoke a feeling or memory, many do not. But the distinction, whether of the wrapping or of the contents, is important as a merchandising and advertising ploy. One such example, 'A selection of pickles from Akita,' contains small plastic sachets of various pickles: tiny Chinese artichokes (*chorogi*), bamboo shoots, wild mushrooms, coltsfoot (*fuki*) and so on. Each sachet is in a separate compartment in a flat box. Alas, the whole is made of wood-painted foam rather than of real wood.

The foods sold as *omiyage* cover the entire range of food products. Traditionally, of course, perishable foods were useless as *omiyage*, and thus traditional *omiyage* tended to be preserves, dried foodstuffs, and others with long shelf lives. The traditional importance of this quality is recorded culturally in two important food artefacts, one of which is familiar to non-Japanese audiences. *Sushi*, the food that is almost synonymous with Japanese cuisine, was created originally as a way of preserving fish for travelling, and for the conveyance of gifts of fish. The vinegared rice was intended to preserve the salted fish. Eventually, with the passage of years, and in a process similar to what happened with peasant foods in France (Mennel 1985), *sushi* emerged as a luxury food in its own right. No less interesting is *noshi awabi* (dried abalone). This valuable shellfish was collected and dried in marine settlements, and used as an expression of regard by inlanders with little direct access to seafood. The delicacy became so prized that it became a required item in important gift-giving events, such as weddings. *Noshi gami*, the latest evolution, are the ubiquitous wrapping papers with which Japanese traditionally wrap or decorate gifts. Each such paper is printed with a stylized image of dried abalone in its own celebratory wrapping.

While the two examples above are not specifically *omiyage* per se, they do indicate the importance of the emotional and memory-evoking qualities of food. Some forms of *sushi* can thus, like the trout example above, benefit from lengthy emotional-historical association of place and travel, while at the same time make culturally valid claims to association with 'tradition', with 'freshness' and with 'naturalness'; all of them, in Japan as in all other modern societies, desirable qualities.

Like all merchandise, *omiyage* must attract a clientele. This means that the association with place of origin must be as manifest as possible, and that the presentation of the food be attractive to the eye. In the Japanese context this often means the display of particular colours which are culturally appropriate: combinations of white, reds and yellows (gold) predominate, for instance, in many *omiyage*, and if not in the food itself, then on the wrapping or backing of the food. Specific items are often wrapped in individual wrappers, which may well be traditional (grass straw for *natto*, paper tissue for certain kinds of biscuits, wooden or fake-wooden box containers for drinks) or innovative. One example of the latter which has always entranced me is an *omiyage* from Anchorage, Alaska. Cross-polar flights from Europe would often make a stopover for refuelling at Anchorage. Japanese tourists would hurriedly make purchases of ready-cut, ready-packed red beefsteaks, each in its cellophane wrapping, nestling in a box with a compartment for dry ice and a cellophane window to show the red meat. The boxes were inscribed with 'PRODUCT OF THE USA' in large letters, and guaranteed, in Japanese, to be (a) suitable for shipping for the flight time, and (b) up to Japanese customs standards.

It is important to remember that the visual qualities are often a matter of entirely subjective interpretation. The emotions aroused in the gift-giver and in the gift receiver may differ substantially. The important thing, as one of my informants, who was waxing lyrical over a particular *omiyage* from his home town, said, was that strong emotions were raised in both.

The power of the home-place idea in Japanese culture must not be underestimated here. Giant food companies – Kentucky Fried Chicken is one marvellous example – utilize the phenomenon by projecting ideas of homey comfort, maternal warmth and grandfatherly advice in their advertisements. That the homes and peoples displayed are almost always non-Japanese (or at best, ambiguously Japanese) is irrelevant: it is the emotional aura that the advertisers are after. At the other end of the scale, small-time local farmers evoke the same sensations by offering 'local produce' packs by mail order (Knight 2000).

The Alaskan steak rush characterizes the modernization of the *omiyage* phenomenon. *Omiyage* are meant to indicate that the presenter has been at a particular place; this, in effect, is one of the benefits of the transaction, an announcement of personal worth. This is undermined, in modern Japan, by the existence of special *omiyage* departments in department stores, most notably the famous (infamous?) one at Daimaru in Tokyo station, where anyone can buy *omiyage* from most prefectures in Japan without leaving, as it were, one's own home. One can, indeed, literally not leave one's home by simply ordering local *omiyage* via the post office. My own catalogues of post office gift selection are hefty 280–300 page, large-format volumes illustrating in mouth-watering detail the pleasures of gifts available from the post office (Royal Mail, take notice!) from Wakanai in the extreme north to Shuri in the tropical south.

The speed of modern communications ensures that one can also order for another, or receive for oneself, fresh items. These range from hairy crabs and fresh salmon (a Hokkaido delicacy) to fresh tropical flowers and fruit. The possibilities are also very tempting. During fieldwork, I sent a friend some particular delicacies I had bought at a local market in Hokkaido, in the depths of winter. While I was mailing them, I was asked by the puzzled counter clerk why I didn't simply order the same, or similar things from the post office catalogue.

The range of *omiyage* foods is enormous. Virtually the entire spectrum of foods available in Japan is represented. This ranges from condiments, particularly those from 'traditional' or 'natural' provenance, to full meals of *sushi* or other set meals, and all the way to raw materials, such as fish, fish roe, steaks, preserves and, of course, liquor. The number of such *omiyage* is clearly uncountable. New ones are added from time to time, and older ones fall by the wayside as tastes change.

One of my own particular research (ahem!) interests, is Japanese confections. These tend to feature in *omiyage* in the form of *senbei* (savoury, sweet, or mixed savoury/sweet dried biscuits or crackers), *manju* (buns or pancakes stuffed with bean jam) or *anko* (sweet bean jelly). Many other forms are available, ranging from *kasutera* (sponge cake) to specialized local delights.

A firm I have been studying for some years produces local confections largely for domestic (i.e. local) consumption. The firm, founded in the previous century, makes a range of traditional Japanese sweets and confections. It also, however, is constantly on the lookout for new marketing opportunities. These, from its point of view, include, among other things, the utilization of local culture. Traditional local festivals are extolled. Thus the local custom of creating *mochi* (pounded glutinous rice paste) figurines of dogs during a winter festival is actively exploited by the firm, which sells, mainly to tourists, small models of the *inukko* dogs, made of *mochi* and sweetened with *anko*. Another festival, in which local children make small igloos, has been commemorated with little igloo-shaped buns of white gelatine stuffed with black bean jam. Local farming dress patterns of blue-on-white are formed into doll shapes. All of the sweets, one must add, are beautifully made and delicious, but, except for their visual appeal, fairly conventional Japanese confections. Significantly, too, many of the wrappers for these include brief descriptions of the local custom, its origins (often hidden in the mists of time) and other forms of connection to the traditional heritage of the area.

'Our traditional heritage'
'Tradition' is an agreed-upon recourse to elements of the past, so that they may constitute the present (Hobsbawm and Ranger 1983; Shanklin 1981; Shils 1981). This is unquestionably true of many of the products which sell as *omiyage*.

Many of these relate, directly or indirectly, to the supposed history of their place of origin. Thus, for example, one of the *omiyage* described, from Ononomachi, in southern Akita Prefecture makes reference to the historical personage of the 'beautiful Akita woman', a courtier who was born in the area in the eighth century.

The creation of tradition is a major industry in any tourist economy. Indeed, so much of an industry is it, that a great deal of time and effort is invested in its creation and preservation (Koyano 1979; Moon 1989). One such is the '*ikura-donburi*'. The northern Island of Japan, Hokkaido, or at least its capital Sapporo, is associated in many Japanese minds with *Sapporo-ramen*, Chinese style noodles. In recent years, however, in Hokkaido itself, a new local food has been advertised. This consists of a bowl of cooked white rice covered over with a glistening layer of fresh salmon eggs. *Ikura-don* is now available as an *omiyage* as well, and can be bought (or shipped) from Hokkaido, where it is touted as the local *meibutsu* (famous product).

Tradition is both created and preserved. One of the most interesting *omiyage* is plain salt. Salt is sold in modern Japan as a government monopoly using modern methods of production. Traditional methods of drying seawater are preserved as a national cultural treasure, and indeed, the last living traditional salt maker was honoured as a Living National Treasure. Shioda City (the name means 'salt fields') sells an *omiyage* of salt 'extracted according to traditional methods'. One can buy a 250 gm bottle separately or elegantly wrapped in a boxed set of two with a bottle of 300 ml of mineral soy-sauce. The latter contains 68(!) sea minerals from its natural salt.

The modern Japanese middle class, which encompasses the vast majority of the population, is an eager consumer of the 'traditional' (Graburn 1995; Kelly 1986). The preservation of the myriads of local cuisines in Japan (Kimura 1974), while not a major preoccupation, is a cultural desideratum that many subscribe to. This is particularly true where, as in the case of the salt *omiyage* cited above, 'traditional' and 'healthy' are clearly elided.

Discussion

In pre-modern Japan, different areas, isolated from one another by geographical features and political circumstances, developed specific local cuisines. Economic and political expatriates hankered after their traditional fare, and often noted that in their letters and diaries, which, when published as they often were, became elements of national culture. Though these local cuisines tended to be variations on general Japanese themes (soup-and-side-dish structure of meals, heavy reliance on vegetable and fish products, preserved foods) they were, of course, the products of unique local ecologies (Kimura

1974; Nôrinsuisanshô 1986). With modernization, both political and technological, and the emergence of a metropolitan state, a general, rather bland 'national' cuisine emerged.

In the past several decades, towns and villages outside the Tokyo to Kobe conurbation have fought back 'metropolitization' by trying to establish their local cuisines or at least particular features of them. The most common strategy is to appeal to features of local history, and to claim antiquity, greater or lesser, of the food in question.

While we may regard the constant appeal to tradition as little more than a marketing gimmick (and indeed, it is that, too) there is an indication here of a greater issue. Modernization tends to destroy memory. Our memories of modernity are of the here and now, perhaps of the future. The speed of new sensation, a product both of the technology we use and the mercantilist philosophy which underlie our lives, means that we are interested in items of fashion for a brief time at best. Indeed, White (1993) indicates that the passing of fads is a conducted, product-created phenomenon. In Japanese culture, the idea of memory, of the recollection of times past, is often tied intimately to food. And in Japanese culture, where the 'natural' and the human-made blend imperceptibly into one, the concept of evoking a 'false' memory by providing a stay-at-home with an evocative gift, is not false at all.

But human memory, for many good reasons, extends beyond the immediacy of a fad or a fashion. Modern fads are made and made intentionally to be forgotten once the next fad comes into existence. The 'McDonaldization' of society (Ritzer 1993) creates a situation where, even in food, we are constantly being faced with a barrage of requirements to adapt our food consumption choices to the needs and will of the marketer. Indeed, we all, at some time or other, fall into the clutches of the merchandizer, and we can't really cope with that.

Attempts to revive and to preserve memories of times past serve many needs in any society. In the case of the Japanese, discussed here, they serve in the fight of local communities against the metropolis, they serve to bolster local economies and pride, and they are excellent merchandising sources of income for the metropolis's most pervasive arm, the post office. But for the people involved, those who actually consume the goods, they do serve a purpose. These 'false memories', however false they may be, help the individual to locate her or himself in the matrix of the society they are living in. In the Japanese view of things, we still can have the false memory of idyllic peace invoked by supposed products of less complicated times, provided by travellers who, whether they were 'there' or not, can at least evoke the memory of simple comfort in some forgotten corner of the world.

BIBLIOGRAPHY

Brumann, Christoph (2000) 'Materialistic culture: The uses of money in Tokyo gift exchanges', in Ashkenazi, M. and Clammer, J. (eds.) *Consumption and Material Culture in Contemporary Japan*, London: Kegan Paul International, pp. 217–240.

Graburn, Nelson H.H. (1995) 'The past in the present in Japan: Nostalgia and neo-traditionalism in contemporary Japanese domestic tourism', in Butler, R. and Pierce, D. (eds.) *Change in Tourism: People, Places, Processes*, London: Routledge.

Hendry, Joy (1993) *Wrapping culture*, Oxford: Clarendon Press.

Hiramatsu, Morihiko (1982) *Isson ippin no susume* [Recommending one village one product], Tokyo: Gyôsei.

Hobsbawm, E. and Ranger, T. (eds.) (1983) *Invention of tradition*, Cambridge: Cambridge University Press.

Kelly, William (1986) 'Rationalization and nostalgia: Cultural dynamics of new middle-class Japanese', in *American Ethnologist*, 13 (4), pp. 603–18.

Kimura, Masayoshi (1974) 'Geographical distribution of local traditional cuisines in Japan', in *Geographical Review of Japan*, 47 (6), pp. 394–401.

Knight, John (2000) 'Sharing Suzuki's rice: Commodity narratives in the Rural Revitalization Movement', in Ashkenazi, M. and Clammer, J. (eds.) *Consumption and Material Culture in Contemporary Japan*, London: Kegan Paul International.

Koyano, Shogo (1979) *Technology of traditional industry and the role of craftsmen*, Tokyo: The United Nations University.

Mauss, Marcel (1966) *The Gift*, tr. Cunnison, Ian, London: Cohen & West.

Mennell, Stephen (1985) *All Manners of Food*, Oxford: Basil Blackwell.

Moeran, Brian and Skov, Lisa (1997) 'Mount Fuji and the cherry blossoms: A view from afar', in Asquith, P. and Kalland, A. (eds.) *Japanese Images of Nature*, Richmond: Curzon.

Moon, Okpyo (1989) *From paddy field to ski slope: The revitalization of tradition in Japanese village life*, Manchester: Manchester University Press.

Nôrinsuisanshô (1986) *Chiiki shokuhin ni taisuru chishiki to kôdô ni tsuite* [Attitudes and Behaviour in Relation to Regional Foods], Tokyo: Nôrinsuisanshô Shokuhin Ryûtsûkyoku Shôhikeizaika.

Ritzer, George (1993) *The McDonaldization of Society: An Investigation into the Changing Character of Contemporary Social Life*, Thousand Oaks, California: Pine Forge Press.

Shanklin, Eugenia (1981) 'Two meanings and uses of tradition', in *Journal of Anthropological Research*, 37 (1) pp. 71–89.

Shils, Edward (1981) *Tradition*, London: Faber and Faber.

White, Merry (1993) *The Material Child*, New York: The Free Press, Macmillan Inc.

The Language of Flavour: Learning and Memory

Anthony Blake

Introduction

The only animal species which does not simply eat the food which it can find or catch is the human race. Evolution and our unique mental capacities have given us the ability to blend, process and cook our foods and ultimately to develop the art of gastronomy. Today all of the foods we eat can be considered a product of human ingenuity, whether consciously planned or evolved as a consequence of human interference with the hybridization of plants or the breeding of animals. Cooking and processing of food is a refinement which has allowed us to make things edible which uncooked would be poisonous, and to enable us to store foods which would otherwise be perishable.

We now recognize that homo sapiens was not the only hominid to evolve upon the earth, and fossil remains from the last two to three million years show that several distinctly different hominid species co-existed (Tattersall 2000). We have no idea whether these creatures modified the foods available to them but it is clear that finally none of them survived contact with our ancestors. The most likely explanation is that these unfortunate near-humans could not compete effectively and had not achieved the profound advantage of the human race – symbolic thought.

We have no idea at the present time how the human brain converts the electrical and chemical signals we receive through our senses into our feeling of consciousness. Language is clearly an important part of consciousness; as I write this article I have a conversation with myself: it is entirely mental and, within myself, I consider and choose the words which I hope will convey to you what I am thinking; as you read you recreate a meaning which is now entirely within your consciousness and hopefully it will duplicate, or at least be close to, my own thoughts. Clearly, however, the precise meaning which you give to the words will be based on your experiences, and my choice of words will depend on the meaning I give to them and how I learned them; in short, our individual consciousness of the idea will be shaped by our separate learned experiences.

So what has all this got to do with food? In this paper I intend to explore what food memory is. All of the people at this conference are passionate about food, all have favourite recipes and can recall eating experiences, some disastrous and some delightful, but what are the processes that go on in our brains that allow us to recollect and convey these thoughts to others, and to what extent do our personal eating experiences modify and determine these thoughts?

Food memory
When we choose to go to a favourite restaurant we are rarely making the decision purely because we are hungry; it will be an advantage if we are feeling somewhat peckish but for most of the people here today hunger is not the driving force. We are seeking a gastronomic experience, convivial company and shared pleasures of taste, flavour, texture and, not least, the appearance of our food. These pleasures are what make gastronomy a uniquely human pleasure; it is the art form intended for our mouths and noses as much as music, song and poetry are intended for our ears or the visual arts for our eyes. Our mental manipulation and appreciation of sounds clearly depends on the information received by our ears; our appreciation of paintings and sculpture relies on the information sent by our eyes to our brain, but our delight in food is more subtle and uses all our senses. All our memories of food arise from its appearance, its odour, its taste, its texture and the sensations it gives in our mouths, and even the sounds made as we eat it; all five senses send messages to the brain which are stored and can be revisited in our thoughts as conscious memories.

Let us then look at the relevance of each of these channels of information, because in very recent years some surprising new ideas have appeared as a result of fundamental research into how the brain uses this information. We do not fully understand how we learn and use our memory of food, but a picture, or should we say a taste, is emerging, which raises some important and intriguing questions.

Our eyes and vision
Sight is arguably our most immediate and dominant sense; it is certainly the sense which allows us to explore our surroundings to the furthest distances. It allows us to detect and identify potential foods and track a route to obtaining them. What is perhaps surprising is that recent work being done here in Oxford (Rolls 1999) suggests that the regions of the brain which receive taste and flavour signals and allow us to correctly identify foods are also interconnected with those parts of the brain dealing with visual signals. What is

even more interesting is that eating a specific food to satiety causes us to dislike the appearance of the food; it appears that we can literally become sick at the sight of food.

In evolutionary terms, it would be expected that for creatures needing a balanced diet a mechanism would be required to stop them gorging to excess on an easily available food source. It has been speculated that such aversion mechanisms would be particularly important to animals such as monkeys with large quantities of fruit and berries available to them. Vision not only plays an important role in the identification of food, but also in deciding the acceptability and pleasure to be obtained from the food. An inappropriate colour or appearance can make food unacceptable even if it smells and tastes perfect.

Our nose and odour

For many animals, smell is the most important sense for finding food or avoiding being eaten. I still have a vivid memory of watching a frightened rabbit zigzag around me as it dashed across a recently harvested corn field; what made the impression was not so much that the rabbit avoided me, but that the hound which appeared nose to the ground some seconds later followed exactly the same course as that taken by the rabbit. We all know how much we use our noses when selecting food, yet we use our noses in two quite distinctly different ways; we smell food before we put it in our mouths and we also get the odour of the food as we chew and swallow it. Smelling our food before we put it into our mouths allows us to make judgements about it and, if necessary, to reject it before we actually make contact with it; the information from the food is transmitted as volatile, odourant molecules, carried into our nose as we breathe in, called orthonasal breath. We then get a second message after we chew and swallow our food; this time when we breathe out, termed the retronasal breath, and it could be the case that our brain processes the signals from orthonasal breath differently to those from retronasal breath.

High up inside the nose, just behind the eyes, is a small patch of tissue called the olfactory bulb. This is a remarkable organ which is in fact an extension of the brain, sending information directly into it, and it contains a vast array of detectors which respond to specific molecules with remarkable precision, and at incredibly low levels. What is even more amazing is that although there are many detectors for thousands of different molecules, all the detectors for one type of molecule appear to be 'wired' into the same receptor cells within the brain How the nerve fibres find the right part of the brain is one of the great unsolved mysteries of our bodies.

What is also remarkable, and only recently understood, is that the genetic coding which controls the construction of our olfactory bulb is the largest sequence of DNA in our genome. Furthermore, we are continually regenerating new olfactory receptors, which are among the fastest replicating cells in our bodies. Within the last few years, remarkable progress has been made at Nottingham University Department of Food and Agricultural Sciences (Taylor & Linforth 2000) in techniques for studying how we receive and process the information carried by our breath to our nose. I will come back to this point later, because there are important issues here related to how we develop a food memory.

Our tongues and taste

We all know about our four basic tastes of sweet, sour, salt and bitter, and we all know that these are detected on the tongue and in the mouth and throat. Our taste receptors are located in the pits on our tongue and in the sides of our mouths – the so called taste buds. Much work has been done to establish how the taste buds work and how they detect chemicals in the mouth and transmit the information into signals which go to the brain, and it will be described later how these signals can affect our overall perception of flavour. Not all animals share the same pattern of taste receptors as humans and these have evolved as yet another sensing and control mechanism, giving information about food before it is swallowed. Humans share with monkeys and apes the appreciation of sweetness which tells us that the food will provide calories.

Salt is important for maintaining our correct physiological balance, and as we sweat, our appreciation of salty foods increases. In a South Wales iron works, heat exhaustion was sufficiently an issue that Thomas and Evans, the local 'pop' manufacturer, produced salty versions of its carbonated drinks, which were much better appreciated by the workers.

Sourness and bitterness seem to have evolved as deterrent senses; acidity in fruits is a sign of immaturity, and many natural toxins produced by plants are bitter; it is only as we become adult that we develop and learn to appreciate which bitter foods to like.

It is now known that we have more than these four taste receptors. Again, from work here in the department of Experimental Psychology, Professor Rolls has strong evidence for our ability to detect the taste of monosodium glutamate as a discrete sensation, and it is speculated that this could be an important signal in food to indicate the presence of protein. It can be added that human's milk is the richest in MSG of all animals', with the specific exception of the chimpanzee's. There are some suggestions that we may also have receptors specific to fatty compounds of foods, but this is still, as yet, not conclusive.

Mouthfeel and sensation

When we eat food, we are not only aware of its aroma and taste, but also know whether it is hot, cold, spicy, cooling or astringent; we know if it is crisp or slimy because our mouths are able to convey remarkably subtle information, about the physical properties of the food, to the brain. Information about touch and temperature is transmitted from the face and head via the trigeminal nerve. We also now know that the heat of chillies is sensed because the capsaicin contained within them directly stimulates the pain cells, which tell us that the temperature of our food is too high. Within the brain this information is integrated with that from the nose and mouth to give the total impression of flavour.

Hearing

Even sound plays a part in giving us information about our food. Celery without the snap would not be celery, an apple without the crunch would not be an apple and we immediately know if the crisps have been out of the bag for too long at the first bite.

The subconscious and conscious experience

From the foregoing, it should be clear that as soon as we sit down in our favourite restaurant we start supplying our brain with information: the smells of the food, the sight of the décor and the presentation of the dish all start to build the experience. Once we start the meal our brain inputs data from all the senses, although not all this is immediately available to our conscious self. It is now apparent that our brains are capable of considerable subconscious processing of this data, sharing information from one sensory channel to another, and allowing our conscious selves to be aware of a selected and edited part of the whole. We are all aware of optical illusions, when the brain will make interpretations which are not an exact representation of the true world. The figure illustrates this very well, in that you will clearly 'see' a curved line in the diagram passing across the triangle and connecting the left and right dark segments; this is a true figment of your imagination, as no such line is in the picture.

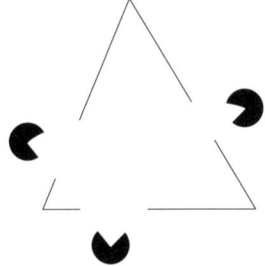

Well, it seems that our brain is also capable of taking information from our food, and, just as it deals with visual data, it can edit, and even change, what we perceive and remember. What has very recently been realized from a number of different scientific groups, working on different aspects of perception, is that much goes on in our heads at an unconscious level, which can modify and even deceive our conscious experience.

The first example I will mention was reported at a recent scientific meeting in San Francisco (Breslin 2000). Dr Paul Breslin, from the Monell Chemical Senses Center in Philadelphia, showed some fascinating results from carefully monitored sensory panels. Without going into all the details, what he demonstrated was the subtle way in which our senses of taste and olfaction are linked within the brain. Using a trained taste panel, he established the lowest concentration of benzaldehyde (the smell of bitter almonds, which is also present in cherries and plums) which the individual members could smell. He also established the lowest concentration of sucrose which they could taste. Now he asked them to smell air containing benzaldehyde at half the threshold level and, of course, they could smell nothing, but (and this is the fascinating bit) if they held a solution containing a sub-threshold level of sucrose in their mouth, they could now smell the benzaldehyde.

What is really important about this work is that it shows that sub-threshold does not mean that a sensation cannot be detected by the brain; we are simply not conscious of it; equally, signals from the taste receptors in the mouth and smell receptors in the nose can reinforce each other within the brain. Dr Breslin reported a further observation which, if confirmed, is even more exciting. He was suspicious that simply having anything in the mouth that was activating taste receptors could perhaps trigger the reinforcement of the odour signal, so he repeated the experiment, but asking panellists to smell sub-threshold benzaldehyde with a sub-threshold solution of MSG in their mouths; this time they could no longer detect the benzaldehyde, apart from one panellist, who was Japanese. Whereas Europeans associate sweetness with plums and cherries, the Japanese are very fond of pickled plums, which are rich in *umami* taste (MSG). I must stress that this is not a rigorous experiment, and is based on a single observation but, if repeated, it suggests that the associations between tastes and aromas in our brains are learned responses from childhood.

Some very recent work has also been done at the University of Nottingham, sponsored by Firmenich. We have been collaborating with a research group for a number of years and have developed an analytical technique, which we call AFFIRM®. Without going into all the technical details, we are now able to directly analyse, in real time, the flavour molecules which are in the breath of a volunteer as a result of eating or drinking. We are able to see exactly which flavours, and their intensities, are passing the olfactory bulb. In other words, we have a direct measure of the flavour input to the person's nose, and the subjects can also describe their sensations. In this way, we have been able to deduce some of the rules about how the nose and brain work.

It seems very obvious in hindsight, but one of the first things we learned is that our noses do not measure an absolute level of a flavour; we detect the rates of change in a flavour. You can easily prove this by holding your nose, or by stopping breathing for a few seconds: in either case you have no sense of smell. It is not that flavour molecules are absent from your nose, but that their concentration is not changing, and no signals are going to the brain. We have also been surprised at how quickly the nose adapts, and ceases to be able to recognize a persistent flavour – this starts after a little over 80 seconds, and within five minutes the ability to smell that flavour is lost. This is essentially why chewing gum loses its flavour; we have shown that after two hours of chewing peppermint flavoured gum, the peppermint flavour in the nose is still as strong as after two minutes, but the nose can no longer detect it.

The lesson from this is that we need variety in our food if we are to experience flavour pleasure, and this is exactly what chefs achieve when they arrange the meals on a plate. We also find some other interesting facts which show that chefs often know intuitively what to do, even if they don't necessarily know why. Our AFFIRM® system allows us to directly measure how a food ingredient can change the release of flavour from the food during eating. One of my colleagues, Edelgard Meyer, has prepared and eaten a variety of cooked vegetables with and without cream, with some surprising results. Eating carrots with cream dramatically suppresses some of the carrot odour which would normally reach the nose in the absence of cream; onions are little affected whether cream is absent or not; but in the case of cauliflower, cream causes more flavour to reach the nose than without it. Isn't it fascinating that we often eat cauliflower with cream sauces?

Another very recent piece of work from the Nottingham group nicely supports the ideas of Paul Breslin. All cooks know that as a sauce is thickened, its flavour decreases. It was a generally accepted belief that as the viscosity of the sauce increased, less of the volatile flavour molecules were released in the mouth and transported, by the breath, to the nose. It was a great surprise when the researchers measured the strawberry flavour reaching the nose, from a series of increasingly viscous strawberry syrups; they found no measured difference whatsoever in the level of strawberry odour molecules in the nose, although the perceived strawberry flavour decreased. When they repeated the experiment with no strawberry flavour, but simply sweetened syrups, they found that the apparent sweetness also declined. In the minds of the tasters, it was the sweet taste perception which was determining the intensity of strawberry aroma perception. Further experiments have confirmed the fact that we have a remarkable degree of interaction within the brain between taste and odour.

The Learning Process

So, if our brains learn how to recognize and like food from its taste and odour, and if our brains learn which tastes and odours relate to each other, when does this learning process take place, and to what extent does it shape our future personal preferences for food? With some notable exceptions this is a little explored area, but a few observations are pertinent. In the USA, a popular flavour is that of wintergreen: it is used in soft drinks, chewing gums and a variety of candies, and is accepted and liked. Here in Europe, with an essentially identical genetic pool in the population, wintergreen in food is generally disliked and is associated with medicines and ointments. At a point in childhood, Americans learn to associate and like wintergreen in foods, but Europeans do not.

This is a very clear cut difference and there are others which are perhaps more subtle. My wife and I grew up in the UK, our daughter was born and grew up in Switzerland; she thinks English vanilla ice-cream is a very strange thing to eat, and anyway, why doesn't it have black specks like real ice-cream? We once spent some time convincing a worried restaurateur in Chester that my then five year old daughter's dislike of his ice-cream was not that she had found a black speck in it, but rather that she hadn't; it didn't fit her mental impression of vanilla ice-cream, either in appearance or taste, and was therefore rejected. So at what age in childhood did she start to learn what foods to accept and which to reject? My belief is that at the weaning stage, and when children first try new foods, they start to learn the patterns of food memories which will largely stay with them all their lives. Clearly, we can experience and learn to like new combinations as we mature, but how does our learning ability change with age?

The work of Leann Lipps Birch, of Pennsylvania State University, and Elizabeth Capaldi, of the University of Florida, has looked at such questions. We are born with some innate predispositions for taste – new born babies like sweet, but reject sour and bitter tastes – but preferences for the aroma of food appear to be learned in an associative way with taste and social occasion, and at an early age.

Menella and Beauchamp, at the Monell Chemical Senses Center in Philadelphia, have shown that flavours ingested by mothers have a positive influence on the amount of milk taken by breast-fed babies. Equally, up until the age of about one year, babies will have a go at eating more or less anything, and it is probably at this stage that the associations between flavour and what is acceptable as food are made. From one year onward, children are increasingly neophobic and will often reject anything that is different or new, which means that children who haven't tasted spinach in the first year of life will find it harder to like it when they grow older.

Professor Paul Rozin, of the University of Pennsylvania, has also written extensively on how children develop disgust for certain foods and flavours, and, for thirty years, has studied the way children develop flavour preferences. The workers quoted above have devoted much time trying to understand what is a fundamental human pleasure, but it is fair to say that most of this work has been conducted from an American perspective and with the American food culture as the norm. Rozin, however, is an exception, and has made specific comparisons of the role of food in American and French life; he claims that the French have a better and more sensible attitude toward food: they enjoy it more and eat better-tasting food. He is also quoted as saying, 'the French think about food when it is in the mouth, Americans when it is in their bloodstream.' The psychology of how we learn to like different flavours is also now being studied in France, and the *Institut National de Recherche Agronomique* (INRA) at Dijon has an ongoing programme of work in this area.

I am fascinated by the parallels which appear to exist between learning to speak and learning what to eat. As one-year-olds we learn the patterns of noise which become language; we do it without effort and start to talk. Young children will easily learn several languages simultaneously if they hear them regularly, but once over the age of three or four the learning of a language becomes progressively harder, so is it the same with flavour? I ask these questions because I am curious as to why we send our children to school, where they learn about music, painting, drawing and self expression, but it seems we never teach our children 'food appreciation'. Of course, all children are finicky and fussy about their food, just as my daughter was with her English ice-cream, but are we not all suspicious when we taste something strange for the first time?

I have never seen a European express delight at first tasting a durian fruit, but these obviously give pleasure to the people who queue for them in Thailand and Indonesia. If, as adults, we are to fully appreciate the flavour of food then we must remember that the process starts early in childhood. If our children are only exposed to the blandest of baby foods, cola drinks and hamburgers as their first eating experiences, then why should we be surprised if they develop into adults with limited acceptance of other foods? My friend, Fritz Blank, talks about the attenuation of the American palate. He has to arrange special evenings for selected customers, at his restaurant in Philadelphia, when he can serve *rognons de veau*, or indeed any form of offal, because his normal clients won't eat them. Almost certainly the seeds for Fritz' frustration were sown forty years ago, in the affluence of the 1960s, and when children neither had to, nor were encouraged to eat the cheaper cuts of meat.

Conclusions

It is becoming clearer that our early experiences with food, and how our brains use the information from our senses, especially vision, taste and smell, create memory patterns which play a major role in later life in deciding what foods are acceptable or unacceptable. Since eating and drinking are arguably pleasures which start at birth and end only at death, it is surprising that so little awareness exists about how this learning process develops and changes with age. Equally, it is interesting how little consideration is given to the training of children in flavour appreciation, nor indeed how the food you give to your toddler might already decide how much pleasure that child will get from food in later life.

BIBLIOGRAPHY

Birch, L.L. (1990) *The Control of Food Intake by Young Children: the role of learning in Taste, experience and feeding*, Capaldi, E.D. and Pourley, T.L. (eds.), American Psychological Association, Washington.

Birch, L.L. et al. (1996) 'The Development of Children's Eating Habits', in *Food Choice, Acceptance and Consumption*, Meiselman, H.L. and Macfie, H.J.H. (eds.), Blackie Academic & Professional Press.

Breslin, P. (March 2000) ACS meeting, San Francisco.

Capaldi, E.D. (ed.) (1996) *Why we Eat What We Eat – The Psychology of Eating*, American Psychological Association.

Menella, J.A. and Beauchamp, G.K. (1993) 'The Effect of Repeated Exposure to Garlic-flavoured Milk on the Nursling's Behaviour', in *Pediatric Research*, 34, pp. 805–808.

———, 'The Human Infant's Response to Vanilla flavours in Mother's Milk and Formula', in *Infant Behaviour and Development*.

Rolls, E.T. (1999) *The Brain and Emotion*, Oxford University Press.

Rozin, P. et al. (1997) 'The Cultural Evolution of Disgust', in *Food Preferences and Taste: continuity and change*, Macbeth, H.M. (ed.), Oxford.

Tattersall, I. (Jan 2000) 'Once we were not alone', in *Scientific American*, 38–44.

Taylor, A.J. and Linforth, R.S.T. (2000) in *Flavor Release: Linking experiments, theory and reality*, Roberts, D.D. and Taylor, A.J. (eds.), ACS Symposium series.

Amarcord: the Flavour of Buried Memories

John F. Carafoli

In the United States we call ourselves 'a nation of immigrants.' One thing that this means for us is that there's often a gap, a break in family memories. People whose families came over from Europe may be almost completely cut off from knowledge of anything earlier than some dividing point when another generation reached America. There's a Before, and there's an After.

As a third-generation Italian-American from the town of Sagamore Village, Massachusetts, I experienced this gap of memory in two ways. One – the break between two continents – might have been something I could put in the back of my mind and only think about occasionally. But the second break with our family past may be the reason I'm here today. I was almost twelve years old when my mother, my maternal grandmother, and one of my two brothers died in a terrible fire from which I barely escaped. Everything in my life belongs to Before or After.

The first way I learned to fill in part of what was missing was through cooking. It was what connected me with our village and part of my parents' world. But before we go further I'd better introduce the village.

Shortly before 1910 a huge construction project was started on what we call Upper Cape Cod, the southern part where the Cape joins the mainland. The idea was to dig a canal between Cape Cod Bay and Buzzards Bay and open a shorter water route to Boston from points south along the Atlantic coast. Construction workers poured into the Sagamore-Sandwich area, many coming almost directly from Europe, lured by the prospect of work. Among them were thousands of Italians who stayed on after the canal was finished to find permanent employment with the biggest local business, a company that manufactured railroad cars. One contingent, including the Carafolis, came from the vicinity of Bologna.

I'm leaving out a lot of earlier local history here, including other job opportunities that started attracting Italian labourers long before 1910 – I want to concentrate on the core group of Italians who founded their own little society in Sagamore Village. You probably know that people from different regions of

Italy can be divided by dialect to the point where they have trouble understanding each other. This happened in our village. So the immigrants communicated in a kind of made-up Italian using words from all their separate backgrounds. They created a world for themselves, a little Italian melting-pot based on the ways of the country districts where they had grown up. Their food was a combination of memories and new inventions – also influenced by prosperity some of them couldn't have dreamed of in Italy. They had the time and money to plant beautiful vegetable gardens and fruit trees. They found which of the old-country crops would grow in the new home, a much colder climate. Someone was always harvesting something, from early spring to late autumn – tomatoes, basil, white peaches, squashes. Many raised their own chickens, rabbits, and even pigs, and they would hold pig-butchering and sausage-making sessions in the autumn just as they remembered from their Italian homes. There was a grape arbour in every backyard, and every year the men crushed the grapes and bottled their own wine. At the same time the women would be making *savor,* a tradition that goes back to Roman times, where you boil down grape must with other fruits for days, to make a super-concentrated preserve that was many people's only sweetener in the days before sugar. Incidentally, I don't know how many of you are familiar with Cape Cod or the American image of Cape Cod, but most of what I'm describing would have been totally invisible to tourists who came from all over the country to visit what they thought was the 'real' Cape Cod of whaling museums or artist colonies.

The unofficial centre of town life was Louis' Market, built in 1914 to keep this community of labourers supplied with imported arborio rice, dried pasta, olive oil, cornmeal for polenta and Italian cheeses. Meanwhile, many in Sagamore found ways to use skills they had learned in their first homes. Men fished for lobsters, clams, mussels, squid, codfish, swordfish and bluefish. Women gathered young dandelions in spring, the native wild cranberries and blueberries in summer, forest mushrooms in autumn.

These people were the contemporaries of my grandparents, bringing to life something they had carried in their minds and hearts since they were born. They would never have thought of not recreating their Italian birthplaces from direct memory when they put down roots in Upper Cape Cod.

Now we come to the other side of the memory coin: forgetting. You can't talk about memory without – in a way – talking about forgetting. Or wanting not to forget. There's no way anybody can remember everything forever, especially when a community or a family is broken apart. Wanting to not forget comes when people see something being lost.

The first memory-casualty in immigrant communities is usually language. This was especially true for people who had done little reading or writing in their own language before coming to America. I described how the first generation in Sagamore learned to talk to each other in a hybrid Italian with words from their different dialects. At home they spoke their own dialect. In the next generation, English became the first language, or at least the one that children were taught to read and write. By my generation, most children spoke only English. I grew up not knowing either standard Italian (Tuscan) or any of the dialects, except for a few words I might have picked up without ever thinking about it or knowing where they fitted into a pan-Italian picture. By this time people were marrying outside the community. My father was Italian, my mother French-Canadian.

By then the Sagamore Village roots that the first immigrants had put down had already started to be torn up. It didn't take long. The railroad-car company that was the economic backbone of the town closed in 1928, the year before the Great Depression began. People moved to other Massachusetts towns looking for work, or left the area completely. It was another break with the past, even if not as drastic a break as crossing the Atlantic. To this day, local history buffs and the few elderly residents of Sagamore who arrived in the early days divide life into Before and After the Keith Car works went out of business. For the dwindling number who remained, memories became extra-precious because there was so much to be forgotten.

This is where I enter the picture. I guess I always had more of a motive to remember the Italian Sagamore Village than Sagamore had to remember itself (especially now that the Italian Sagamore is nearly 100 per cent gone). My Before and After was the fire. I clung eagerly to my memories of a safe, stable family life when I was quite young and we were living with my Carafoli grandparents.

The Carafolis came from near Bologna, a little town called Renazzo. There were a lot of people in Sagamore from Bologna and nearby parts of Emilia-Romagna. At that time I only vaguely understood that 'Italy' meant many regions and sub-regions, not just one place on the map. So the meaning of its culinary tradition in relation to other culinary traditions was beyond me, at the time. But the meaning of food as love wasn't. What happened was that after the fire some of the women who had been neighbours and friends of my parents befriended me. They let me and my baby brother (I had to be a kind of parent to him) spend hours in their kitchens after school, watching them cook and sometimes being allowed to help.

This was an incredible gift to me, because food was my most treasured link with Before (before the fire, that is). Many of these women shared the regional traditions the Carafolis had brought across the Atlantic. My joy was to remember my grandmother's polenta, her risottos, her version of a simple *bollito misto* that would be our Sunday dinner, or the tortellini that she would make later, filled with beef or chicken from the leftovers of that meal. The few household possessions that hadn't been in the fire became revered objects for me – both those brought from Italy and those that my grandparents bought in America when they set up housekeeping. I still have the garden bench where my grandmother used to sit, picking over a basket of spring dandelions. I have my grandmother's wooden polenta board and spoon, her Hoosier cabinet ('The Hoosier State' is a nickname for Indiana, where these cabinets were manufactured around the turn of the last century), her olive oil cruet ('S.S.P.' stands for S.S. Pierce, a renowned Boston purveyor), my grandfather's brass corkscrew, and his glass dish for *pinzimonio* (olive oil seasoned with salt and cracked pepper, served with raw vegetables or bread for dipping). They were then, and are, links with everything I've lost. They were allies in the mission not to forget.

Generally speaking, I don't think anyone in our community made a big point of food and memory when Sagamore was at its height. The women who taught me to cook, several decades later, didn't do any song and dance about it, either. They were too busy cooking – from memory of course. They rarely wrote down a recipe. To them it was all second nature, which may be another name for memories so strong and instinctive that people can't even imagine them being lost. It's only an accident that a child happened to be around, a child with a desperate need to remember. I absorbed their way of putting together any dish without recipes. I absorbed things I didn't know I was absorbing – like the Bolognese passion for *ragù*s and the Italian love of fresh greens, when Rose Sorenti made her ravioli filled with Swiss Chard and topped with what we called 'Bolognese sauce'. Like the northern Italian reverence for polenta, when Alba Papi served her polenta with stewed rabbit. Like the wisdom that Rosina Boffetti passed down to me one day when I wanted to know why she cooked wild mushrooms (picked only an hour or two earlier by herself) with a silver dollar, a sprig of parsley, and a slice of bread. 'If the silver tarnishes and the parsley turns a strange colour, the mushrooms are not good,' she told me in her broken English. 'But what about the bread?' I asked. She threw up her hands expressively and said, 'You feed the bread to the chicken. If the chicken dies, you throw the mushrooms out!' I never thought I'd be almost the only person from our village who's still around to bequeath this piece of medical science. Everybody just knew these things, and it seemed eternal.

People start worrying about food and memory when they realize that the food they've loved might not be around forever. As a kid learning to cook from the women of Sagamore, I had a feeling that they were helping me to remember the best of my own family life from Before. The meaning was personal. But it wasn't until many years later that I realized how easy it is for food to be forgotten by a whole community. Or let's put it another way – how easy it is for a community to disappear and be forgotten, along with its food.

I had grown up and moved away from Sagamore, then eventually moved back to Massachusetts and studied cooking at Madeleine Kamman's school near Boston. I became a food professional (specifically, a photography stylist). After that two things began happening: (1) I saw that my parents' contemporaries were dying out together with the food traditions they'd brought and re-created; and (2) my work and study had given me some of the necessary knowledge to look at those traditions and draw connections instead of just passively taking our village food for granted.

A good example is the bread that used to be made at Louis' Market in the old days when Louis' still had bread ovens in the cellar. People in Sagamore just called it 'horn bread' in English; I never knew any Italian name for it. I just thought that was what good bread was supposed to be like. But, coming back years later with a wider knowledge of food, I realized how unusual it was. It had four points, like horns, belonging to two segments of bread jointed in the middle like Siamese twins.

I am not by any stretch of the imagination a culinary historian, but it dawned on me that this bread must have a past. It didn't seem as if it had much of a future. After Louis' Market closed down their bread ovens they started importing 'horn bread' from a bakery in Plymouth about twenty miles away. I tried inquiring about it there. But at this point the original owner was too old to be much help, and the younger woman running the bakery didn't know anything about the bread's history. I have a feeling that in a few years no one is going to be making horn bread – and it used to be almost the staff of life in Sagamore! The key to helping it survive has to be somewhere on the other side of the ocean, though it took me a while to know that.

I decided that I had to start working on behalf of more memories than just mine. It was time to learn Italian. Well, another thing I'm never going to be is a linguist. But in my spare time I started studying the language with a teacher – that is, studying Tuscan, the 'standard' Italian. I see now that for most of my life I was totally cut off from a big part of the village memory and the Carafoli family experience coming to America, because I was 'deaf' to the talk that flowed around me unless it was in English. If the older people had an Italian name for our 'horn bread', it went right past me.

And I'm afraid that this loss also is a big part of why I'm here today – because it's all too typical of something that happens with the movement of people around the globe. Not just Italians, but people of all ethnic backgrounds, tend to forget their ancestral language by the time the third generation is growing up. It's not necessarily that we're ashamed of the group we started out belonging to, it's that when we get to school age, somehow everything keeps us from belonging to the group of speakers. I was too young at the time to understand that this is almost like losing a parent. Or let's say that I was too young to understand the nature of the loss until I was too old to get the full benefit of study. It's a loss of memory, including important culinary memories tied to language.

I know that I'll never be able to get the nuances of our family's home dialect. But at least I can communicate now, after a fashion, when I go to Italy – for that was probably the most important step I took. I saw that if I wanted to re-forge a broken chain of memory, I would have to go to Italy. Now you have to understand that European travel wasn't always an automatic thing for American grandchildren of European immigrants. It all depended on a million different factors in a family's situation, like whether somebody appointed himself or herself the international social secretary and kept the different branches in touch. We didn't have anyone like that, and in our family, there wasn't any possibility of any of us visiting Europe. So my opportunities for figuring out where my folks fit into a larger family picture beyond Sagamore were limited.

I did remember that a very nice elderly great-uncle and his wife would sometimes visit our home and that he was a professional cook somewhere in Connecticut who used to make the most terrific lobster *cacciatore* (among other things) when he came. I registered his name as 'Zio Carabing'. Maybe I thought 'Carabing' was some sort of nickname – it was one of those things that kids don't really pay attention to. I knew that 'Zio Carabing' and Tessilla, his wife, somehow had disappeared by the time of the fire, but I never knew the rest of their story.

Now, let me try to wrap up all these issues of food and memory in the Italian community of Sagamore Village, Massachusetts, as quickly as I can. It all started coming together for me about a year and a half ago when I made my first trip to Bologna and neighbouring regions in the spring of 1999. I've been back three times since, and I'm on my way there now. I have just begun my mission to take vanishing memories of food (vanishing in my home community, that is) and understand them as I never have, hoping that it will make a difference for people with even fewer first-hand memories than I have.

Someone had told me that a bread like our 'horn bread' still existed in Emilia-Romagna – and I found it! The original bread is still being made in Ferrara, Modena, and Bologna. They call it *la coppia* ('the couple' or 'the pair') or in dialect *ciupita*. The shape is a little different, because the Siamese-twin halves are rolled into thin crescents. The texture is somewhat drier. But when I saw and tasted *la coppia*, I knew, 'That's it!' Now that I can talk to people in

Ferrara and Bologna who have living knowledge of this bread, I just may be able to take home what I've learned and interest New England-Italians in producing it, so that the memory of our Plymouth and Sagamore 'horn bread' doesn't perish when the last of the old bakers dies in Plymouth.

I feel that with each trip I make I'm recovering from a kind of amnesia. Some piece of memory is filled in every time. It might be going to a restaurant in Ferrara and eating a dish of ground-up sausage over mashed potatoes and realizing why my Aunt Mary used to serve a dish of hamburger meat (ground beef) over mashed potatoes. It might be going to the cemetery in Renazzo accompanied by a distant relative whose mother was a Carafoli and seeing the name of my 'Zio Carabing' in writing for the first time by the picture on the vault. My own grandfather's brother, the prince of cooks in our family, and we had nothing in Sagamore with his name actually written down! His real name was right there engraved on the vault, Cherubino Carafoli, which my child's ear had turned into 'Carabing'. And when I was eleven, Cherubino and Tessilla, his wife, had returned to Renazzo, where they lived until the 1960s.

Remembering, forgetting, and learning to remember again – my community and I are not unique in this pattern. The wave of immigration that brought the Carafolis to America is over. But now there are other waves coming from different places. People are moving around the globe looking for jobs, stability, democracy, or just a better life. It's one of our big political issues in America – and now in England, too. I won't go into that. But I can imagine some other family in a few years trying to look back and saying, 'How did we ever forget?' I hope that small attempts like mine to recover memory through cooking can be a future help or model to other people fighting amnesia – because food will always be a powerful magnet to draw out buried memories.

I would like to acknowledge my gratitude to Anne Mendelsohn for helping me sort out my memories.

Spice Memories

Fred Czarra

'Be still! Oh north winds, and come, oh Southern Breezes, and blow upon my garden, that the spice trees therein may blossom and bear fruit!'

'His cheeks are as a bed of spices, of sweet flowers.'

The Song of Solomon

I was born in Washington, DC on the backside of World War II. Since the effects of the Great Depression were still very strong, and money was tight, my father and I lived with my mother's father and her two sisters while my father worked at the Washington Navy Yard. Grandfather owned a grocery store, across the street from our three-level brick home on Florida Avenue and his three daughters worked at the store. As a young child I spent a great deal of time there and, as a result, began my lifelong love of spices.

My grandfather had opened his store in the 1890s and was only a few years away from celebrating his 50th anniversary at the same location. Since I was there almost every day the smells of the grocery were part of my sensory heritage. When the food from the store crossed the street and became part of a meal, the senses of smell and taste combined and peaked in a full awareness of spices.

One of the first meals that I recall consisted of a half-ham with a crossing square pattern etched in its top across a fatty layer of skin. In each of the squares was a clove which collectively formed a chess-like pattern of very small spikes studding the surface. When the ham came out of the oven the smell was wonderful. I took great pleasure in removing some of the charred cloves and chewing on them. When the ham was cut for serving I took more cloves from the top and pierced them into my piece of ham. As I grew older cloves gave me relief from occasional toothaches. Although the relief was for a short period of time, the pleasure of the clove was very satisfying. Other parts of the meal were peas with nutmeg sprinkled on top and baked apples with cinnamon. Pumpkin pie would be for dessert with its ample supply of ginger, cinnamon, nutmeg and vanilla.

During the later years of World War II we moved to Cove Point on the Chesapeake Bay, in southern Maryland, an hour south-east of Washington. It was here, in the land of blue crabs, oysters and fish, that a new sense of spices floated into my life. Crabs are the mainstays of this region. The Chesapeake Bay Blue Crab is always steamed, usually from 30–40 minutes in a large pot which may contain about two dozen crabs. Once steamed, the crabs emerge orange-red and are placed on a large table with a newspaper base. They may then be eaten one by one, or picked to make crab cakes, crab soup or crab salad. Some people find it very difficult to pick the crabs without consuming most of their work. The pot has three parts: a bottom section about eight inches high, a middle section about eighteen inches high with holes in the bottom and a lid. The pot is put on the stove and the bottom section is filled about three-quarters full with water. Vinegar is added as well as Old Bay Seasoning. When the water comes to a boil and the steam is strong, the top section is added and the live crabs are placed inside. Many people sprinkle a lot of Old Bay on the crabs as they go into the pot. As a child I remember the occasional crab that 'slipped' out of its thongs on the way to the pot and hit the floor with its dual claws looking for victims. For young children, this was a time of panic and squealing delight and I must admit that I let 'slip' a few crabs on the kitchen floor for my own children. The key to the taste of the steamed crabs was the Old Bay Seasoning. The ingredients were: celery salt, paprika and a variety of spices, including mustard, red pepper, black pepper, bay (laurel) leaves, cloves, allspice, ginger, mace, cardamom and cinnamon. Old Bay is made by McCormick and Company, one of the leading spice producers in the world, who make the spice 60 miles north, via the Chesapeake Bay, from Cove Point at the end of the Port of Baltimore.

After World War II my grandfather died, his store was sold and we moved across the Patuxent River from Cove Point, to government housing in St. Mary's County. Within a few years I was sent to an upper elementary military school, where I lived in a dormitory for three years. My food and spice memories from these years are blank; institutional food does not promote fond food memories. During high school I went away to school again; this time 100 miles to the north, to a Catholic boys boarding school in Baltimore. Again the memories are very dim. The food was cooked by a group of German nuns and I am only able to recall bowls of plain white potatoes, *sans* spices.

Through college, more of the same food, which many times was found on the ceiling of the dining room – a result of frustrated collegiate eaters. As I studied history in college and later in graduate school, my interest in world history increased after I had developed a strong base in United States history and literature. After teaching senior high school for a few years I started working on my doctorate, and my interest in world history increased with a doctoral field of study in Latin American and Spanish and Portuguese history.

However, it was not until I started working with groups of teachers that I began to see the connections between spices and world history. From that point forward I was hooked. Every trip to a new city was climaxed by a trip to old bookstores to search for books on spices. My collection grew as did my knowledge of these wonderful additions to food.

What are your memories of spices? Do they stand out in your mind or do they blend into your eating habits?

My memories of spices in history go back long before the Common Era to Pliny, who, in his *Natural History*, reflected on pepper, 'It is astonishing that its use has met with such flavour. In other foods it is their sweetness that enchants us, or else it is their appearance that beguiles; but, as for pepper, neither its fruit or its berry has anything to recommend it. To think that it is just for its bitterness that people like it, and that they go to India in search for it.' Over time pepper became my spice of choice and my major focal point for research and understanding spices and the spice trade.

Pepper is one of the sovereign spices, along with cloves and nutmeg, which will be the subject of this paper and presents a starting point for individual memory. Our senses, especially through our taste buds, crave soft, sensual caresses, but they also need stronger, more fiery spices. We would be incomplete without both in our memory. In south Asia, where the world's memories of pepper begin, perhaps over two millennia ago, Indians call peppercorns *kalo marich*. To them, peppercorns will sweat the secrets out of you. Pepper, like other spices, first entered the memories of people as a medicine. Hippocrates recommended it, combined with honey and vinegar, for use in the treatment of feminine disorders. Pepper owes its pungency to a resin and its flavour to a volatile oil. For those who raised the pepper over millennia as well as for those that came from Europe to find pepper, the sensual memories must have been strong. In India pepper began on the Malabar or west coast in the state of Kerala. High up in the western Ghats, or mountain ranges, along the coast of the Arabian Sea, there are many waterfalls, and herds of wild elephants roam in an area where soft mists fill the air. Watching a recent PBS series on Indian Religions, with it colourful filming of the Malabar coast, has increased my desire to visit the historical sources of pepper. I want to watch the green bunches of peppercorns being detached by hand and then dried in the sun, shrivelling and puckering as they turn black. It would also be fun to develop the white peppercorns: picking the berries when red and fermenting them in salt water until the fragile outer shells can be removed by hand and then sorted and dried. White and black pepper give you different sense memories. Most of the piperine, the pungent substance found in pepper, is found in the skin around the seed, whereas the aroma of its essential oils is contained within the seed itself. This fact explains why white pepper is less fiery, but richer in flavour, than black.

My memories of pepper in restaurants are varied and ongoing images of different peppermills and degrees of knowledge about the black, white or green spice that is being served. Sometimes I will sense a waiter is knowledgeable and actually knows about pepper and so I engage the server in a discussion of pepper. At other moments I get a blank, functional stare that tells me to avoid discussion and eat my food. My memories are of black pepper on salads, especially when spinach is the food; the pungent black contrasts well on the tongue with the dark green vegetable. Since I live in a major fish-catching area I look forward to white peppercorns on my meaty rockfish and, when I travel to the north-west, the goodness of line-caught halibut with a pepper spray is a treat. Once or twice a year I may encounter a green peppercorn sauce on a nice piece of steak; a treat not to be enjoyed too often for very obvious reasons, which have nothing to do with mad-cow disease. I must admit that I have a very traditional view of consuming pepper in its classical forms as I have outlined above. However, I would also be tempted to try Black Pepper Biscotti the next time I visit a Portland, Oregon restaurant, or move to a more Asian/southwestern venue by trying Suzanna Foo's Pork with Poblano Chili, Grapes and Cracked Pepper, at her Philadelphia restaurant.

As I noted earlier my memories of nutmeg were sensed from pumpkin pies and the topping of peas. Both were wintertime memories. Additionally I remember nutmeg sprinkled on the top of eggnog, that heady Christmas drink with heavily creamed milk and sharp American whiskey. Although I was allowed a taste of the eggnog, my upper lip and tongue got more of the nutmeg on top than the whisky down below. Seeing the nutmeg that comes out of cans and bottles belies that fact that its origin is a pulpy, peach-like plant surrounding a hard brown nut, surrounded by a fiery red, loose-weaved membrane netting of mace. Nutmeg grows on several Indonesian islands as well as in India and Sri Lanka, and, to a large extent, on the island of Grenada, one of the Windward Islands of the West Indies.

For over a millennium cloves have been used for purifying and as an antiseptic. Their essential oils possess anti-bacterial, anti-fungal, and analgesic properties that are used in dentistry. I remind my son-in-law, a dentist, of his debt to the world of spices. On the food side cloves blend well with ginger, peppercorns and cardamom, which are found in Indian *masalas*, which I especially enjoy on my too infrequent visits to south Asian restaurants, not found in my home port of St. Mary's City, Maryland.

My home memories of cloves find me grinding them on orange juice. Try it! My wife, Betty, cans peaches in the late summer of each year and pierces each whole peach with spikes of cloves. By midwinter, the clove has done its work and winter nights become spicier and sweeter, with the scent of clove peaches.

What did people from the northern Hemisphere sense and feel when they came upon the clove islands of the Moluccan East Indies? There are five islands, all within sight of each other and about 100 miles long from north to south. The most noted of these islands are Ternate and Tidore. They are described by a Portuguese explorer, Barros, as summarized by historian Donald Lash.

> Climate and landscape are both unpleasant and healthy. Because of the equatorial location of the islands, the sun is always near, even when at its northern and southern solstices. Constant heat combined with high humidity encourages the growth of heavy vegetation everywhere and produces clouds that hang near the tops of the mountains. The moisture laden air, so good for vegetation is unhealthy for humans. Most trees are never without leaves, though the clove puts forth its leaves only every second year because the growth is usually crushed at harvest time. On the sides of the volcanic mountains of the interior, the atmosphere is healthier than in the marshy and disease-ridden lowlands. The soil on all of the islands is usually black, dry and highly porous. No matter how much it rains, this thirsty soil (lava) seemingly absorbs all the water. Even rivers which rise in the interior dry up before reaching the sea. Several of the islands have active volcanoes...

Cloves, like other spices, have lost the high value that they had attained during the medieval and renaissance worlds. Today, cloves are limited to a few specific uses in Europe, such as with onions, studded with a few cloves, in braised and boiled meat dishes; pastries with honey and dried fruits. In India and China they are included in several mixtures of spices. However, for many of us cloves retain their high value as a spice enhancing peaches, hams or wine.

For most of us our work and our families have consumed the time of our lives. Many of us will have to live with local memories of food and spices as we create our own world of culinary enjoyment or live vicariously through the writing of others. However, for some of us there still lingers the possibility of visiting the island of Run to see and smell the nutmeg and mace; to go to the island of Tidore and watch the clove trees being harvested; and to venture up in the Ghats on the Malabar coast of India to see, smell, and touch the best pepper in the world.

What are your sense memories of spices? Do you take them for granted in the dishes you are served or do they take on their own identities through your senses? Perhaps you might look into one or two of your favourite spices and find that they have their own world histories, their own geographic settings and their own sensual processes to get to your table.

BIBLIOGRAPHY

Corn, Charles (1998) *The Scents of Eden*, New York: Kodansha International.
Divakaruni, Chitra Banerjee (1997) *The Mistress of Spices*, New York: Anchor Books.
Gibbs, W.M. (1909) *Spices and How to Know Them*, Buffalo, New York: Composition, presswork and binding by the Matthews-Northrup Works.
Lash, Donald (1965) *Asia in the Making of Europe, Volume I: The Century of Discovery*, Book 2, Chicago: The University of Chicago Press.
Milton, Giles (1999) *Nathaniel's Nutmeg*, New York: Farrar, Straus, and Giroux.
Stefla, Akaub (1998) *The Book of Spices*, New York: Flammarion.
Tannahill, Reay (1973) *Food in History*, New York: Stein and Day.
Tidbury, G.E. (1949) *The Clove Tree*, London: Crosby, Lockwood and Son, Ltd.

Dining with the Caesars

Andrew Dalby

Memories, archives, conversations over dinner

The author of the *Lives of the Caesars* was not an unimportant man. His grandfather knew some people who knew the emperor Caligula. His father had been a military tribune, a liaison post, during the Year of the Four Emperors (AD 69). As for Gaius Suetonius Tranquillus himself, he nearly became a military tribune like his father; he got an appointment to serve with the new governor of the wild and wintry province of Britain around AD 101, but changed his mind just in time and did not go. He became a close friend of the writer and provincial administrator Pliny 'the younger'; he himself was in his heart a writer, or rather a scholar, and eventually found in the Imperial secretariat a post that suited him much better than anything in Britain would have done. Suetonius was *ab epistulis*, in charge of the correspondence; we do not know for how long. As such, and as one of the people who didn't get on with the empress Sabina, he was a victim in a round of sackings under Hadrian in AD 121.

He wrote many books. They were scholars' books; some of them were little encyclopaedias or dictionaries: *Greek Games, Roman Festivals, Names of Clothes and Shoes, Physical Blemishes, Greek Terms of Abuse, Roman Customs*; and then a couple of other unusual topics that clearly suited this particular author: a history or manual of the *Imperial Civil Service* and a guide to *Manuscript Signs and Abbreviations*. He wrote little biographies, too, gathered under the general title *On Famous Men* and subdivided into themes: poets, orators, historians, philosophers, scholars and teachers. We should notice this list of themes; they show that Suetonius' 'famous men', like Suetonius himself, were not men of action. Much more significantly, they and he had lived in the same world. His sources of information for many of his books, including some of these biographies, must have been varied and impressive. He drew on his own professional knowledge, the gossip of his seniors and his colleagues, revealing documents that he had had in his hands, and tireless note-taking in the course of a lifetime's reading of history and literature.

Some of his little biographies still survive: the scholars, the teachers and a few of the poets. The other books are lost, although his glossary of Greek terms of abuse has been lovingly reconstructed from what may be extracts in later Greek dictionaries.

Apart from these, Suetonius wrote one book that survives and is a perennial best-seller. He applied his own special biographical method, his personal knowledge of the Imperial household, his extended memory (through family and contacts) of recent history, and his familiarity with the archives, to the *Lives of the Caesars*. The range of source materials used and explicitly credited by Suetonius in this book is unusual, possibly unique, in ancient writing. What he produced is a scholar's book, almost an archivist's book, but it is on a topic that cannot fail to attract masses of readers. With the *Lives of the Caesars*, as with his other books, his strong suit is that he lived in the same world as his subjects. The difference, this time, is that his subjects were men of almost limitless power: the twelve autocrats who successively ruled Rome, beginning with Julius Caesar and ending with Domitian.

We will see that food and wine, meals and banquets recur continually in Suetonius' biographies. This is in no way surprising. In Roman society, perhaps even more than today, meals and drinking parties were the environment in which one interacted with others and revealed oneself. Biography, as Suetonius practised it, was about revelation and self-revelation. Naturally – unavoidably – he visualized his subjects as they ate and drank.

To whet the appetite, here are three of the 'memories', his own and his family's, that went into Suetonius' book.

At the fashionable seaside resort of Baiae, near Naples, the emperor Gaius 'Caligula' once built a bridge of ships, three miles long, across the bay. He galloped across it on horseback, held a torchlit banquet on it and, with the sense of humour for which he was so famous, tipped a good number of the banqueters off it into the sea. Not many were drowned. But what on earth gave him the idea? After suggesting other possible reasons, Suetonius adds: 'As a boy I used to hear my grandfather tell this story. According to insiders at court, there was one simple reason for the bridge. Years before, Tiberius was pondering the future and was inclined to name young Tiberius, his grandson, as his successor. Thrasyllus the astrologer commented: "As for Gaius here, he has no more chance of becoming Emperor than of riding a horse across the Bay of Baiae"' (Suetonius, *Gaius* 19).

Why did Otho, during that nightmare year AD 69, having seized the empire from Galba, give it up with hardly a struggle when challenged in turn by Vitellius' army? Suetonius recalls a telling detail: 'My own father, Suetonius Laetus, who wore the narrow stripe, served as tribune with the Thirteenth Legion on this campaign. He often used to say afterwards that Otho had so deeply abhorred the thought of civil war, even as a private citizen, that he would shudder if over dinner anyone should happen to mention the fates of Brutus and Cassius; and he only challenged Galba because he was confident that he could manage it without any fighting' (*Otho* 10).¹

I asserted that Suetonius lived in the same world as his subjects. This was no undocumented claim. Just once in his best-selling book, this self-effacing author allows the reader to observe that a principal private secretary is on reasonably close terms with his Emperor: 'In thus stating that Augustus had the *cognomen* Thurinus as a child I am sure of my facts. I once owned an old bronze figurine of him as a boy, which bore an inscription in iron letters, by then scarcely legible, giving him this name. I presented the figure to the Emperor [Hadrian], who now honours it among the Household Gods in his bedroom' (*Augustus* 7).

This paper explores how Suetonius used his own memory and those of others. In doing so it will focus on several of the 'twelve Caesars' in turn: Domitian, Vitellius, Nero, Claudius, Caligula, Augustus, Julius. They are in reverse chronological order, because we are working from the emperors under whom Suetonius had lived towards the ones who died many years before he was born. And since Suetonius himself was able to compare emperors with one another, and to interpret the character of one in the light of another, we are free to do the same.

What Suetonius knew

If you write the social history of your own time – and this is what Suetonius was doing, though he cast it in the form of a series of biographies – you will take a great deal for granted: things that seem natural, things that you know and every reader must know as well. You will focus on what seems unusual, unexpected or at least noticeable. Here, for example, in the course of sketching the daily life of Augustus, a hundred years before his own time, Suetonius quotes one of Augustus' private letters:²

> We had the same company for dinner, my dear Tiberius, except that Vinicius and the elder Silius were also invited; and we gambled like old men all through the meal, and until yesterday turned into today. Anyone who threw the Dog or a Six put a *denarius* in the pool for each of the dice; and anyone who threw Venus scooped the lot.
> Suetonius, Augustus 71.³

Perhaps we want to know where they put the gaming board, or how they stopped the dice getting mixed up with the food? Suetonius knows perfectly well, and so should we. Do we want to know what 'The Dog' and 'Venus' are, and the regular rules of the game that Augustus is obviously varying? Suetonius was just the man to write a book on the subject, but this is not that book.

Perhaps we want to know how the Imperial family arranged itself around the dinner tables? We must take care. Suetonius will not tell us the everyday practice among the nobility of his own time, because that is taken as given; he will only tell us what surprises him. Whenever Augustus' grandsons, Gaius and Lucius, dined with him 'he had them sit by him on his own couch' (*Augustus* 64). This comes in a sequence of anecdotes on the care Augustus took personally over the boys' education; it tells us that Suetonius would have expected, in his own time, to see 'princes' such as these brought on more quickly, not perched on a parental couch but reclining at dinner like young adults. Augustus was old-fashioned, so it seemed to Suetonius; Caligula, when we come to him, had a more liberal attitude to family relationships: 'It had become his custom to commit incest with all of his three sisters. At big dinners he arranged them all in order below him, while his wife reclined above him' (*Gaius* 24). If a man were less godlike than Caligula (Suetonius is certainly thinking) he might well place his wife to his left at dinner, or his girl friend to his right, but probably not both at the same dinner; again, if he had three girl friends, or sisters, it would be the action of a thoughtful host of a dinner party not to place all three together.

Certain relatives of this same emperor were less circumspectly treated, such as his uncle Claudius:

> Claudius' new honours did not protect him from frequent insults. If ever he arrived a little late for dinner, he just had to go around the couches in search of a space; and when he nodded off after dinner, as he very often did, the company would pelt him with olive and date stones, and the buffoons would give him a sudden blow of a whip or cane to stir him up. They even used to put slippers on his hands as he lay snoring, so that when he woke suddenly he would rub his face with them.
>
> Suetonius, *Claudius* 8.

Let us be aware that there is nothing strange in the presence of buffoons or jesters at dinner; nothing strange if the most despised member of the family is unable to find a place on the couches; nothing strange about practical jokes. The social historian is immensely grateful for these everyday touches, but they are only given space by Suetonius in order to bring out the one unexpected and important point. The only thing that made this story worth telling by Suetonius' grandfather (or whoever was his source here) and worth retelling by Suetonius, is that uncle Claudius was destined to be emperor.

Less fortunate even than Claudius were the slaves who hung about behind the couches, with nowhere to sit and nothing to do until the moment when the master or mistress wanted something; and with nothing to eat till it was all over, unless an old-fashioned and paternalistic master gave a thought to this detail in the course of dinner. There was even such a one among the first twelve emperors. Galba, Suetonius tells us, 'was a heavy eater, in winter always breakfasting before daylight. He had a habit, at dinner, of gathering up left-over food in his hands to be passed on to the slaves standing by' (*Galba* 21). Galba was even more old-fashioned than Augustus; this detail of his behaviour, which would no doubt have been just right for a Roman householder of about 120 BC, seemed so monstrously inappropriate in an emperor two centuries later that Suetonius can only deal with it under the rubric of 'bad habits'.

To conclude this section, let us picture one of those small imperial dinner parties. There are three large couches, offering nine places, on three sides of the dining room; in the centre there are several small tables, and waiters forever coming and going to serve food and wine. Here is how Augustus used to do it:

> He gave frequent dinner parties, always formal ones, and each time taking great care over social status and personality. Valerius Messala states that Augustus never on any occasion invited a freed slave to dinner, except Menas, to whom he had awarded the citizenship for betraying Sextus Pompey's fleet to him. Augustus himself, though, writes that he did sometimes invite a former bodyguard, the man whose country place he used as a retreat. At his dinner parties he would sometimes arrive late and leave early, letting his guests start before he had reclined and finish after he had left. The meal would usually consist of three courses, or, at his most liberal, six: there was no excessive extravagance. Yet the atmosphere was extremely convivial. If there were guests who did not speak, or whispered to their neighbours, he managed to bring them into the general conversation; and he laid on entertainment by providing actors, people who did Circus acts and street shows, and, even more frequently, professional storytellers.
>
> Suetonius, *Augustus* 74.

It will have seemed to Suetonius very antiquated that Augustus scarcely ever invited freedmen to dinner: in the century that intervened between Augustus' death and Suetonius' researches, freedmen had become ubiquitous at court and in the Imperial service. So, once he had noted this provocative assertion on the subject by Valerius Messala, it is no wonder that Suetonius hunted through Augustus' letters to come up with another example. The informality of Augustus' entertaining – for example, the guests starting to eat before the Emperor has reclined – will also have charmed Suetonius.

He insists on the small number of courses. At the end of this paper we shall find evidence that an extravagant kind of gastronomy had begun to peak under

Augustus; Augustus himself was no doubt consciously reacting against it, if (as I suppose) his own letters are Suetonius' source of information on this detail. That costly gastronomy had rather died away by Suetonius' time, but meanwhile the fashion of serving a larger number of separate courses at dinner parties had become established, and it persisted. Thus a three-course meal, in the context of Imperial entertaining, will have seemed very Spartan to Suetonius.

Domitian, or the perfect host

We have already seen that Caligula liked a joke. It is one thing that Caligula had in common with the twelfth of the Caesars, Domitian – not a bad emperor in some ways, though he fell victim to a palace revolution in the end. Here is one of Domitian's jokes:

> On one occasion Domitian entertained the leading senators and knights to dinner. He prepared a room that was completely black all over, ceiling, walls and floor. On the bare floor were bare couches of the same colour. He invited his guests to enter alone, without their attendants. Beside each of them was set a stone slab like a gravestone, on which the name was inscribed, and a small lamp such as people hang in tombs. Then beautiful boys, naked, and painted black, entered just like ghosts, and after performing an eerie dance around the guests took their places at their feet. Then all the foods that are offered to the spirits of the dead were served to them, all black, in dishes of the same colour. Every one of them was naturally in fear and trembling that he would be butchered any moment, especially because everyone except Domitian himself was as silent as the dead, and Domitian chatted all evening about death and sacrifice. At length they were dismissed, but he had meanwhile taken away their own attendants, who had been waiting in the vestibule; instead he consigned them to others whom they did not know to take them home in carriages or litters. This was even more frightening. Each guest had scarcely reached home, and begun to breathe again, as it were, when a message from the Emperor was announced. Now, they thought, they were certainly doomed. Then a first messenger brought them their slab – which turned out to be silver – and others brought them various other things, including all the tableware that had been set before them at dinner, all of which was of very costly manufacture; and last of all the very boy who had been each guest's 'spirit', now washed and dolled up. So, after a night of terror, they were given all these presents; and that was Domitian's 'Triumph', or rather (as ordinary people said) his funeral feast for those who had died in his Dacian War and in Rome.
>
> Dio Cassius 67.9.[4]

This famous story is one that Suetonius does not tell: I translate it here from a history of Rome written, a century later, in Greek by Dio Cassius. In reading it one realizes with stark clarity that an emperor who likes a practical joke is his own worst enemy. The nightmare that his guests had lived through before getting their gifts is well described and easily imagined. On whose side would these guests be when Domitian's wife decided it was time for a change at the top?

Yes, there may have been some leading senators and knights who were looking forward to Domitian's death. Among ordinary people, none the less, he was highly popular. To them Domitian was truly the perfect host, at his best when presiding divinely while everyone around him gradually became happier and happier. Let me begin with an eyewitness report of a magnificent Saturnalia feast given by Domitian in the Colosseum. This description is by Statius, the almost-laureate poet of Domitian's principate, who calls on 'drunk December' and other temporary Muses to help him narrate 'the fine day and the bibulous night that our cheerful Caesar arranged for us'. I will curtail him slightly, while adding a few explanations to help us savour Domitian's picnic:

> Scarce had Dawn got out of bed when sweets began to rain down on us, a rare dew distilled by the rising East Wind. The finest harvest of the hazel orchards of the Pontus and of the date palms of Idume, all that devout Damascus grows on its boughs [prunes or damsons came from Damascus], all that thirsty Caunus dries [figs were dried in Caunus], all these fell on us in profusion: there was a veritable shower of little cheeses and fritters, must-cakes and enormous *caryotis* dates from invisible palms [these were even juicier dates]. A second 'audience', at least as good-looking and well-dressed as we who were sitting down, now threaded its way along every row. Some carried baskets of bread and white napkins and more elaborate delicacies; others served languorous wine in brimming measure: you would think each one a divine cupbearer from Mount Ida [Ganymede, Jupiter's own cupbearer]. The same table served every class alike, child, woman, plebeian, knight and senator. You yourself – most gods could not have managed this! – you, Caesar, condescended to share our feast.

At this point Statius notices what was going on in the arena – a mock battle between 'Amazons', a hunting display in which dwarfs or pygmies were the hunters and cranes were the quarry, and then variety acts. Meanwhile, 'great clouds of birds swoop suddenly down through the air, birds from holy Nile and frozen Phasis, birds that Numidians capture under the watery South Wind.' Birds from the Nile are flamingos, those from Phasis are pheasants, those from

Numidia are guinea-fowl; this was not the first time that a Roman audience had been presented with exotic birds by a generous emperor.[5] As night fell there were fireworks, and 'who,' Statius asks rhetorically, 'could describe the scene that ensued, the wild partying, the merriment, the food that no one had to pay for, the broad rivers of wine? I'm beginning to feel weak. Caesar's wine was too much for me, and it's time I staggered off to bed' (Statius, *Silvae* 1.6). The various delicacies descended like rain from a sunny sky, Statius assures us, and by the end of this entertainment the average spectator would be fairly sticky – whether or not this was one of those shows at which the whole auditorium was sprayed, to improve its aroma, with a jet of white wine scented with saffron.

We cannot doubt that the official poet enjoyed himself; but do we know whether such entertainments as Domitian's Saturnalia feast were sufficiently notable to be remembered after his death? The answer is that they were not easily forgotten:

> Domitian was an enthusiastic presenter of magnificent and costly entertainments both in the Amphitheatre and in the Circus... There were hunting displays and gladiatorial combats, sometimes nocturnal ones illuminated with torches – and there were women warriors in these shows as well as men... Once, in the course of the show to celebrate the Feast of the Seven Hills, he gave a splendid banquet, with hampers for senators and knights, and smaller baskets of food for plebeians. He took the first bite himself. Next day he scattered tokens for all kinds of gifts, and since most of them fell in the seats occupied by the plebeians he had 500 additional tokens thrown into each of the sections that were reserved for senators and knights.
>
> Suetonius, *Domitian* 4.

Suetonius is writing perhaps 25 years after the events. Incidentally, if Domitian had not fallen, then Nerva, Trajan and Hadrian, under the last of whom Suetonius wrote, would never have taken their turns as emperor; so Suetonius usually takes the safe course and is critical of Domitian. For all that, he gives a great deal of space – much more than I have quoted here – to Domitian's generous entertainments.

Some details in the passage by Suetonius remind us closely of the very show that Statius enjoyed so much: the programme running through the night, the women warriors, the fact that Domitian himself ceremoniously shared the meal ('most gods could not have managed this,' said Statius with his usual obsequiousness). Other details show that the precise arrangements at the Feast of the Seven Hills (as sketched by Suetonius) differed from those at the Saturnalia (as painted in by Statius); in the former, senators and knights got bigger picnic hampers than the plebeians did, while in the latter everyone was equal.

Even the free wine at these shows, though it goes unmentioned by Suetonius, was long remembered. A hundred years later this is one of the details that Dio Cassius thought worth restoring to the collective memory: 'Domitian once gave the spectators a dinner while they stayed in their places, and at night he provided wine on tap in several places in the Amphitheatre' (Dio Cassius 67.4.4).[6]

Vitellius, or the best possible taste

In approaching dinner with Vitellius, last of the failed emperors of AD 69, we must first step gingerly around the vomiting question. No one who studies Rome through the medium of Suetonius can quite forget those vomiting emperors. Julius Caesar, so far as we know, had kept his food and wine down, but Augustus, in this as in many other ways, had set a new pattern for his successors.

> As regards wine, Augustus was by nature very abstemious. During the siege of Mutina, according to Cornelius Nepos, he never took more than three cups with his dinner. Later he would not go beyond a pint – if he did, he would throw up. He particularly liked Raetian, but he rarely drank between meals; instead, he would take a bit of bread soaked in cold water; or a slice of cucumber, or the heart of a young lettuce; or perhaps an apple (freshly picked, or dried) with a wine-like flavour. After luncheon he used to rest for a while without removing clothes or shoes; one hand shading his eyes, his feet uncovered.
>
> Suetonius, *Augustus* 77–8.

The Raetian wine that Augustus liked came from the hills around Verona (Valpolicella, more or less). No one else liked it much, and Augustus is showing quite remarkable prescience. It was perhaps the only wine available in Greece or Italy that was matured in wooden barrels. Augustus, like a modern Californian or Australian, loved the taste of oak.

In the passage just quoted I have to take issue with Suetonius' classic translator, Robert Graves. Graves over-translates this passage. He makes the three cups 'wine-and-water', probably because three cups of wine would have seemed far too much in England in the 1950s, even if it didn't in Majorca. More boldly, Graves says that Augustus 'would deliberately vomit' if he took more than a pint of wine. The 'deliberately' isn't there in the Latin: the verb *reicio* means literally 'throw up', and it's for the reader to decide whether Augustus made a conscious decision or found himself overtaken by events.

We follow the tradition forwards from Augustus to later emperors. Tiberius liked to drink, as we shall see, but he drank for keeps. Caligula, an aesthetic type, was not a heavy eater or drinker. But Claudius was, or so it seemed to Suetonius seventy years later:

> No matter where and when, Claudius was always hungry for food and wine. One day, sitting [as judge] in the Forum of Augustus, he was tempted by the scent of lunch being prepared for the Salian priests in the neighbouring Temple of Mars. He abandoned the tribunal, crossed the way and reclined with the priests to share their meal. Claudius was unlikely ever to leave a dining room except bloated, sodden, and ready to fall asleep supine with his mouth wide open so that a feather could be put down his throat to bring up the surfeit from his stomach.
> <div align="right">Suetonius, <i>Claudius</i> 33.</div>

Not a pretty picture. A detail of the life of Nero, Claudius' successor, supports it. He wanted to be a singer, and 'conscientiously undertook all the usual exercises for strengthening the voice. He would lie on his back with a slab of lead on his chest, use enemas and emetics to keep down his weight, and refrain from eating apples and every other food considered deleterious to the vocal chords' (*Nero* 20). Notice the emetics: Nero, too, habitually vomited, in order to keep his weight down.

Now the fastidious Seneca, stoic moralist and tragedian, was a man about court just at this time, having been engaged as tutor to young Nero himself. Seneca, I believe, took a good look at the bloated, sodden and stertorous emperor, and peeked round the bathroom door at his weight-watching pupil, before striding back to his desk to condemn his entire generation in the memorable words, 'They vomit in order to eat, they eat in order to vomit: the whole earth supplies their meals, and they do not even bother to digest them' (Seneca, *Consolation to Helvia* 10.3). I respect Seneca's opinion, as a man who was able to colonize both sides of any moral question ('Seneca was critical of other people's extravagance but he himself had five hundred cedar wood tables, with ivory legs, all matching, to serve his banquets on', claimed Dio Cassius,[7] who disapproved of him) but how many other Romans really treated their food in the same cavalier fashion as Claudius and Nero? I am still not sure.

Still, I do know one other person who did. The future emperor Vitellius was a courtier just at this same time. As a charioteer he was admired by Caligula; he used to play dice with Claudius (by what rules is not recorded)[8] while Seneca, no doubt, was sitting in the corner and getting on with his reading. During Vitellius' own brief principate, which was to follow in twenty years' time, 'the one and only avenue to influence was to glut the insatiable appetites of Vitellius with lavish junketing, expenditure and debauch. The emperor himself, content to enjoy the present and thoughtless of the morrow, is held to have squandered 900 million sesterces in a very few months' (Tacitus, *Histories* 2.95).[9] That is all that the sardonic Tacitus, writing his history of this period thirty years after, cares to say. The topic was closer to the heart of his younger contemporary Suetonius. What follows is one of Suetonius' finest pen-portraits of a Roman emperor at dinner. From it we can see that Vitellius admired and imitated Claudius' way with food:

> Devoted to gluttony and cruelty in equal measure, Vitellius took at least three, often four meals a day, breakfast, lunch, dinner and then a drinking party. He managed it all easily thanks to his habit of vomiting. Often he invited himself out to these various meals, each one of which cost his hosts at least four hundred thousand sestertii. More notorious than any of the others was the banquet given him by his brother to welcome him to Rome, at which two thousand of the choicest fish and seven thousand birds are said to have been served. Vitellius himself surpassed this with a single dish that he invented, named from its immense size 'Shield of Minerva the All-Protecting'. In it he mixed together parrot-wrasse livers, pheasant and peacock brains, flamingos' tongues and *murenarum lactes*,[10] fetched for him by naval commanders in triremes from as far away as Parthia and the Spanish straits.
>
> He was a man of vast, inappropriate and unwholesome appetite. He would satisfy his greed while a sacrifice was in progress, with lumps of meat or cake off the altar, still sizzling from the fire; and when on the road, with smoking-hot morsels, or cold left-overs and half-eaten scraps, from wayside cook shops.
>
> Suetonius, *Vitellius* 13.[11]

That is the evidence in Roman texts about vomiting as a way of life: one queasy wine-drinker, two binging emperors, one obsessive slimmer and a sweep of Seneca's pen. Let us return to the food. As for that enormously costly dish, the 'Shield of Minerva the All-Protecting', it was memorable enough to leave other traces in the collective memory and to recur in the historical record a century later. Here is the Greek historian, Dio Cassius, once more:

> Vitellius ate greedily and regularly vomited it up again, as if this short-stay food were all he needed for nourishment… All the most expensive foods were fetched in – from the Ocean, or I might almost say beyond it, and from every land and sea. They were prepared in such an extravagant way that, even now, some cakes and other dishes are called

'Vitellian' after him… He once invented a dish that cost 250,000 denarii, a mixture of the tongues, the brains and the livers of various fish and birds. It was impossible to make an earthenware cooking pot large enough, so he ordered one of silver. It survived for a long time as a sort of object of worship, till eventually Hadrian came across it and melted it down.

Dio Cassius 65.2.2–65.3.3.[12]

We see that Dio has another piece in the jigsaw puzzle of evidence about that wondrous dish invented by Vitellius: just the kind of evidence that Suetonius himself liked, but this time Suetonius failed to obtain it. Maybe Suetonius had had his little disagreement with the empress and left the Imperial household before that fateful day on which Hadrian peeked into the kitchens, was shown the awesome silver cooking pot and had it melted down.

Dio, like Suetonius, says how far Vitellius' luxury foods had travelled, but he says it in a different way. For Suetonius, they had come from Parthia and from the Spanish straits. For Dio, they came from every land and sea, from the Ocean 'and even beyond it'. To take these geographical clues one by one: Parthia was the source of plenty of aromatics used in Roman cooking, notably asafoetida. Together Parthia and the Spanish straits stood for opposite ends of the Mediterranean, the normal range of the Roman navy. Dio's 'Ocean' may well have represented the same as Suetonius' 'Spanish straits', since one led to the other, and so they denote some delicacy that Vitellius sent for from outside the Straits of Gibraltar. But what about Dio's 'beyond the Ocean'? I have wondered whether 'beyond the Ocean' means India, source of Roman pepper and of several other spices. Against this idea, what we call the Indian Ocean, Romans called a sea, the *mare Erythraeum* or 'Red Sea'; to their way of thinking, India was not 'beyond the Ocean'. I believe there is only one other possibility: if Dio's meaning is to be pressed, Romans were already importing British oysters in AD 69, or Dio thought they were. There is independent literary evidence that British oysters had reached Rome by Vitellius' time.[13]

Dio adds another detail of interest, that in his time certain dishes were named after Vitellius. This we know independently: Apicius supplies recipes for Vitellian peas, Vitellian beans and Vitellian sucking pig. We have seen that Vitellius was at court in Caligula's time; the invention of costly dishes was a hobby that these two emperors shared. 'No parallel can be found for Caligula's far-fetched extravagances,' writes Suetonius (I am borrowing Robert Graves' translation here). 'He invented new kinds of baths, and the most unnatural dishes and drinks – bathing in hot and cold perfumes, drinking valuable pearls dissolved in vinegar, and providing his guests with golden bread and golden meat' (*Gaius* 37). But it is Vitellius who must be seen as the true emperor of all gastronomes, and our picture of him is charmingly completed by Suetonius' little sketch of his attempted disappearance from the Roman scene: 'Sneaking into a sedan chair he made for his father's house on the Aventine Hill, intending to escape to Campania. He took only two companions, his pastry-cook and his chef' (*Vitellius* 16).

Nero, or the sharing of pleasures

Human beings want to be lots of things, and Roman emperors were in a better position than most other people to make their ambitions come true. They all, for example, wanted to be gods, after their deaths if not before. Caligula actually 'established a shrine to himself as God, with priests and with the costliest possible victims...Flamingos, peacocks, black grouse, guinea hens, and pheasants were offered as sacrifices to him, each on a particular day of the month' (*Gaius* 22). Even Augustus, modest man as he was in many ways, had a hankering after divinity. We remember his private banquet, known as 'The Feast of the Divine Twelve', which caused a public scandal; the guests came dressed as gods or goddesses, Augustus himself representing Apollo. Our authority for this [adds Suetonius] is a spiteful letter of Mark Antony's which names all twelve (*Augustus* 70).

Caligula wanted to be a charioteer; Claudius wanted to add some new letters to the Latin alphabet; Nero wanted to be a slim singer and win all the musical prizes. Needless to say, they all achieved their aims. But Nero wanted other things too. He wanted to be one of the boys: 'After dusk he would snatch a felt cap or leather hat, go down to the cook shops, and range the city looking for fun – not always innocently, because one of his games was to attack men on their way home from dinner, stab them if they offered resistance, and then drop their bodies down the sewers. He would also break into shops, afterwards holding a midweek market at the Palace with the stolen goods' (*Nero* 26).[14]

Nero was, quite simply, the most successful singer of his day. When he sang, everybody listened. When he competed, though suffering agonies of nervousness beforehand, he always won first prize. In fact he did not need to compete: all the juries sent him first prize anyway. He was also the most successful and the most generous gangster of his day, for he soon realized that these rowdy pleasures, too, could be enjoyed on an Imperial scale, and could be shared with all his friends:

> He now made his dinners last from noon till midnight, varied with an occasional swim in a heated bath or, in summer, in snow-cooled water. He held public dinner parties, too, in the *Naumachia* (temporarily

drained)[15] or the Campus Martius or the Circus Maximus, and these were attended by whores from all over the City and Syrian dancing-girls.

Suetonius, *Nero* 27.

We might like to know a little more of these dinners. Fortunately their memory, like that of Domitian's entertainments, survived through more than one channel. Dio, writing 150 years later, can tell us of one particular banquet held in the artificially flooded Colosseum:

> In the middle, sunk in the water, were big wooden wine barrels. A wooden platform was fixed on top of these, and there were taverns and disorderly houses all around it. Nero, Tigellinus and their fellow-diners were feasting in the middle, lying on purple rugs and soft cushions, while everybody else enjoyed themselves in the taverns. They could go into the brothels, too, and have sex quite freely with any of the women who were on display; and these were the most beautiful and the most admired women in Rome...
>
> Dio Cassius 62.15.1–6.[16]

We will leave to Dio his additional details concerning activities in the brothels. Nero's assumption of the grand style expressed itself eventually in the *Domus Aurea*, his new palace occupying half of central Rome (which had conveniently burnt down just before):

> All its dining-rooms had ceilings whose fretted ivory panels could slide back to allow flower petals to fall on the diners, and were fitted with pipes to shower them with perfumes. The main dining-room was circular, and its roof revolved slowly, day and night, in time with the sky.
>
> Suetonius, *Nero* 31.

Nero's influence on later gastronomy has been partly good, partly bad. The facts come to us from three widely separated passages[17] of the encyclopaedic *Natural History* compiled by Pliny 'the elder', uncle of the Pliny who was Suetonius' friend. Inventions and 'firsts' were not the kind of detail that Suetonius looked for; Pliny was fascinated by them.

The bad news first: Nero's transport policy was what killed the wine of the *Ager Caecubus*, the unrivalled great name in wine in earlier Rome. Pliny in fact attributes this catastrophe to 'the grower's neglect, the smallness of the terroir, and more still the ship canal begun by Nero that was to link the lake of Baiae to Ostia.' The ship canal never materialized, but the vineyard was abandoned – the first recorded case of planning blight. So it came about that the great physician Galen, about a hundred years after Nero's time, is the very last person on record to have tasted *Caecuban*: he found it, reasonably enough, 'too old'. Another great flavour that Nero crossed off our list is that of silphium, the spice from north Africa that resembled – but was so much better than – asafoetida. It had once been 'worth its weight in silver,' said Pliny, but 'for many years now no silphium has been seen in its native region...The single stem found within living memory was sent to the emperor Nero,' who, presumably, ate it without a second thought. No one will ever know what it tasted like.

But now the good news: until Nero's time the only safe way to add water to wine was to add it recently boiled, still hot. The Romans knew this, although, unaware of microbes, they had no idea why it was. They liked to add ice to wine, and even carried snow to Rome and stored it there for the purpose, but they knew that it would sometimes make them ill. Nero's great idea was to boil water, to seal it in a jar, and then to embed the jar in snow. This produced ice-cold water that was more or less sterilized, to add to wine, and I think it will be agreed that it was a significant contribution to human happiness, or at least to the happiness of those in Rome who could afford large quantities of snow in summer.

I am not alone in believing this to be one of Nero's greatest achievements. Nero himself thought as I do, to judge from the fact that his great invention was at the front of his mind on his very last day on Earth. Expecting to be captured at any moment, Nero was hiding alone in a garden not far from Rome. Lacking any other supplies, 'he scooped up water from a pool to drink from his cupped hands. "Here is Nero's very own iced water," he said' (*Nero* 48).[18] Whatever Suetonius' immediate source, the story, if true, must come from the memories of the few slaves who had remained with Nero during his flight.

Claudius, or how to ensure the succession

Those who dined with emperors accepted a certain risk. Already in those days there was a long history of the use of poison in royal households. No wonder that Agrippina, wife of the murdered hero Germanicus, was chary of biting into an apple politely handed to her, at a private dinner, by Tiberius in person – and no wonder Tiberius was offended at her refusal. She died soon afterwards.[19]

Some said that Livia murdered her husband, Augustus, by smearing poison on the figs that he was about to pick from the tree. As for Claudius, his wife Agrippina the younger (daughter of Germanicus and Agrippina) was a suspect:

> There is consensus that Claudius was poisoned. Where, and by whom, is not agreed: some state that it was the eunuch Halotus, his taster, while he was dining with the priests in the Citadel; others that Agrippina

herself, at a family banquet, poisoned a mushroom, one of the foods he would eat most greedily. What happened next is similarly disputed. Many people say that immediately after taking the poison he lost his power of speech, was in frightful pain all night long, and died shortly before dawn; others that he became unconscious, but his stomach was so full that he vomited it all and had to be poisoned a second time: it is not clear whether this was by means of a gruel, which he was persuaded would revive him, or by means of an enema, given on the grounds that his digestive tract must be cleared by emptying his bowels.

Suetonius, *Claudius* 44.

You may think that Suetonius has done his best here: if Claudius was poisoned, and anyone at all ever said so afterwards, the true story is in that paragraph somewhere. Yet Dio Cassius, much later, while evidently going with one particular version among those offered by Suetonius, seems able to fill in some additional facts, notably the name of the technical expert involved:

It was difficult to poison Claudius, because of the large quantity of wine he habitually drank... Agrippina sent for Locusta, a well known druggist recently convicted of poisoning, and prepared with her help an effective poison, which she inserted in a mushroom. She herself ate other mushrooms from the dish, but arranged it that Claudius should eat the biggest, which was the one containing the poison...he remained speechless and insensible, and died that same night.

Dio Cassius 60.34.2–3.[20]

We cannot really know how to take the stories of imperial poisonings. These tales of the murder of Claudius cannot have been published until after the death of Nero, because Nero – Agrippina's son – had benefited directly. Suetonius gives us evidence, in fact, that the rumours were in circulation just after that time, when Domitian was a sensitive young man and his insensitive father Vespasian was emperor:

Domitian had long known the year and the day, indeed even the hour and the method of his death: the Chaldees had predicted all of this. His father once teased him openly at dinner for refusing some mushrooms: had he forgotten, Vespasian said, that it was steel he was supposed to be afraid of?

Suetonius, *Domitian* 14.

To return to the death of Claudius: because these were necessarily rumours rather than attested facts, I am more inclined to approve Suetonius' method here (listing them all without explicitly accepting any) than Dio's. I have two particular quibbles with Dio: one, that the business of the marked mushroom, good story though it is, is altogether too close to his version of the murder of Augustus, which, so he says, was done by poisoning one particular fig; two, that Locusta was a well known poisoner under Nero and evidently worked her way into this story because of her later fame.

Once the poisoning business was under way, it grew. Everyone was quite sure that this was how Nero got rid of his inconvenient half-brother, Claudius' own son Britannicus. In dealing with the death of Britannicus, Suetonius recalls the earlier death of Claudius and, this time – we notice – he nods through the same version of the story that Dio Cassius would later accept: evidently it was already the most popular:

> Even if not himself the murderer of [the deified] Claudius, Nero knew about the plot and did not pretend otherwise. The poison had been administered in mushrooms, and it would amuse Nero to quote the Greek proverb which calls mushrooms 'the food of the gods'. [Locusta is now introduced, described as 'a certain poisoner': as far as Suetonius is concerned, this is her first appearance in Imperial history. The researches of Nero and Locusta are narrated colourfully: they develop a very strong poison, testing it at each stage.] Nero had it brought to the dining room that very day and served to Britannicus. Britannicus collapsed at the first mouthful: he had always suffered from these epileptic fits, said Nero lyingly to the other diners.
>
> Suetonius, *Nero* 33.

Curiously enough a future emperor was present at this scene, or so the story ran. When Suetonius, later in his work, is describing the youthful life of the emperor Titus, he reverts to the event: 'The two boys were such good friends as to make it credible that when Britannicus drank his poison and died, Titus, reclining at his side, also took a drink of it and was seriously ill for a long time' (*Titus* 2). Do we believe this, or is it a story put about by the Titus groupies when Titus was heir apparent? It *may* be true – but it is significant that neither Suetonius nor any other historian uses it when narrating the death of Britannicus. It supports the poison theory, but not the story of the increasingly strong poisons being tested in advance by Nero and Locusta. If they had done their work properly, Titus should have died as well...

Caligula, or the patron's privilege

Caligula, like Nero and Domitian, felt that it was a major part of his duty as Emperor to make his people happy. His methods were similar to those of his successors. For example, 'he twice invited the whole Senate and the order of knights, with their wives and children, to a very generous banquet. At the second of these he gave every man a toga and every woman and child a red or purple scarf', and to put happiness on a more permanent footing he made the Saturnalia holiday five days instead of four. 'Again, he staged a great number of different theatrical shows of various types, sometimes at night, with the whole city illuminated. He gave out a basket of food to each man attending, and also scattered vouchers for all sorts of gifts. Noticing how happily and hungrily a knight seated opposite dug into this picnic, he sent him his own share as well' (*Gaius* 17–18).

On his own last day on earth Caligula was engaged in this same heart-warming occupation, presiding at a theatrical festival at which 'plenty of fruit was distributed to the audience, and plenty of birds rare enough to be of value to those who got them. Gaius was amused by the fighting and jostling to get hold of these prizes' (Josephus, *Jewish Antiquities* 19.1.13). According to a much later source, 'even Pomponius Secundus, who was then consul, was having a go at the food, sitting at the Emperor's feet and frequently leaning over to kiss them' (Dio Cassius 59.29.5).[21] If that happens to be true, it is quite in character. More than any other emperor, Caligula felt that it was equally his people's duty to make him happy.

A patron's power depended totally on what he could do for his clients. Caesar, and successors, all gave public dinners – symbols, whether they knew it or not, of all the other things that a patron did for his clients – and if Caligula regarded the current Consul as his client and as such qualified to kiss his feet, can we presume to disagree?

In a well-developed system of patronage, the rights that the system confers sometimes come into conflict with the law. The Roman law, for example, said that if a man married a woman, she stayed with him (till divorce or death). A man's patron knew otherwise, and, as just explained, Caligula was everybody's patron:

He attended the wedding ceremony of Gaius Piso and Livia Orestilla, but had the bride carried off to his own home... Others state that he told Piso, who was reclining opposite him at the wedding feast: 'Don't keep touching my wife!' and took her home with him from the party. Next day he announced that he had taken a wife as Romulus and Augustus had done.

Suetonius, *Gaius* 25.

He did not keep her very long; there were so many others:

> After inviting a number of noblewomen to dinner with their husbands he would slowly and carefully examine each in turn like a slave dealer as they passed his couch, even reaching out to lift up the chin of any woman who kept her eyes modestly cast down. When he felt so inclined, he would call for whoever pleased him best and leave the dining room with her. A little later he would return, making it quite clear that he had just been making love, and would praise or criticize her good and bad physical features and her sexual performance.
>
> Suetonius, *Gaius* 36.

What was all that about Romulus and Augustus? Romulus, along with his followers, seized the Sabine women; but that was eight hundred years ago, when Romans were rustic country folk. Augustus was quite different, and as it happens Suetonius owed his insight into Augustus' youthful sexual adventures to a collection of letters by Mark Antony to Augustus, both of whom were Caligula's great-grandfathers. There is every reason to suppose that Caligula knew these dining-room scandals as well as or better than Suetonius:

> Mark Antony threw back at Augustus the great haste in which he had married Livia, and that he had once fetched a former consul's wife from her husband's dining room into the bedroom before this husband's eyes: he brought her back to dinner blushing to the ears and with her hair in disorder.
>
> Suetonius, *Augustus* 69.

In later versions of the story Livia herself, Augustus' wife and widow, was seized from her former husband in just this way: perhaps this was already what Caligula believed.

Even in his own time, Augustus was probably not the only powerful patron to have taken advantage of his client in this way, for the Augustan poets are aware of such power games: Horace disapproves of them; Propertius claims to have played himself; Ovid even dares to write advice for the dinner-party seducer.[22]

Augustus, or not being fussy about food

Most of the emperors, from Augustus onwards, had their personal food preferences and their dietary fads. Tiberius' preference would appear to have been for wine:

> When already Emperor and busily engaged on the reform of public morals, he spent two whole days and the intervening night in an orgy of food and drink with Pomponius Flaccus and Lucius Piso, at the

conclusion of which he made Flaccus Governor of Syria and Piso City Prefect – actually describing them in their commissions as 'convivial friends at all hours of the day or night.' Being invited to dinner by Cestius Gallus, a lecherous old spendthrift whom Augustus had ignominiously removed from the Senate and whom he had himself reprimanded for his ill-living only a few days previously, Tiberius accepted on condition that the dinner should follow Gallus' usual style, in no way altered or diluted, and that the waitresses should be naked.

Suetonius, *Tiberius* 42.[23]

Domitian preferred the upside-down life:

He used to bathe in the morning, and then fill himself up at lunch, so that a Matian apple and a small jug of wine were generally all he wanted at dinner time. His many generous banquets were never greedy affairs, and never went on beyond sunset or turned into drinking parties.

Suetonius, *Domitian* 21.

Anyone who is not immediately struck by the oddness of this must recall that Suetonius and his readers took little or nothing at breakfast, a very light lunch, then a leisurely afternoon including a bathe, and a heavy evening meal which often did go on after sunset and often included no small quantity of wine. Domitian's father, Vespasian, had an enduring reputation for stinginess and no reported dietary views at all except that he would 'fast one whole day every month' (*Vespasian* 20). Galba, briefly Emperor in AD 69, was quite his equal: 'when an especially lavish dinner was set before him, he groaned aloud' (*Galba* 12). On his journey towards the capital, 'for his formal dinners he had at his disposal a full array of the imperial table-service and attendants, selected from Nero's and sent to him by his agent in Rome. Galba ignored them' (Plutarch, *Life of Galba* 11–12).

Along with the grand entertainments and the lavish meals offered to others, the tendency not to care too much about one's own food has, of course, a fine Roman pedigree. Suetonius thinks it slightly wrong of Domitian (so that Robert Graves may be translating Suetonius' thought, if not his words, accurately when he has Domitian take 'enormous' lunches and thus maintain a critical tone of voice). Suetonius thinks it very odd of Vespasian and Galba to be so 'common' or so old-fashionedly frugal in their style of eating. But Augustus – we must remember that Augustus died half a century before Suetonius was born – Augustus is the legendary founder of the monarchy, a hero from another time, and every feature of his life is potentially matter for admiration:

> As regards food Augustus was very sparing, almost plebeian, with a liking for brown bread, whitebait, soft, spongy hand-pressed cheese, and green figs from a twice-bearing tree. Sometimes he would eat before dinner time, whenever and wherever he felt hungry. Here are his own words, quoted from his letters: 'I had a snack of bread and dates while out in my carriage to-day...' and: 'As I came home from the *Regia* in my litter I ate a bit of bread and a few *duracina* grapes.' And again: 'Not even a Jew fasts so scrupulously on his Sabbath, my dear Tiberius, as I have done today. Not until an hour after sunset did I touch a thing; and that was at the baths, before I had my oil rub, when I swallowed two mouthfuls of bread.' This irregular timetable often resulted in his eating alone, either before or after dinner, and taking nothing at all while he was reclining with his guests.
>
> Suetonius, Augustus 76.

Those *duracina* grapes are the firm-fleshed, thick-skinned kind that the more sensible growers used to produce to send to the Roman market, because they would stand travel and storage and still look good. Shall we compare them with 'Golden Delicious' apples? An emperor, if he cared to, could very well get nicer and fresher ones.

Julius Caesar, or the roots at Dyrrachium

In not caring to, Augustus is following precisely the philosophy of his much-admired great-uncle and adoptive father, Julius Caesar, subject of the first of Suetonius' biographies. Caesar was famous for his tasteful and generous banquets (a menu survives) and for his fine selection of wines (a wine list survives). But that was wholly political. Personally, Caesar is confidently said to have been not in the least interested in his food, as Plutarch shows from the following story:

> When Valerius Leo was entertaining him to dinner at Milan, he served up asparagus dressed with myrrh instead of with olive oil. Caesar ate this quite calmly himself and reprimanded his friends when they criticized the dish. 'If you didn't like it,' he said, 'there was no need to have eaten it, but to criticize another for ineptitude is inept.'
>
> Plutarch, Life of Caesar 17.9–10.[24]

Plutarch is a fine character biographer, but he can occasionally fail to get across a detail of social life. What is going on at Valerius Leo's dinner table? We need a second opinion, and here is Suetonius', telling what is clearly the same story through a different intermediate source:

Even Caesar's enemies admitted he drank very little. Caesar was the only sober man who ever tried to overturn the constitution, is the way Marcus Cato put it. Gaius Oppius implies that he did not care much about his food either: when a host served up to him perfumed oil in place of green olive oil, other guests were disgusted but Caesar helped himself rather generously, so as not to seem to criticize his host either for carelessness or for ineptitude.

Suetonius, *Julius* 53.

Now we see. The mistake of Valerius Leo, in the small and isolated provincial town that Milan then was, was to think that because perfumed oil (perfumed with myrrh, in this case) was hideously expensive, grand people must use it in place of ordinary green olive oil to dress their asparagus. The greatness of Caesar was to accept his hospitality in the spirit in which it was intended.

There has been some over-indulgence in this paper. I will conclude it by showing that dining with the Caesars was not all fun. At the siege of Dyrrachium (now Durres in Albania) in 48 BC, Caesar's troops were less well supplied than those of Pompey whom they were besieging. It was his lowest point in the Civil War. They would have run out of food completely but for a stroke of luck here described by Caesar himself in his war notes.

There is also a kind of root, soon discovered by those on potherb duty,[25] which is called *chara* and – mixed with milk – it considerably relieved the shortage of food. They made it into a kind of bread. There was a lot of it: when Pompey's soldiers were talking to mine and teased them with being hungry, they used to throw these loaves at them in reply. It made them less cocky.

Caesar, *Civil War* 3.48.

To us now, Caesar's war notes are among the most memorable legacies of the whole century. Romans of succeeding generations admired them too, but they had a wider range of memories to draw on. The encyclopaedist Pliny 'the elder', writing in the AD 60s, appeals not to Caesar but to Caesar's rowdy troops in pinning down the facts on this same vegetable. It became famous, he tells us, 'mainly because of the satirical choruses of the soldiers at a Triumph of Julius Caesar. He was so stingy with their wages – they complained in one of their part-songs – that they had to live on *lapsana* at Dyrrachium. This is a kind of wild cabbage' (Pliny, *Natural History* 19.144). Now the legionaries called it *lapsana* ('charlock') because it sounded good in their songs, but the root at Dyrrachium was actually not this, nor any kind of wild cabbage. Georg Veith, a German officer whose troops used the same roots while on campaign in Albania in 1917–18, is sure that it was *Arum italicum*,[26] a species of cuckoo-pint or lords-and-ladies and a European relative of taro, not bad food if thoroughly cooked.

But I want to pursue the memory of the root at Dyrrachium through later Roman writers. Next in order is Plutarch's *Life of Caesar*, written in good long Greek:

> Caesar's soldiers dug up some kind of root, mixed it with milk, and used it for food. Kneading this into loaves, on one occasion they ran up to the enemy outposts and tossed the loaves among the men inside, adding the taunt that as long as Earth produced these roots they would go on besieging Pompey. But Pompey would not let the mass of his army see the loaves or hear the taunt: his soldiers were losing heart, disturbed by the savagery and the persistence of their wild-animal-like opponents.
>
> 39.1–2.

I suspect, but I cannot prove, that Caesar's notes are the only primary source underlying this story. Plutarch, or his immediate source, found it easier to suppose that the taunting only happened once, and developed Pompey's own reaction to the affair out of a brief hint by Caesar. Now we move to the next round in this game of Chinese whispers: shortly after Plutarch, Suetonius got down to work on his biographies. Suetonius read Plutarch (or the intermediate source) and took just as much as he wanted from the earlier author:

> Caesar's legionaries were prepared to put up with a lot, not only when besieged, but when they were the besiegers. When Pompey was shown the bread, made out of some plant, that was keeping them going at the siege of Dyrrachium, he said he was pitted against wild animals. He ordered it taken away and not shown to anyone – in case his own troops' morale were to be undermined by the enemy's stubbornness in adversity.
>
> Suetonius, *Julius* 68.2.

Thanks to the incident of the roots at Dyrrachium, I have been able to show you Suetonius warts and all. He speaks elsewhere very highly of Caesar's war notes and he could have used them here – but he does not. He quotes elsewhere verbatim several of the rude verses that Caesar's troops sang at his Triumphs, and surely he could have quoted the couplet about *lapsana* here – but he does not. Instead, since a recent historian gave him the angle he wanted, he sharpened up the narrative and left it at that. Modern historians trust Suetonius on this little story at their own risk.

The rise and fall of Roman gastronomy

Suetonius is a great biographer because he does not try to draw general conclusions or to see long-term trends. If his readers wish to do so, that is up to them. His older contemporary Tacitus is a great historian who is able to see long-term trends, even in the distorting mirror of what was to him very recent history, and sometimes he is right about them. Let us conclude this survey by quoting Tacitus on the rise and fall of early imperial gastronomy – a subject that arises in his *Annals* in connection with a sudden scare about the inflated price of luxury foods in the course of Tiberius' principate. Should new legislation be rushed through? Tiberius was for letting things be:

> When Tiberius' letter had been read in the Senate, the aediles were allowed to set the problem aside. And in fact the gastronomy on which so much was spent between Augustus' victory at Actium [31 BC] and the war that brought Galba to power [AD 68] has gradually died away. It is worth asking why. In the past, rich families...used to ruin themselves in the struggle to show their wealth, because it was acceptable for ordinary Romans, allied states, and even foreign kings, to seek patrons and to be sought as clients. The importance of any person notable for his money, his property or his style of life was evaluated according to his occurrence in popular talk and the number of his clients. Then came the random executions; popularity was suddenly deadly. Those who were left behaved more wisely. Meanwhile, newcomers from...the provinces, rapidly recruited to the Senate, introduced their own domestic frugality: many, by luck or hard work, were rich in old age, but they retained their original attitudes. More than any other, Vespasian set the example of a simple way of life: he was old-fashioned in his behaviour and his eating habits. Deference to the Emperor and the desire to emulate him were more powerful than legal penalties or threats.
>
> Perhaps, after all, there is a kind of revolution in all human affairs, and social behaviour goes in cycles just as the seasons do. Not everything was better in the old days.
>
> Tacitus, *Annals* 3.55.[27]

These two paragraphs are, if I am not mistaken, the only explicit history of the zenith and decline of Roman patronage to be found in any ancient work; few other authors give the impression of noticing the matter at all. But Suetonius' series of biographies is (though he does not say so, and may not have thought so) a detailed history of exactly this, the heyday of Roman patronage.

This is what all the dinners were about that Julius Caesar had once presented so generously. 'He spent money recklessly,' Plutarch, his Greek biographer, tells us, 'and many people thought that he was purchasing a moment's brief fame at an enormous price, whereas in reality he was buying the greatest place in the world at inconsiderable expense' (Plutarch, *Life of Caesar* 5). Rome had a history of great men who rivalled one another to become even greater. Tacitus has it exactly right. But Caesar was so good at it that eventually he had no rival.

Caesar's immediate successors were truly everybody's patrons, and it was this that gave them their power, for there was no constitutional position of 'emperor'. The great men had transmitted their patronage to sons or adopted sons; Caesar did the same, by adopting Augustus. Augustus adopted Tiberius, Tiberius adopted Caligula. The system faltered at Caligula's assassination in AD 41: he had adopted nobody. The Praetorian Guards seemed to put matters right by choosing Claudius, the only suitable survivor of Caligula's family. Claudius adopted Nero. And from Nero's death in AD 68 (Tacitus has it right again) patronage, as Rome had known it, can truly be seen to be in decline. The real power (to call it patronage would be to overstretch the term) was with the soldiers, as they had truly shown in AD 41 and would show over and over again in the following centuries, as Rome slid from one weak emperor to the next.

So Domitian's glorious, endless, sticky public dinners are mere relics of a gastronomy that was dying, fossils of a system of imperial patronage that was already dead. Which of Julius Caesar's dinners was a truer sign of the future: the generous public entertainments with four kinds of wine, or the roots at Dyrrachium?

BIBLIOGRAPHY

Translations of and commentaries on Suetonius' *Lives of the Caesars*
Bradley, K.R. (1978) *Suetonius' Life of Nero: an historical commentary*, Brussels.
Hurley, Donna W. (1993) *An historical and historiographical commentary on Suetonius' Life of C. Caligula*, Atlanta: Scholars Press.
Martinet, Hans C. (1981) *Suetonius Tranquillus, Divus Titus: Kommentar*, Königstein am Taunus: Hain.
Maurer, Joseph A. (1949) *A commentary on C. Suetonii Tranquilli Vita C. Caligulae Caesaris*, Philadelphia [Dissertation, University of Pennsylvania].
Sueton (1992) *Leben des Claudius und Nero*, Kierdorf, W. (ed.), Paderborn: Schöningh.
Suetonio (1991) *Vita di Domiziano*, Galli, Francesca (ed. and tr.), Roma: Edizioni dell'Ateneo.
Suetoni Tranquilli, C. (1927) *Divus Vespasianus*, Braithwaite, A.W. (ed.), Oxford: Clarendon Press.
Suetoni Tranquilli, C. (1927) *Divus Iulius*, Butler, H.E. and Cary, M. (eds.), Oxford: Clarendon Press. Reissued with new introduction, bibliography and additional notes by Townend, G.B. (1982) Bristol: Bristol Classical Press.
Suetonius (1993) *Caligula*, Lindsay, Hugh (ed.), London: Bristol Classical Press.

Suetonius (1986) *Claudius*, Mottershead, J. (ed.), Bristol: Bristol Classical Press.
Suetonius (1982) *Divus Augustus*, Carter, John M. (ed.), Bristol: Bristol Classical Press.
Suetonius (1996) *Domitian*, Jones, Brian W. (ed.), Bristol: Bristol Classical Press.
Suetonius (1992) *Galba, Otho, Vitellius*, Murison, Charles L. (ed.), London: Bristol Classical Press.
Suetonius (1999) *Nero*, Warmington, B.H. (ed.), London: Bristol Classical Press.
Suetonius (1995) *Tiberius*, Lindsay, Hugh (ed.), London: Bristol Classical Press.
Suetonius, with an English translation by Rolfe, J. C. (1913–4) London: Heinemann.
Suetonius Tranquillus, Gaius (1957) *The Twelve Caesars*, Graves, Robert (tr.), Harmondsworth: Penguin. Revised by Grant, Michael (ed.) (1979) London: Allen Lane.
Svetonio Tranquillo, C. (1977) *Vite di Galba, Otone, Vitellio*, Venini, Paola (ed.), Torino: Paravia.
Wardle, D. (1994) *Suetonius' Life of Caligula: a commentary*, Brussels: Latomus.

few other useful books
Baldwin, B. (1983) *Suetonius*, Amsterdam: Hakkert.
Dalby, Andrew (2000) *Empire of pleasures: luxury and indulgence in the Roman world*, London: Routledge.
de Coninck, Luc (1983) *Suetonius en de archivalia*, Brussels: AWLSK.
Elsner, J. and Masters, J. (eds.) (1994) *Reflections of Nero: culture, history and representation*, London: Duckworth.
Gascou, J. (1984) *Suétone historien*, Rome.
Grieve, Mrs M. (1931) *A modern herbal*, Leyel, H. (ed.), London.
Veith, Georg K. and Hauptmann, K. (1920) *Der Feldzug von Dyrrhachium zwischen Caesar und Pompejus, mit besonderer Berücksichtigung der historischen Geographie des albanischen Kriegsschauplatzes*, Vienna.
Wallace-Hadrill, A. (1983) *Suetonius: the scholar and his Caesars*, London: Duckworth. Second edition (1995) entitled *Suetonius*, London: Bristol Classical Press.

REFERENCES

[1] All quotations without author's name are from Suetonius' *Lives of the Caesars*. Brutus and Cassius were of course fated to be among the murderers of Julius Caesar, and to die by violence not long afterwards.

[2] Suetonius uses several of Augustus' letters, some addressed to his successor Tiberius, some to his wife and eventual widow, Livia.

[3] Acknowledgements to Robert Graves' 1957 translation which I have adapted, here and for some other quotations.

[4] The text of Dio Cassius does not survive: it is reconstructed from the Byzantine author Xiphilinus [pages 219–220 Stephanus].

[5] For the presentation by Caligula, on the very day he was to be assassinated, see Josephus, *Jewish Antiquities* 19.1.13, quoted below.

[6] Xiphilinus 218 Stephanus.

[7] 61.10.3 [Xiphilinus 152 Stephanus].

[8] Suetonius, *Vitellius* 4.

[9] Translation by Kenneth Wellesley.

[10] 'Lamprey-milt', according to Robert Graves. I hope that symposiasts will tell me what these 'milks of *murenae*' (either morays or lampreys) may be.

[11] Murison (1992 p. 162) suggests that the introduction of the parrot-wrasse to Misenum by Ti. Julius Optatus Pontianus, while he was prefect of the fleet under Claudius, is a precedent for Vitellius' use of military resources to transport his luxury foods. The parallel is

interesting, but we notice that Pontianus, by contrast with Vitenius, was importing the parrot-wrasses to breed in fish farms, and thus at least investing in the future.

[12] Xiphilinus 193–194 Stephanus.

[13] Juvenal 4.140–2, written slightly later, suggests that British oysters were known during Nero's principate.

[14] Cf. Tacitus, *Annals* 13.25.

[15] The *Naumachia* was an artificial lake, surrounded by seating for spectators, designed for mock sea-battles.

[16] Xiphilinus 166 Stephanus.

[17] Pliny, *Natural History* 14.61, 19.38, 31.40.

[18] Cf. Dio Cassius 63.28.5 [Xiphilinus 185 Stephanus].

[19] Suetonius, *Tiberius* 53.

[20] Based on Zonaras 11.11; cf. Xiphilinus 145–146 Stephanus.

[21] Xiphilinus 172 Stephanus.

[22] More details and references in Dalby 2000 pp. 257–8.

[23] Generally following Robert Graves' translation.

[24] Translation after Rex Warner.

[25] The phrase 'on potherb duty' translates my conjectural reading *ab oleribus*. The manuscripts read *a valeribus,* which is meaningless.

[26] Butler and Cary 1927 p. 129 citing Veith and Hauptmann 1920 p. 254 note 54a. On earlier work agreeing with this identification see Mrs Grieve (ed. Leyel, 1931, p. 237).

[27] Acknowledgements to Michael Grant's translation.

Journeys through Smell and Taste: Home, Self, Identity

Ferda Erdinç

A few years ago, a very dear friend of mine, Amila, a Bosnian woman living in Canada, announced that she would make a list of the faces, smells and tastes from Sarajevo. This was after losing her sister and father during the war. In the face of forgetting and pain, this was what she thought of doing to retrieve her memory of Sarajevo, her home which was being ruthlessly destroyed.

Tracing faces, smells and tastes in memory – where would a journey of this nature take one? To a multitude of recollections in memory: the more intense and loaded smells and tastes, the more deeply inscribed ones, those cherished, those not. Childhood, inevitably, is a major stop; a site of the initial recordings. Then you move away from childhood into later stages, from more distant to less. This is how it worked for me, when I sat down and submerged myself in the process of remembering guided by smells and tastes. The faces appeared along with these and, of course, what completed the picture were feelings, settings, locations and situations.

As a person whose memories of food, wittingly or unwittingly, have become an integral part of her work, I took this opportunity to look back into my personal history, focusing on certain recordings of smells and tastes in memory to share with you, and suggesting a way of looking at these revealing connections to notions of self, identity and home. At each instance of remembering, events and feelings of the past are re-ordered: each is a new configuration. It is the contact of 'now' with 'then' that takes the mind's eye on a journey. 'Remembrance of things past' thus conveys to us the perceptions and feelings of now, as well. When my friend Amila sat down to trace the tastes and smells down memory lanes, hers was an act of resistance, an urgent need as her memory was forced to be brutally dispersed. In my case, the dispersion is caused by time and distance alone, and the need is drawing yet another picture of the self as it is here and now.

It is hard to pinpoint the earliest 'recording' of a taste or a smell in memory. But one can tell among many those which are more intense and basic. The smell of bread is one such in my case: for instance, the smell of flat brown bread from the tandoor, a primitive oven dug into the earth, where the heat is obtained by the fire piled at the bottom. The flat bread is stuck to the inner walls to bake. In the huge garden in my father's family homestead in Erciş, a town by Lake Van in the eastern part of Turkey, bread-making was a weekly affair, carried out by my Kurdish grandmother in a little room in some obscure part of the garden where the tandoor was located. There was a kitchen in the house, yet the 'tandoor house' as it was called, was outside and a somewhat forbidden zone for kids. There was fire, a possible source of danger, but the kids were shooed away also because bread-making was a hassle and the womenfolk involved did not really want to deal with the kids while labouring hard to make the weekly bread for the entire household. The household meant seventeen adults, descendants of my grandfather and his brother, together with wives or husbands and offspring, and the elderly folk such as great-aunts and my grandmother. Of these seventeen cousins, most of whom were living in the two big houses in the garden, a few, like my father, had moved away and thus were there only for summers. The weekly bread for the entire household was a lot of bread, to say the least, especially if you also add the unknown number of guests which would show up daily. Those two mansion-like houses operated like inns, and the womenfolk had a lot of cooking and baking to do. Years later, at another instance of remembering for an interview, something else about the 'tandoor house' struck me: that it was also used as the 'cell' the old aunt was locked in during her 'crazy' days; the Mrs Rochester of the family. 'Tandoor house' was a truly 'female' quarter of the estate; the locus of the 'natural' yet 'hidden' aspects of life: bread-making and insanity under the same roof. Nothing to be exposed to the public eye. Looking back at these, years later, considering what was allowed for women in such a social structure of strict rules of right and wrong, public and private, it makes sense to me now; the odd combination of women's labour and insanity, both sharing the same niche. They were both 'natural', given, yet to be pushed far away or kept hidden, to remain unacknowledged.

A very strong and intense taste lingering in my mouth from those days is the taste of my grandmother's bread dipped in olive oil. The taste takes me immediately to a 'picture' in memory where in the dim hall of the second floor of the house in Erciş, sitting alone by the table in the silence of the evening, I am dipping the bread in olive oil. The dimness is most probably due to either lack of electricity, or just the poor quality of it. There is nobody around because we have just arrived from Erzurum, and my mother has put these on the table for me, because I am too hungry to wait for supper. And the most unusual component of this picture, tastewise, is the juxtaposition of this bread with olive oil.

Olives belong geographically mostly to the Aegean and Marmara regions of Turkey. Olive oil is thus produced and consumed mainly in those areas. Today it is almost natural that any food item can be shipped and consumed anywhere in the world. In the Turkey of the early 1960s, as in most other places in the world, this was not the case. Neither people nor food travelled as much. Also, the regional differences in climate and geography very much determined everything else that happened in each region, with limited, if any, interaction in between. And the cleavage between the east and the west of the country was a lot deeper than that of today. That was the pre-television era, to say the least. Olive oil was almost unknown, and, even if barely known, hardly acceptable and of very poor quality in that distant part of the country; the land of herds, snow-capped mountains and tough people. They were the butter and meat people. How did olive oil make its way into our house, and into my taste repertoire? Because of my truly modern, innovative and city-educated mother. As a young bride from Istanbul, she introduced not only olive oil but also home-made mayonnaise and New Year celebration dinners: Russian salad, hors-d'œuvre, cakes, cookies...The 'tango', that is to say modern, young woman, put them in touch with a world far away and hardly imaginable for them all, these young men and women who had grown up in that vast garden. How was olive oil obtained in that town? Most probably through the efforts of my kind-hearted, food-loving, eldest uncle.

I was probably the first one combining the taste of the fire-baked bread of my grandmother with that of the ancient treasure of the far-away Aegean culture, and to do justice to this unique meeting, my mouth kept the taste all along my journeys thereafter, without my awareness of its existence. Taste memory travels with you in such a way that awareness of it is usually discovered in the absence of that taste in real life. So it was decades later and countries apart, while learning to make bread in the mountains of Tennessee, that I did start recalling these. When I sort out my 'taste memories' now, finding the smell of that bread, and the intensely strong taste of it dipped in olive oil to be one of the most deeply inscribed, it makes me wonder what makes it so distinct. It certainly is not associated with my love for the person who made it. I did not have a special attachment to my grandmother, nor necessarily to the taste of that bread. They were just there, as part of the life in that garden. Yet, the taste captures that moment so well, triggering an association of images from the past that it refers to more than just the taste itself. That taste alone connects me to the garden, the 'tandoor house', the crazy aunt, insanity, my grandmother and my somewhat isolated position, different from that of the rest of the kids, as the city girl versus the 'garden' bunch; activating a series of pictures, directing my act of remembrance to various other points. It offers me a chance to 'read' my own story, as the little girl in whose taste buds the homemade bread meets the olive oil. What I see in this picture is also the combination of the two distinctly diverse traditions which are the major constructive forces of my 'self' and how I relate to food and life today. These are all probably why I remember it so well. Also, when I think back, I realize that my grandmother, a woman quite estranged from her Kurdish identity as the daughter of the tribal leader up in the highlands, far away from 'home', without realizing, was probably putting so much of herself into the bread she was making that, maybe through her bread, this was also registering in our mouths.

We had supper every day in my uncle's quarters. If I think long enough I would recall many dishes, but they are not among those which come vividly upon first call like the meat and vegetable stew my uncle made every once in a while. Usually made for lunch, his famous *tava* (the name of both the unglazed pot it was cooked in and the dish itself) was rather hot and spicy, and meant a festive gathering of the family at large around a long table set up in the garden, rather than at the regular dinner table in the house. I remember that taste well because it was a somewhat rare event, at least not part of the routine, the food itself tasted great, and my uncle was an adorable person. And he truly enjoyed food in all its aspects: choosing, buying, cooking and eating it.

The garden was full of fruit trees of all kinds, most of them apricots. They were not the small, well-tended fruit trees in a dreamy orchard scene. These, like most other fruit trees in that garden, were tall and overgrown with branches freely wandering in any direction up in the sky. Nobody really did much tending. It seemed they were there for ages and, as anything else in that garden (that is, the kids, shrubs and flowers), were thrown in there to grow on their own and bear fruit if they so pleased. We ate the fruits day and night, not necessarily making an effort to climb up to pick them. They were so abundant, falling on our heads while wandering around in the garden. In the mornings, they would be on the ground and we would share them with the geese, the chicken, the dogs, insects and of course the birds, as we pleased. It was mostly the wind and the birds in charge of the apricot fall; who could know which apricot would drop on whose head? Call it your luck, or your lot. This was part of the garden 'wisdom'. Unless, of course, you would get so bored with this random apricot fall, as we kids did, and start climbing up the trees one by one, and be picky about which apricot to put into your mouth.

Another apricot activity, in that time of the summer, was the endless cracking of apricot stones to eat the kernels. After all these casual activities, centred around apricots, came the big event: a rigorous apricot picking one early morning, organized by mothers, carried out by kids. The day after, there would hardly be any apricots left on the trees, as they were all in buckets, to be washed and halved to cover the flat rooftops of mud houses to dry. The rooftops of houses would turn into a darker shade of orange for the rest of summer; the sign of the apricot drying season. Apricots were not just fruits simply eaten in that town. They appeared in many instances, in various forms, and made their presence felt all year round. In my taste memory, what is retained is not the taste of regular apricots, though. What is recorded as precious is the taste of unripe apricots. As kids, we loved to eat them when still green, or when they started turning barely yellow. This was a taste only kids enjoyed, outside the realm of adulthood and apricots sold in grocery shops; a taste memory connecting me to the whole lore of apricots and childhood in that garden.

The summers were spent in Erciş, the rest of the year in Erzurum, a very cold and conservative city where nature had not much to offer but the snow and high mountains. Two distinct tastes from this city I never managed to like were tea and *çaşir*, a bitter tasting wild green. Tea was more than an issue of gastronomy. It was a social ceremony, an art to excel in, and a way of learning your responsibility and place as a woman. In the public space, it belonged to the male kingdom. Teahouses were no places for women to hang out; you wouldn't even want to walk by them, as young women. Inside the houses, it was the women's utmost responsibility to prepare and serve. And, unlike cooking, young girls in the family were expected to join in. One samovar after another had to be prepared to keep the men, elderly womenfolk and guests drinking excellent tea.

For me, as a young girl growing up in that city, endless tea sessions were nightmares. As soon as a little tea glass is emptied you were expected to rise up to your feet, fetch it, fill it up and return to the tea-drinking party before his tea-glass-searching hand hit its absence. This was my experience of tea, socially and culturally. Although I must admit the smell of nicely brewed tea, mingled with the smell of burning charcoal from the samovar, managed to sneak into my memory as one of the very pleasant smells from that time. But I had to move far away from all these before I could remember, appreciate and even miss this. The same goes for the awful smell of *çaşir* boiling in huge pots, and the strong bitter-sour taste of it when brought to the table after being kept in brine as a seasonal condiment – almost to celebrate for. That was how my mother and aunt cherished this unusual taste, while we kids would watch them in utter amazement. The revenge of the *çaşir* was felt many years and journeys later, though. It is a taste I now crave.

I came to Istanbul at the age of fifteen for my education, leaving my home and family behind in Erzurum. Passing a special exam, I was admitted to the most prestigious school of the country, an American school, which was a distinctly 'free' environment compared to the rest. Life in this school, and in this city, was very different from that in the countryside. As a bunch of boarding students, having just left home and having made our way into that 'top' school, coming from different regions of the country, from good stock nonetheless, but still from the countryside, we were thrown into a very unfamiliar environment. Being in that school, and in the dormitory, thirteen girls in one room, we felt as if we were almost in another country.

Partially culture-shocked, mostly homesick, in a totally new environment and being subjected to mass-produced food, we couldn't help but seek refuge more and more in food. Every night, after study, we made sure that the big dormitory kettle was on the stove, with the teapot on top and, inside, the tea leaves steeped just right. That latter bit was mostly my concern alone; the rest of the girls did not care much about the steeping and how it affected the taste of the tea. They were not from a family of tea worshippers. The distance had performed its trick: I no longer dreaded the tea ceremony. The tea drinking now was a different story. Feeling quite lost, for the first time outside the realm of family, and faced unexpectedly with the question of who we really were, gradually, our longing for home pulled us together more and more around the smell of the tea. This is how I made my peace with tea. Years later, leaving home again to go to Montreal, a little tea pot was to accompany my journey across the ocean, and to stay with me all along; clustered around it, my friends as a new group of tea-worshippers.

Our 'close encounters' with food in that boarding school were soon almost bordering on obsession. Coming back from each holiday, we carried food in bulk, and stored it in our room. Whenever we felt exam-stressed, homesick or lovesick, we would pull the tables together in the middle of our big room and set up a feast. That was also our initiation to regional food. Each one of us brought the best of home cooking and regional specialities back from home. During this exchange of food, family stories were exchanged as well, and the knowledge of mothers' cooking. Through new tastes and smells, a new life of our own in the dormitory was starting to unfold. Through food, we shared and expressed our stories and our identities. Before leaving home, there was no need to think, know and express who you were. In the countryside, even if it is a city, people knew each other through families. That was simply home, and you took part as the child of the family. Here, away from home and family, our identities were initials sewn on our bed sheets, towels, and a bunch of personal belongings in our individual closets in this room. Away from home, we were missing all that was familiar, and food was an essential part of it.

Our food stocks were obviously not endless. When they were gone, we were again at the mercy of the tasteless and meagre food from the cafeteria. Our only supply of food then was the slices of bread smuggled from the cafeteria to the dormitory for late night snacks. If well organized, we could manage to get them toasted on the stove to accompany our after-study tea ceremony. And the smell of the toasted bread was bliss. As a result of our obsession with food, our room was declared a forbidden zone on special days, when the dormitory was opened to important visitors. Our room was not just a messy sight, with all the food piled up on the shelves, but it also had an additional uninvited guest, a little mouse, who was as fond of food as we were. For the four years that we were there, the conflict between the administration and the inhabitants of our room remained unresolved. We would not give up on our food; they would not accept us as presentable 'Robert College' girls. We could just not be moulded. After our graduation, the school administration reconsidered their policy of admissions from outside of Istanbul.

I had to cross the ocean some four years later, to have further and more intense encounters with food, in memory and in life. Much deeper, more intense and voluntary 'journeys' down memory lane, tracing smells and tastes on the one hand, discovering more about the food and food memories of 'the other', on the other hand, took place in Montreal. In fact, the encounters with the smells and tastes from the past began almost spontaneously without necessarily my efforts to remember. Many smells and tastes of home started coming back to me unexpectedly. Mostly, upon waking up, I would detect a certain smell in my nose or a taste in my mouth. Far away from home once again, this time really far away and in an altogether different country, smells and tastes from a past long disappeared, not just those from Istanbul but those from Erciş and Erzurum, started visiting me. Nothing around me had any resemblance to home to trigger the remembrance. On the contrary, I was surrounded by difference and unfamiliarity. And it was all that physical distance from home that created a vacuum, a space of release and relaxation, a time for forgetting that was activating the counter process of remembering. In the absence of all that is familiar, whatever was inscribed in memory, unnoticed before, was being missed and somehow coming up to the surface. Memory of taste and smell was at work very intensely, maybe also because now I was living on my own and quite involved in cooking.

We were a bunch of graduate students in social sciences in the conservative 1980s, in a conservative school, in a cold climate and far away from home. No longer a teenager leaving home for the first time, I was in my early twenties and this time voluntarily leaving my family and my country behind to discover myself in a totally different setting. It was an experience I cherished every moment of. During the six years spent in Montreal, engaged in endless struggles in the conservative Department of Sociology, making friends of various nationalities, I found myself yet again clustered around a table cooking and sharing food.

Guided by tastes and smells registered in memory, a dear friend of mine, a Bengali woman, and myself were wandering around in Montreal, from Middle Eastern grocery stores to Indian shops, from fish markets to Jewish bakeries. Matching the tastes with names in a foreign language: this is how I learned most of my spices. Tracing the smells and discovering herbs, condiments, vegetables, grains... Inevitably, all this detective work and expedition led to cooking together and learning from each other. She hated to cook at first; I loved to. Through food we exchanged stories of ourselves, our families and countries. I learned to cook her mother's five-spice stew; she learned how to make my mother's pickles. She was living in a big house with other students where I was a frequent visitor. Dimitri's grandma was almost our spiritual leader, with her recipes. Our daily dinner gatherings around the table were further crowded with all the mothers, aunts and grandmothers present through their cooking, as demonstrated by us. Sharing food on many occasions, a rich menu of tastes and smells became part of our collective memory. Being far away from home, we built up a happy 'home' of our own.

During a summer spent in the mountains of Tennessee, I found myself baking bread out in the garden, on a fire, almost like my grandmother used to do. It took me a while to see the resemblance. I had never baked bread before. When my hands touched the dough, after the initial timidity, I was surprised to see the knowledge my hands possessed. Quite confident in no time, they knew what to do with the dough. Bread making became an indispensable activity, in time, and the taste of my bread was now making its entry into others' taste memories.

More than a decade since then, back in Istanbul in a small restaurant I have owned for seven years now, we are offering food to people. 'Zencefil' is a pioneer restaurant, the first in Istanbul with a menu based on vegetable dishes alone, together with two kinds of bread baked on the premises. The breads we make are neither my grandmother's nor mine. Each has a story of its own, like most dishes we make, although I must admit the food served in our restaurant has its roots mostly in my journeys across the country, the ocean or across the memory.

The smells and tastes, each time I trace them, in various phases of my own story, like the pebbles in the Hansel and Gretel story, take me home. Putting the pieces together, the picture appears as yet another rendering of the narrative of the self. In some instances, it is a taste of something strongly disliked, like that of çaşir, which somehow in time becomes a taste craved for; or a taste of something like my uncle's stew, which I cannot forget because of its association with a person I deeply cared for. From among the pile of memories, the taste of my grandmother's bread emerges as a significant one, after I witness the knowledge of my hands in bread-making, miles and oceans away from home. Of course 'mom's cooking' is unforgettable for almost everybody, but in my own story, through the journeys I shared with you briefly, I feel the inscription of tastes and smells, and what they evoke, trigger, and mean to the individual, may have reasons far beyond a simple habit. Remembrance of those are instances, welcoming one not just into the familiarity of a taste or smell; rather, through these they welcome you to an entire 'slice' in time filled with endless details. Each time you pass through this welcoming 'door', you can come up with yet another story. And all these stories from these recordings, for whatever reason and in whichever fashion they get to be recorded, all say something about home to me: 'home', which is not just the physical environment you open your eyes to; 'home' as a mental construct as well; 'home' as the locus of familiarity; 'home' as the place you feel aligned and connected with your past, your lineage, your identity and dreams; and as the niche of comfort and sense of belonging.

And it all starts with a simple association of faces, smells and tastes, like I was told by my friend Amila recently. She was having a picnic out in a park in Toronto this spring with her three year old daughter Asya. They were in Istanbul the summer before, and we all spent some time down south by the sea. That was when Asya and myself met for the first time. Out in the park in Toronto, eating fruits with her mother, Asya turned to her mother all of a sudden, and with a big smile on her face, said, 'just like eating grapes on the beach with Ferda.'

Grapes, beach and myself in Asya's memory: what a comforting, simple and pleasant place to be!

Whisky Sours, Flapjacks and Woodsmoke: a Century in the Life of an Adirondack Picnic

Elizabeth Field

As a kid, I think I knew instinctively that the portal to my mother's soul was a black and white photo that hung opposite her bed, framed in a rustic, pine-bark frame. In it was a rude archway over an open gate that spanned a dirt road, deep forest on both sides. There were no people in the photo, just a handcrafted stick-work message in the archway, beckoning: 'Welcome to Kildare'.

This place, Kildare, took on a mythological proportion, as Mom told stories about the overnight train ride from Manhattan to deep into the Adirondack region of upstate New York, every summer during the 1920s and 1930s; the long drive down the sixteen-mile road, into her grandmother and great-aunt's 'camp'; the lapping of its lake beside a lean-to festooned with balsam-stuffed red pillows; the fun of kids putting frogs in each others' beds and spying on the grown-ups – and the release and freedom of being 300 miles north of their city apartment, a metaphorical delivery from what sounded like a pretty gloomy, although materially comfortable, childhood.

I went to Kildare at about age seven – my mother and her brothers had sold out their share of the place to an uncle about eleven years before, but our family would get occasional invites – and remember sitting at a small square table in the corner of the long dining-room, whose floorboards were varnished incredibly shiny and covered with bearskin rugs, and whose dark green-painted dining table sat under a dramatic ten-foot chandelier made from stags horns, anchored into a peeled-bark ceiling. There were always cosy smells of wood fires from the enormous stone fireplace, a comforting sense of flannel against the skin on cold mornings, a hum of a generator outside, dew on the grass. I think I went on an elaborate picnic with my mother there – but maybe it was a dream.

The dreamy quality that always struck me about Kildare was its sense of isolation, of being literally in the middle of the wilderness on a 10,000 acre tract, surrounded by nature. This incredibly solacing environment was a real boon for several members of my mother's family who, painfully shy, took great pleasure in fishing, walking in the woods and painting.

But there was another dynamic at work. My great-grandmother and her sister, born into one of New York's illustrious 'old' German-Jewish banking families, were absolute products of their time. Surely their sense of entitlement contributed to their purchase of Kildare, a former Vanderbilt hunting and fishing club, in 1896. At that time, among the rich it was considered fashionable to retreat with family and friends to the 'simple rusticity' of the North Woods – but in delightfully luxurious style.

The so-called great camps of the period, distinguished by their architectural use of native materials, like logs and stone, were as much a triumph over nature as an embrace of it. To support each compound's self-sufficient world of main house, covered sleeping tents, bungalows, barns, workshops, boat houses, ice houses, wash houses, tennis courts, gardens and untrammelled wilderness acreage required enormous servant-power and money. And in such situations of power, there are always social protocols, hierarchies and rituals that get played out.

A perfect example of the 'civilized rusticity' that governed Kildare was the elaborate picnic its owners held several times during each summer season. In the account below, my mother, Jane Field, now 81, beautifully captures both the children's straight-up enjoyment of the event, and the worldly realities that drove its execution.

> This ritual has been going on, with only a few variations, several times a summer since 1896. One morning when we were children, we would wake up at our summer 'Camp' (one of the fabled 'great camps' or rustic estates of the Adirondacks in upstate New York) and my grandmother would say right after breakfast, 'Well, I think today is a fine day for a picnic.' She would study the cloud formations, glance at the weather vane over by the tennis court. 'All the signs point to excellent weather!' The picnic would mean Pirates Point. That would be taken for granted.
>
> Soon we children could see dozens of ears of corn being shucked by the 'Men' (the hired help, or 'guides') as they sat by the Big House's kitchen door. There were busy preparations, baskets being readied, crockery packed. All was ahum with activity.
>
> Around noon, there was the usual discussion. My grandmother stated, 'The picnic will start at one p.m. Who will paddle over to the point? Those who want can walk to the picnic around the lake, and others can swim.' The food, the Men, the cooking utensils and some of

my grandmother's more decrepit guests could ride in the large motorboat.

So the picnic party would start out. Most of us took canoes, for the lake on a picnic day would be calm and fresh and inviting. As we neared the Point a small spit of land on our lake about a mile away, covered with many pine trees and blueberry bushes we could see the smoke of the cooking fire through the branches of the trees. Before our canoe landed on the little sandy beach, we children would lace our hands in the soft water and pull up long stalks of white or yellow water lilies. These we were allowed to decorate the eating space with.

There were about twelve to fifteen people at the picnic, on average. The cast of characters was theme and variations, including: My grandmother in her loose, raggedy, tan cardigan, floppy hat and knickers (American-style loose-fitting breeches that are gathered at the knee). My parents, aunts, uncles, brothers and cousins of all ages. Semi-members of the family such as 'Giggly', as we kids called him, also in knickers, with a silver-plated cocktail shaker; the Buck sisters, maiden ladies; and the Bohemian types such as 'Smoke', a prolific novelist, and his current lady friend.

And the Men. Often the head guide, rather portly, who had a distinctive air of command. Lawrence: tall, handsome, totally shy, with unruly curls which peeped out from his hat. And often some young buck in his late teens. We'd get out of the canoes and climb up on to what seemed like a huge rock (but actually wasn't) to see how things were getting along.

Yes, there was either the linen damask cloth spread on pine needles and anchored with heavy white plates, or the trestle table, covered with the tablecloth, and benches alongside it. We'd look down from the rock where the eating would take place, and there was the fire, doing nicely now, and the Men with blue or red bandannas tied around their foreheads or necks to ward off smoke. Then beyond on all sides the gentle soft lake. We'd be standing about watching the Men cook when Giggly would appear beaming, with the cocktail shaker filled with whisky sours. He shook it with relish. Glasses were proffered. There was no soda for the kids (at Pirates Point it was an inter-generational, not a child-centered world). The Men would pass grilled toast, striped from the grill, spread with sardines.

After a while and a good bit of whisky sours, it would be time to sit down. The serious eating began. Luscious individual steaks were brought up by the Men. Steaks that also, like the toast, had a pattern of stripes from the grill. They were seared by the fire, crusty on the outside, pinkish inside. With the steaks came the big favorite – razor-thin sliced potato chips briskly cooked in oil and salted. These chips only appeared at Pirates Point picnics. They were delectable and their supply seemed unlimited. They curled invitingly. There would be a kind of happy silence as people munched and crunched the food. It was no time for serious conversation, especially since mounds of delectable ears of corn would then appear, accompanied by plates of butter.

We'd sit there under the solacing midday sun; it was rarely too hot even at noon in the Adirondacks. We felt warm breezes, the lapping of the lake, warm wood smoke. My grandmother would light her one cigarette of the year, which would ward off those giant flies that buzzed around, attracted by the feast. Citronella, to ward off mosquitos, would be passed around.

The eating went on a long time. Finally, we stretched a bit, wandered about and watched the little kids constructing tiny twig houses next to the blueberry bushes. We complimented the Men, who quietly acknowledged our praise. When did they eat at this picnic? Did they? And then it was time to sit down again. The inevitable round pancakes arrived; we called them flapjacks. They were golden brown and accompanied by our own maple syrup that had been culled from nearby trees. We anointed them with maple syrup and butter, and then our sticky fingers and forks got to work. Then, strong coffee, which had been carried over in the rowboat in an enameled pot, was delivered. It was slightly burnt with a pleasant bitter taste.

There was not much sitting after the final cup of coffee. There was no cleaning up to do. We watched the Men drink the strong coffee and carry the baskets with dishes back to the motorboat. They loaded in the cutlery, glasses, dinnerware. Very heavy work. But, 'Oh,' said the kids, 'where are the marshmallows?' Sure enough, there they were. The Men whittled sharply pointed sticks to hold them. The marshmallows were pierced, and kids slowly toasted them in the ebbing fire. Some turned out golden brown, some were black and burnt, but considered delicious if they didn't fall into the fire.

And so when it was time to go back to the Big House across the lake, the same discussion ensued. Who had the strength after all that food to paddle back, or sit in the middle of the canoe and be paddled back? Who would walk around the other side of the lake? No one was up to swimming back. After an hour, everyone returned. They pulled up the canoes beside the boathouse. The Men in the motorboat had also returned, leaving the heavy plates for the kitchen staff to deal with, and they were, hopefully, relaxing.

Soon tennis balls would be heard bouncing about on the tennis court, the outside swing in the summer house would be creaking back and forth, and the little kids would be allowed to go swimming or digging at the beach below the Big House. Frothy chocolate milkshakes might be brought down to them in the late afternoon. Another day – a picnic day! – had passed.[1]

Where did the menu originate?

There are precedents in the camp-cookery manuals of the late nineteenth century. Miss M Parloa, in her *Camp Cookery. How to Live in Camp*, published in 1878, offers recipes for simple, manly dishes like fried boiled potatoes, broiled beef steak ('on the gridiron'), griddle cakes, and the adored home-made potato chips, called simply 'fried potatoes'.[2] Her book's directive, as stated in its preface, is: 'to give only dishes that any gentleman, be he ever so ignorant of the combinations of the most common dish, will have no difficulty in cooking for himself or friends.'[3]

In a similar genteel-rustic vein, *The Hunter's Handbook. Containing a Description of All Articles Required in Camp with Hints on Provisions and Stores and Receipts for Camp Cooking*, by 'An Old Hunter' (published in 1885), devotes ample space to building a proper campfire, choosing cooking utensils (a tin tea kettle, a tin potato kettle, an iron rice kettle, one or two frying pans and a Dutch oven are considered appropriate for a duck-shooting excursion, via water, in canoes for a party of four for ten days).[4]

There are recipes for baked, boiled, raw-fried and boiled-fried potatoes and potato fritters; fried onions, flour pancakes and Indian meal (cornmeal) pancakes, among other simple kettle, skillet and open-grill preparations.[6]

Again, the book is aimed toward the gentleman hunter, who is engaging in his pursuit for fun or pleasure, rather than necessity. According to the author, '...the amateur will gather that all that is required to render his life in Camp pleasant, and to crown with success his efforts at house-keeping in the wilderness, is some small stock of neatness and activity, and in fact that he follow, in some degree, the well-recognized customs of civilized households.'[7]

The notes of Dr Arpad G. Gerster, owner of Camp Oteetiwi in Raquette Lake, New York, in 1895–6, detail a late-summer 1896 'Sybaritic feast' as follows:

When Charley [a guide?] came, we concerted a fine woodsmen's breakfast: brook trout and rashers of bacon, and some excellent griddle cakes concocted by myself with glee (done with understanding to a turn), then some freshly roasted coffee called 'pisen' by Charley, whose notions on coffee were considerably evident and enlightened by my endeavors. The syrup out of our cache came in beautifully. I found that a pint of flour will yield exactly 24 cakes.[7]

A luncheon taken on 2 September 1895 beside 'a tall, open, hardwood forest, with shady mossy banks, between which gurgled the crystalline waters of our rocky little stream,' consisted of potatoes, steak and bacon. After tea was made, 'our frugal repast was consumed in regal style with regal appetites.'[8] Sound familiar?

Recalling the 49 years she spent as a kitchen girl and then chief housekeeper at Kildare, Lois Sanford, 78, of Potsdam, New York, says that her husband, Lawrence, who became head guide, always prepared the picnic's flapjack batter himself, in the guides' house, and transferred it via large containers to the picnic site. She doesn't know the recipe's origins.

Certainly, the kitchen women were as heroic as the men in terms of masterminding the wilderness picnic.

At some point before Lois Sanford's tenure (which began in 1943), she notes that the dazzlingly thin home-made potato chips had evolved into a less labour-intensive (for the men) dish of pan-fried potatoes with onions. On the morning of the picnic, she would boil, peel, slice and fry untold numbers of potatoes, with onions and shortening or oil, in big cast-iron skillets on the kitchen's coal-burning range. The skillets were later transferred by truck to Pirates Point and reheated over the fire.[9]

Margaret Mannion, who arrived in 1948 from Ireland as housekeeper for one of the camp owners' families, describes preparations which began at ten a.m. on picnic day:

> First, one of the men would go over and start the fire. We'd pack the old blue dishes in newspaper in a couple of great big wooden boxes in the kitchen. First came the smaller plates for toast and sardines, then cups and saucers, another set of plates for the pancakes.

Also to be packed were a set of stainless steel picnic cutlery, salt and pepper shakers, pitchers for milk and maple syrup, sugar bowl, butter dishes, napkins, tablecloth and paper towels. There were chests of ice for the soda and beer – which, at some point, had replaced the whisky sours – a water jug, grills for the steaks, a big old black enamel coffee pot (coffee was made in advance), a huge pot for the corn, kitchen knives and forks and other serving utensils.

The meal started sometime after one p.m. and continued until three o'clock. The men would then clear up, and bring back all the dirty dishes to the pantry between half past three and four p.m. 'It was an awful mess with all the grease and pancakes,' says Margaret Mannion. Of course, the kitchen staff would 'pray for a picnic,' she says, because then 'you got the afternoon off.'[10]

In recent years, I have gone to a couple of Pirates Point picnics, thanks to my cousins' hospitality. The original participants are getting fewer and older – there are hardly any young kids – and new faces have replaced the old retainers. Since the original family has grown too large to summer at Kildare collectively, they now divide their stays into two-week blocks. I don't know what the future generations of owners' plans are for Kildare.

But, save for the changing cast and some obvious concessions to modernity (like dishwashers in the big house), the picnic's menu and atmosphere remain true to its roots. There is still the guests' witty conversation – like something out of a Woody Allen movie – the same debate over whether to swim, walk or canoe to the event; the enjoyment of the absolutely marvellous food taken in the great outdoors. On the return to the main shore, there is the comforting thwack of tennis balls, but, prisoners of this driven age, guests more often retreat to their laptop computers, where work calls, than to a nap in the lean-to by the lake.

Yes, I wax unapologetically nostalgic – for a 'lost' time I've never known: for my mother's memories of her youth, and for my own experiences of Kildare, which are as dreamy as woodsmoke.

BIBLIOGRAPHY

'An Old Hunter', *The Hunter's Handbook. Containing a Description of All Articles Required in Camp with Hints on Provisions and Stores and Receipts for Camp Cooking*, Boston: Lee and Shepard, and New York: Charles T. Dillingham, 1885.

Gerster, Dr A.G., *Notes Collected in the Adirondacks, No. 1, 1895–1896*, collection of the Adirondack Museum Library, Blue Mountain Lake, New York.

Kaiser, Harvey H., *Great Camps of the Adirondacks*, Boston: David R. Godine, 1982.

Parloa, Miss M., *Camp Cookery. How to Live in Camp*, Boston: Graves, Locke and Company, 1878.

REFERENCES

[1] Jane Field's account written in 1996.
[2] Parloa, 1878, pp. 51, 43, 10, 50.
[3] Ibid, from the Preface, p. 4.
[4] 'An Old Hunter', 1885, pp. 23–27; 39–43.
[5] Ibid, pp. 88–90; 94–95.
[6] Ibid, p. 38.
[7] Gerster, p. 88.
[8] Ibid, p. 22.
[9] Conversation with Lois Sanford, April 2000.
[10] Conversation with Margaret Mannion, April 2000.

Memories of M.F.K. Fisher

Geraldene Holt

Late one afternoon, in June 1985, I drove into Aix-en-Provence looking for a quiet hotel where I could spend a few days writing. I found the ideal place, parked, and booked into a cool, pretty room. Then I set off for an evening stroll. At the end of the street I discovered its name: Rue Cardinale. With a glow of pleasure I realized I was staying almost opposite the town house of Madame de Sévigné's daughter, where, in the mid-fifties, in an attic bedroom, M.F.K. Fisher had lived.

Her book about Aix, *Map of Another Town* (1964), was in my hotel room and later I re-read her essay about 17 Rue Cardinale. It is, of course, not just a portrait of a house and its occupants, but a brilliantly observed account of female conduct.

Before leaving Aix I posted a card of the Four Dolphins fountain[1] – which stands at one end of the Rue Cardinale – to Mrs Fisher, at the address of her English publisher. I thanked her for making my stay in Aix so particularly enjoyable.

A few weeks later I was astonished to receive a reply from Mrs Fisher, forwarded by my publisher. When I returned to England, Mary Frances – as she preferred to be known – and I began to correspond and she invited me to her home in California. Four years later, when she was about to write the preface to the American edition of one of my books,[2] Mary Frances telephoned and asked if we could at last meet.

I followed the road out of San Francisco, over the Golden Gate bridge and north to the Sonoma Valley. On Highway 12, just before Glen Ellen, I turned right onto the drive to the Bouverie Ranch. A low Spanish-style house sat squarely at the foot of the Oakville range, surrounded by live oaks and madrona trees. At its back stood a monumental bell tower amid vineyards carpeted with wild flowers. Pinned to the front door, a scrawled notice read, 'Friends – ring bell and come in. Foes – enter any old way.'

Knowing that both of us thought first impressions significant made me feel distinctly nervous.[3] But, bearing gifts – flowers and wine from France, and bread from San Francisco – I was taken into the large study to meet Mary Frances.

To begin with I couldn't see her, the room seemed so dark after the brilliant Californian sunlight, but then I made out the smiling face of a slim, fine-boned woman sitting in an enormous leather chair with her legs resting on a support. Her low, careful voice welcomed me and we embraced warmly. She asked me to sit in the wheelchair beside her, saying, 'Then you'll know how it feels,' and we began to talk. We drank local white wine. 'It's just a goes-down-easy wine,' she said, and we ate a light meal of vegetable soup and a salad served on trays on our laps.

Some time later, as I began to say good-bye, Mary Frances stopped me and stated firmly that I was to stay as long as possible, and certainly until three days later, when her younger sister Norah would be arriving. 'You can sleep on the couch in the living room – it's delicious the first night, bearable the second and increasingly uncomfortable after that. Of course, the cats will want to share it with you.'

During the next few days we talked at length about writers and writing. 'I never intended to be a writer, although I've always enjoyed writing,' she said. 'I simply write as I speak. I think about it for a long time, then I write fast with little revision. I grew up with a father who ran a newspaper and wrote two thousand words a day come what may. Writing is the thing I do best; that, and cooking.'[4]

At that time in 1989 Mary Frances still wrote every day, in her words, 'slowly and with great pleasure'. She was then the author of twenty titles though she rarely read her earlier work; in *Dubious Honors* (1988) – a commentary on the prefaces she had written to other authors' books – she describes the dire results when she does so.[5] But since I had several of her books with me, she kindly inscribed them in her almost illegible hand and we discussed each volume. *A Cordiall Water* (1961) was the book she liked most – she considered it contained her finest writing – alongside her translation of Brillat-Savarin's *The Physiology of Taste* (1949).

Then she asked me to go to the deep cupboard at the far end of her study to select copies of her titles that I had not yet acquired. They included *Sister Age* (1983), whose jacket illustration was of a small painting that she bought in 1936 when she was in Zurich with Dillwyn (Tim) Parrish, 'the love of my life'. The strange, dark painting was now hanging on the wall behind her desk. And she gave me a copy of *As They Were* (1982), a collection of essays which she inscribed, 'And as we are, Thank God.' When it was time for Mary Frances to rest, I took the new titles and sat in one of the big cane chairs, surrounded by pink geraniums, on the long balcony overlooking the valley. I remember reading the final essay in *As They Were*, entitled 'Nowhere but Here'.[6]

The piece describes the house, named Last House, in which I was sitting: how it came to be designed and built by David Pleydell-Bouverie, the English architect who was her neighbour and friend, and her decision to move there.

She concludes: 'It is plain that creature comforts are an acceptable part of my choice to live here in my later years. Aside from them as well as because of them, I find this house a never-ending excitement, and I think this is as necessary when a person is in the seventies as in the teens and twenties. What is more, knowing *why* and *where* is much easier and more fun in one's later years, even if such enjoyment may have to be paid for with a few purely physical hindrances, like crickety fingers or capricious eyesight.'[7]

Two days later Norah Kennedy Barr arrived. She was, and is, a tall, imposing woman with grey hair, a naturally serious face but a ready and generous smile. While Norah prepared the meal for the three of us in the kitchen on one side of the big, sun-lit living room, she told me about her family and her adult sons. The main dish was of braised veal in a delicate wine sauce, served on the same green pottery plates bought in Provence and described in *As They Were*.[8] While Mary Frances slept we talked about how close both sisters had always been. 'For Norah, again and always,' reads the dedication of this same book.

To one side of the table where we sat, a long chain of interlocking chicken wishbones swayed slightly in the breeze from the open windows. Near the door a large-format book of modern French painting stood on a lectern, and I remember that each day the book was left open at a different page. Just beyond the door, what looked like a complete collection of the works of Georges Simenon[9] filled a long bookshelf. Further along, towards the front door, was the handsome and totally seductive bathroom described in *Nowhere but Here*.[10]

At the time, it didn't strike me as odd that the description written by Mary Frances of 'Last House' should be so accurate and truthful: that there was no attempt to portray anything beyond reality, no attempt to gild the lily. Now, years later, and after reading all her work several times, I appreciate that this is a defining aspect of her writing, her commitment to complete and sometimes painful honesty. Often writing from notes made decades earlier, she observes: 'By now some of my notes sound like fabrications, invented to prove a point in an argument. This is because it is my way of explaining, and it has always been a personal problem, even a handicap. When I tell of a stubbed toe or childbirth, or how to serve peacocks' tongues on toast it sounds made-up, embroidered. But it is as it happened to *me*.'[11] One is reminded that Antony Powell once said to Kingsley Amis: '*In vino veritas* – I don't know, but *in scribendo veritas* – a certainty.'[12]

Yet, even for a writer blessed with near perfect recall, MFK found writing from memory an arduous business: 'I sweated like a stevedore, literally, over the actual turmoil that I'd made for myself, because I was determined to prove that most of us do not remember the real facts of something from our childhood, but instead recall what we were told we remembered by our parents and teachers. It was as Hell itself to strip down all the wishful dreams of what had really happened.'[13]

Nor did MFK find imagining or inventing any easier. In conversation, she told me: 'I tried writing a novel once. It was no good, but I got it out of my system.'[14]

'I have always been a reporter and perhaps a writer,' says Mary Frances in *Long Ago in France* (1991),[15] the book she was working on while I was there. She and Norah would set aside some time each day to look through cardboard boxes of papers, letters and postcards, dating from the time that Mary Frances and Al Fisher were living in Dijon in 1929 and newly married. 'I learnt to study and to think,' she said[16] of the three years she lived there, on little money, in the gastronomic capital of France. 'It was there, I now understand, that I started to grow up, to study, to make love, to eat and drink, to be me and not what I was expected to be. It was there that I learned it is blessed to receive, as well as that every human being, no matter how base, is worthy of my respect and even my envy because he knows something that I may never be old or wise or kind or tender enough to know.'[17] Norah later joined them in Dijon, and so the two sisters would talk about those days and recall events and people of their shared past.

On the last day of my stay, I drove over the Oakville Grade to the Napa Valley to visit the little museum devoted to Robert Louis Stevenson – Mary Frances and I were both admirers of his writing. Coming back in the twilight, over a level crossing, I accidentally drove off the road and onto the parallel railtrack so that my nearside wheels were on the sleepers and it was impossible to drive back over the rail. I knew the Napa Valley wine train would be approaching quite soon, and I was beginning to panic about the fate of my hired car, when four local people pulled up to help. Two drove ahead to stop the wine train, and another 'phoned a garage to lift the car off the track and change the damaged wheel.

Two hours later than expected, I returned to Last House. Mary Frances was waiting anxiously and was very concerned by what had happened. She sat in her wheelchair, craning forward, to hear every detail of my escapade. While I sipped whisky to calm my nerves, she put her hand on my arm and looked at me intently. 'I know it was a dreadful thing for you to experience,' she said, and, looking away, added quietly, 'but, you know, it couldn't happen to me.'[18] This was the only time Mary Frances referred to the Parkinson's Disease which was already restricting her activity to the house.

By the time of my last visit to Mary Frances in May 1992, the illness had deprived her of most movement and her voice was hardly audible. Norah Barr had urged me to visit her sister while I was staying in San Francisco. Mary Frances was now very frail and confined to the high-sided bed at the far end of her study.

As I walked into the room she waved her arm to greet me in the usual way and I saw that she had asked her nurse to dress her in a pale silk dress. She looked even more beautiful, her ivory skin remarkably unlined, her grey-green eyes undimmed. She lay in her table-high bed, smiling, serene, but very weak. Yet, she insisted on talking for some time and I had to hold my ear right against her mouth to hear her. I hoped she couldn't see how very upset I felt. After a while she invited my husband and myself to go onto the balcony for a glass of wine. I knew I'd never see her again, and the sadness I felt was deepened by the sight of her and by yet another reminder of her indomitable spirit and unfailingly generous nature.

It was this generosity, allied to her integrity and insight, that made her such a fine writer. Writing is inevitably about sharing, and MFK Fisher shares her thoughts like no other writer on gastronomy. Her sensibilities make her fastidious with words, cajoling from them fresh nuances that awake and enlighten the reader. 'I do love words, their connotations, their uses and abuses.'[19]

Even in her lifetime she was described as a national treasure; she was praised by W.H. Auden, and dubbed 'a poet of the appetites' by John Updike. Her writing does indeed celebrate our capacity for sensual pleasure; she relishes the complex and redemptive nature of love, and she savours hunger in all its forms. For many of us, her prose is itself sustenance.

M.F.K. Fisher died at Last House on 22 June 1992. A neighbour and good friend of Mary Frances wrote to me about the funeral and described movingly how her ashes were scattered in a place in the Californian countryside that she loved.

Since her death, two more books of her letters and journals have been published which shed further light on her writing. *Stay Me, Oh Comfort Me – Journals and stories, 1933–1941* (1993) is a continuation of the earlier volume *To Begin Again – Stories and memoirs 1908–1929* (1992). In her introduction, Norah Barr writes: 'Mary Frances put this manuscript together...because she wished her life to be read as it really happened to her and as she felt it at the time, not interpreted later by a biographer or even by her older self.'[20]

M.F.K. Fisher's legendary desire for simple food was evident in her writing well before publication: 'One of the reasons I am glad to go to Laguna tomorrow with Larry is that then it will be easy to eat simply, of milk and lettuce and yeast and vegetables.'[21]

And because her work is principally concerned with eating well – in all senses of the word – the occasional reference to eating badly is specially memorable: 'The supper chez Hinchman was one of the worst meals I've ever eaten, but the people were good. There was a great tub of spaghetti cooked with cheap oil and hamburger meat and no imagination, a salad so badly mixed that the salt and the oil and the garlic came in gobs, and, most god-awful, saucers of pink gelatin. I was almost too depressed to be revived, but the people were quite interesting.'[22]

It is, of course, her moral values which contribute such strength to her writing. These values are, as one would expect, even more freely expressed in her journals and letters. Her understanding of the actions and motives of herself and others is shown in a journal entry for 22 November 1933 about the disadvantages, when adult and married, of living with one's family: 'But I did want to go *away*. I do these people no good – open a few car doors for Mother, run errands, be present for talk and this and that. But they get along as well, sometimes better, without me. And when I'm here, I worry and scheme and stir up and smooth down, and when I'm away – away too far to telephone or summon – I am all in one piece. That is what I want, to be whole.'[23]

It is also plain that MFK clarified her thinking through writing itself. From Switzerland in 1938 she wrote two letters[24] to Lawrence Powell about the failure of her marriage to Al Fisher: the first is intense, agonizing, and unsent; the second is calmer, more controlled, and was posted.

M.F.K. Fisher – a Life in Letters, correspondence 1929–1991 was published in 1997. This volume is dedicated to 'Lawrence Clark Powell, an unfailing friend and colleague of M.F.K. Fisher from 1929 until her death in 1992.' Powell is the recipient of a great many of her published (and unpublished) letters, and he himself contributes *MF: A Reminiscence.* This collection of letters covers the whole period of her published writing life from the appearance of her first book, *Serve It Forth* (1937), which immediately established the author's extraordinarily mature and wise voice, although she was only 29 years old.

A Life in Letters illuminates the life and thinking of Mary Frances in a way no biography could. And, to my mind, few of its readers would not feel renewed respect for the overriding courage of Mary Frances, both as a person and as a writer, in living according to her convictions.

After a lifetime of words, a book of photographs of M.F.K. Fisher appeared in 1997. *A Welcoming Life – the MFK Fisher Scrapbook* contains 240 family photographs, compiled and most ably annotated by Dominique Gioia, working from MFK's published writing and from the unpublished papers bequeathed to the Schlesinger Library at Radcliffe College. The epitaph of the book is the one chosen by Mary Frances to her fourth book, *The Gastronomical Me* (1943), a quotation from George Santayana: 'To be happy you must have taken the measure of your powers, tasted the fruits of your passion, and learned your place in the world.'

Now that we are able to read the full corpus of M.F.K. Fisher's published work, it is abundantly clear that her books and articles not only reveal the true measure of her powers, but unquestionably confirm her pre-eminent place in the world of gastronomic writing.

REFERENCES

[1] *Map of Another Town*, p. 130.
[2] Preface to *French Country Kitchen*, Simon and Schuster, 1990.
[3] *A Considerable Town*, p. 47.
[4] G.H.'s personal notes, 11/89.
[5] *Dubious Honors*, introduction.
[6] *As They Were*, p. 251.
[7] ibid, p. 260.
[8] ibid, p. 95.
[9] *Last House*, pp. 41–2; *A Considerable Town*, p. 7, 104.
[10] *As They Were*, p. 257.
[11] *Sister Age*, p. 5.
[12] *Memoirs*, Kingsley Amis, introduction.
[13] *Dubious Honors*, p. 144.
[14] G.H.'s personal notes, 11/89.
[15] *Long Ago in France*, preface xiii.
[16] G.H.'s personal notes, 11/89.
[17] *Long Ago in France*, preface xiv.
[18] G.H.'s personal notes, 11/89.
[19] *A Welcoming Life*, p. 31.
[20] *Stay Me, Oh Comfort Me*, introduction vii.
[21] ibid, p. 10.
[22] ibid, p. 24.
[23] ibid, p. 13.
[24] ibid, p. 164.

Memory as a Culinary Skill and Necessity

Philip Iddison

Introduction

Flanked by food reference books and with a selection of culinary classics from several different periods to hand, often loaded with recipes, it is difficult to imagine working in a culinary environment with no printed or even hand-written records available. Complete reliance on memory to establish one's culinary credentials is a rather disturbing prospect. Knowing that the grey cells have to provide the detail to resource, prepare, cook and consume the daily intake of food at anything above a subsistence level seems a daunting prospect in the information age.

Before writing developed and printed material became readily available there was no choice. Food traditions were passed by memory from generation to generation. To our modern minds this oral tradition may seem to be characterized by transience and instability. We have come to trust only hard facts, and even those with circumspection. Historical evidence, however, shows a different reality. Classics of folklore and religion, as well as culinary traditions, were successfully passed down from generation to generation, faithfully detailed, because they were revered as immutable truths or records. Our modern flirtations with dissimulation, mutation and even downright lies were not acceptable. The maintenance of a true record of essential details in a strong oral tradition was possible for a number of reasons: the narrator was often a respected member of the social group; narrators were usually well known to their audience; justified challenge was always imminent from any quarter, for instance if there was a stranger in the audience.

Tradition can, however, be varied in detail. Individual character is inserted by the narrator, whether by experiment, opportunity or simply by individual flair, to enrich and diversify. However, the key details remain true to the tradition whether they are the recitation of a lineage, the tale of a battle or the description of food at a wedding celebration.

How far back in time does a communal memory extend? It is closely interwoven with knowledge, traditions and local culture. For instance, the antiquity of food processing skills indicates that some aspects of this memory resource probably date back to prehistory. In the Arabian Gulf countries there is archaeological evidence that date storage and processing have not changed over the last 5,000 years.[1] Similarly, the processing methods for milk have a long history, well attested by travellers in Arabia over several centuries.

Before written records, memory was just one of a number of complimentary skills which would contribute to culinary competence:

- judgment of weights and measures by eye, hand or simple measuring tools;
- heightened sensory ability, particularly taste and smell;
- knowledge of what was edible and what was inedible;[2]
- ability to judge cooking temperatures;
- dexterity in handling foodstuffs;
- knowledge of basic culinary chemistry;
- understanding of food hygiene.[3]

Resources, in the forms of instant reference to books, specialized tools such as thermometers, and processing equipment, have now replaced these skills for many cooks. These suit a more casual and time-conscious approach to food and cookery. In the absence of memory of how a dish should look and taste, we rely on a written description or a highly stylized photograph in a glossy cookbook.

Our experiences of taste and smell also rely substantially on memory, as there is no method to record or reproduce standards for these senses. Can we be sure that the essential taste and smell of, say, cardamom has not changed significantly over the years of selective cultivation, since it was first tasted in the West? The loss of taste and aromas in produce from modern plant cultivars, animal breeds and factory processing has undoubtedly consigned many subtle memories to oblivion.

The development of a culinary tradition must have depended initially on the memory function, whether it was based on ethnic, regional, national or religious characteristics. While memory was the only recording resource, a culinary tradition might be constrained to a small locality, encouraging diversity.[4]

At this stage, a culinary tradition is in a vulnerable condition, with no written records to detail its characteristics. Any study must rely on available artefacts, archaeology and folklore. In a stable environment, with no social, economic or political upheaval, a cuisine will survive. Media reports of political or natural disasters, showing refugees fleeing from their homes and living in camps, usually also show evidence of temporary or even permanent displacement of food traditions. International aid organizations provide some new form of food and cooking methods, often at odds with local traditions. Store-cupboard foods and local produce are no longer available and cooking methods have to be adapted to new resources. Refugees may become reliant on international aid to the detriment of their own food traditions. Memory can ensure that the desire to regain former traditions is kept alive.

United Arab Emirates and culinary memory

General literacy in the United Arab Emirates is a recent development. The ability of the older generation of nationals to remember events and facts is prodigious. This is to be expected in a society with practically no written records, a tribal structure and little in the way of outside influences. The Emirates had a true 'paperless' society, but not in the modern computer-driven idiom of this phrase. Even today, apart from the paper needs of government bureaucracy, this particular medium has little use in most people's lives.

This reliance on memory was evident in several aspects of life, such as traditional medicine, crafts like dhow building, the farming calendar[5] and the culinary repertoire.

The culinary repertoire is varied, rich in the use of a limited palette of resources, and has also borrowed from neighbouring sources, due to a strong trading tradition.

Food traditions appear, at present, to be in a robust condition, at least in parts of the community. I found a good example recently on a visit to a modern desert village, in the company of the under-secretary of the local municipality. When the morning's business had been concluded, all in attendance were invited to a late breakfast at a village leader's *majlis*.[6] After preliminary cold drinks, coffee and the passing of incense, we assembled in the eating area, where the food had been laid out on the floor. Nearly all the key dishes of the national food heritage were present: *harees, ballaleeth, laham meshwee,*[7] *wagafi* with *assal* and *samn*, and *aseeda* were served. Only *thareed*[8] was missing. The presentation of the food was also thoroughly traditional and the guests well-versed in the niceties of accepting apparently casual hospitality. The preliminaries to the meal were conducted with elegant haste and the food was eaten in sufficient quantity to register appreciation, but not in such quantity as to deprive the unseen family members of their lunch, for that is what we were offered.

Another aspect of the local interaction between food and memory is the special dishes which are prepared for the main festivals or *eids*.[9] In Al Ain the population has mixed roots in Oman and the UAE. *Shuwa*[10] is an important festival dish of Omani origin which is only prepared at *eid*. This is pit-roasted, well-spiced meat, comprising a whole beast or large cuts. The meat is sewn into palm-leaf sacks, placed in a pit which has been fired with timber and left to cook for 24 hours. It is then eaten with rice and honey. The cooking process imparts a particular combination of smoke and ash flavours to the meat, which are much appreciated by Omanis.[11] Having to wait for nearly eleven months through the year for such a special dish must sharpen and intensify the memory, as well as the cultural and religious significance of the food experience. The effort involved also ensures that this is a communal affair, with many families placing their food in the same roasting pit.

Concern for the future is a serious consideration. The current generation leading the country and acting as cultural arbiters is only a part-generation away from its pre-development-era roots. They were children in an undeveloped, undisturbed country[12] which now has one of the highest per capita incomes in the world. They are therefore still in touch, through their memories, with a solid cultural background based on centuries of collective memory.

However, significant changes are already recorded. The traditional wedding celebrations have changed dramatically. Less than twenty years ago, the wedding celebration for a sheikh's son would have extended to five days of communal social gatherings, including singing, dancing and eating.[13] This year, the wedding of one of the ruler's sons appears to have been concluded in one day.[14] At an even more extreme limit, the wedding receptions held in the major hotels include a formal meal, where everyone troops in, eats their food and departs, in a typical duration of seventeen to twenty-five minutes.[15] It would be simplistic to conclude that this was the impact of the fast-food culture, as far more complex factors are involved.

The lack of written resources for culinary information will be a particular problem when the inevitable change to written sources occurs. Any remnants of oral food tradition will then have to compete with written food resources from around the world. This is already evident: translations into Arabic, of western food recipes and Chinese cookery, are already on the bookshelves.

Memory can be fugitive, or perhaps just hopeful. William Lancaster was positively advised in Ras Al Khaimah that he would be able to get locally grown *bir abyad* (white wheat) in the Buraimi suq.[16] This is the wheat grain used in *harees*. It was once grown locally, but has now been displaced by imported Australian wheat. A thorough check around the Buraimi suq this spring, seeking older and older inhabitants, finally found an octogenarian who said that the last locally grown *bir abyad* had disappeared from the Buraimi suq before the Second World War!

The nationals are only just beginning to write their autobiographies. Men's biographies concentrate on their business and social success. Very little mention is made of the routines of life, such as food. In her autobiography, Mariam Behnam admits to never having learned to cook. She was the daughter of a wealthy Iranian Arab merchant and the kitchen was out of bounds to her as a child.[17] Her autobiography is therefore starved of food references and the cooks in her childhood household will not have left any written record.

Contemporary records from Saudi Arabia

One form of food research which is not generally accessible is the work done by market researchers.[18] Whilst the research is often focused on particular new food products and concentrates on the marketing aspects to probe perceptions and attitudes, the researchers ask their focus groups a broad range of questions, to build up a general picture and also to encourage free participation. It is in this context that interesting snippets of information are found. A chance to review some of this research on dairy products in the Kingdom of Saudi Arabia revealed some evidence of the function of memory and its importance to food traditions.

The Arabian peninsula has long been a focal point for travellers through the Islamic traditions of Haj and Umrah, when people from the whole Muslim world travel to the holy cities, Mecca and Medina. In their turn, the coastal populations have been significant traders, for instance there are strong connections between Oman and East Africa and the Yemeni Hadramaut and Indonesia. As a result, the food culture has been exposed to many external influences. Whilst some of these have been adopted,[19] the traditional food culture appears to be holding up, with traditional and regional foods still well appreciated, although now alongside many new dishes.[20]

The contributors to the study were grouped by economic status and sex. Most interviews were arranged with groups of women, usually mistresses of households. There was a hesitant consensus on the issue of what constitutes 'traditional food'. Often memories had to be stirred to confirm the group's knowledge. There was a quite distinct division between 'historical' foods, more recent adoptions largely from the Arab world, and thoroughly modern foods, usually from Western or Far-Eastern sources.

Aggressive advertising and promotions have had an impact on the Saudi attitude to food. Women note that children are readily affected by television advertising. This could be the reason for the children's shunning of traditional foods, particularly at breakfast. Milk drinking has been a casualty of this trend: most contributors say their children will not drink milk unless it is flavoured, usually with chocolate. One result of this will be a lack of the important childhood memories of traditional foods which can shape later preferences in life so markedly. On a similar theme the research records the frequent breakdown in the tradition of taking of meals as a communal family event: 'in the early morning the children open the fridge and have a Pepsi without eating anything.' Overseas travel is also cited as a reason for changed food desires and habits.

On the other hand, the culinary traditions in the neighbouring provinces of the Kingdom are often only vaguely known. Statements such as, 'they keep their own goats and sheep in Nejd and use the milk', indicate that food traditions are on the wane. A generation ago, everyone in the Kingdom had access to their own livestock. The most frequent modern reference for the source of milk is the cow, a relative rarity in Arabia in the past due to the abundance of camels, goats and even sheep.[21] No doubt this short memory has been precipitated by the flood of imported dried milk products, followed by the development of local dairy farms, creating a dislocation in the food chain.

Reliance on foreign maids working in the household also has an impact on the retention of traditional memories. Foreign foods and attitudes are introduced more easily into family life through daily contacts. In some cases, maids are not allowed to cook traditional food, while in other cases the contributors were proud of the fact that they had trained their maids to cook traditional dishes.

Conclusion

Memory has served the food traditions of the UAE and Saudi Arabia well in the past. It has been the main recording medium for the maintenance of culinary heritage.

The last quarter of the twentieth century has been an era of major change in the lifestyles of the people of these countries. It was a period when reliance on the oral tradition was substantially replaced by many new inputs into the food equation. This change to written or other media sources will relegate the oral tradition to a subsidiary role.

The survival of the memory-driven oral tradition which has relied on memory for centuries, if not millennia, is now in question.

BIBLIOGRAPHY

Al Taie, Lamees Abdullah (1995) *Al Azaf – The Omani Cookbook*, Oman: Oman Bookshop.
Behnam, Mariam (1998) *Zelzelah – A Woman before her Time*, Dubai: Motivate Publishing.
Brock-Al Ansari, Celia Ann (1994) *The Complete United Arab Emirates Cookbook*, Dubai: Emirates Airlines.
Højlund, F. (1990) 'Date Honey Production in Dilmun in the Mid 2nd Millennium BC: Steps in the Technological Evolution of the Madbasa', in *Paleorient*, Volume 16/1.
Holton, Patricia (1997) *Mother Without a Mask*, Dubai: Motivate Publishing.
Iddison, Philip (2000) 'Dairy Food in the UAE', in *Milk: Beyond the Dairy: Proceedings of the Oxford Symposium on Food and Cookery 1999*, Totnes: Prospect Books.
Perry, Charles (1998) 'A Nuanced Apology to Rotted Barley', in *PPC* 58, London: Prospect Books.

——— (1998) 'Medieval Near Eastern Rotted Condiments', in *Taste: Proceedings of the Oxford Symposium on Food & Cookery 1987*, London: Prospect Books.
——— (1999) 'More Rotted Barley', in *PPC* 61, London: Prospect Books.
Sexton, Regina (1999) 'The Re-discovery of Gammelsaltet Sei', in *PPC* 63, London: Prospect Books.
Thesiger, Wilfred (1964) *Arabian Sands*, Harmondsworth: Penguin.

1977 Statistics Yearbook, UAE Government, 1977.
Unpublished market research interviews with Saudi nationals, Gulf News.

REFERENCES

[1] *Mudibsa*, date storage buildings, were a common construction in Gulf countries. The dates are packed into sacks or baskets woven from date palm leaf and stacked in a pile inside the building. The floor has channels to collect any date syrup, dibs, exuding from the dates and direct it to a collection receptacle. Stacking the dates two or three metres high hastens the dibs production by a combination of pressure and heat mass. There are examples of these date storage cellars, in the restored Omani forts at Nizwa and Jabrin, which date from the seventeenth and eighteenth centuries respectively. Archaeological excavations in Bahrain, Oman and on Failaka island off Kuwait have uncovered *mudibsa* dating from the second millennium BC through the Islamic period (Højlund). Their purpose was identified from the ridged floors found in the excavations and the provision of sumps for the dibs collection. The simple technology required for the food processing was the key to identifying the purpose of the remains.

[2] Charles Perry's reporting on rotted barley products is a good example of modern investigation of past practices, reference *PPC* 58 & 61 and *OSF&C* 1987.

[3] An example of this knowledge is the wet salting of surplus fish in the UAE markets. The process for tuna is to gut the fish and cut off the head, but not completely clean the guts and blood. The carcass is then split along the backbone, covered with salt and packed into containers, rather at odds with our modern conception of food hygiene. Interesting comparisons can be drawn with the Norwegian practice reported by Regina Sexton in *PPC* 63. Another example is the air drying of quite large tuna specimens which have simply been split open and left in the sun. They are discernible from a long distance due to the smell of the drying flesh (personal communication from Mark Beech after a visit to Dalma Island in 1998).

[4] Nevin Halici's records of traditional food recipes in rural Turkey demonstrate this diversity well. The recipes are credited to individual cooks, and even in a small geographical area display subtle variation in ingredients for dishes with the same local name, a characteristic of a cuisine relying on memory, rather than books.

[5] Holton records that an elderly female member of a sheikh's family kept an account of the farming almanac, based on the lunar calendar, positions of stars and numerology. In the 1980s this was recorded in writing, but was probably a memory exercise for previous generations.

[6] The *majlis* is the public reception room or suite of rooms in an Emirati home.

[7] It was perhaps fortunate that the choice morsel that was offered to me from this dish of cooked lamb was a piece of boiled liver and not the eyeball of travellers' tales. *Harees* is a porridge made from wheat grains and meat, *ballaleeth* is sweet noodles with an omelette, *wagafi* is the local flat bread served traditionally with honey and clarified butter, *aseeda* is browned flour pudding.

[8] *Thareed* is a stew served on a pile of paper thin bread.

[9] The two main *eid* festivals occur after the end of the fasting month of Ramadan (Eid al Fitr), and on the tenth to fourteenth days of the month of Dhu'l-hijja (Eid al Addha), some

66 days after Eid al Fitr.

[10] Recipe in Lamees Abdullah Al Taie.

[11] The rosewater from the Jebel Akhdar region is heavily impregnated with this characteristic smell of smoke and ash. In Nizwa, one Friday morning, the fish market was redolent with this same smell as large roasted and charred tuna were broken into chunks and sold to eager buyers by the kilo.

[12] Wilfred Thesiger noted, during his travels in the UAE and Oman in the period 1946–50, that he was observing a people and lifestyle which was about to change irrevocably with the arrival of oil exploration.

[13] Recorded in Holton, the date is imprecise, but the wedding described appears to have been in the early 1980s.

[14] The list of attending sheikhs was published in the local press. One tradition was, however, upheld, that virtually anyone could attend if they so wished. Open invitations were issued through various institutions.

[15] Personal observations at a number of these commercial events.

[16] Buraimi and Al Ain are adjacent cities on each side of the Oman/UAE border.

[17] Mariam Behnam.

[18] The research is organized for a specific product, funded by a client and as such is considered confidential to that client; it is therefore archived at the end of the research campaign and is rarely ever used again.

[19] Examples are: the general use of olive oil in Saudi cooking (it is not a native product) and the adoption of biryani/pillaff in the United Arab Emirates.

[20] Macaroni and chips & ketchup are examples.

[21] Animal populations in the UAE as recently as 1976 outnumbered humans, and cattle were outnumbered 20:1 by other milk-producers (Iddison).

Remembrance of Meals Past: Cooking by Apicius' Book

Cathy K. Kaufman

The antique banquet has been a favorite subject of speculation and recreation, as witnessed by our own Saturday night fête. In 1788, the French painter Louise-Elisabeth Vigée-Le Brun hosted an impromptu recreation of a Greek banquet, inspired by an afternoon reading of Jean-Jacques Barthélmy's *Voyages d'Anacharsis*, with its description of an extravagant Athenian dinner. She had at her disposal everything she thought necessary: rich fabrics to drape the dining-room, tunic-swathed beauties bedecked with garlands, antique vases, a guitarist whose instrument was transformed into a golden lyre and, most importantly, a cooperative cook willing to make 'a certain sauce for poultry and another for eels,' supplemented with 'two vegetable dishes and a cake made with honey and Corinthian raisins...[and] a bottle of old Cyprus wine.' By her account the effect was picturesque, although we learn no more of the gustatory pleasures. Curiously, she declined invitations to repeat her little 'joke', which lead to scandalous rumours, inflating the banquet's expense.[1]

Guests have dined less well at other recreations, both real and fictional. The eighteenth-century classicist Mme Dacier allegedly suffered from hallucinations and believed that she had brought back the exact recipe for a Spartan black broth from the banks of the Eurotas; on serving it to six academicians, they thought themselves poisoned.[2] Tobias Smollett's doctor-host of a Roman dinner (no doubt a reference to Dr Martin Lister and his 1705 edition of Apicius' *De re coquinaria*) had to dismiss five cooks:

> because they could not prevail upon their own consciences to obey [the doctor's] directions in things that were contrary to the present practice of their art; and that although he had at last engaged a person, by an extraordinary premium, to comply with his orders, the fellow was so astonished, mortified and incensed at the commands he received that his hair stood on end, and he begged on his knees, to be released from his agreement.

The doctor held fast, dinner was served over the caterwauling of the cook, and the brave marquis who gamely swallowed the soup suffered, 'until his stomach was so much offended, that he was compelled to...[fly] into another apartment...puking and crossing himself with great devotion...'[3] The encyclopaedists provided academic cover for the Roman-bashing, claiming that decadence of French cookery in the sixteenth and early seventeenth centuries could be traced to the Italians, and especially Catherine de Medici's 'corrupt mob', who, as inheritors of the 'debris' of Roman cookery, forced an overly-spiced amalgam upon the French.[4]

These brutal critiques continued in the nineteenth and twentieth centuries. *Kettner's Book of the Table* moralizes that, 'Roman cookery is a warning...Mines of wealth were spent upon it; infinite pains were wasted upon it; the uttermost parts of the earth were ransacked...and to what result? Any Picardy kitchen-maid will turn out a better dish for a few francs.'[5] Mary Ella Milham cautions that any host of an authentic Roman dinner had better have a hefty supply of hamburgers at the ready, as most people will be put off by the excessive mixtures of spices and condiments.[6] Even the usually sympathetic translators of *De re coquinaria*, Barbara Flower and Elisabeth Rosenbaum, opine that the Romans abhorred simple flavours: 'There is hardly a single recipe which does not add a sauce to the main ingredient, a sauce which changes the original taste *radically* (emphasis added).'[7] . These anecdotes tell us more about the biases of the writers[8] than anything else, supporting Theodore Zeldin's observation that every generation reinvents its memories.

It is easy to understand how such an unflattering image of Apicius' cookery emerged. Reading Apicius, even as a professional chef, is hardly a mouth-watering journey into gastronomy. The recipes do not read like anything that modern cooks expect. In addition to puzzling over flamingos' tongues and sows' wombs, that ubiquitous *garum* stinks up everything. Techniques are scanty and quantities infrequent, allowing the cook to imagine the worst. But, as every professional cook knows, the written recipe is only a starting point for executing a dish. Few recipes explicate every step that must be taken to complete a dish, and the competent practice of cookery requires the cook to draw on resources beyond the page.[9] These resources include the cook's artisanal memory, that is, the understanding of the physical processes of cooking and the skilful handling of ingredients that comes from experience. One function of cookbooks is to act as mnemonics for these artisanal memories:

> Every particular Art hath its proper Terms and certain Rules and Methods, which through disuse are easily lost and forgot. The Memory, like polished Steel, the more it is used, the brighter the Reflection, but

neglected, rusts and dulls. This Manual therefore will be a necessary Companion to several Persons to refresh their Memories of those Excellent Things which they shall at any time happen to forget...'[10]

The centrality of these artisanal memories explains why Smollett's cooks objected so strenuously to the doctor's insistence on an 'authentic' Roman meal. Technique provides the paradigm for judging the cook's efforts.

Consider the following hypothetical recipe: 'Meringue: combine six eggs and one and a half cups sugar.' Two things will immediately cross the practitioner's mind: firstly, that the recipe means to use only the egg whites and secondly, that the sugar and egg whites could be combined in any of four ways to produce an acceptable meringue. The cook must determine from his artisanal memory which technique to use, as each technique will result in a meringue with slightly different qualities, more or less appropriate for different dishes. Will the cook slowly add granulated sugar while beating raw egg whites, or will he fold the sugar into the already-beaten whites? Will he beat the whites over heat (and, if so, over a *bain-marie* or direct heat?) before adding the sugar, or will he drizzle a hot syrup of melted sugar into beaten whites, continuing all the while to beat rapidly? And what about using an icing sugar instead? The permutations on even a simple recipe can be daunting. The historian must, therefore, construe the recipe by analysing the language and inferring details of technique from his knowledge of the equipment and ingredients available, and any other sources that suggest what the finished dish might be.

Apicius is often no more explicit than my hypothetical meringue recipe, and cooking from Apicius is nearly impossible without relying on artisanal memories. The recipes are written haphazardly, as if someone familiar with the workings of a kitchen was jotting down notes for a colleague – not necessarily in the order in which the cook would need the information – to prepare the various dishes.[11] Some explicitly rely on the cook's judgment, acknowledging that the executed recipes will vary from one cook to another: 'Taste; if something is missing, add it.'[12] Others are baffling without reference to their titles. Recipe 3.4.8 for marrows with fowl contains neither marrows, nor fowl, nor even a verb to suggest what to do with the list of ingredients that are given; presumably the cook will infer that he should make a sauce. Given these inadequacies and corruptions in the text,[13] the exact nature of many of the finished dishes is uncertain. I have thus experimented with a variety of techniques that could have been available to a Roman cook to prepare recipes from Apicius' Book 4, Chapter 2, *patinae piscium holerum pomorum*, or dishes of fish, green vegetables and fruit.

A *patina* is a round, relatively shallow dish, and, like the terms tagine or terrine, signifies both a cooking vessel and a category of dishes prepared in such vessels. Of the 37 *patinae* in Apicius 4.2, 23 contain eggs that are used in some way to bind the dish. These recipes have been construed as frittatas, omelettes or custards.[14] Undoubtedly, many such dishes graced Roman tables for centuries. However, the vocabulary used to describe the technique by which the eggs are incorporated in these dishes varies widely. Although this may simply be the product of a careless scrivener or result from the fact that many hands contributed to the Apician manuscripts, I believe that these language differences indicate that a great range of cooking techniques was used, including a technique for a soufflé.

Apicius uses eight different verbs to describe techniques for incorporating eggs into *patinae*. The terms are: *obligo*, to bind, *frango* and *confringo*, to break, *misceo* and *commisceo*, to mix (together), *agito*, to stir, *temperatio*, to mix in proportion,[15] *infundo*, to pour in, *missio*, to release from captivity and, most critically for my hypothesis, *dissolvo*, to break up into component parts, disintegrate, undo, dismantle or separate.[16] Some of the *patinae* are missing verbs in the key passages and the noncommittal 'to cook' has been supplied, while others use more than one verb to communicate the technical use of the eggs. Variations on *frango* and *confringo* are used most often, appearing in eleven of the 23 recipes; the binding function *obligo* appears in seven recipes, *misceo/commisceo* is used in five recipes, and my favorite *dissolvo* shows up four times. The remaining verbs appear only once or twice. In seventeen of the 23 recipes, the term *ova* is used without indicating whether the eggs are raw or cooked; the remaining six specify raw eggs for the binding function, and one recipe requires hard-cooked eggs.[17] The context generally indicates that raw eggs are to be liquefied and poured, blended or stirred into the dish. *Dissolvo* also appears in several recipes outside of Apicius 4.2, which in context suggest that the eggs should be beaten.

Recipes 4.2.14, the gourmet *patinam Apicianam*, and 4.2.15, the more mundane *patina cotidiana*, are two versions of the twentieth-century *gâteau aux crêpes* or, perhaps, fresh lasagne. Both recipes use *dissolvo* in what appears to be the preparation of ghastly sounding 'oil-cakes'. While Flower and Rosenbaum translate '*ova vero cruda cum oleo dissolvis*', (recipe 4.2.14) as 'then stir raw eggs into oil', as a cook, I believe that the eggs first must be well beaten to trap air and thicken slightly, before being sautéd in oil, thereby giving delicate texture to the layers that will separate the rich filling. This, of course, betrays my personal biases as a cook, as I judge the results against the standards of my modern palate. Yet, other Apician recipes do imply a beating function with the term *dissolvo*. Recipe 7.13.8, for *ova spongia ex lacte*, or egg sponge with milk, uses *dissolvo*, and the name 'sponge', surviving today in cakes made with airily-beaten eggs, implies that the cook must do something to lighten the egg mixture before cooking it. Obtaining a 'sponge' by briskly beating the eggs would be an easy task for kitchens populated by slave-cooks, with their copious perforated strainers.[18]

My proposed soufflé is recipe 4.2.27, the *patina zomoteganon*,[19] in which the cook poaches some fish in a flavourful broth, purées the fish and adds back some of the broth. The crucial step of incorporating the eggs follows: '*ova cruda dissolves, temperas. exinanies in patinam, facies ut obligetur.*' Mesdames Flower and Rosenbaum translate this passage as 'stir in raw eggs [into the hot fish-broth], blend. Pour into the pan and allow to set.' Yet, if *dissolvo* can mean 'to separate', and also implies beating, then I propose the following expanded cook's meaning for the passage: 'separate the raw eggs. Temper [the yolks into the hot fish-broth and beat the whites], blend. Pour into the pan and allow to set.'[20] This interpretation yields a soufflé[21] and gives independent meaning to *temperas*, which otherwise appears somewhat redundant of *dissolvo*. The question is: whether a late Roman cook had the technical ability and knowledge to beat the egg whites into a foam and fold them back into the tempered purée to yield a tender and light treat? I believe so, based on artifacts and other works written shortly after the presumed date of the later parts of *De re coquinaria*.

Mesdames Flower and Rosenbaum illustrate their translation with a suggested *patina* that is a round dish approximately twice as wide as it is high.[22] If they are correct, it resembles our modern soufflé dish and would support the eggs as they rise in cooking. Furthermore, the early sixth-century work of the physician Anthimus, *De obseruatione ciborum*,[23] contains two recipes for soufflé-like dishes:

> 34. What is called in Greek *afrutum* and in Latin *spumeum* is made from chicken and egg whites. Lots of egg white must be used so that the *afrutum* becomes foamy. It should be prepared in a mound on a shallow casserole with a previously prepared gravy and diluted fish sauce underneath. Then the casserole is set over the charcoal and the *afrutum* cooked in the steam of the sauce. The casserole is then placed in the middle of the a serving dish, and a little wine and honey poured over it. It is eaten with a spoon or small ladle. I often add to this recipe some good fish or even some sea-scallops, because they are extremely tasty and are particularly plentiful around where I live. From clean scallops are made 'snow balls'.

40. Pike is good too. Egg white should be mixed into the dish called *spumeum* which is made with pike, so this dish may be quite soft rather than hard, and wholesome when mixed together.

If we indulge my expanded reading of recipe 4.2.27, the *patina zomoteganon* sounds like the *spumeum* of Anthimus.

Admittedly Anthimus' vocabulary is very different from recipe 4.2.27. *Spumeum* itself means foam, and Anthimus specifically requires egg whites, rather than whole eggs, to make the dish. He uses no verb to describe the actual process of whipping the eggs, assuming that the cook's artisanal memory will supply that step from the description of the eggs' texture. His otherwise detailed recipe is consistent with his medical training and dietetic purpose in writing the book. Although I have not found earlier examples of *afrutum* or *spumeum*, Anthimus' reliance on both Greek and Roman terms for an egg white foam proves that this dish was not unique in Roman Europe. Even if the specific recipe for *spumeum* was unknown to the cooks using *De re coquinaria*, years of kitchen observation would surely have taught the more conscientious among them of the foaming properties of eggs and their delightful rise when placed in a *patina* among the hot ashes. Thus the soufflé could have been 'invented' independently by cooks interpreting *dissolvo* to mean 'to separate.'

Cookbooks are imperfect tools for recreating recipes, for two people participate in the process: the cookbook writer, who sets for himself the task of giving instructions to an unknown audience, and the practitioner, who interprets the instructions to recreate a dish. The final product depends on the skills of both. The best expressions of a cuisine, however, are not found in slavishly following a recipe, for no two kitchens or sets of ingredients are identical. The artisanal memory allows the cook to adjust and create according to what is at hand. William King summed it up nicely:

> 'Tis a sage Question, if the Art of Cooks
> Is lodg'd by Nature, or attain'd by Books:
> That Men will never frame a noble Treat
> Whose whole Dependence lies on some Receipt.
> Then by pure Nature ev'ry thing is spoil'd,
> She knows no more than stew'd, bak'd, rost and boyl'd.
> When Art and Nature join th' Effect will be
> Some nice Ragoust, or charming Fricasy.[24]

We will never be certain whether any cook made a fish soufflé based on Apicius 4.2.27. Yet, if the thought that Apicius' Romans were tucking into that quintessentially elegant 'French' soufflé seems anachronistic, the historian ignores evidence that the cook, with her artisanal memory, appreciates.

REFERENCES

[1] Vigée-Le Brun, Louise-Elizabeth (1926) *Memoirs*, trans. Shelly, Gerard, London: J. Hamilton, pp. 43–47.
[2] Gottschalk, Alfred (1948) *Histoire de l'Alimentation et de la Gastronomie*, vol. 1, Paris: Éd. Hippocrate, p. 143.
[3] Smollett, Tobias (1936) *The Adventures of Peregrine Pickle* (1751), Oxford University Press, pp. 232–235.
[4] See the articles on 'Cuisine', 'Assaisonment' and 'Gourmandise' in Diderot and D'Alembert's *Encyclopédie ou dictionnaire raisonné des sciences, des arts et des métiers*, Paris 1751–1757.
[5] Dallas, E.S. (1968) *Kettner's Book of the Table* (1877), London: Centaur Press, pp. 389–90.
[6] Milham, Mary Ella (1966) 'In Defense of Hamburger: Apicius and Roman Cooking', 12 *Vergilius* 46.
[7] Apicius (1958) *De re coquinaria*, trans. and eds. Flower, Barbara and Rosenbaum, Elisabeth, London: Harrap, pp. 19–20.
[8] My own biases as a cook in our politically correct times are that (i) any culture sophisticated enough to write cookbooks and make some form of alcoholic beverage shares enough in common with our palates to have made food at least somewhat appealing to us; (ii) we tend to exaggerate the differences rather than the core similarities in western cuisine; and (iii) differences in cuisine are most striking in the use of ingredients that we politely consider 'acquired tastes'.
[9] Escoffier's *Guide Culinaire* is a classic example of the *aide-mémoire*, in which nearly 3,000 recipes are crammed into a bit over 800 pages, useful mainly to trained cooks.
[10] Howard, Henry (1729) *The British Cook's Companion: Being a Collection of Four Hundred of the Newest and Best Receipts*, 5th ed., London: from 'to the Reader'.
[11] Recipe 4.2.14 shows the poor construction of the recipes, in which a number of steps are given when the scribe suddenly interrupts himself: 'But first add all the different meats and let them cook...Before you put all these meats with the sauce into the saucepan you should have bound them with eggs.'
[12] Apicius 5.2.2, 5.2.3, 5.3.1.
[13] Scholars report that the oldest extant manuscripts are ninth-century and date the original compilation to the late fourth or early fifth century. Mesdames Flower and Rosenbaum believe that a healthy 60 per cent of the recipes come from first-century sources, perhaps from the notorious Apicius who lived in the reign of Tiberius. Given differences in the recipes' detail, the book is believed to be liberally sprinkled with recipes from Greek and Latin dietetic and agricultural works, in addition to later culinary delights.
[14] *Patinae* of this sort are in Bober, Phyllis Pray (1999) *Art, Culture and Cuisine: Ancient and Medieval Gastronomy*, Chicago: University of Chicago Press; Dalby, Andrew, and Grainger, Sally (1996) *The Classical Cookbook*, J. Paul Getty Museum; Ricotti, Eugenia Salza Prina (1995) *Dining as a Roman Emperor*, Rome: 'L'Erma' di Bretschneider; Giacosa, Ilaria Gozzini (1992) *A Taste of Ancient* Rome, trans. Anna Herklotz, Chicago: University of Chicago Press; Edwards, John (1988) *The Roman Cookery of Apicius*, London: Random House; Solomon, Jon and Solomon, Julia (1977) *Ancient Roman Feasts and Recipes*, Miami: E.A. Seemann Pub.
[15] Modern culinary lexicon uses the verb 'to temper' to instruct the cook to incorporate a hot liquid slowly into eggs to thicken the liquid, avoiding a lumpy coagulation. Ancient cooks likely observed this same phenomenon.

[16] All definitions come from Lewis and Short (1966) *Oxford Latin Dictionary*, Oxford: Clarendon Press.

[17] Recipe 4.2.13 specifies hard cooked eggs *(ova dura)* as part of the filling for a complicated layered dish that finally is bound with a custard *(lacte colas, cui cruda ova commisces)*.

[18] Flower and Rosenbaum additionally translate *dissolvo* to mean 'beat' in recipes 2.1.5 (*'adicies ova quinque et dissolves diligentur*: Add five eggs and beat well.') and 4.2.15 ('*ova confringes in caccabum et dissolves…reexinanies in caccabum, facies ut ferveat*: Break eggs into a saucepan and beat…pour [liquids] into the saucepan, bring to the boil, and thicken').

[19] The *Glossary of Later Latin* (1966),Oxford: Clarendon Press, defines *zomoteganon* as a dish of boiled fish, citing Apicius. The definition is both inadequate and, of course, circular, in trying to get at the nature of this particular dish. Liddell's *Greek-English Lexicon* (1968), Oxford: Clarendon Press, offers two definitions: fish stew or a fat, greasy fellow.

[20] Andrew Dalby suggests in his introduction to his translation of Cato's *De agricultura* [On Farming] that in translating Latin, the reader must add 'padding' to the spare language used to obtain the full meaning.

[21] Joseph Dommers Vehling's translation of this dish also takes some interpretive liberties, although he thinks that the dish is a stew in which the sauce is bound with only the egg yolks. He interpolates *dissolvo* as 'break and beat egg yolks for a liaison…binding the sauce with the yolks.' Apicius (1977) *Cookery and Dining in Imperial Rome*, trans. and ed. Vehling, Joseph Dommers, New York: Dover.

[22] Flower & Rosenbaum, p. 17.

[23] Anthimus (1996) *De obseruatione ciborum* [On the Observance of Foods], trans. and ed. Grant, Mark, Prospect Books.

[24] King, William (1709) *The Art of Cookery in Imitation of Horace's Art of Poetry, with some Letters to Dr. Lister and Others: Occasion'd principally by the title of a Book published by the Doctor, being the Works of Apicius Cœlius concerning the Soups and Sauces of the Antients*, London: Bernard Lintott, p. 123.

The Diet of the Greeks: 'Genetic' and Recent Memories

Sotiris Kitrilakis and Lidia Kitrilakis

'Genetic' memory

Humans have existed as a genus for over two million years and have been hunter-gatherers for 99.9 per cent of that time.[1] Their diet consisted of mostly fruits and vegetables, was high in fibre and included lean meat and fish. It was a diet low in fat, even lower in saturated fat, high in longer chain polyunsaturated fatty acids, with a ratio omega-6 to omega-3 fatty acids of between one and four. There is strong evidence indicating that the human genetic constitution, well adapted to this diet, has changed very little over the last 40,000 years.[2] Consequently, the foods which were commonly available to pre-agricultural man were the foods that determined modern man's genetic nutritional requirements. Our diet, however, has changed dramatically since the advent of agriculture 10,000 years ago.[3] Cereal grains, which have become a staple, are a relatively recent addition to the human diet and represent a dramatic departure from those foods to which we are genetically adapted. Nevertheless, they have been staples for every highly developed civilization in history and now are the base of the food selection pyramid recommended in the United States.[4]

Notwithstanding such official endorsement, there is a significant body of evidence which suggests that cereal grains are less than optimal foods for humans, and that the human genetic make-up and physiology are not adapted to high levels of cereal grain consumption. Many studies indicate that the discrepancy between humanity's genetically determined dietary needs and its present-day diet is responsible for many of the chronic degenerative diseases so prevalent in industrial societies. In other words, our body retains a 'genetic memory' of a very different diet.[5]

In general, as hunter-gatherers abandoned their fruit, vegetable and animal based diet, replacing it with cereal staples when they became early farmers, there were characteristic reductions in stature, increased infant mortality, a reduction in life-span, an increased incidence of infectious diseases and an increase in iron deficiency anaemia, an increased incidence of bone mineral disorders, and an increase in the number of dental caries and enamel defects.[6] In a review of 51 references examining human populations from around the earth and from different chronologies as they made the transition from hunter-gatherers to farmers, Cohen[7] concluded that there was an overall decline in both the quality and quantity of life. There is now substantial empirical and clinical evidence to indicate that many of these deleterious changes may be directly related to the predominantly cereal based diets of these early farmers. Cereal grains are devoid of key nutrients, such as vitamins A, B12 and C and beta-carotene, to mention only a few of the most familiar. In addition, humans are unable to physiologically overcome cereal grain anti-nutrients (phytates, alkylresorcinols, protease inhibitors, lectins, etc.).[8]

Obviously, cereal grains can be included in low to moderate amounts in the diets of most people without any noticeable deleterious health effects. Moderate consumption of cereal grains requires that a substantial portion of the caloric intake and protein be obtained from other foods: fruits, vegetables, dairy and animal sources. Our genetic memory that mandates this diet goes back to 300 to 500 generations for most of us, a rather short interval in evolutionary terms. Until the early 1960s the majority of the population of Greece obtained little of their caloric intake from cereal grains. This factor, and a high degree of physical activity, may have been primarily responsible for low incidence of chronic diseases observed in the early studies in Crete.

Lifetime memories

In the in last 100 years there has been a change in our food supply and diet which may be even more profound than the one associated with the 'agricultural revolution'. The industrialization of our food supply is driven by the desire to produce low-cost food that can be easily preserved and transported. Mass production and processing of food by industrial methods, using high technology, is now widespread in every corner of the earth. Increasingly complex technology is accelerating the changes in the food supply and the diet of humanity. Unlike the changes related to the agricultural revolution that span our 'genetic memory', these changes are happening within a single life-span. In our lifetime we have witnessed the radical changes that are taking place in the 'Mediterranean Diet'. We would like to examine these by describing the changes that have taken place in the last 25 or so years in five basic foods that are very common in this much-touted diet.

Chickens and eggs

Eggs have been a staple in the Greek diet since antiquity. In the countryside, during my childhood, each household had a few chickens, minimally confined, that roamed around the yard. Raw eggs were given to the young to help them grow strong and healthy. I remember getting an egg, warm from the hen, puncturing a hole in the shell, and sucking the contents. Another children's favourite was to whip a raw egg with honey or sugar into a sweet pleasant paste, which was closer to dessert than to 'food that was good for you'. Eggs with bright, almost orange yolks, fried in olive oil, made a great lunch. Used in sauces, baked goods or home-made pasta, eggs imparted a kind of luxury of flavour.

The majority of chickens and eggs consumed in Greece today, as elsewhere, are mass-produced on industrialized farms. Animals are confined in tiny compartments, are formula fed, and their daylight period artificially determined. These conditions brought about the threat of salmonella and other pathogens. Nobody dares eat a raw egg and the loss of flavour in both chickens and eggs is astounding. The pale yellow yolks of supermarket eggs have virtually no taste. The natural balance of omega-3 to omega-6 fatty acids has been destroyed in the mass production of eggs.[9]

There are still households in the villages were chickens are allowed to forage in the fields and are fed various grains and scraps from the table. On the island of Zante, our friend Maria has about 30 chickens that spend most of their time in the family olive orchards. The flock furnishes chicken for the family meals as well as eggs. It is always a special treat to be invited to Maria's table for chicken *krasato*, the Greek equivalent of *coq-au-vin*. Chickens and their eggs are most flavourful in the months of January and February, when they have been eating ripe olives falling off the trees. Apart from the wonderful flavour, these eggs also show the beneficial balance between omega-6 and omega-3 fatty acids. In recognition of the importance of these essential nutrients, several companies have started producing eggs of a similar composition by allowing the chickens freedom and feeding them a more natural, balanced diet. These omega-3-rich eggs are available in the US and now in Greece.

Cheese

Cheese owes its existence to the need to preserve milk and must be almost as old as the domestication of ruminants. Like all ancient foods it has undergone many embellishments in response to local conditions, climates, tastes and preferences. Hundreds of different cheeses have evolved in Europe and at least a few dozen different types existed in Greece at the end of the Second World War. The prevalent cheese in the country has always been *feta*, a soft to semi-soft cheese preserved in brine. Prior to widespread availability of refrigeration, *feta* cheese was kept in cool cellars in brine with a relatively high content of salt, about ten to twelve per cent. An alternative to high salt concentration, practised in the Ionian Islands, was to transfer the cheese, after a short time, from the brine to an olive oil bath. Cheese submerged in oil lasted for more than a year although with time it hardened and became increasingly sharp. In the early 1950s, when this was still a widespread practice in the Ionian Islands, it was a treat for city dwellers to receive a small head of cheese still coated with olive oil. *Ladotyri*, oil-cheese, has all but vanished as a commercial product. It rarely reaches towns and cities beyond the islands and has become a farmhouse product consumed by the family.

Friends in the Ionian Islands still make it with milk from their own ewes and goats in January through April. Its flavour peaks after two to three months of aging in oil. The natural culture and the extra-virgin oil give the cheese a hard to describe unique aroma and taste. Peak flavour develops in the summer months making the cheese the perfect companion to summer salads.

Wild greens

In the lean years of the 1940s and 1950s, when street vendors still plied the neighbourhoods of Athens, a familiar sight was the donkey loaded with two baskets of wild greens, one on either side. Wild greens became available with the first rains and continued until late spring. The variety of greens changed as the season progressed. Dandelions were the first to come up and they were the perennial favourite. Many other types, including pungent mustard greens, amaranth, and many aromatic, sour, and bitter varieties, whose English names I could not find, followed them. By January, when the rainy season was in full swing, the prices dropped and mixtures of various greens were offered, each vendor proclaiming superiority for his particular blend of greens. Elderly aunts and uncles attributed great therapeutic value to these greens and claimed to have been cured of many ailments. It would not be true to say that I liked all these varieties. No child could tolerate the bitterness of young dandelions. But the aromatic greens that came in spring were a delicacy when lightly steamed and drenched with fresh olive oil and lemon. Wild arugula, purslane, rocket and watercress were great in raw salads. Mixed wild greens and new onions were often used as pie fillings in spring and early summer. The crust, simple home-made country crust, using olive oil and the smoky flavour imparted by wood burning ovens, was a further enhancement of the pies' flavours.

The 'agricultural revolution' aside, modern Greeks seem to have retained the gatherer aspect of the hunter-gatherer up to contemporary times. The itinerant wild-green vendors and their donkeys have long disappeared from both the cities and the countryside, but older country people are often seen roaming the hillsides, collecting greens. Occasionally they will sell the excess in the open-air farmers' markets, earning pocket money in the process. If you are lucky enough to come across one of them, you're in for a feast.

Memories and actions

Those who live in large towns and cities have little access to such foods. Older people have memories of them, the younger ones have only heard about them.

Occasionally, when city dwellers visit relatives in the country, they get to taste what used to be everyday food just 30 years ago. But in the Greek countryside, in the villages, families continue to make traditional foods and small dairies are producing ancient cheeses. While the forces of industrialization continue to eliminate small producers, there is a growing movement to preserve and strengthen what is left of traditional food production. This, of course, is not just a Greek phenomenon; it has happened in many other countries and it is beginning to take the shape of a movement. The movement is driven by memories of the great flavours and diversity of food that were available just a few decades ago. It is also powered by concerns over the long-term health effects of high technology industrial food. Organizations such as Slow Food are co-ordinating the actions of interested groups and individuals in many countries and are providing a platform for promoting these values. The issue has surfaced at this Symposium many times.

REFERENCES

[1] Simopoulos, A.P. (ed.) (1999) 'Evolutionary Aspects of Nutrition and Health', in *World Rev. Nutr. Diet*, vol. 84, Basel: Karger, pp. 19–73.

[2] Eaton, S.B. and Konner, M. (1985) 'Paleothithic nutrition, a consideration of its nature and current implications', in *N Engl J Med*, 312:283–289.

[3] Sinclair, A.J. and O'Dea, K. (1990) 'Fats in human diets through history: Is the Western diet out of step?', in Wood, J.D. and Fisher, A.V. (eds.) *Reducing fat in meat animals*, London: Elsevier Applied Science, pp. 1–47.

[4] Achterberg, C., McDonell, E. and Bagby, R. (1994) 'How to put the food guide pyramid into practice', in *J Am Diet Assoc*, 94:1030–1035.

[5] Eaton, S.B., Konner, M. and Shostak, M. (1988) 'Stone agers in the fast lane: Chronic degenerative diseases in evolutionary perspective', in *Am J of Med*, 84:739–749.

[6] Eaton, S.B. and Nelson, D.A. (1991) 'Calcium in evolutionary perspective', in *Am J Clin Nutr*, 54:281s–287s; Angel, J.L. 'Paleoecology, paleodemography and health', in Polgar, S. (ed.) *Population, Ecology and Social Evolution*, The Hague: Mouton, pp. 167–190; Nickens, P.R. (1976) 'Stature reduction as an adaptive response to food production in Mesoamerica', in *J Archeol. Sci*, 3:31–41; Cohen, M.N. (1987) 'The significance of long-term changes in human diet and food economy', in Harris, M. and Ross, E.B. (eds.) *Food and evolution. Toward A Theory Of Human Food Habits*, Philadelphia: Temple University Press, pp. 261–283; Cassidy, C.M. (1980) 'Nutrition and health in agriculturalists and hunter-gatherers: A case study of two prehistoric populations', in *Nutritional Anthropology*, Pleasantville: Redgrave Publishing Company, pp. 117–145; Diamond, J. (1992) *The Third Chimpanzee: The Evolution and Future of the Human Animal*, New York: Harper Collins, pp. 180–191; Lallo, J.W., Armelagos, G.J. and Mensforth, R.P. (1977) 'The role of diet, disease and physiology in the origin of porotic hyperostosis', in *Human Biol*, 49:471–473; Turner, C.G. (1979) 'Dental anthropological indications of agriculture among the Jomon people of central Japan', in *M J Phys. Anthropol*, 619–636.

[7] Cohen (1987) pp. 261–283.

[8] Simopoulos (1999) vol. 84, pp. 19–73.

[9] Simopoulos, A.P. The International Conference on the Return of Omega 3 Fatty Acids to the Food Supply 1997, Bethesda MD, The Center for Genetics Nutrition and Health.

Food as a Vehicle for Remembering: the Case of the Thessalonikan Jews

Vasiliki Kravva

Introduction

It is not only individuals that forget; modern 'cities' tend to forget as well. Thessaloniki, a city situated in northern Greece, with a population of almost a million inhabitants, doesn't seem to have escaped collective amnesia. I often recall scenes from my early childhood when older members of my family talked about their lives in pre-war Thessaloniki. All these narratives included Jewish friends and invitations to attend *Bar Mitzvah*[1] ceremonies at the Synagogue. The stories ended quite abruptly with the following comment: 'All our Jewish friends were sent to the concentration camps...' For a child's imagination such a comment provided no real answers and generated further questions about the fate of those people: Why? Who sent them? Why didn't they refuse to go? What happened in those camps?

Greek state education provided no further answers to my questions. During my years at school I heard nothing on this and during my time at the Aristotle University of Thessaloniki there was hardly any mention of the Jewish presence in the city. Years later the situation was similar in my work and social environment. No one seemed able, or at least willing, to give me a clear picture of the city's past. The municipal and other authorities of the city of Thessaloniki have not proved particularly keen to highlight any evidence of the city's multi-ethnic past. Thus there are no Jewish streets and no monuments apart from the Square of the Jewish Martyrs, a square that was dedicated to the victims of the Holocaust quite recently, in 1997.[2] Collective amnesia has been transformed into ignorance, in the interests of a 'homogeneous' present, a present without non-Christian citizens. However, since I have been engaged in a research project concerning Salonican Jews, I have come to realize that my childhood narratives were neither fairytales nor figments of my imagination. They proved to be true stories of the Jewish presence and pictures of everyday life in Thessaloniki prior to the Second World War.

This essay will be an exploration of people's memories and the identities they experience through food. Sephardic[3] cuisine constitutes an important marker of a shared past and present and a repository of shared memories from before and after the war. My interest focuses on two age groups: the Holocaust survivors and the second generation of Salonican Jews, meaning those people who were born after the *Shoah*[4] and who today constitute the middle-aged population in the city. The nexus between memory and food acquires special attention in my overall account. Therefore, I strongly suggest that food functions as a mnemonic device, as a basic ingredient in the process of creating sameness and solidifying the sense of belonging to a group.

A brief historical overview

The Jewish presence in Thessaloniki dates back to the foundation of the city in 316 BC by Cassandrus. Several historical sources, including the ancient historian Strabo and the Acts of the Apostles, indicate that in this famous port a significant Jewish population lived, uninterruptedly, from the Hellenistic period up to the Byzantine era. This population was strongly Hellenized and gradually was culturally assimilated. Nevertheless, the *Romaniotes* – the Greek-Jewish people – maintained some religious features. During the Middle Ages a strong wave of anti-Semitism emerged. In particular, the building processes of Western monotheistic states legitimized by religion and the Crusades that followed from these rendered the Jewish presence in the Christian world marginal and insecure. As a result of this anti-semitic climate the edict of Granada[5] was issued by the Catholic kings of Spain in 1492. According to the edict, all the Spanish Jews, who refused to be baptized as Christians, had to leave Spain within three months. A massive exodus of Jews from Spain followed. It is estimated that 50,000 people converted to Christianity and remained, but more than 250,000 left the Spanish peninsula. The majority of them found shelter in the lands of the Ottoman Empire and almost 20,000 chose Salonica as their home, which was at that time under Ottoman rule.

These Spanish Jews, known as Sephardic Jews, gradually came to possess a significant economic power in the port of Salonica. The local language they developed over time, *Ladino*,[6] was a mixture of Spanish, Hebrew, Turkish and Greek. Sephardic culture marked the life of Thessaloniki and its influence was continuous until the Second World War, when 46,000 Thessalonikan Jews were sent to the death camps of Auschwitz, Birkenau and Bergen-Belsen. This number represents 96 per cent of the Jewish population of pre-war Thessaloniki. Today the community counts almost 1,000 members and maintains two Synagogues, a primary school, a home for the elderly, a summer camp, two museums and a community centre, which serves as an administrative centre, but also as a cultural club and 'brotherhood', organizing various activities.

'We were expelled from Spain'

During my fieldwork among the Jewish community of Thessaloniki, people expressed a strong tendency to establish links with the Spanish past. This past stood for something that was felt to be not necessarily distant but, on the contrary, familiar and intimate. Memories of Spanish cultural heritage formed a common point of reference, a starting point for differentiation with the rest of the city's population. Remembering the past was not only a way to denote distinctiveness, but also a source of communal pride. This privatized notion of the past was evident in most of my interviewees' accounts:

> Sepharad means Spain, so we are Jews of Spanish origin. Our ancestors left Spain to avoid conversion to Christianity. Many of them came to Thessaloniki, which was under Ottoman rule. The Ottoman Empire paid no attention to our religious beliefs as long as we paid our taxes.[7] For more than 400 years until the Second World War in this city there was a lively and powerful Jewish community which maintained many synagogues and schools and created an admirable civilization.

This strong affiliation with Spanish culture was evident among the majority of my interviewees and covered many aspects of life and various cultural products, such as language, music and cuisine, and often a combination of these elements. In fact, many housewives explained to me that the Sephardic dishes they prepare have *Ladino* names, so 'they definitely have Spanish origins,' and they were 'authentic Sephardic dishes.' This was the case for salty dishes like *sfougato* or *sfougatico*, *pesce en salsa*, *keftikes de prassa de patata* and *de spinaka*, or sweet dishes like *tupishti* and *sutlach*. The preparation of these dishes represented a bridge connecting them to their origins and, as such, it constitutes a powerful statement of identity. But the most interesting thing is that preparing and serving these dishes generated discussions about sameness and difference and served as the starting point for the expression of differences between the Jewish and the Christian populations in contemporary Thessaloniki. I was often invited during the end of my fieldwork to 'taste' this difference: 'Try some of our dishes. This is the way we do it and this is based on the way our mothers and grandmothers used to cook. You[8] cook differently.'

Eating and remembering...

The legitimization of present social realities, via food preparation and consumption, was one theme I came across during my fieldwork. The topic of food proved to be more than a mundane pursuit, since it generated important symbolic discourses. As far as family was concerned, food practices and narratives enacted a whole series of nostalgic recollections about the lost families, an idealized childhood but also memories, about the Jewish past, of 'the mother of Israel'.[9] By recollecting family life people reproduced boundaries and reaffirmed their identities in a rapidly changing world. Throughout my paper I avoid making use of the dichotomy of private (family) versus public (community institutions) as, in the case of Salonican Jews, such reductionist binarism distorts the complexity of everyday realities. The boundaries between the two spheres are never fixed because both contexts are conceived as a continuum. Both private and public domains are loaded with notions of privatized history and identity. Within a common context privatized memories of a Thessalonikan-Jewish past constitute the basis for present discourses on identity.

The connection between taste and childhood memories is the first issue to be explored. In many of my informants' words, there was an evident recollection of a harmonious past through remembering tastes of childhood. A 40-year-old man commented:

> I remember a sweet that I can't find any more called *tupishti*. It looks like your walnut cake. My aunt used to make it dark with a lot of syrup; I called her Nona. She used to make it for the day of Yom Kippur. Generally I am a great fan of sweet tastes but believe me, this was something else. I am still looking for this taste but I can't find it anywhere.

The term 'tasty' became equated with the term 'familial'; people searched for tastes that were familiar to them and reminded them of their childhood. Mrs Lea, an 80-year-old woman, still cooks for her son although he has his own family now; in order to marry a Christian woman he converted to Christianity. During the Christian Easter he had to fast as his wife did. Mrs Lea explained to me:

> During Christian Easter my son was fasting. I cooked some of our food for Pessach, which is called *pesce en salsa*. My daughter-in-law cannot bear to even taste it but my son loves this dish and he wanted to have his portion. So I gave him some to take home. He loves it because it is tied with memories. Food you know is something that ties in with memory. My children love this dish because they were raised with this taste. They remember tastes. The food that someone loves is definitely the one he used to eat as a little child...

In some discussions food was associated with memories of married life and family bonds. Rosa, a 50-year-old woman, used food narratives to reveal aspects of married life and her relation to her mother-in-law:

As far as cooking is concerned I learned a lot from my mother-in-law. My mother was a rebel. She refused to keep traditions. For my mother-in-law cooking was a kind of ritual. She cleaned up, washed herself and then she cooked for hours. I remember I first tasted a sweet called *sutlach* at her home. At the beginning I thought it was a bit burnt but I found it so delicious. Of course I was embarrassed to say anything. Then I realized that the more burnt it is the more tasty it becomes.

The ritual of commensality provided an excellent opportunity for releasing memories of past family life. While conducting my fieldwork I had the opportunity to share such a situation with several people. 'Sharing the same table'[10] proved for my informants an ideal vehicle for memory release. Once, while eating with friends at a local restaurant, Rachel made the following remark: 'I like garlic but I don't use it when I cook. I prefer onions. My mother used to cook like that. This is the taste I've been brought up with.' Taste evoked a matrix of recollections concerning childhood, motherhood and the idealized image of a lost family life.

All the discussions I had with older men and women eventually turned to the 'glorious' past of Thessaloniki. Food discussions proved a powerful channel for memories and nostalgia about the good old days of life in the city:

Me and my husband love salted fish. We call it *souimekos*. It is very difficult to find this kind of fish in the market nowadays. Native Thessalonikans know it is the best *meze* (appetizer) for ouzo.

My ignorance about life in the city surprised my informants, but it was a good excuse for them to recall the past and narrate how their lives used to be and which are the tastes that they miss in contemporary Thessaloniki:

Oh, I remember the old pastry shop, the hotels, the centre. Life used to have a different quality in those days, beauty and luxury. Nowadays I don't even want to leave my home. Everything seems so cheap...

The ethnographic data presented in this paper highlight that food, apart from constructing family boundaries, and thus sociability, has the power to evoke memories concerning past family relations and sentiments of belonging to a city. By this token the past blends with the present and food narratives function as a repository of shared sentiments. After all, shared history is partly the internalization and the employment of shared experiences and sentiments and, if this is the case, food serves as an important marker of creating and recreating shared histories.

Food, memory and the construction of identities are strongly interconnected. In particular, food is often the locus of recollections and memories of a family or community past. The mnemonic qualities of food and eating consist of retrieving memories of time, place and belonging. It has been stressed that:

> If identity is constructed through memory, the memories of time and place linked to food, eating and nurturing play a key part in retrieving significant memories. Food could be seen as the sensory point of entry into a web of sentiments, memories and fantasies which largely constitute a sense of identity...
>
> Goddard, 1996: 213

Shadows and silences

The picture that I have presented so far is one of idealized life, with happy memories from childhood and idealized recollections of a past city life. Of course, this is only one part of the picture. All these recollections belong to settled spaces of memories and spoken past experiences. But in the individual's life there are also unspoken memories or, more accurately, unsettled spaces of memories. This was the case for the Holocaust survivors in Thessaloniki: food narratives became the starting point for expressing their experiences at the camps, but also a way to mourn the lost members of their families. The Second World War was, for them, a strong dividing line, which separated time, space and memories in a pre-war and a post-war Thessaloniki. Such a past consisted for many years of 'traumatized' and 'unspoken' memories (Jeleniewski-Seidler, 2000: 6).

More than 50 years separate us from the *Shoah*. Last year, when I was carrying out my fieldwork in Thessaloniki, I realized that people had started to put in order the tragic experiences that marked their personal, family and community lives. Food discussions were used by Thessalonikan Jews, who were either survivors or children of survivors, as a vehicle to remember the painful past and evaluate the effects of that tragic ordeal upon their lives. Although my initial intention was not to collect Holocaust experiences, the narratives of food made people overcome their reluctance and made them comfortable enough to share their experiences with a young Christian woman. It seemed to me that food was a vehicle for speaking about the painful past, of sharing it and of putting some order in this 'unsettled space':

> Oh, life before the War was so beautiful. Here we are again. I am going to tell you the story of our deportation to the Concentration Camps. Everything happened so quickly. My father was trying for months to

get us foreign passports. But ironically the same day we managed to get them we were already on our way to Bergen-Belsen. All my family. I remember I was just a young girl then…

As an epilogue

Taste acquires a central position in the formulation and evaluation of present life experiences. It enacts past memories of childhood and family life. In the case of Thessalonikan Jews, such memories are happy and idealized but, to a great extent, they also constitute a source of sadness and discomfort. In any case, food practices and narratives proved a valuable means of evaluating the past and, thus, of release as a web of sentiments and experiences for the present. It could be said that food functions as a mnemonic device, which enables individuals to place themselves in the present and 'manage' aspects of their identities. The same applies not only to taste but even to the thought of certain dishes: they seem to carry a powerful baggage of recollections. Food serves as a starting point for the elaboration of differences and a reaffirmation of boundaries. Through past memories Thessalonikan Jews express their membership in a community and at the same time state issues of belonging and denote quite strongly the feeling of 'being a Salonican'. I end this discussion with the words of one of my informants:

> After the War many things kept me here. I love my city so much that I could not live anywhere else. I feel that this is my home. I feel that every change that happens in this city also happens in my home. Thessaloniki is my home…

Recipe
This recipe was given to me by Lina Perahia. *Pesce en salsa* is a dish that Thessalonikan Jews consume during the celebration of *Pesach* (Passover). According to Judaic dietary law, only the use of *matsah* (unleavened bread) is allowed. Old Thessalonikan Jews argue that this dish represents 'the city and the history of Thessaloniki'.

Pesce en salsa

Fish fillets (preferably carp) • Walnuts chopped (one cup)
Eggs beaten (one or two) • Olive oil (one small cup)
Matsah (almost two cups) • Salt, Pepper
Vinegar (one cup)

Dip the fish fillets in the egg and then roll them in the crumbled *matsah* in which you have added salt and pepper. Fry the fillets in the oil and vinegar adding some *matsah*. When fried place them on a platter and spread over them the chopped walnuts.

BIBLIOGRAPHY

Barth, F. (ed.) (1969) *Ethnic groups and boundaries: The social organization of Cultural Difference*, Boston: Little Brown.
Barthes, R. (1975) 'Towards a psychosociology of contemporary food consumption', in Foster, E. and Foster, R. (eds.) *European diet from pre-industrial to modern times*, New York: Harper and Row.
Beardsworth, A. and Keil, T. (1997) 'Food, Family and Community', in Beardsworth and Keil (1997) *Sociology on the Menu: an invitation to the study of food and society*, London: Routledge and Kegan Paul.
Bell, D. and Valentine, G. (1977) *Consuming geographies: We are where we Eat*, London: Routledge and Kegan Paul.
Caplan, P. (1994) 'Feasts, Fasts and Famine: Food for thought', Berg Occasional papers.
——— (ed.) (1997) *Food, Health and Identity*, London: Routledge and Kegan Paul.
Connerton, P. (1989) *How Societies Remember*, Cambridge: Cambridge University Press.
Delamont, S. (1995) *Appetites and Identities: an Introduction to the Social Anthropology of Western Europe*, London: Routledge and Kegan Paul.
De Vault, M. (1991) *Feeding the Family: The Social Organization of Caring as Gendered work*, Chicago: the University of Chicago Press.
Douglas, M. (1975) 'Deciphering a Meal', in Douglas, M. *Implicit Meanings*, London: Routledge and Kegan Paul.
Fischler, C. (1988) 'Food, Self and Identity', *Social Science Information*, 27 (2): 275–292.
Goddard, V. (1996) 'Food, Family and Community Memory', in Goddard, V. *Gender, Family and Work in Naples*, London: Berg.
James, A. (1997) 'How British is British food?', in Caplan, P. (ed.) *Food, Health and Identity*, London: Routledge and Kegan Paul.

Jeleniewski-Seidler, V. (2000) *Shadows of the Shoah: Jewish identity and Belonging*, Oxford: Berg.
Levi-Strauss, C. (1965) 'The Culinary Triangle', in *Partisan Review*, 33: 586–95.
Lewkowicz, B. (1994) 'Greece is my Home but...Ethnic identity of Greek Jews in Thessaloniki', in *Journal of Mediterranean Studies*, 4 (2): 225–240.
Molho, R. (1994) 'The Jewish presence in Thessaloniki', (in Greek) in *O Paratiritis, series of language and art, Thessaloniki*, 25–26:13–51.
────── (1998) 'The Judaeo-Espagnol: an everyday Mediterranean language of Thessaloniki during the 20th century', (in Greek) in *Historical issues*, 1998, 28–29: 123–146.
Roden, C. (1994) 'Jewish food in the Middle East' in Zubaida, S. and Tapper, R. (eds.), *Culinary Cultures of the Middle East*, London: I.B. Tauris.
────── (1997) *The Book of Jewish Food. An Odyssey from Samarkand and Vilna to the Present Day*, London: Viking.
Stavroulakis, N. (1986) *Cookbook of the Jews of Greece*, Athens: Lycabettus Press.
Van Den Berghe, P. L. (1984) 'Ethnic cuisine: Culture in Nature', in *Ethnic and Racial Studies*, 7 (3): 386–397.

Other bibliographical sources
'The Jews in Greece: approaches to the history of Modern Greek minorities', (in Greek) in *Sinchrona Themata*, 1994: (52–53).
Special edition of the Greek newspaper *Kathimerini* on Sunday 3 March 1996 with the title: 'The Jews of Greece'.

REFERENCES

[1] The Jewish ceremony of coming of age, which takes place publicly at the Synagogue.
[2] In 1997 Thessaloniki was the Cultural Capital of Europe. During that year a series of publications and talks concerning the Jewish presence in the city took place. Moreover, a monument to the Jewish victims of the Holocaust was inaugurated and the whole square was named after it, 'Square of the Jewish Martyrs'.
[3] *Sfarad* in Hebrew means Spain. Accordingly, Jews with Spanish origins are called Sephardi.
[4] *Shoah* in Hebrew means destruction. In the literature the term Shoah is more commonly found than the Greek term Holocaust. In my discussion I make use of both terms.
[5] The edict of Granada was the outcome of the *Reconquista*, meaning the recovery of the Iberian Peninsula from the Arabs by the Christians. This edict was influenced by the Catholic Inquisition.
[6] According to historian Rena Molho: '...most of them were forced to leave all their belongings except the Spanish civilization that in later times proved an indispensable part of their Jewish identity. If the mother tongue of a people describes its national belonging then the fact that the Spanish-Jews preserved the Spanish language even after their destruction by the Nazis proves the deep roots of their cultural patriotism' (Molho, 1998:123).
[7] The Ottoman Empire was based on the *millet* system according to which all the non-Muslim populations were allowed to practice their religion but were obliged to pay heavy taxes.
[8] In all our discussions the distinction 'Us/Them' came up quite frequently as people differentiated Jewish from Christian Thessalonikans.
[9] In 1552 the poet Samuel Usque wrote: 'Near the big sea that surrounds the Ottoman Shores God raised the mace of mercy and stopped the river of misery, people of Jacob! Thessaloniki is a faithful city. The exiled Jews run to your protection and are welcome as if this city was our holy mother, Jerusalem.'
[10] Christine Delphy (1979), 'Sharing the same table: Consumption and the Family'.

Notes on an Eighteenth-century Manuscript Recipe Book

Janet Laurence

For many of us memories are bound up with food. Dishes we have eaten in childhood, later in life conjure up atmospheres, events and people, not all of them special or even enjoyable. If we are interested in cooking, when we leave home, we take copies of recipes with us. I still have a battered ring-file stuffed with scrawled-on pieces of paper – the recipes I was able to wrench out of my mother - together with newspaper and magazine cuttings.

My mother was Swedish and a marvellous cook. She was born with a fantastic palate and an innate sense of how to handle food. Ask her why she did something a particular way and she'd say, 'Oh, I don't know, it's just how it should be done.' Almost the only piece of technical advice I ever had from her was not to salt liver before cooking – even then she didn't know why, just that in her opinion it tasted better.

My mother was a devil as far as giving away recipes was concerned. She truly believed that if someone else had her recipe, they could cook like her, and she thought cooking was her only real talent. So she guarded her dishes. The first year I was married, I wanted to cook the Christmas cake she'd made for us for many years. I asked her, very nicely, for the recipe. She got very po-faced and said she didn't think she'd give it to me. Incensed, I told her if she didn't, I'd go to the person I knew she'd got it from in the first place and ask her! She gave me the recipe. Later she was much more helpful. I finally got her to teach me how she made Gravad Lax, a great speciality of hers. She measured out all the ingredients entirely by eye and we had to weigh them as she did so in order that I could recreate and publish her recipe.

Memories of meals as I and my two brothers and little sister were growing up centre mostly on the incredible buffet feasts she achieved for special occasions. She'd spend three days cooking her special dishes. Three days of hell, as far as the rest of us were concerned, as we were bullied and shouted at to do this, do that (mostly housework) and asked, 'what were we thinking of to be enjoying ourselves whilst she was working so hard?' What, indeed! It should have put us off cooking for ever but because the results were so wonderful, we all grew up with a deep love of food and all four of us learned to cook. One brother entered the hotel world and for many years was Managing Director of the Ritz in London, later adding the Stafford to his responsibilities.

In the 1940s and 1950s, when I was growing up, my mother cooked with what was, by today's standards, a very limited range of ingredients, and an equally limited budget, though food had first call on whatever money was available and she never skimped on quality. Her daily repertoire, as distinct from that for entertaining and special occasions, mainly consisted of roasts for Sundays (even with meat rationing, we managed that), stews, herrings cooked in any number of ways, tripe (not much of that, we all refused to eat it), shepherd's and cottage pies, meat loaf and macaroni cheese. If I go to my ring file, however, what is in there are the luxury recipes: almond cake, Swedish meat balls, fillet of beef, Norwegian fish mousse with prawns, *pommes dauphinoise*, *paella* (donated by an uncle in catering who spent half the year in Spain), Tosca cake, etc., etc.

I didn't get far with these when I started running a household. Indeed, when I got married and acquired two stepsons, I was staggered by the catering requirements. In order to cope, on Sunday evenings I would write out menus for the following week together with the shopping lists. I kept a book and on average my husband and I entertained twice a week over the first year of married life. The dishes that I'd taken from my mother were exhausted in the first month! Over that year I cooked my way through the *Cordon Bleu Cookery Course*, published in weekly instalments, hardly ever repeating a dish but filing away in my mind the ones I thought particularly successful.

Today, interest in food and cookery has never been higher and the world is plundered for new tastes, ingredients and ways of cooking. Whenever I and my siblings get together, though, the dishes we talk about and remember are those our mother produced. Looking back I can see that they were influenced by several factors: her Swedish background, which meant a very high standard of food preparation and presentation, a love of dairy produce and meat, especially farces and casseroles, fish, spices such as peppercorns and bay leaves (she wouldn't have anything to do with cardamom, so dearly loved by most Swedes), and baking – her Danish pastries were to die for. My father's taste was for highly flavoured dishes (his palate was very poor – my mother flinched every time he reached for the pepper pot before he'd even tasted her beautifully balanced dishes), and he encouraged her to make curries – though she never learned to mix her own spices.

All this is an introduction to the fact that, some years ago, I acquired a most beautiful folio manuscript 'Receipt Book'. In the front of the gold stamped leather cover is pasted a label which states:

Margaret Foulkes
This Book was given me by my dear
Mother Catherine Clough
April the 2nd 1770

The antiquarian booksellers I bought it from could only tell me it had been sold by someone in the south of England who had no connection with the original owner. There was no background information.

Compared with this book, my ring file is a frayed petticoat beside a magnificent court dress. And if my recipes conjure up memories of my childhood and the way we lived, how much more, surely, a book such as this must contain; not only the owner's culinary memories but those of the mother who gave it to her and whose collection it must be, and probably also some of her grandmother's as well. The collection, indeed, must be the mother's rather than the daughter's. Here are recipes that have suited a particular family living in a particular way. Is it possible, so long after the book's creation and with no background details, to retrieve some of these memories and to understand something of Catherine Clough, the conditions under which she lived and her culinary background?

First of all, the date of the book: the antiquarian booksellers thought the collection was earlier than 1770; a faint pencil notation inside the front cover says: 'Early 18th century? late 17th century?' However, one of the recipes in the book is entitled: 'Lady Sundon's Marrow Pudding made for Q. Caroline.' George II assumed the throne in 1727 and his wife, Queen Caroline, died in 1737.

Another indication of date can be gathered from the fact that the collection contains three trifle recipes. The first, called simply 'Trifle', is made with macaroons soaked in Mountain (Mountain Wine, a variety of Malaga, is made from grapes grown on the mountain[1]), layered with sweetmeats, some 'thick boiled' custard, finely cut almonds and candied orange and lemon peel, covered with a solid syllabub then garnished round the edge with more candied sweetmeats. Very close to the best sort of trifle made today, in fact. The second recipe, 'A Cold Trifle much in Fashion', has 'scalded' apples, beaten up with sugar and nutmeg, covered with a solid syllabub, and includes the recipe for this. The third recipe, 'A Trifle to eat Hot', is made from slices (called 'shives') of bread with hot white wine poured over, and sprinkled with grated cinnamon. Four yolks of eggs, a pint of good milk, and sugar and nutmeg to taste are cooked in a skillet on the fire until 'as thick as custard', then poured on the wine-soaked bread, and the whole is served up to the table.

According to Alan Davidson's monumental tome, *The Oxford Companion to Food*, it was during the middle of the eighteenth century that trifle developed, from a spiced and sweetened cream, latterly thickened by renneting, into these sorts of recipes.[2]

Manuscript recipe books, such as this collection, by their very nature cover a family usage of many, many years (some of my mother's recipes date back to the 1930s and no doubt some of my Swedish cousins have some of our grandmother's that go back to the start of the century). Collections will be handed on to succeeding generations, who will gradually discard what is no longer wanted, adapt others and add their own. However, it would be impossible to prepare a dish for Queen Caroline before 1727 and it seems unlikely that this sort of collection would include three such trifle recipes before the middle of the century. The collection, therefore, that Catherine Clough handed on to her daughter, Margaret, almost certainly was made some little time after the mid-eighteenth century. The date of 1770 seems accurate and I think is most likely to have been her daughter's wedding day.

The appearance and nature of the book suggest at the very least a reasonably comfortable existence. The ornate leather binding may well have been added at a later date as otherwise the inscription would not have needed to be pasted onto the inside front cover. The page edges are gilded. The book is written in the most beautiful script with each recipe title decorated, some very elaborately, with scrolls and fancy work. Each recipe is separated from the next by neatly drawn double lines in ink. As far as content goes, most of the recipes are written very clearly and in what seems a uniform style. This suggests that, though the scribing of the book could have been carried out by someone else, Catherine Clough herself worded the recipes, no doubt reworking some of those garnered from various sources.

Some of the recipes contain comments from Catherine (for it must surely be she). In the first trifle recipe mentioned above, for instance, there is an N.B. added: 'When the Maccaroons are thoroughly soaked you must pour away the Wine before you put in the Custard.' After a recipe for 'House Pudding', a simple dish of suet, raisins, currants, flour, eggs, milk, salt and nutmeg, the last line states: 'Experience has proved three hours will boil it as well as five.' Then in 'Orange Pudding *tres Excellent*' (no grave accent), a recipe that calls for peeling the skin of oranges without any pith and then shredding and beating them, we find:

> I think grated Peel saves Trouble, and does it finer and thinner, than you can shred or beat it: But you must beat up the Butter and Sugar with it, and the Eggs withall, to mix them well.

Education is also displayed in other ways. The recipes are very well organized. They are divided into various sections with three final sections: Potting,

Collaring and Pickling, headlined but empty of recipes. In most of the sections, the recipes are more or less ordered alphabetically by main ingredient, though under Preserves, Apricots come before Angelica and Apples, and under Jellies and Creams, Flummerys and Blamanges come after Syllabubs. In the Cookery section, which covers meat and fish dishes, the only apparent organization is that it starts with 'soops', and there is a run of recipes for stews. The other recipes are much more hugger-mugger, as they would normally come in a personal collection. Since it is the last section, there is a possibility that there wasn't time for a more elaborate sorting out. All of the pages are numbered and, at the back of the book, there is an index listing all the recipes, in the order given, with their page numbers.

There are indications of foreign influences. French invades some of the titles, such as the one noted above, 'Orange Pudding *tres Excellent*'. Then we get 'Beef *Alamode*' and 'Cutlets *Alamaintenoy*'. Beef, or *Boef, Ala Mode* appears in most cookery books of the time. I have not, though, found references to the other recipes (a list of those consulted is given at the end of this paper. I am the first to admit that it is not comprehensive and maybe someone else can come up with a reference not only for these but also other points I raise). Also included is 'Turkish *Dutma*' (which turns out to be a version of *Dolmas*) and two recipes for '*Piloe*', the first of which boils two pounds of veal and two pounds of mutton, and then adds rice; the second cooks rice then adds a fowl.

The recipe for *Dutma* is, in many essentials, the same as appears in *Adam's Luxury and Eve's Cookery*, a book of vegetable and fruit cookery (its subtitle is *The Kitchen-Garden display'd*) published in 1744, but there the recipe is merely called, 'Another Way to farce a Cabbage,' and lacks both rice and various flavourings. The only other reference to a similar recipe I've found in an eighteenth-century (or earlier) recipe book is in *The Receipt Book of Ann Blencowe*, which includes, 'To Make a Delma,' with a recipe which is very close to Catherine Clough's. Born in 1656, Ann Blencowe married in 1675 and her recipe book, dated 1694, was published in a limited edition in 1925 with a foreword by George Saintsbury. In it, he comments, 'If he (the reader) knows what a "Delma" is, if he has even ever heard or seen the word before, he has the better of this Introducer.' Which says a great deal about the general culinary memory of those not particularly interested in food, even the well educated, in the 1920s.

It's impossible to know if Catherine Clough had access to those whose business involved foreign travel, maybe merchants who were connected with the East India Company, but the scarcity of such recipes in other collections suggests that she may well have done. On the other hand, it may merely indicate that she, or her mother, or mother-in-law, had friends who had such connections.

A Floating Island (135)

Take the white of two Eggs and three quarters of a pound of Sugar & sifted; beat it together as for Icing, then put in as much Pulp of Rasberries, or what you please, as your Sugar looks to be; and beat it till it will stand up a Mount, in the middle of a convenient Glass or Bason. It will take a great deal of whipping, and must be lead out by spoonfuls, still turning the Spoon and drawing it upwards, that it may stand up high in the Middle; then put the Cream in softly, it will float about. This is the way fruit Cuffs are made, put out in little Cakes turn'd out with a Spoon by degrees; it may lie high upon white Paper, they will dry in the Sun in two or three Days, on a Roome Window.

To Make Orange Posset

Squeeze the juice of two Seville Oranges and one Lemon, into a china Bason that holds about a quart; sweeten this Juice like a Syrup, with double refin'd Sugar, put to it two spoonfuls of Orange Flower Water, and strain it through a fine Sive; boil a large Pint of thick Cream, with some of the Orange Peel in it cut thin; when it is pretty cool, pour it into the Bason of Juice through a Funnel, which must be held as high as you can from the Bason. It must stand a Day before you use it. When you use it to Table, stick slips of Candied Orange, Lemon, and Citron Peel on the Top.

A Custard Sack Posset

Take a quart of Cream, boil it and season it well with Sugar; then take ten Eggs with two whites beat in very well; strain them to half a pint of Sack, stir the Eggs and Sack with Care over the fire till it is very hot, then pour in the Cream, hold it very high & stir all very well together; cover it very close, and set it over a kettle of Water till it is come as thick and smooth as a Custard. It is by much the best sort of Posset that is made.

A Sack Posset

Break sixteen Eggs take eight of the whites out, beat them well and put in a pint of Sack and half a pound of Sugar, mix it very well; put it on a chafing Dish till it is so hot that you cannot hold your finger in it. Take a quart of Cream, boil a little Mace in it; when it is boiling pour your Milk hot holding your skellet high; cover it close with three or four fold of Flannel; let it stand three or four Hours.

A page from Margaret Foulkes' recipe book (not full-sized).

I have four printed sets of personal recipe collections of the late seventeenth and eighteenth centuries in my library: *In an Eighteenth Century Kitchen* (dated 1698 with 85 receipts in one hand plus another 85 receipts added later in different hands), *The Receipt Book of Ann Blencowe* (last quarter of seventeenth century – 89 cookery receipts), *The Compleat Cook or the Secrets of a Seventeenth Century Housewife by Rebecca Price* (compiled between 1681 and 1740 – 494 receipts), and *Elizabeth Raper's Receipt Book* (1756–1770 – 123 receipts). The Rebecca Price collection seems astonishingly industrious until Catherine Clough's recipes are counted. They come to an even more astonishing 629, in sections as follows:

Wines	85 recipes
Shrubs, Spirits & Cordials	12 recipes
Preserves & Candies	52 recipes
Preserves	134 recipes
All Sorts of Cakes	75 recipes
Jellies & Creams	67 recipes
Pastry, All Sorts of Puddings, etc	66 recipes
Cheese Cakes	19 recipes
Pancakes	8 recipes
Tansey	7 recipes
Fritters	20 recipes
Cookery	84 recipes

There are no recipes for medicines or household requirements. These essential aids to any eighteenth-century housewife were no doubt covered in another collection. The breadth of the recipes, wide as it is, does not include such basics as pastry or bread, other than a few for speciality breads such as French. Such skills must have been assumed to be so well known as to make recipes redundant.

The wine recipes give some idea of the sort of estate that Catherine Clough and her unknown husband must have owned. Apart from dried currant wines, the ingredients include: apricots, red, black and white currants, red and black cherries, damsons, gooseberries, quinces, raspberries, turnips, oranges and lemons, apples (for cider), sage, gillyflower and barley. There are also recipes for birch, balm, clary, cowslip and elder flower wines. Some of the quantities called for are vast. Black Cherry wine specifies 24 pounds of cherries and six gallons of spring water, then two pounds of loaf sugar for every gallon of liquid obtained after the cherries have been marinated in the heated water for 24 hours. Cyprus wine calls for three hundredweight of Zantz currants and 66 gallons of boiling water (Winchester measure – which may give a clue to the location of the Clough estate). Apricots, though, are used in smaller quantities; there are three recipes calling for, respectively, one and a half pounds of apricots to every quart of water, six pounds of apricots to three quarts of water and eight pounds of apricots to two gallons of spring water (with various amounts of sugar). The careful housewife adds that 'the Apricots made marmalade and are very good for present spending (after they've been boiled in the water).'

Obviously Catherine needed to provide large quantities of wines for a sizeable household. Not only that, most estates of the time would be more or less self-sufficient in foodstuffs. Apart that is, from such items as sugar, dried fruits and spices. The stated quantities would have been very expensive. I think it is safe to assume that the Cloughs were very comfortably situated.

In the mid-eighteenth century very little water or milk was drunk. Ale was the most usual beverage. But home-made wines were very popular. Sir Kenelm Digby, in his *Closet Opened*, has around 115 recipes for various wines, mostly for Meath (a form of mead) and Methegelin (a spiced and medicated sort of mead). It's delightful to contemplate the Clough family, friends and household quaffing these delicious-sounding drinks produced from what I suggest must have been home-grown ingredients.

The preserve sections demonstrate a careful husbandry that makes sure the most is made of summer's abundance against winter's bleakness as fruits and even flowers are preserved and candied in many different ways. One can imagine blazing log fires and merry gatherings when summer delights are served for both drinking and eating.

That Catherine Clough entertained is certain, from such recipes as 'A Floating Island for the middle of the Table', 'Moon and Stars', and 'A Hen's Nest', for which blancmange is added to emptied egg shells, then turned out when set, placed in a basin with calves' foot jelly and shredded lemon peel to represent straw. When completely set, the Hen's Nest is turned out onto a glass Salver. Even more fun is 'To make Harlequins. A middle Dish for Supper'. For this, blown eggs are filled with a cream, rolled in comfits about the size of mustard seeds, topped with prunes studded with white caraway comfits to represent eyes, nose and mouth, then topped with ratafia drops for hats. The harlequin eggs are then set on heaped-up icing sugar. It is suggested that one set of eggs will last a person's life – though I wonder what happens to the cream! 'Hen's Nest', 'Floating Island' and 'Moon and Stars' can be found in Hannah Glasse and Elizabeth Raffald, but I haven't found the harlequin eggs elsewhere yet

There are a number of ingredient omissions. Unlike many collections, venison isn't mentioned. An indication that there were no deer on the estate? And though crabs and shrimps make an appearance, lobster doesn't. An aversion, or was there some other reason? Neither tea nor coffee is included but these are beverages whose preparation, like that of pastry and bread, might be reckoned to be thoroughly understood without a recipe. Chocolate is included. Not only are there recipes for Chocolate Creams and Chocolate Wafers, but Catherine suggests that the best way to whip a syllabub is with a chocolate mill, one, she advises, reserved for that purpose. A chocolate mill had a barrel shaped head, heavily notched, on a long handle. The mill was spun between the hands to beat liquid into a froth.

Catherine not only had glass salvers for serving chicken nests on, she also mentions glass for cooking in – heavy glass jars were produced in the eighteenth century that apparently withstood certain oven temperatures.[3] The chocolate mills were available from the turn of the eighteenth century.[4] Another item of cookery equipment she mentions is a charcoal fire. These were small fires used for sautéd and chafed dishes, techniques that required a control not possible on the large fire used for roasting and stewing in cauldrons. Catherine obviously appreciated the necessity for cooking equipment that catered for sophisticated effects. 'Wafer Irons' also receive a mention.

There is one, all-purpose, recipe for ice-cream. This goes into considerable detail on the breaking up of the ice and placing of the tin 'Icepotts' in a mixture of ice and bay salt, but does not ask for the mixture to be beaten as it freezes. There is nothing to indicate whether there was an ice house in the estate grounds or whether the house was sufficiently near the sort of town that would sell large blocks of ice. Elizabeth David wrote that:

> When Hannah Glasse remarked, in her *Compleat Confectioner*, published c. 1760, that ice cream was 'a thing us'd in all deserts [her own spelling] as it is always to be had at the confectioners', she was not, I think exaggerating. By the second half of the eighteenth century cream ices – as they were then usually called – had become quite a craze in fashionable London.[5]

The inclusion of ice-cream and the new type of trifle suggests that Catherine was well up to fashions and may well have spent part of her time in London. Incidentally, Hannah Glasse's 1747 cookery book does not contain an ice-cream recipe.

Catherine's meat and fish recipes cover a vast range of dishes, from the elaborate 'To Dress a Turtle' to the simple 'To Stew a Hare'. One wonders, in fact, whether Catherine ever did dress a turtle. The recipe, which is probably the longest in the book and goes into considerable detail, seems to be have been given by a professional cook, for it ends:

By this method of dressing the turtle, your ladyship will have the fine flavour of the Fish, and a rich gravy, in quantity sufficient for the whole, at a little Expense... P.S. I generally bring my Turtle to the Table in the dish in which it is baked, in order to keep it warm, while it is eating; but I don't know how this will agree with yr Ladyship's delicacy [the dishes mentioned are described as 'the common brown Ware'].

'Yr ladyship' may refer to a friend who gave Catherine a copy of her recipe. I feel Catherine would have had some comment to make on the directions if her kitchen had attempted the recipe.

Many of the recipes are expressed simply but suggest that the result, in the hands of an experienced cook, will be excellent (I have yet to try some of them). Much use is made of herbs and such spices as cinnamon and nutmeg. Almonds figure largely. In the Cookery section, such ingredients as morels, truffles and cock's combs are mentioned, but usually in such a manner as to suggest they are optional. In the manner of the eighteenth century, simple recipes employ lavish quantities of quality ingredients. For instance, here is the recipe for 'Family Soup':

Boil about three pounds of Beef in three pints of Water, and skim it very well, then add three or four carrots, two Parsnips, few Onions, according to their bigness, stuck with two heads of Cloves; put few Leeks, a Lettuce, Sellery, and Sorrel; boil all together, and add a small knuckle of Veal, first scalded; and boil it for about two hours; serve your Broth and the Knuckle in it.

The manuscript as a whole suggests the recipes come via a housewife, running a large household on a sizeable estate, living a life of comfort, who is unlikely to have carried out much of the cooking herself, but with a 'hands on' approach; an intelligent, practical and educated woman with considerable facilities at her command, probably running a large household and with a home that affords modern conveniences. She may well have spent some time in London.

The big question for me, as far as the manuscript is concerned, is why it ends with three sections that have undecorated headings but no recipes.

The fact that the inside label was written by the same hand as the recipes suggests that it was Margaret Foulkes, the daughter, who scribed it. If so, she was very skilled. On page 175, after the recipe for 'Ragged Pancakes', the little waves, that are generally used to fill up the line when the writing ends short of the edge of the page, have been overwritten with: 'Garnish with orange' with, underneath, 'M. Clough'. The writing is careful and could be the same as has been used for the manuscript, but it lacks just a little of the same control. Under the end of the recipe above, a short and simple one for plain, though rich, pancakes, are the initials 'M.C.' Was this to identify a recipe of Margaret's? After 'To Stew a Hare', a very shaky hand, very unlike the rest of the manuscript, says, 'my Mothers Rect'.

A couple of the recipes are accredited at the time of writing out the recipes. 'Beef Collops' has at the end, in small letters, 'Lady Clarges'. Another recipe for 'Beef Collops' has, 'Mr Church – Cook – Grayson'. 'To Preserve Oranges' ends with, 'pr. ME Clough'. Margaret again? Or some other Clough?

Though the writing is reasonably consistent, the decorations of the recipe titles vary. It's as though the scribe is experimenting with various styles. There are several gaps, one for a whole recipe, 'Black Currant Wine', others for the amount of eggs or some other ingredient; it's as though the scribe wasn't able to read what he or she was copying and needed to check with the original author.

Was it Margaret who wrote out the recipes and then wasn't able to complete the task? It seems unlikely it was Catherine, for surely she would not have had to leave gaps. And would a professional scribe have experimented so delightfully with the various decorations? And did Catherine lose her daughter very soon after marriage, perhaps in childbirth?

Whoever wrote out the manuscript, we owe them a great debt. What exists today is, I suggest, a most valuable record of mid-eighteenth-century recipes for wine and food cookery. One that holds many memories of the life that was lived by a family belonging to the wealthy landed gentry.

BIBLIOGRAPHY

The Receipt Book of Ann Blencowe, 1694, published in a limited edition by The Adelphi, Guy Chapman, 1926, introduction by George Saintsbury.

Grant, Bartle (ed.), ill. Grant, Duncan (1924) *The Receipt Book of Elizabeth Raper, 1756–1770*, Soho: The Nonesuch Press.

Price, Rebecca, intr. Masson, Madeleine (1974) *The Compleat Cook or the Secrets of a Seventeenth-Century Housewife (1683-1740)*, London: Routledge & Kegan Paul.

Rhodes, Dennis (ed.), preface Nichols, Beverly, ill. Grant, Duncan (1968, reissued 1983) *In An Eighteenth Century Kitchen*, London: published in a limited edition by Cecil Woolf.

Other books consulted:

Adam's Luxury and Eve's Cookery or The Kitchen-Garden display'd, (1983) London: Prospect Books, printed for R. Dodsley in Pall-Mall & sold by M. Cooper at the Globe in Paternoster Row, 1744.

Bradley, R. (1980) *The Country Housewife and Lady's Director,* London: Prospect Books, a facsimile edition of the London edition printed for D. Browne, 1736.

Carter, Charles (1984) *The Complete Practical Cook or, a new System of the Whole Art and Mystery of Cookery*, London: Prospect Books, a facsimile edition of the London edition printed for W. Meadows in Cornhill, C. Rivington in St Pauls Church-Yard, and R. Hett in the Poultry, 1730.

Glasse, Hannah (1983) *The Art of Cookery Made Plain and Easy*, Prospect Books, a facsimile of the first edition, first published London, 1747.

——— (1971) a facsimile of the 1796 edition, published S. R. Publishers, Wakefield, Yorkshire.

Macdonell, Anne (ed.) (1910) *The Closet of Sir Kenelm Digby Knight Opened*, London: Philip Lee Warner.

Nott, John, int. and glossary David, Elizabeth (1980) *Cooks and Confectioners Dictionary, 1726*, London: Lawrence Rivington, a facsimile edition.

Raffald, Elizabeth (1771) *The Experienced English House-keeper*, second edition, London.

Smith, Eliza (1983) *The Compleat Housewife: or, Accomplished Gentlewoman's Companion*, Arlon House Publishing, a facsimile of the sixteenth edition, 1758.

Verral, William (1948) *The Cook's Paradise, 1759*, London: Sylvan Press.

REFERENCES

[1] The compact edition of the *Oxford English Dictionary*.

[2] Alan Davidson, *The Oxford Companion to Food*, Oxford University Press, 1999, p. 805.

[3] Rebecca Price, p. 21.

[4] Rachael Field, *Irons in the Fire, A History of Cooking Equipment*, The Crowood Press, 1984, p. 159.

[5] Elizabeth David, *Harvest of the Cold Months, The Social History of Ice and Ices*, Michael Joseph, 1994, p. 310.

Food History and the Death of Memory

Gerald Mars and Valerie Mars

> My mother-in-law came to England – but only once! She saw frozen fish in the supermarket – and dried pasta. She says that the only good fish is the fish that jumps! And she gets up at 5 a.m. every day to prepare her own pasta.
> *A London woman's comment on her Sardinian mother-in-law.*

Introduction

Social historians have trouble with food. It is so peripheral. After enjoying even the most substantial of banquets, the most corporeal of feasts, after relishing flavours and aromas – there is nothing left! Nothing, that is, except our defective and vulnerable memories.

This peripheral character of food, and the resultant burden it imposes on memory, applies to individual meals as it does to whole cuisines. It is this that offers food historians their prime challenge and their most useful function: to move from being mere recorders of past foods and foodways to becoming active campaigners in the detection of 'commercial dilution, intellectual fraud and dishonest imitation'.[1] These aims are easily stated; unfortunately, less easily achieved! The first step, however, is perhaps to uncover the processes by which cuisines are fostered, then move to identify the means by which they are eroded. In doing so, we hope to explain the mechanisms and processes which govern the shift from established tradition to denatured false provenance. Bear with us if some aspects of this route appear self-evident.

Knowledge of a cuisine and its structure is like knowledge of a language: it extends beyond mere individuals and resides within a people's culture. When a culture is involved in fast change or otherwise loses its distinctiveness, its cuisine suffers, just as its language does. And though cultures are the repository of knowledge about cuisine, it is in face-to-face groups within a culture – in its villages, neighbourhoods and families – that cuisines are fostered. At this level a thread of continuous knowledge underpins standards of traditional production, preparation and consumption. These are passed from one generation to the next. When these groups weaken, the thread is broken, transmission ceases and the cuisine atrophies.[2]

Our own culture has now moved, from the relatively traditional and homogeneous, to acceptance of change and variety. Innovation and competition increasingly dominate our interests and fix how we organize our lives. Time becomes an important commodity. Groups like the family and the neighbourhood are less significant to us than in more traditional societies. Above all, our focus has shifted from social processes that occur within groups to a more isolated and competitive individualism. Instead of strongly structured groups, set within cultures on which cuisines are based, and instead of incremental change, we have an explosion of multiple changes. The path is cleared for 'flux and fragmentation', where historic provenance is discounted. This is the world of post-modernism.[3]

Foodway flux and fragmentation
The idea of post-modernism, when applied to cuisine, signifies an end to the dominance of any overall belief in what is appropriate and correct. No longer is there an overarching and unitary view about food (or indeed anything else). Instead, 'a thousand flowers bloom', and society is a battleground for the survival of each of them: post-modem society is a state of continual flux. This is not to suggest that the cuisines of traditional cultures are static or homogeneous, or that they lack the dynamics of competitive change. For a start, 'traditional' and 'post-modernist' are archetypes – that is, extremes. They represent two ends of a cultural continuum. Traditional society frequently manifests competition – but its competition is very different from competition in post-modernist society.

'Traditional competition' is illustrated by the family's pride expressed for their mother's ragoût in De Philippo's play, *Saturday, Sunday, Monday*. Her ragoût was thought a better ragoût by far than the generality of ragoûts. This kind of competition takes place in an understood, limited and bounded context with historic provenance set in the family group, and where change is incremental.

Competition in our kind of society is very different. At its sharpest, it is essentially innovative and concerned with creating the new, rather than being adaptive of the old. Here, competition is unbounded: new dishes are created from mixtures of ingredients, eagerly sought from far away or long ago. New styles of cooking are embraced and old styles adapted. The more novel the source, the more the competitive advantage.

This contrasting duality is not offered to praise the one or condemn the other. But one thing is certain: for the contenders in this field there is a foreshortening of time and a distortion of provenance. Instead of foods having a linked provenance to their pasts, we find rhetorical, and frequently spurious, claims to an authenticity that often has never existed. It is against this background that the following themes will be explored.

'The Habit of Hands': marshalling memory[4]

In a lecture on traditional cooking crafts, J. Marc Meltonville referred to the way a trainee woodworker was taught to build a workspace around him:[5] how to place his tools, where to put his materials, how to develop styles of work that adapted to different actions. The idea was that by the time he had developed his craft he would have evolved both knowledge and practice into a vocabulary of ideal and practical routines. This learning process involves acquiring what is called 'the habit of hands',[6] a way of relating ritually to objects and the processes they are set out to serve. Learning cooking crafts, as Meltonville observes, similarly involves acquiring 'the habit of hands'.

Learning to cook a traditional cuisine, just as learning to be a woodworker, also involves verbal instruction. In this respect, learning the habit of hands is an aspect of oral tradition. It acts as a prompt or mnemonic without needing the support of texts (or with only simple lists of ingredients).[7] Jack Goody, the anthropologist, has noted that for people to learn their roles in ritual performances they, too, have to be taught orally to relate to objects and graphic signs, and that this similarly acts as a mnemonic prompt.[8] The way dishes are prepared and cooked can be said to have its own mnemonics that is reiterated by the 'habit of hands'.

Distorting memory

A change of technology, such as a new heat source or a change in ingredients, can easily disrupt the habit of hands. This is likely not just to involve the loss of a traditional routine, but can imperceptibly change the whole nature of a dish and result in an entirely different process. A prime example is the move from the English tradition of roasting meat in front of a fire to baking it in an oven. Until the final demise of the Victorian kitchener, at the beginning of the last century, meat was roasted in front of a fire, yet it now seems as distant a taste and skill as cauldron cookery. Although the process is still called roasting, the method has changed completely. Common memory of traditional roasting, possibly with the exception of occasional country pig roasts, has all but vanished in England. This can occur with great rapidity, though the last bottle jacks (the most usual domestic jack), were still being manufactured as late as 1938.[9]

Baking has, for many people, also changed its nature, again without changing its name. In our study of consumption and ways of life among suburban households,[10] we found a housewife who asserted that she baked like her grandmother. But her baking was not like her grandmother's, whose baked bread, risen with yeast, was baked weekly as a staple. Her granddaughter baked cakes made from self-raising flour, eggs and margarine, that were mixed in a square tin then baked in an electric oven. Substituting industrially processed ingredients to cut the time and skill required by traditional techniques is not new; just more plentiful.[11]

The flight from the natural: a scale from traditional cuisine to the rise of post-modernist 'assemblage'

To return to the Sardinian grandmother and her assertion that, 'the only good fish is the fish that jumps': frozen fish, in her opinion, is unhealthy and living by the sea makes her contemptuous of anything but the freshest of fish. These are social, not just personal, values. They do not arise in a timeless vacuum but are passed on and reaffirmed through the face-to-face groups in her culture. To cook her traditional cuisine demands *socially* transmitted knowledge – knowledge of cultural continuity and context. She needs to know the sources, characters and qualities of her raw materials, as well as the cooking process that is the 'habit of hands'. These practices are integrally time based. They are set in the daily, weekly, calendrical and life-stage cycles. For her, preparing pasta is the task that starts her standard day, with other dishes similarly embedded in their socially determined times and places.

Once awareness of traditional practice is broken, however, and cooks become distanced from cultural continuity, cookery becomes removed from its essential definition – 'applying knowledge to the selection of raw produce and transforming it'. Instead, there is a concentration on 'assemblage'.[12] In assemblage, food preparation focuses only on the final presentation. Knowledge of continuity atrophies and preparation times are telescoped. Assemblage is pseudo-cookery removed from both context and process.

The road to assemblage is graduated. Many Italians buy frozen fish when they cannot get fresh and inland fish shops[13] are filled with frozen, unpacketed, identifiable and whole fish, which the cook scales and cleans. They are partway along the road. Fish fingers and other processed fish dishes can also be found in Italian shops, but they appear outside the acknowledged national ideal of cookery. The end of the assemblage road is well represented in the United States. Once, when shopping at a market fish stall in Venice, we met an American woman who'd never in her life seen a whole live fish and who couldn't bear to look. For her, fish were essentially rectangular and frozen.[14]

During the twentieth century we have seen an accelerating move from nature to culture. One end of this scale is illustrated by our traditional Sardinian peasant. Dependent on local products, she cooks them according to her cultural traditions. At the scale's other end we find the modern American, separated from local culture, lacking group conformities or group set standards and normless in matters of food. She is accordingly amenable (vulnerable?) to eclectic assemblage. Divorced from place, time and tradition, her cooking is part of the 'flux and fragmentation' of post-modernism. In the middle of this scale, as he uses new technologies and products, we have the urban, inland Italian.

Assemblage and the post-modern vacuum

G.K. Chesterton observed that 'when a person loses the faith, they don't then believe in nothing: they are liable to believe in anything.' When a culture becomes detached from its provenance, it is open to a range of competing and shifting claims. A vacuum then exists, that is too readily filled by assertions from the heritage industry and food manufacturers (and perhaps, more positively, by the creative and the innovative). In this arena of explosive change, the food historian's role is surely to tease out and reveal the techniques and practices – the habit of hands – of past cooks.

REFERENCES

[1] Mason, Laura with Brown, Catherine (1999) *Traditional Foods of Britain: an inventory prepared for GEIE/Euroterroirs*, Totnes: Prospect Books, p. 11.

[2] We are grateful to Rodney Saunders for a fascinating account of his Italian mother's failed attempts as an isolated immigrant in the UK to sustain her native cuisine, despite the availability of its raw materials.

[3] See Watson, Nigel (1998) 'Postmodernism and Lifestyles', in *The Icon Critical Dictionary of Postmodern Thought*, ed. Sim, Stuart, Cambridge: Icon Books Ltd.

[4] It was Dr B. Cotton, a teacher of vernacular woodworking methods, who coined the phrase 'habit of hands'.

[5] Personal communication from J. Marc Meltonville: 'The original concept of "Habit of hands" with regard to all jobs, crafts and tasks was brought to our attention during a course on English vernacular furniture and identification of wood types given by Dr B. Cotton. It was here that Dr Cotton discussed the concept that a person builds around him a workspace with all his tools of the trade, positioned in an order that is both comfortable and practical. To an outsider this layout of objects will appear random. We were told to look at the way in which craft demonstrators worked compared with the set-up used by people who lived from the product of their work, not the showing of how it was done. This can be applied to any working situation, and is now something that we are starting to look at when using historic kitchens.' See in particular the work of Peter Briers and Ivan Day.

[6] In this text we have expanded the concept to cover the repetitive routines that are integral to cookery. Marc Meltonville suggests the use of illustrations for evidence, but with the caveat: 'One has now to start looking at illustration engravings etc. to look at the layout of equipment around a worker to see if anything can be learnt from that. (Presuming that the artist has copied a workshop and not just moved things around to make things look good). Luckily for the later Victorian era one has photographs to help. It is pleasing to think that this study of the way in which people worked is starting to attract some interest.'

[7] Grundmann (née Feltzenthal), Hedwig (c. 1877–1960) *Manuscript Recipe Book*. She spent her younger married life near Hameln, and kept a recipe book that was simply a list of ingredients for baked goods. There are few quantities; she worked from memory using her eyes and hands to judge quantities.

[8] Goody, Jack (1998) 'Memory in the Oral Tradition', in *Memory*, eds. Fara, Patricia and Patterson, Kararalyn,Cambridge: Cambridge University Press, pp. 73–94.

[9] Ivan Day, Lecture at Kenwood, London, July 2000. We are not certain if production was only for use in this country, but they were certainly in use in Wales in the 1930s, so it is probable some were made for home market use.

[10] Fieldwork in the late eighties/early nineties. See Mars, Gerald and Mars, Valerie (1993) 'Two contrasting Dining Styles: Suburban Conformity and Urban Individualism', in *Food Culture and History*, eds. Mars, Gerald and Mars, Valerie, The London Food Seminar, pp. 49–60.

[11] A claim may be made to make a tart by use of ready-made pastry and a tin of fruit tart filling, or by using Betty Crocker's cake mix and 'just adding an egg'. These are all part of a repertoire of 'cookery by numbers'. (From the practice of 'painting by numbers' – making outline drawings with areas numbered according to the paint colour to be used).

[12] A stage beyond assemblage is the microwaving of manufactured packaged products.

[13] Typical examples are found in Siena and Volterra.

[14] Middle-class Newfoundland housewives in the 1960s chose not to buy fresh fish at the harbour, but preferred genteel frozen packets from the supermarket – whereas the self-conscious anthropologist preferred to buy from the harbour. Both chose non-traditional transactions, the first as moving away from tradition and the other as the exercise of professionally based ethnographic 'expertise'. See Bourdieu, where he examines choice in France and describes it in relation to social status. Bourdieu, Pierre (1986) *Distinction, A social critique of the Judgement of Taste*, tr. Nice, Richard, London: Routledge & Kegan Paul, p. 291.

The Digest of Memory: Food, Health and Upbringing in Early Childhood

Stephen Massil

The starting point of this paper must, under the inspiration of last year's Symposium, be the memory of horse-drawn milk delivery in the London suburbs of the 1940s and 1950s. In East Finchley (London N2), the United Dairies had a massive stable-yard just up from the Northern Line tube station on the High Road (the old A1 proper), opposite the Rex Cinema. It was not to the films that a small boy often urged the direction for a walk, but to the stables, where the straw-scattered yard with its farmyard smells and the stomping of hooves was the attraction. On the roads roundabout, the milkman pacing his horse, the vestiges of straw and oaty trail, and the manure left behind (scooped up for the season of my father's tomato plants) made a bonding between the product and the lifestyle of the day. What remains are the lingering folk myths of the milkman as a suburban character and the fact that milk, along with a newspaper, is probably still the only delivery left inviolable on the doorstep. In Hampstead there is Yorkshire Grey Walk, alongside the residual Express Dairy, and at Stroud Green there are architectural facades displaying dairying scenes, which always conjure up those days on my regular routes.

Other directions for after-school diversion led through the Market Place of Hampstead Garden Suburb, where Myer, the grocer, Greenspan, the butcher and Grodzinski, the baker, supplied their Jewish clientele, to the Express Dairy Farm at Henleys Corner on the North Circular Road where the milking of the cows in the byre was a regular entertainment. It was not for nothing that I took readily to summer holidays, a few years later, on a farm in Kent, where on the first visits the reaper-binder produced sheaves to stook and then to build into a stack, and at half-term in late October came the threshing machine to watch in action; subsequently to be replaced by the combine harvester and the immediate stacking of the bales, a cardinal moment in the development of English farm practices. For me, the harvest and the picking of fruit in orchards, which exalted the pleasure of Schumann's *Farmer's Boy* as one of my piano tunes, fed my imagination when it took hold of these scenes.

My earliest memories mostly have associations with food: the visit to the clinic for a dose of ultra-violet, prancing on a table under the lamp, wearing dark glasses, and the spoonful of concentrated orange juice that followed – our wartime precursors of the National Health Service in action. Rosehip syrup is another lost taste of the era. Also a wartime experience, and perhaps now my earliest memory of all, was a late summer holiday at a trade union resort at Maiden Earley, near Reading, in 1943, where my mother danced with Barbara Castle, in the wartime absence of fraternal partners, and where, placed atop a ladder and while the adults about me all tried to enforce their pickings on me indulgently, I endeavoured to feed myself with the mulberries that stained fingers, cheeks and clothes in glorious colours, and I am not sure that I consumed very many at all.

Lurid colour of another sort stands now for the memory of a spell in hospital when I was about three, when we were evacuated to Wargrave, near Coventry, and I had scarlet fever; there were sandwiches of a spectral greyness, smeared with dire raspberry jam, and I have rarely since allowed myself to consume anything so vile (a British Rail sandwich at Birmingham New Street on a delayed journey to Shrewsbury, three years ago, was the last such occasion when Brenda and I succumbed, through desperation of delays on Virgin Rail).[1] Just after the war, when my uncle Len on demob got married, I can remember only the ice-cream, in a tall silver goblet, as the high point of the celebration.

The counting of stones from prunes, cherries and plums was always a ritual and field of sibling debate. By contrast, and here we approach one of those curious afterthoughts of childhood which repeatedly considers and fails to comprehend just what method it was my parents had in our upbringing, when each of my sisters was born, I was consigned to the Norwood Orphanage, for tending, while my mother was confined: the first occasion at age two and a half, when my sister Marilyn was born, and I can only remember a night-time sickness and a low lamp glowing; the second, the two of us together when Janet was born and I was nearly six. As non-residents at the orphanage, Marilyn and I were excused the dismaying rigour of the watercress that the other children had forced upon them at tea.

This dispensation takes on the character of a minor epiphany, because what has to be said is that the predominant texture of my childhood and early upbringing was, indeed, salad, with all regularity. And it was precisely at this point, the birth of my sister Janet in August 1947 (under the Truby-King regimen), that my mother went over to a vegetarian diet, from which we did not depart until a period in 1954–55, when fish and meat were re-introduced and the full gamut of home-Jewish cooking (never entirely eliminated, I seem to remember) regained the pride of the table. This was after a singular episode, at a phase when we three children came home from school for lunch, my mother pregnant with her last child and at odds with Marilyn, who constantly rebelled at mealtimes, when, in exasperation, my mother tipped a plate of spaghetti cheese-and-tomato over Marilyn's head, to the awe of Janet and to my great amusement.

Perhaps I should pass the word to Janet to describe here her first recollection of fish, which would have been after this date in 1955, our sister Rosy being born in June that year when Janet was nearly eight. My first notion of fish, and a rare trauma of my own at table, dates from much earlier, when I was sat over to finish a portion of hake, which would have taken only 'two spoonfuls', but which I wretchedly carved up to make five. Generally I was a ready finisher of my sisters' groats and other leavings, and standing by to lick the bowls when cakes were a-making was one of my delights before the use of a spatula put an end to that.

The subject of watching my mother at work in the kitchen would extend this paper inordinately, but three reflections arise for specific evocation: the darning of socks and the sewing of the stuffed neck (*helzel*), which were among the most fascinating things she did; it is doubtful whether many modern middle-class Jewish mothers bother to darn their children's socks or can stuff and sew a blanket-stitch to close a chicken neck; the nestling clamour we children would make on being served an egg or a chicken foot in our soup; I do not suppose one can even buy a chicken with giblets, let alone any pre-laid eggs, these days, and the texture of these in soup is now lost for ever (in this country, I surmise) and remains a poignant vortex of childhood memories at table; techniques for the preparation of gefüllte fish, stuffings and the fillings for blintzes ensured that the vegetarian stodge of nut cutlets and the like (the stuffing of a marrow) came in superior form, too, and I am not sure that this is just a commonplace or the pleading of filial memory.

Two reflections on the lavishness of my mother's kitchen come from much later dates, but may be permitted on circumstantial grounds as comments by two of my girlfriends. One of these commented to her mother on the large cut of the lamb chops we had had, so all credit to Sam Greenspan (who, when my sister Rosy, by chance, dropped into his shop for a boiling chicken a few years ago, still remembered our mother – for which affection I included his obituary among the names of the great and the good, listed in the Jewish Year Book, which I edit, in the year of his death). The other reported to her mother that the salmon rissoles (made from tinned salmon) had not been bulked out with potato, but with egg and onions and only a sparing of matzo meal, for texture (no wonder that was a short engagement!).[2]

The character of these memoirs has political overtones, and it is not for nothing that the retreat to the socialist haven, at Maiden Earley, featured in

Horatian retrospect above. Rambling groups into the Chilterns, the Surrey hills and the Weald were a phenomenon of the 1930s, when the East Enders and disciples of Toynbee Hall, of the day, betook themselves for weekend country jaunts ending at Leatherhead, where the Hungarian food reformer (self-styled paneubiotist or cosmotherapist) Edmond Székely[3] lived and lectured; or to Jordans (teetotal villages of that ilk) for country teas and romance and the hilarities of random photographs. My parents figured in these and my father sat down to consume record numbers of cups of tea at journeys' ends. He was briefly a member of the SPGB (which, right through to the late 1950s, regularly polled 211 for their candidate in the Hampstead constituency at the General Elections of that era). At their wedding, while the guests consumed the standard roast chicken menu of the day, my parents apparently treated themselves to plain salad.

The rambling gave my father a hankering for the spaces of Princes Risborough, for industrial development (in fact, he took the family wood-turning business from Hoxton out to a site near Hatfield after the war's end), the salads a notion of diet which matured into a serious endeavour to practise food reform under the tutelage, first of Stanley Leif at Champneys, and then James Thompson of the Kingston Clinic in Edinburgh, and Blunham House in Bedfordshire, run by Peter LaBarre, Thompson's son-in-law. Maurice and Tilly Golding, friends from the Toynbee rambling days, opened a vegetarian guesthouse in Swanage where we holidayed after the war one summer (a novel establishment in that era, but a suitable place to meet the Reverend S. Lipson and his wife, happy to enjoy the assurance of uncomplicated kosher observance). Other years, we took a summer house of our own at Minnis Bay, so as to be sure of vegetarian provision, and stayed vegetarian at Leigh-on-Sea in 1946, and later in Folkestone, H.G. Wells's erstwhile home (so it was possible to find such places). Later, my parents would stay at a vegetarian guest house when they visited the Edinburgh Festival in the early 1950s (and we children were on our farmyard holidays under the eye of a German or Swiss or Scandinavian *au pair* – of all these, it was Swiss Irmgaard who augmented my mother's Passover dishes with a hazelnut torte, in ingredients all kosher and correct, which outdid the homely *plava* she brought from her mother's kitchen).

The regimen (monitored by Dr Parkes) included cold-compresses, for any childhood infection, and homeopathic remedies; and the sovereign dish that proclaimed we had come through the measles or the chicken pox and were on the way to recovery (after fasts and juices) was always a trayful of poached egg on spinach and an agar fruit-jelly (sticky jellies were allowed for treats). At table it was regular salads for tea and fruit as staple. Not water to drink, but generous consumption of fruit and greens to provide the necessary fluids. Also Jersey milk, fresh juices and eggs (each studiously inspected as much through Jewish scrupulosity as pre-war experience of unreliable provision), wholemeal bread – from what must have, in those days, been the only health food shop in north London (at Temple Fortune, NW11) – of texture as delicious as velvet and dotted with oat flakes for effect. No wonder, then, that I was rounded up one day, when, walking from school (also experimental under Beatrix Tudor-Hart, free-wheeling, progressive, and curiously undisciplined) I was seen strolling, with a penny bun from the bakery next to the Rex, on my way to Hebrew classes; my mother and the *au pair* were shepherding my sisters and other girls on the way home and I was hauled in for a proper tea, before being sent on to my class. I don't think my mother was aware that the Hebrew school indulged its pupils with sticky buns from Grodzinski's by way of enticement to attend (an extension, I believe, of the Continental schoolchild's first-day experience of school-going). Day school, of course, saw us assured of our quarter bottle of milk of a morning, a taste not easily forgotten.

Another lapse that my mother may not have considered, except perhaps when she, too, found time to help out at father's office a couple of days a week and took tea with the secretaries there, with iced cup-cakes, was during my holiday visits to the factory, where I would clock in for timber-yard work. At the morning tea break the relish was for airy, crusty rolls filled with grated cheese, and a mug of thick-brewed tea in the fug of the canteen. It was, perhaps, the canteen cakes that made the highlight of a school visit to the factory when our teacher Vernon Hamilton and a party of twenty boys and girls came, by charabanc, out to Marshmoor, and a slice of battenberg cake took the biscuit.

Meals down at the farm at Idleigh, at Nanny Delaney's, the doyenne of foster-mothers and a friend of Beatrix Tudor-Hart, who took in Council children and the waifs of embassies and divorcees for a living, and also the children of middle-class families for the summer holidays, were hearty, but if you asked for seconds she gave you a large slab of bread and butter. She would butter the bread before slicing it, something I had never seen at home. The farmer in question, Martin Boswell, one of her erstwhile charges from days of private childminding, moved eventually from Kent to the Isle of Wight, where he pioneered successively the growing of sweetcorn (as King Cob on the island) and then garlic. From him I learnt how to pick peas, raspberries and strawberries, with that care which fills a basket, within a yard from where PYO summer folk tend to complete a row without so great a harvest. My father's devotion to our garden manifested itself in a keen effort for the raising of tomatoes and the exhortation to consume home-grown produce. The aroma of tomato plants, well watered and pinched, is the lasting fragrance of childhood.

Dates, packed in boxes, needed to be inspected for maggots. They came with wooden boards that I used as field markers and tracks for my model farm animals. The quintessential iced cake of our childhood was Fuller's walnut cake, with its incomparable and unreproduceable thick, smooth icing, no longer found. Favourite chocolates were the coffee selection in Terry's and Black Magic, and Cadbury's burnt almond dark chocolate bar, also long-since dropped from the market. The other indulgences of the era were the visits to Apenrodts in Golders Green after matinées at the Hippodrome and lunches at the Vega, London's high class vegetarian restaurant at the corner of Leicester Square, after Saturday morning Children's Concerts (Robert Mayer's), and the dish of choice was always mushrooms on toast. Shearns in Tottenham Court Road, which also sold fresh produce, less often favoured, was the more earthy, but did not survive as long (though the Vega, where Gandhi had been feted in the 1930s, when it closed endured the ignominy of becoming a steakhouse). I was eleven when uncle Len (also on the vegetarian kick and a devotee of the 'Salad Bowl' at J. Lyon & Co.'s corner-house emporium at Coventry Street) took me to lunch there after rowing on Regent's Park lake.

A break in the proceedings for a morning coffee or (these days especially) an afternoon cup of tea is one of my father's priorities and will be one of his family legacies. White-bread toast and lurid jams featured also at post-match teas my uncle Ben took me to in the neighbourhood of Highbury in those days. The greatest treat of all for a seven-year-old was to be taken to a Piccadilly movie-house for the cartoons, followed by salted almonds at the eponymous Trocadero night spot! Such experience was later boosted, in my teens, by regular birthday celebrations at the White Tower in Percy Street, where my father and the uncle 'accompanying us on these occasions' were known from the 1940s; but this takes us too far forward in a childhood account. However, you get the picture...and window-gazing at Heal's furniture after the meal.

I had my first experience of foreign food only at the age of twelve, when I spent a month in France with Georges and Lili Garel and their cohort of children, a Parisian family with whom my uncle David had had wartime and post-war connections in the shepherding of refugee children, which regularly dispersed to a villa in the Hautes Alpes for the summer. Their oldest boy, Jean-Renaud, had stayed a month with us in July (and we managed to give him a weekend at Brancaster); we two were met at Le Bourget by his father and we stayed the night in Passy with the venerable grandparents (presided over by an *arrière-grandmère*, which immediately tested my first-year French) who entertained us in stylish Russian emigré rooms with a delicate soup, off old-fashioned plates.

The journey to the mountains, via Lyons and Grenoble, took us two full days. The first night on the road we had a meal, where I was confronted with the thinnest matchstick chips I have ever seen and meat so pink I couldn't face it! And, arriving at Aiguilles and beset by a crowd of younger children, I was bewildered by a platter of sliced tomatoes laced with oil refulgent of the sun. If I was not prepared for such fare, I ended the month fully acclimatized and ready, when Georges drove me back to Paris to meet my father, to eat cheese at breakfast and to enjoy the wonders of a Russian restaurant off the Champs Elysées, where Georges took us on our last night. One reflection concerns the fact that the young Garels were under instruction, for table manners, that required having the hands on the table at all times, whereas I was a well-brought up English boy, keeping my hands, when not occupied with knife and fork, under the table, a fact drawn to by my assiduous host who knew well how to turn a pun, in English and French (is life worth living? – it depends on the liver).

It was a couple of years later, in Brussels, that I encountered for the first time how one turns down an unsatisfactory dish. I had accompanied my father on a machine-buying trip to Liège and Malines and it was at a famous restaurant, where I was aghast to see an elegant woman browbeat a waiter with aplomb when she sent back her steak. I have the menu still (as I do that of the White Tower in its heyday) but when I went back to the Grande Place in 1990 it had been superseded by a tourist establishment. So endeth one's childhood in food!

After the resumption of fish and meat, a promotion of more traditional Jewish fare; nevertheless, my mother managed to retain the good sense of the food reform regime and the balance of diet. *Griblekh*, the onion shreds fried in chicken fat, a cook's perk at the end of the production line for a sabbath or festival meal, she always shared. Onions and garlic she deemed to be life-savers and never did without these. The gribles (Hungarian: *Töpötyü*) surfaced, surprisingly, when Elizabeth Morrison, whose ex-husband had been of Magyar stock, came from Australia to live with me for a year in 1981, and other delicacies learnt from a Hungarian mother-in-law enlivened our fare for a while.

The questions of diet, health, fitness and longevity: like all children in post-war Britain we were exhorted to clean our plates by way of acknowledging the privations of the starving children of Asia (and not to display our 'dining-room furniture' and talk while eating), but the more enduring message at meals, and the embargoes on sweets between meals and the like, with refusal of regulated innoculations in infancy and the preference for a naturopath, rather than the local GP, at times of sickness[4] were the questions of right-eating and the preservation of health with minimal recourse to medicines.[5] White bread was anathema, tea or coffee were denied (except an occasional milk-and-a-dash) and smoking was always spoken of in horror; the evils of processed food and too much sugar were drummed into us by way of contrast to the food prepared.

My mother, who had had a hysterectomy and an operation for gall bladder, nevertheless died of a stroke at 58; she had troubled over her weight and her bowels all her life (and memories of the measures of public health of the post-1918 era and of folk-treatment for constipation in her own childhood, at a time when her mother, burdened after much childbearing, had come to rely on her, sole daughter, to maintain the kitchen and household), hence the concern for diet, nature cure and food reform. Along with the salads for tea, we children always had to endure twice-daily sessions on the toilet, and my sisters remember enemas with horror. Of her six brothers, one died of a cancer and four of them, variously, at ages over 70, have also died of heart conditions. Three of them were notably athletic, if not actually professional, at tennis or boxing and field sports; while one, the other vegetarian, survives, still now in his 80s. My father, second-born of five and now the last surviving of his family in his late 80s, suffers from arthritis and the combat of spondilitis anchylosis, and he recently endured a gall-bladder operation. He swears by a morning cold bath and exercise, as an ex-golfer, but reminisces of the jug of cream that, on early visits, was always left on the White Tower table with the dessert; I remember a pipe rack at home, in our earliest childhood, and the occasional cigar with the uncles, up to about 1960, but never a cigarette, which killed his wood-turner father at 65, who died of cancer of the bladder in the winter of 1946–47, at the time the purchase of the site at Marshmoor was being negotiated.

Hitherto, I have put together a string of reminiscences encompassing all the incidental references to food that I retain from my childhood. These cohere and indicate as much of the *Bildungsroman*, on the one hand, or the Proustian unravelling of a life, in time, as those of the next man. Many things are braided together in a life and I suppose that what are usually omitted from biographies are the nursery and the breakfast table; also such things as the taking of vegetarian food to school and the impact that has on character formation in the playground, and under the eyes of masters and prefects in charge of jostling boys at table in the dining hall, and where this made a further margin, since the Jewish boys were already set (benignly) apart. Nostalgia is a permitted ingredient in these reminiscences, also a condition shared with anyone writing autobiographically, but leavened, I hope, with a dispassionate view of the structures and conditions that frame and interfuse the life one has led.

That Brenda, my wife, has been a dedicated vegetarian for many years may appear to be significant in this story. It is not necessary to stress how it is clear that food and meals are of the circumstance in the entertaining of guests; likewise in the wooing of a partner they mediate powerfully. As well for Mann and Proust and Joyce, so also for Dorothy L. Sayers, food and circumstances figure significantly; and Levi-Strauss's intuition, that his Indians would square exactly with the semiotics of the picnic basket, on the boating trip that ended in the engagement of Peter Wimsey to Harriet Vane, makes one of the most satisfying connections.

If I were to devote paragraphs to my mother's Jewish cuisine and the spread she always laid on when entertaining the family or guests or the audience at home film shows and recitals, I could vie with *Buddenbrooks* in setting forth her table. All I think I need say on this score is that my mother kept a book of recipes, cullings from magazines, drafts in impeccable office shorthand of recipes offered by her friends and other jottings from Champneys and Edinburgh (the Misses Davies's *Bircher muesli*, for instance). What the book does not have in it are any of the recipes for the traditional Jewish fare learned from her mother's kitchen.

There is a nuance here: my grandparents made a mixed marriage, that is, my grandfather was from Satanov in Podolya, from Belarus in the Pale; my grandmother was from Khalarash, near Kishinev in Bessarabia (Russian Moldova). It is not inappropriate to add the detail that he was, at the time (the 1880s) when they met, a travelling lemonade vendor (subsequently in London he was a tailor); hence the possibility of making such a match, whereas his brothers and sisters married more locally, or amongst *landtsmen* when they dispersed to America. It meant that their Yiddish crossed the linguistic isophemes and their diet crossed the salt/sugar isophemes. Having a wife from Bessarabia means *mamaliga*, also that ground almonds go into the gefüllte fish and the Passover *kneidlakh*. And so on. It means that my mother won my father's heart (a son of a mother from Kiev and a father from Belarus) as much with *potlejonas*[6] as with scones or fried fish and chicken soup. Because her recipe for the Bessarabian version of roasted aubergine, mashed to a thick purée with onion (Israeli *Hatzilim*), is not extant (and no-one reproduces a version in any of the published works), it remains virtually the only dish of memory that I cannot now reproduce for my father. The other dish that I cannot reproduce is *hubergrits*, for my own delectation, made with kasha, I presume.

I shall stray outside of my time scheme for one further instance, since the mixed marriage and the *potlejonas* form a strand in Brenda's story, too. Her father settled in Rhodesia, from Romania, before the first-world war, coming from Vasluj, which is only as far to the west of the River Prut as Khalarasch is to the east. He married, in Bulawayo, the daughter of a Dutch–Jewish South African, and Brenda's mother must have learned her recipe for *potlejonas* from her mother-in-law; it figured regularly on the family lunch table in Brenda's childhood.

This essay, then, is a writing about food in memory; incidentally, it puts up markers for a consideration of the topography of vegetarianism in post-war

London and the English holiday resorts, as well as of the Jewish butchers and bakers of that era, and evokes probably lost kitchen practices and expertise. It could serve, as the naturopath tells me, as lay witness on the tradition of the regimen laid down by Leif, Benjamin, Thompson and their line of 60 years ago, now under neglect, in food reform circles. The inspiration to me arising from all this is to make a study of vegetarianism and food reform and, thanks to Cooks Books, I have begun to compile a bibliography that starts a surprisingly long time ago, in the eighteenth century. What with the references to Sir Stafford Cripps and other socialist braidings in the story, there will be much in it to help explain the public stereotyping of the rambling, be-sandalled and bearded vegetarians. It puts down a marker, I suggest, for a Symposium to elicit consideration of the questions, hitherto subsumed but latent in many of our deliberations, of food, diet and health in the public, as well as private, domains. It does honour to my parents and evokes names again of those I wish to remember. It shows how food maketh the man, also how the attitudes with which it is served up can exert considerable influence and how even the ways to a man's heart can be settled very early; and though I have not given an overt autobiographical account, I have shown what also deserves to go into biography and how the slightest remembrance of past tasting can remain in the mind, over time.

REFERENCES

[1] It is W.G. Sebald in *The Rings of Saturn* who describes perhaps the worst meal in all English literature at his Lowestoft hotel.

[2] To which I might add that the taramasalata that I make with a small addition of rye-bread crumbs was also dismissed, for shortcomings less to do with thriftlessness than as being apparently less appetizing than the pallid version, made with white-bread crumbs that she was used to!

[3] Székely, Edmond (1936) *Cosmos, man and society: a paneubiotic synthesis*; tr. and ed. Weaver, L. Purcell, with drawings by Wragg, Arthur, London: C. W. Daniel Co.

[4] My mother dated her copy of Benjamin, Harry (1936) *Everybody's Guide to Nature Cure*, Health for All Publishing, in April 1946; it is dedicated to Stanley Leif.

[5] If I make mention of Dr Parkes as naturopath of choice, it is not inappropriate also to mention recourse to dental treatment from Dr Braun at his august surgery in Queen Anne Street, a fearsome experience under the old-fashioned beam of an Austrian practitioner.

[6] *Patlijan* is the form given in Nina Kehayon's recent book on the aubergine: *Essentially Aubergines*, Grub Street, 1994.

Damra Bound: Indian Echoes in Guyanese Foodways

Gaitri Pagrach-Chandra

They were a motley bunch. Among them were wild Dhangar hill tribals, aloof Brahmins, proud Rajputs, Sepoys who deemed it politic to absent themselves temporarily from the scene, and wives who sought to escape domestic tyranny. Coerced, cajoled or kidnapped; fleeing justice or injustice; persuaded by the tempting tales of silver-tongued recruiters or by the stark reality of poverty, famine and scarcity. They crossed the Kala Pani,[1] on their way to Damra, as they familiarly dubbed it,[2] Demerara, British bastion on the verge of financial ruin now that the newly emancipated slaves had proven unwilling to continue working in the sugar industry. They had a destination, each one of them, bound by indentureship to a specific plantation. Of course, they weren't coming forever: as soon as their term had expired they would make use of the repatriation clause in their contract and return to India as men and women of substance. But they stayed,[3] all but a handful, motivated at first by dire necessity. By the time they had come to terms with the hollowness of promises made, they had lost all urge to return and many had found a new straw to clutch at: the settlement and colonisation schemes that were being set up by the government. After a few unsuccessful attempts, the project got off the ground in 1880 and Indian labourers were encouraged to commute their passages for land grants,[4] which many willingly did, realizing that the new colony had more to offer than they could realistically hope to achieve in India.

Stereotypically, but nonetheless prophetically, an Immigration Agent named Duff had observed at the time that, 'the natives of India with their love of land and fondness of agriculture and pastoral pursuits will probably have a greater impact on the future of the colony than all the other races put together.'[5] Despair and hopelessness were soon replaced by a vigorous determination to get ahead, and a new offshoot of India took root and started to bloom, leaving a rich heritage of Indian-based culture: music, dance and religion and, more especially, food.

The pattern of their diet was set from the start. From the initiation of indentureship,[6] it had been customary to issue each passenger with daily rations which were to be cooked by him or herself. This bounty consisted of:

	lbs.	oz.	dr.		lbs.	oz.	dr.
Rice	1	4	0	Onions	0	2	0
Dholl (sic.)	0	4	0	Garlic	0	2	½
Ghee	0	1	0	Chillies	0	0	¾
Mustard oil	0	0	8	Black Pepper	0	0	1½
Salt	0	1	0	Coriander Seeds	0	0	2
Salt Fish	0	2	0	Mustard Seeds	0	0	½
Tamarind	0	0	4	Tobacco, Smoking	0	0	8
Turmeric	0	0	4	Firewood	2	0	0[7]

In the 1870s, in the interest of economy, hygiene and orderliness, the Demerara depot at Calcutta introduced the *bhandara* system, serving cooked food instead of doling out rations.[8] Professional cooks were installed on board the outbound vessels, chosen from the higher castes to allay lurking fears of caste-contamination. When they arrived at their destination the immigrants were once again issued with daily or weekly rations, whose cost was deducted from their earnings. Children under fifteen received half the rations at half the cost and those under ten received a third of the rations, free of charge. It was extremely basic fare, as the following table shows:[9]

	Chittacks[10]	*Kanchas*
Rice	12	0
Dal	2	0
Coconut oil or ghee	0	2
Masala	0	1½
Sugar	1	0
Salt	0	1

Salted or dried fish and onions were sometimes issued[11] as well as cheap flavourings, like tamarind. Supplementary items could often be bought from small shops, operated by labourers in a better position,[12] but it is uncertain as to when this practice started and how openly it functioned; an ordinance from 1891 strictly forbade the selling of rations by an immigrant or the buying of rations from another immigrant or any person.[13] It is noteworthy that this English word, 'ration', remained firmly wedged in the minds of many, long outlasting indentureship. I remember it as a word used by rural Indians, in particular, as a synonym for groceries.

The new immigrants were housed in wooden barracks, referred to as 'logies', with one family or group to a cramped room and several rooms to a barrack. Cooking was done under the verandah, on *chulhas*, fireplaces made from clay, dung and straw.[14] Later, when people began to build houses of their own, the *chulha* was either put under the house[15] or in a jutting alcove separated, at least partially, from the main kitchen with, ideally, ventilation slats on three sides, as cooking on a *chulha* is a smoky business. Up to today many rural households still own one which is used for dishes like *baigan chokha*, as no oven, grill or gas flame can reproduce the flavour imparted by the *chulha*. Daily cooking was generally done in a family context if there was a family to speak of, or small groups were formed by those without attachments. The sparse celebratory dishes, financed by the pooling of meagre resources, were generally cooked communally. This communal cooking, with its melding of styles,[16] together with the limited availability of foodstuffs are perhaps the two most important single factors that have combined to produce the style of cooking known as 'Indian' in Guyana.

Communally cooked Indian food continues to bind people together on festive or sad occasions, acting as a great equalizer which temporarily cuts through class and social barriers. Secular events always seem to require the slaughtering of a sheep or two, with duck and chicken appearing lower down in the culinary hierarchy. Muslims eat beef, a practice most Hindus still refrain from. In Hindu circles, religiously-tinted occasions, wakes and weddings are vegetarian in nature. Word of the event travels at the speed of a bush fire and, before you know it, all sorts of willing helpers have descended on the house of celebration or mourning.

Catering is a fairly recent innovation and has not yet become matter-of-course, the spectre of religious and dietary taboos forever hovering in the wings. As a concession, a few strong men, always available in such situations, are hired for heavy work. They man the huge *karahis*, often more than a metre in diameter, which are perched on halved oil drums packed with blazing firewood. Shirt-less, wielding wooden implements the size and shape of oars, they give the fiercely boiling pots vigorous stirs. This is often all they are required to do as the ladies enjoy doing the rest themselves. Chopping, slicing, kneading and rolling, they deafen each other with an endless flow of gossip, chatter and witticisms, often bursting into snatches of Hindi melodies warranted by the occasion, tongues persistently going at the same pace as their hands. Few things are as delicious as this communally-cooked food where everything is tossed in 'by average' and the overall atmosphere contributes substantially to the general enjoyment. Sitting cross-legged on the floor, with a lotus leaf on your lap, a train of servers passes by, each depositing a dollop of food on your leaf: curried pumpkin, *katahar*, *channa*, potato, rice, *dal*, *puri* and *kheer*, among others. The green, leafy scent permeates the warm food, giving it an unmistakably festive flavour.

There were enough ingredients from the beginning to give the food an Indian peasant character. It is interesting that *masala* was issued, ready-mixed, as part of the ration package. It would have helped cut costs significantly, cheap bulky spices being substituted as a matter of course. This standardization, coupled with the subsequent use of proprietary brands of 'curry powder' have given Guyanese curries their consistent, though by no means uniform, taste.

By the time most people could afford to have reasonably good food on a regular basis, some had forgotten how such dishes were made; others had never known any but the most basic kind of food. Dishes recreated from memory, especially after a period of culinary fallow, are bound to contain inconsistencies. Substitution was inevitable and ingredients that were difficult to obtain were often left out. Curry leaves, fresh coriander and mint were forgotten – they had no place in the survival kitchen. Cooking with *ghee* was a luxury not routinely enjoyed by many, though it has always remained indispensable for religious occasions; while vegetable oil is fine for mortals, holy fires must be fed on best quality *ghee*. Imported *ghee* may be bought for this purpose, or it may be made at home, from the cream patiently and painstakingly skimmed off milk during the preceding weeks. Imported mustard oil was too precious for everyday cooking, so it was kept for flavouring pickles.

Later, those who might have been able to afford to make rich Indian dishes using authentic ingredients, eschewed them for more westernized food, seen as a sign of sophistication. For a long time, there was a social stigma attached to being too closely associated with Indian food and Indian culture in general. It may have reached its peak in my generation, by which time the connotations of deprivation had begun to fade, making it permissible to show a tentative interest. By tradition, Indian food was confined to the family kitchen, rarely used when entertaining. Adding to that the Guyanese penchant for hospitably, giving guests the kind of food to which they are accustomed, it comes as no surprise that non-Indians in Guyana had to wait quite long to be privy to the meals previously considered too homely to set before them.

Indo-Guyanese food is characterized by curry powder, *garam masala*, hot peppers and coconut. One or all of these ingredients is bound to find its way into any savoury dish. Many people still prefer to blend their own *masala*, roasting, mixing and grinding it in bulk to be stored for subsequent use. To make a curry, the curry powder is mixed with a smaller proportion of *garam masala* and enough water is added to make a paste. Onion, garlic and chillies are laboriously ground on a '*masala* brick', as the grinding stone is invariably called. Modern cooks pounced upon the food processor with great joy, but it doesn't grind the flavourings as finely as the stone does and consequently subtly alters the texture of the finished dish. The ground seasonings are sautéd in a generous amount of oil, then the curry paste is added and cooked for a few minutes. Meat or vegetables are put in and stir fried on a high heat. Once there is barely enough sauce to coat the contents of the *karahi*, salt and liquid are added and the dish is left to simmer. If you think that time might be saved by letting the food cook in its own moisture, put that thought resolutely out of your mind.

This 'burning out the rank', for meat dishes in particular, is an integral part of the whole process and Guyanese cooks swear by it. The quantity of liquid, water or coconut milk depends largely on the amount of gravy the cook desires. These curries are generally fiercely hot, but that does not deter many people from eating spicy pickles as an accompaniment or from taking a bite out of a fresh chilli with each mouthful. Tomato, tamarind or green mango can also be added to a curry to vary the flavour. The latter two are usually reserved for fish curries, when they contribute a welcome tartness. Fish is particularly enjoyed by country dwellers who have ready access to fresh, sweet-water fish from the abundance in surrounding irrigation canals and rivers. Much of it is literally there for the taking, and a glut often results in a burst of home-drying to produce the local version of Bombay duck. Sea fish, which usually has to be bought, is more of a luxury.

Vegetables are often cooked together with meat or fish and there are several popular combinations, like chicken and squash, duck and potato, mutton and aubergine, shrimp and pumpkin, green beans and dried fish and crab and aubergine. When they are not curried, vegetables are usually sautéd in oil with garlic and chillies. It is interesting that, with the exception of potatoes, vegetables normally associated with temperate climates (cauliflower, peas, carrots etc.) continue to be rejected by Indo-Guyanese as a component for Indian meals, even by those who now live in countries where they are standard. The collective memory apparently ceased to remember that regional sub-continental cooking uses a wider range of vegetables as a matter of course, this block arising from the fact that most of them had been unavailable at first and were later too costly for everyday use, so they never managed to become a part of the tradition. Although they formed the backbone of Indo-Guyanese diet in the past, vegetables were pushed into the background as prosperity and meat consumption began to travel at corresponding speeds. Now they are most popular as side dishes. Potatoes are treated as a vegetable, not a staple, and leafy greens are often eaten in combination with *dal*, which most people enjoy in a fairly thin, liquid form. Chick peas and split peas are the most widely-used pulses; lentils and kidney beans never caught on in Guyana the way they did in Trinidad, for example.

Roti and rice are the standard accompaniments to savoury dishes. *Roti* comes in several forms: thick, leavened *sada roti*, *parathas* stuffed with potato or split peas, as well as the extremely popular and time-consuming layered *paratha*, often referred to as 'oil *roti*'. Although the middle class turned to bread and breakfast cereals several decades ago, in the not so distant past, when it was still common for extended families to live together, it was often the task of the newest daughter-in-law to produce the enormous piles of hot, flaky *parathas* required each morning and evening. The dough is kneaded and left to rest, then rolled out thinly, spread with oil and folded into a cone, whose centre is pressed downwards to form a bun shape. These are left to rest again and are then rolled out and cooked on a griddle. The hot *paratha* is flung into the air and caught between both hands with a clapping movement; this typically Guyanese refinement[17] is repeated a few times. In addition to getting crumbs in every possible nook and cranny of the kitchen, it loosens up the flaky layers.

Fried savoury snacks are made from mixtures of wheat, gram and split pea flour, but gram and split pea flour have never been popular for sweets. Rich milk dishes and sweets are eagerly devoured, but very concentrated semi-solids, like the *khoa/khoya* popular on the Indian sub-continent, are unknown. Fresh milk is sometimes boiled down to the desired consistency and tinned evaporated, condensed and powdered milk have found their niches in Indo-Guyanese sweets.

Indo-Guyanese cooking was given a new impulse in the 1980s when the Indian Cultural Centre founded a women's club. It resulted in the meeting of the two sides, both equally suspicious of the other at first, each convinced of the other's presumed arrogance. There were the 'Nationals', on the one hand, Indian High Commission staff and delegates, as well as the Indians who had been living in Guyana in the course of their professional activities and, on the other, Indo-Guyanese women of the social elite. They met, and surprised themselves by liking each other. They sang and danced together, even going on to give charity concerts to filled halls. More importantly, though, they shared food.

Delicacies like *paneer*, hitherto unknown in Indo-Guyanese mainstream cooking, date from this era. 'Entertaining' is a popular Guyanese pastime and most people are accustomed to catering for a variety of dietary preferences, as every gathering is likely to include a non-meat eater, a non-fish eater and a vegetarian or two. *Paneer* was immediately clutched to the culinary bosom of many an Indo-Guyanese hostess as its versatility offered a new perspective on vegetarian cooking, its novelty untainted by the homeliness that had characterized vegetarian dishes in the past.

But this was only the beginning. In 1991 it became concretely evident how much of this subtle 'new wave' influence was at work. The women's club produced a cookbook, *Culinary Delights*. It is not merely a cookbook: properly read, it is a telling social document. Forty-two ladies from both sides of the Kala Pani contributed their favourite recipes and, while a few are inevitably Guyanese mainstream, most have a definite Indian or Indo-Guyanese flavour. Cassava Puffs and *Phulourie* rub shoulders with *Chakkuli* and *Khasta Kachourie*. *Dhokla* is followed by blandly flavoured Chicken Patties. Stuffed *Paratha*, known in Guyana simply as Potato or *Alu Roti*, is followed by a very Anglicized *Dholl Puri*, the socially acceptable pronunciation of *Dal Puri*. *Nan*, practically unknown in Guyana, is obligingly subtitled 'Baked Bread'. Mutton Curry, made with curry powder, ground coriander and *masala*, precedes Mutton Curry with a list of more than a dozen unmistakably Indian spices, which have to be ground to a paste first, but there is a concession to local tastes: a little curry powder and *garam masala*, Indo-Guyanese staples, are added. *Mithai*, a generic term for sweets that has come to mean a particular deep fried delicacy in Guyana, shares space with *Sandesh* and *Mohanthall*, which the vast majority of Guyanese would be hard pushed to visualize. The book ends on a somewhat puzzling note, as the chapter on the mind-blowingly hot pickles, so loved by both sides, is supplemented by two recipes for fruity, exceedingly sweet, British-style chutneys, eaten by neither. The uncharitable thought that immediately crosses my mind is that this is yet another misguided attempt at the culinary sophistication that long marred the acceptance of Indo-Guyanese food as anything other than a stomach-filler for agricultural labourers.

The formerly unfamiliar recipes in this book, along with other similar ones, have already become standard fare in trend-setting circles and are beginning to diffuse from there. For generations proximity to Indian culture has always seemed to form an encumbrance to the newly found upward mobility of the socially insecure, so it is extremely heartening to note this development. At the same time, this new wave of awareness now threatens to tip the balance the other way, as simple and plain Indo-Guyanese food is increasingly disguised by a pseudo-Indian veneer. Although it rests substantially on the collective memory of our indentured ancestors, Indo-Guyanese cooking nevertheless has its own character and even though we refer to it as 'Indian' food, this is not the right adjective to describe it. 'Indian-style' comes closer, much as sour pickles, salt beef and cheesecake are often termed 'Kosher-style' in the United States. We have made it evolve to a modest extent, necessity and deprivation uniting styles in a way that would never be possible on the vast sub-continent. This Indo-Guyanese food has embarked on a new journey, taken to Britain and North America by Guyanese immigrants, but whether in Guyana or abroad, it remains primarily Indo-Guyanese territory and has never significantly fused with other cuisines. This food, spawned from subsistence cooking, later enriched by hazy memories, limited by the initial paucity of ingredients, symbolizes our entire background and continues to function as a major component of Indo-Guyanese identity.

Food-related terms used by Indians in Guyana
ACHAR Hot pickle, usually green mango or lime.
ALU Potato.
ANAR Pomegranate (*Punica granatum*).
BADAM LACHHA A spun-sugar sweet with no trace of the almonds of its name.
BAIGAN Aubergine/egg plant (*Solanum melongena*).
BAIGANI Batter-coated aubergine fritter, like the kind referred to as *bhaji* in Britain.
BAIR Dunks (*Ziziphus mauritiana*).
BARA Fritter made from a split pea paste, often called *vada* in India.
BARTAN Pots, pans, metal dishes.
BAYLAY To roll out, e.g. *roti*.
BELNA Rolling pin.
BESAN Chick pea (gram) flour.
BHAJI Leafy greens like spinach etc. Some examples: *Amaranthus gangeticus* = *chowrai bhaji*, *Basella alba* = *poi bhaji*, *Brassica juncea* = mustard *bhaji*.
BHANDARA Mass feeding/eating, usually to mark an occasion.
BHUNJAL Dry-frying meat or poultry in *masala*.
BHUSI Rice husk, often used as animal fodder or mixed with clay to make a plastering agent.
BORA Yard-long beans (*Vigna unguiculata sesquipedalis*).
CHALNI Sieve.
CHALAY To sift.
CHANNA Chick peas.
CHATNI Hot pickle, usually finely chopped. The Anglicized spelling 'chutney' is also popular.
CHAUNKE Verb, meaning to finish off a dish by adding sizzling seasonings, like garlic and whole cumin seeds, e.g. in *dal*.
CHA'UR Bastardized version of *chawal*, rice.
CHIMTA Tongs used for raking cooking fire.
CHOKHA Highly seasoned (roasted) vegetable dish, e.g. aubergines or coconut.
CHOWKI Pastry board used for flatbreads.
CHULHA Clay fireplace used for cooking, now often with metal reinforcement. It is popularly referred to simply as a 'fireside' nowadays.

The holes upon which the pots are set are called *aila* and the bumps around the hole which make ventilation possible are called *uchkun*.

CURRY Cooked dish made with curry powder.

DAHI Curds, yoghurt.

DAL Split peas or soupy split pea dish.

DAL GHOTNI A large wooden 'swizzle stick' used to break up the grains of *dal* to give a smoother texture.

DAL PURI *Paratha* stuffed with seasoned pureed split peas.

DHANIA Coriander seeds.

DOSA A sweet pancake made from wheat flour, not fermented rice as in southern Indian recipes.

DUDHPITHI Dough strips cooked in sweetened milk.

GHEE Clarified butter.

GHOJA Coconut-stuffed fried pastry similar to *gujjiya*.

GHOTAY To stir.

GHUGRI Boiled blackeye peas, refried with seasonings. An Oriyan (sub-continental) recipe for *Ghuguni* is made along similar lines.

GULAB JAMUN Fried milk balls steeped in syrup.

GULGULA Banana fritters.

GURUMA Half-ripe mangoes stewed with sweet spices.

HALDI Turmeric, also called 'dye'.

HALWA Sweet made with wheat flour and a particular mixture of spices referred to as *halwa masala*. The texture of the dish is fairly loose and it is generally eaten with *roti*.

HING Asafoetida.

JAMOON Tart olive-shaped purple fruit (*Eugenia cumini*).

JEERA Cumin.

JHINGI Ridged luffa (*Luffa acutangula*). Ridged squashlike vegetable.

JILEBI Fried dough spirals in syrup.

KALONJI Used to mean nigella in Hindi, *kalonji* is stuffed bitter gourd in Guyana.

KARAHI Local pronunciation of *kadhai*, woklike cooking vessel.

KARAILA/KARELA Bitter gourd (*Momordica charantia*). The marble-sized variety is known as *karaili*.

KARHI Fried gram or split pea balls in a split pea soup, not unlike *kadhi* from Uttar Pradesh. No curds, yoghurt or buttermilk are added in Guyana.

KATAHAR Jackfruit (*Artocarpus integer*). Ripe jackfruit is often referred to as '*khoa katahar*'. Unripe jackfruit is used in curries. (*Kathal* is Hindu for jackfruit.)

KHEER Rich rice pudding.
KHITCHRI Rice cooked with split peas.
LAUKI Guava bean (*Benincasa hispida*). A squashlike vegetable.
LAWA Balls of puffed rice bound with syrup.
LOI A bun-shaped coil or piece of dough which is to be rolled for *roti*.
LOTA Brass drinking vessel, generally only used symbolically nowadays.
MAHANBHOG A dish made from wheat flour, *ghee*, milk and sugar, usually served at religious functions.
MASALA Mixture of ground spices added to curries or used as a flavouring in its own right.
MITHAI Hindu *mithai*: crisply fried sticks of dough coated with a thick syrup which immediately crystallizes on the surface.

Muslim *mithai*: Made from a richer dough including a generous addition of butter or *ghee*, baking powder and grated coconut. Is cut into chunkier pieces and has a cakelike texture. Also coated with syrup.
MULTANI Spicy split pea-based broth flavoured with tamarind.
NENWA Sponge luffa (*Luffa cylindrica*). Fibrous squashlike vegetable.
PACHOUNIE Sheep's tripe and liver fried with *masala*.
PARATHA Multi-layered flatbread often referred to as 'oil *roti*'.
PARSAD Often used interchangeably with *Mahanbhog*. Generally speaking, the term refers to the collection of edibles given to each guest (like a loot bag) at a religious function. Can include *Mahanbhog, roht, puri, mithai* and fresh fruit.
PERA Individual cookie-shaped milk sweets, like rich fudge.
PEYNOOS Colostrum.
PHULOURIE Savoury deep-fried balls made from a mixture of gram/split pea and wheat flour. Is usually eaten with 'sour', a spicy fresh green mango relish. Popular with all races and often sold in school canteens.
PHUKHNI Metal pipe used to blow cooking fires to life.
PURI Wafer-thin unleavened fried bread, seldom eaten outside religiously inclined situations.
RASGULLA Milk balls cooked in thin syrup.
ROHT A thick pastry-like sweet bread usually eaten at celebrations with a religious tinge. It is fried, not baked like the Afghan bread of the same name and similar composition.
ROTI Flatbread, generic term.
SADA ROTI A thick leavened *roti* made from a dough which often includes finely chopped onion and chillies.
SAIJAN Vegetable drumsticks (*Moringa oleifera*). The young leaves of the tree, referred to as '*saijan bhaji*', are also eaten.

SAKAL The process of toasting a *roti* over an open flame, usually done with thick ones like *sada roti*.

SATWA Seven grains (or as near that as possible; *sat*: seven) ground together, toasted and cooked with milk and sugar to make an almost solid porridge that can be scooped up with the fingers.

SEWAIN Toasted vermicelli cooked with milk, sugar and spices and left to set so that it can be cut into squares. Sometimes called 'vermicelli cake'. Although eaten by both Hindus and Muslims, this dish is essentially considered a Muslim delicacy. Hindus prefer a porridge-like consistency which can be eaten with a spoon and which is usually simply called 'vermicelli'.

SURWA Gravy, usually from a curry dish.

THARIYA Bastardized local pronunciation for *thali*, high-rimmed brass dining plate whose use is now solely ceremonial.

TAWA Perfectly flat griddle used for cooking flatbreads.

BIBLIOGRAPHY

Culinary Delights (1991) The Indian Cultural Centre, Georgetown: Women's Club.

Dabydeen, D. and Samaroo, B. (eds.) (1987) *India in the Caribbean*, London: Hansib.

Mangru, B. (1988) *Benevolent Neutrality. Indian Government Policy and Labour Migration to British Guiana 1854–1884*, London: Hansib.

'Mother India Children Abroad', in *Research Journal of the Antar-Rashtriya Sahayog Parishad*. Vol. II, No. 1, January 1988, New Delhi.

Ruhomon, Peter (1998) *Centenary History of the East Indians in British Guiana 1838–1938*, facsimile reprint, Georgetown.

Williams, R.O. and Williams R.O. Jnr. (1951) *The Useful and Ornamental Plants in Trinidad and Tobago*, revised 4th edition, Port of Spain.

Internet sources:
www.nre.vic.gov.au/trade/asiaveg
www.hear.org/pier/scinames.htm

REFERENCES

[1] Literally 'black water', the endless, unknown stretch of water that divided the Indian subcontinent from the rest of the world.

[2] Damra appears as a place name and a surname in India.

[3] About 51 percent of Guyana's population of approximately 730,000 is of Indian descent.

[4] Ruhomon, p. 155.

[5] As quoted in Ruhomon, p. 161.

[6] The first ship sailed for Demerara in 1838.

[7] B.E.P. 28 December 1864, as reproduced in Mangru, p. 244. These rations were for passengers bound for the West Indies (including Guyana). Children above two and under twelve received half rations.

[8] Mangru, p. 133.

[9] Ibid. p. 248, part of contract made with immigrants in India before leaving for Demerara, dated October 1875.

[10] One chittack is roughly 2½ oz.

[11] *Mother India Children Abroad*, p. 26, Dr Vidya Sagar in 'Indians in Guyana'.

[12] Mangru, p. 248.

[13] See Ruhomon, p. 300, Ordinance XVIII (1891), Clause 6.

[14] Ruhomon, p. 114.

[15] Most Guyanese dwellings are built on stilts or pillars a storey high.

[16] The labourers were recruited primarily but not exclusively from Uttar Pradesh, Bihar, Bengal and Madras.

[17] Some Trinidadian Indians also flake their *parathas* to make 'buss-up-shut' but more often than not they use other aids than their bare hands: wooden spoons, tea towels, etc.

A Scientific Approach to Flavours and Olfactory Memory

Marcia Levin Pelchat and Fritz Blank

'I love the taste of chocolate'

When we eat, we have the impression that food flavour sensations arise from the tongue and, in colloquial speech, we refer to these sensations as 'tastes'. In fact, taste is only a small, though important, part of flavour. The misidentification of odour as taste is known as taste-smell confusion (Murphy et al. 1980; Murphy et al. 1977; Rozin 1982).

Although there is disagreement on the exact number of taste qualities, everyone acknowledges that the number is small. The usual list includes sweet, sour, bitter, salty, and umami (*Physiology and Behavior*, 1991). So, if taste were synonymous with flavour, the number of flavour experiences would be limited as well. Beef would be interchangeable with lamb. In terms of taste alone, raspberry, mango, grape, and peach would all be sweet and tart and would be difficult to distinguish from one another. It is the odour component that makes their flavours unique, that gives a seemingly endless variety of flavour experiences.

The nose and the mouth are connected (see figure 1). This concept is critical to understanding the role of olfaction in flavour. As evidence for the connection, most people are familiar with what happens when someone laughs while drinking milk. A neater way to demonstrate the anatomy is to inhale through the nose with the mouth closed. There will be a sensation of cool air at the back of the mouth. So, during eating, food odours reach the olfactory epithelium (the site of the olfactory receptors) by both the orthonasal pathway (from the front of the nose) and the retronasal pathway (from the back of the nose; figure 1).

Demonstration
To demonstrate the importance of olfaction in flavour, you will need three or four differently flavoured and coloured jelly beans for each person. They must be of good quality. Avoid flavours with a strong sour or 'hot' component. Good choices include: banana, root beer, coffee, cherry and licorice. Identify the flavours for your audience. Instruct each subject as follows: 'Close your eyes,

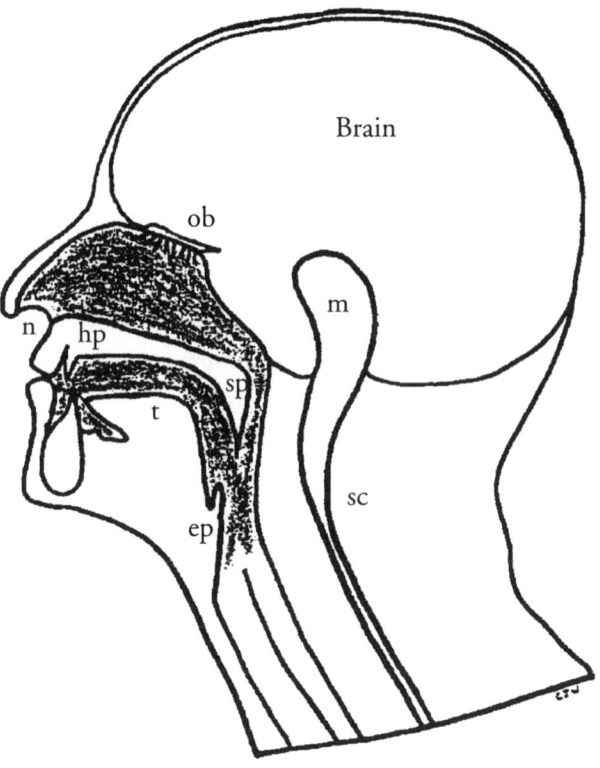

Figure 1. Cut-away side view of the human head. ob = olfactory bulb; n = nostril; hp = hard palate; sp = soft palate; t = tongue; ep = epiglottis; sc = spinal cord; m = medulla. The nasal and oral cavities are shaded to emphasize the connection.

mix up the jelly beans, put one in your mouth and, while holding your nose, begin to chew and try to identify the flavour. Let go of your nostrils before swallowing. Is it easier to identify the flavour with nostrils open or closed?' In such demonstrations, most people heartily agree that it is easier to identify flavour with the nostrils open (that is, with retronasal cues) than with nostrils pinched (without retronasal cues). Interestingly, many participants will express great surprise and delight at this finding, despite the fact that they have frequently experienced diminished 'taste' sensation when they have colds.

Thus, one of the great mysteries in the study of flavour is why people are so astounded that the nose plays a role. Generally speaking, sensory experience is perceived as coming from an object in the environment rather than from a sensory organ. So, light is perceived as coming from the lamp on the table, not from the eyes, and sound is perceived as coming from the orchestra, not from the ears. But at the same time, adults are aware that if they cover their eyes or ears, the sensation will be diminished. By analogy with these other sensory systems, it is not surprising that flavour is perceived as coming from the mouth, rather than from the nose and the mouth. The sensory experience is being localized to the food on the tongue in much the same way that light is localized to a lamp (Murphy et al. 1980). The interesting twist here is that people are so surprised that holding the nose reduces flavour. This is analogous to being surprised that covering the eyes reduces light or that covering the ears reduces sound. Also puzzling is the observation that odours that are unpleasant on the outside of the mouth can be highly preferred food flavours. For example, it is not uncommon for a cheese with a repulsive odour to have a fabulous flavour.

A number of explanations have been proposed for this enigma. One promising idea is that orthonasal and retronasal odour may indeed be qualitatively different. In support of this, Rozin (1982) reports that exotic fruit or soup odours that were easily recognized when sniffed were much harder to recognize when placed in the mouth. One possible mechanism for a qualitative difference is that retronasal odour intensity or quality could be affected by adsorption or absorption by nasal, oral or pharyngeal tissues. Consistent with such a view are data which show that women who wore dentures that covered the palate, even partially, had poor retronasal olfactory perception as compared with women who were dentate or who wore dentures that did not cover the palate (Duffy et al. 1999).

In contrast, Pierce and Halpern (1996) argue that poor identification of odours during retronasal testing is due to use of an inefficient breathing technique and that there is no qualitative difference. This conclusion was based on the observation that retronasal performance could be improved simply by modifying the style of retronasal breathing. Still others (Burdach et al. 1987) have argued that mouth movements and swallowing play the same role in retronasal olfaction that sniffing does in orthonasal olfaction. Thus, in laboratory studies, in which subjects do not actually ingest the stimuli, the efficiency of retronasal perception may be reduced.

An intriguing possibility is that the central nervous system may process olfactory information differently depending on whether an object is present in the mouth. There is support for this view from a PET (Positron Emission Tomagraphy) study in which cerebral blood flow to cortical areas involved in the representation of olfactory and gustatory events differed during simultaneous presentation, as compared with independent presentation of the same stimuli (Small et al. 1997).

Remembrance of things past

Given the important role that olfaction plays in flavour and the amount of information that it conveys, it follows that memory for food will rely heavily on the properties of odour memory. There are a number of interesting attributes of odour memory. Some of these characteristics are reflected in neuroanatomy. All sensory systems other than olfaction follow the same basic plan for central neural connections. They synapse (connect) first in the brainstem or spinal cord, have a further connection in the midbrain and thalamus and then project to some part of the neo-cortex. The olfactory pathways are much more closely associated with the more primitive, emotion-laden parts of the brain. Neurons project from the olfactory epithelium directly into the olfactory bulbs at the base of the brain. (These projections go directly through a series of tiny holes in the skull, called the cribiform plate, in much the same way that strands of spaghetti might go through the holes in a colander. This is why head injury so commonly results in loss of olfaction: during trauma, the brain, which is floating in cerebro-spinal fluid, moves relative to the olfactory epithelium at the roof of the nasal cavity and the bundles of nerve fibres are sheared off as they pass through the cribiform plate.) From there projections go directly to limbic structures involved in emotion and memory, with more minor projections to newer parts of the cortex. So, for example, odours can be consciously detected even with damage to cortical projection areas, whereas visual stimuli may not produce conscious sensations when cortical projection areas are damaged.

Odour memory is emotional

In keeping with the anatomy, responses to odours are inherently evaluative, and odour memories are highly emotion-laden. And so Suskind writes in his dark mystery, *Perfume*, 'The persuasive power of an odour cannot be fended off, it enters us like breath into our lungs, it fills us up, imbues us totally. There is no remedy for it' (Suskind, 1986). This is seen also in Proust's (perhaps hackneyed, though highly relevant) recounting of his childhood experience with the madeleine:

> She sent out for one of those short, plump little cakes called 'petites madeleines', which look as though they had been moulded in the fluted scallop of a pilgrim's shell. And soon, mechanically, weary after a dull day with the prospect of a depressing morrow, I raised to my lips a spoonful of the tea in which I had soaked a morsel of the cake. No sooner had the warm liquid, and the crumbs with it, touched my palate than a shudder ran through my whole body, and I stopped, intent upon

the extraordinary changes that were taking place. An exquisite pleasure had invaded my senses...

                        Marcel Proust, *Swann's way*, ed. Gallimard.

There is not only a richness of detail in his account, but the 'remembrance' is also accompanied by a flood of emotion, by an 'exquisite pleasure'. In a more prosaic vein, in laboratory studies, in which words, sounds, odours and images were used as cues for memory of paintings, all were equally effective in terms of accurately cueing recall. However, the odour cues produced the most emotion-filled descriptions of the paintings (Herz 1998). For example, a non-emotional description might read, 'a girl with a dog'. An emotion-laden description of the same painting would be, 'a girl hugging her beloved puppy'.

Odour memory is long lasting
We are frequently asked whether odour memory is superior to visual memory. One could equally well answer this question as 'yes' or 'no'. One can truthfully state that there is very little forgetting of odours. Once an odour is committed to memory, the passage of time has very little effect on it. This contrasts with paired associate memory in which pairs of words are learned and, at recall, the first word serves as a cue for the second. In the latter type of task, there is a gradual fading with time. As Trygg Engen, the father of modern odour memory research, says, 'Ability to learn odor associations in the laboratory is relatively poor, but whatever the strength of an odor association, weak or strong, the passage of time does not affect it. Odor perception is better characterized as *a system designed not to forget*, rather than one designed to remember.' And, 'In contrast to learning in other modes, odor associations are characterized by pro-active inhibition whereby first associations are protected and new ones inhibited' (Engen et al. 1991).

Odour memory is context-specific
Odour memory is highly episodic as compared with verbal memory. In psychology, episodic memory is often contrasted with semantic memory. An example of a semantic memory would be the information that cousin Sadie is married to a man named Bill, or that the battle of Hastings took place in 1066. This is the type of memory that we rely upon throughout our school years and academic careers. An example of an episodic memory would be your recollection of being at cousin Sadie's wedding. Thus, odours are remembered very much within the contexts in which they occur. As a result, the types of errors that we make when identifying odours tend to be more episodic than errors made when identifying verbal/visual stimuli. So, for example, when

attempting to identify a face, we might come up with an incorrect name that is fairly close in sound to the one we seek, for example, Thrusher instead of Thatcher. When odours are misidentified, the incorrect answer often has no relationship to the correct one, save that they frequently occur together. So, for example, one might identify oregano as garlic because these flavourings occur together in Italian cooking, or identify a pine odour as lemon because both are used to scent cleaning products. The episodic nature of olfactory memory may account for the vividness of the recall that it evokes and may also account for the resistance to forgetting.

The tip-of-the-nose phenomenon

Alternatively, one could just as readily argue that odour memory is vastly inferior to visual memory, if the task were naming of an odour versus naming of a picture. This is another reflection of the neuroanatomy of the olfactory system. The olfactory system does not have the kind of direct connections to the linguistic circuits of the brain that the visual system enjoys. This is illustrated by some of the results of the National Geographic Smell Survey (Wysocki et al. 1989). For those not familiar with the Survey, in 1986 a questionnaire containing six scratch-and-sniff odour samples was shipped with an issue of National Geographic Magazine. Participants were asked to provide demographic data as well as to answer several questions about each of the odour samples. There were over 1.4 million respondents worldwide. One of the questions that subjects were asked was to identify the category to which each of the odours belonged. As can be seen in figure 2 (results are presented as a function of age in decades), performance was extremely poor. Young adults scored dismally: on average just over half of the items correct. Performance got worse as participants aged but women were better at the task than men. The identification task in the National Geographic survey was fairly easy. It was a multiple choice task and respondents were not asked to give the name of the actual odour, but rather to indicate the category to which it belonged. Performance is much worse in free recall tasks.

The result is the 'tip-of-the-nose' phenomenon. When we sample an unknown dish, its characteristics, in terms of taste per se, sweet, sour, bitter, salty, umami, are fairly obvious. The real challenge is to identify the aromas present. We know that they are familiar, that we have eaten food like that before, but we can't name them. This is the tip-of-the-nose effect. Why do we need to name them? We need to name them in order to describe our experience to others and to buttress our own memory of the experience by bringing it into a verbal format with which we are more comfortable.

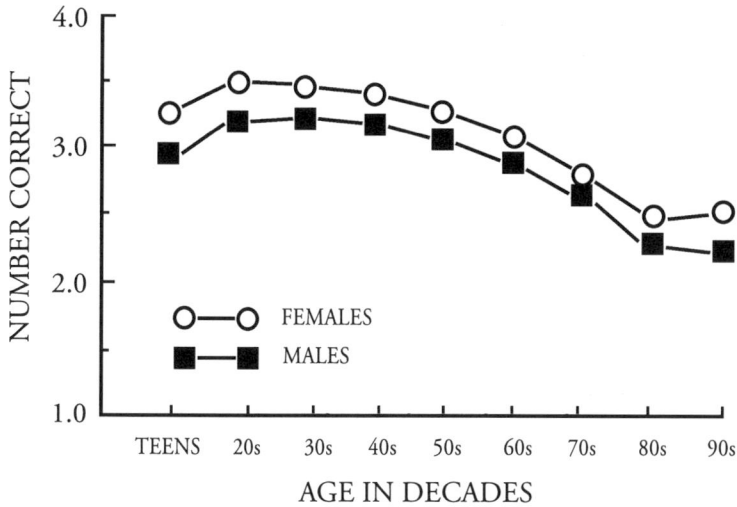

Figure 2. From Wysocki & Gilbert, 1989. Odour classification as a function of age. The figure shows number of stimuli accurately identified out of a possible six correct.

BIBLIOGRAPHY

Burdach, K.J. and Doty, R.L. (1987) 'The effects of mouth movements, swallowing, and spitting on retronasal odor perception', in *Physiology and Behavior*, 41, 353–356.

Duffy, V.B., Cain, W.S. and Ferris, A.M. (1999) 'Measurement of sensitivity to olfactory flavor: application in a study of aging and dentures', in *Chemical Senses*, 24, 671–677.

Engen, T., Gilmore, M.M. and Mair, R.G. (1991) 'Odor Memory', in *Smell and Taste in Health and Disease*, 315–328, eds. Getchell, T.V., Doty, R.L., Snow, J.B. and Bartoshuk, L.M., New York: Raven Press.

Herz, R.S. (1998) 'Are odors the best cues to memory? A cross-modal comparison of associative memory stimuli', in *Annals of the New York Academy of Sciences*, 855, 670–674.

Murphy, C. and Cain, W.S. (1980) 'Taste and olfaction: Independence vs. interaction', in *Physiology and Behavior*, 24, 601–606.

Murphy, C., Cain, W.S. and Bartoshuk, L.M. (1977) 'Mutual action of taste and olfaction [Abstract]', in *Sensory Processes*, 1, 204–211.

Physiology and Behavior, (1991), 49(5), whole issue.

Pierce, J. and Halpern, B.P. (1996) 'Orthonasal and retronasal odorant identification based upon vapor phase input from common substances', in *Chemical Senses*, 21, 529–543.

Rozin, P. (1982) 'Taste-smell confusions and the duality of the olfactory sense', in *Perception and Psychophysics*, 31, 397–401.

Small, D.M., Jones-Gotman, M., Zatorre, R.J., Petrides, M. and Evans, A.C. (1997) 'Flavor processing: more than the sum of its parts', in *Neuroreports*, 8, 3913–3917.

Suskind, P. (1986) *Perfume. The story of a murderer*, New York: Washington Square Press. Translated by John E. Woods from *Das Parfum* (1985).

Wysocki, C.J. and Gilbert, A.N. (1989) 'National Geographic Smell Survey: Effects of age are heterogeneous', in Murphy, C., Cain, W.S. and Hegsted, D.M. (eds.), *Nutrition and the chemical senses in aging. Annals of the New York Academy of Sciences*, 561, pp. 12–28.

Learning by Mouth: Edible Aids to Literacy

Gillian Riley

This paper is part of a wide-ranging investigation of edible letterforms: some are pure kitsch and some are serious art history. Here I discuss one aspect of edible alphabets: those made in a gingerbread mould and said to have been used as an educational tool to help little children learn their letters.

There was once a boy named Milo who didn't know what to do with himself – not just sometimes, but always.

When he was in school he longed to be out, and when he was out he longed to be in. On the way he thought about coming home, and coming home he thought about going. Wherever he was he wished he was somewhere else, and when he got there he wondered why he'd bothered. Nothing really interested him – least of all the things that should have.

'It seems to me that almost everything is a waste of time,' he remarked one day as he walked dejectedly home from school. 'I can't see the point in learning to solve useless problems, or subtracting turnips from turnips, or knowing where Ethiopia is, or how to spell February.' And, since no one bothered to explain otherwise, he regarded the process of seeking knowledge as the greatest waste of time of all.

As he and his unhappy thoughts hurried along (for while he was never anxious to be where he was going, he liked to get there as quickly as possible) it seemed that the world, which was so large, could sometimes seem so small and empty.[1]

Milo, a self-absorbed, over-indulged and lonely little boy, passed through a magic tollbooth and had amazing adventures and a lot of fun exploring the town of Dictionopolis. Along with a friendly, clock-like dog, Tock, he ventured into a busy marketplace where, to cut a boisterous story short, he came upon stalls selling succulent words and one:

with 26 bins filled with all the letters of the alphabet from A to Z. 'Here, taste an A; they're very good,' said the stall-holder. Milo nibbled carefully at the letter and discovered that it was quite sweet and delicious – just the way you'd expect an A to taste.

After many adventures, Milo got back home – literate and happy, and never looked back. Life was so full of books to read and things to do, once he had really tasted the joys of reading.

Milo was not the first child to eat his words. St Columban got off to a good start with a caring Irish mum feeding him alphabetic oatcakes for breakfast, thus inaugurating the intellectual supremacy of Ireland throughout the Dark Ages.[2]

Long before that, however, we find schoolchildren in ancient Greece learning to read and write with the help of waxed wooden tablets.[3] Textual references and the survival of the tablets themselves need to be seen in the context of wider studies of the non-printed book and the history of literacy. A tall order when the most I hoped for was to find an entertaining link between gingerbread and alphabetic cookies, and was lulled into complacency by the obvious link between horn-books and edible ABCs. As we shall see, things are not so simple.

A horn-book consisted of a printed or written alphabet or text, like the Lord's Prayer, secured under a protective sheet of thin transparent horn. It usually had a handle at one end, often pierced for a string to hang it up with. Inevitably, antiquarians were not slow to see these picturesque objects as 'collectables', and thus horn-books found themselves tossed up on the wilder shores of bibliography, somewhat insulated from reality, pulling in ridiculous prices in the sale-rooms[4] and even giving rise to 'suspectibles', as one enthusiast put it. The indefatigable Andrew Tuer built up an impressive collection of them and wrote the definitive work on the subject, bringing the alphabetic gingerbread mould, that other desirable bygone, into line with horn-books.[5] Another collector, Pinto, amassed a magnificent quantity of wooden objects, from treen to domestic objects and furniture. Among them are several single and multiple alphabetic gingerbread moulds.

Gingerbread moulds are functional objects with considerable visual appeal and, as such, preserved in huge quantities in collections of folklore and 'kitchenalia'. They hang in museums, or as ornaments in the kitchens of people who never use them, quite detached from their original purpose – the making of festive, celebratory cookies. The gingerbread men we know today, shaped by hand or stamped with a metal cutter from spongy cake mixture, with unwinking currant eyes their only form of decoration, are a different kind of animal. A firm impression from a historic mould, a richly dressed couple or a galleon in full sail, needs a stiff paste which will keep the intricate design intact and not distort too much in the baking. The elegant, etiolated cavalier who emerges from the oven a corpulent overweight buffoon might taste good, but his gross bulk betrays the intentions of his creator; so an understanding of the mixture formed in these moulds is of the first importance.

Another word for gingerbread is honeycake, which gives us insights into this mixture. Ancient honeycakes, from votive offerings during harvest or sowing rituals, to mere treats for festive occasions, were made of a stiff mixture of honey and flour or breadcrumbs which would keep its shape while baking and keep well, too. Honey is the key: sweetness and light, pleasure and illumination, treats and candles; all from the industrious bee. It can be no coincidence that the area around Nuremberg, 'the bee-garden of the Holy Roman Empire', provided the ideal microclimate for apiculture, and it has been argued that it is from there that a tradition of making honeycakes, formed in beautifully carved wooden moulds, spread to surrounding areas of Europe.[6] Tuer illustrates small pretend coins, tokens with the alphabet on one side and Pythagoras, in the guise of a money-changer, on the reverse, manufactured in Nuremberg, indicating a possible link between literacy in the counting house and its gastronomic rewards, with St Ambrose as the patron saint of honeycake makers.[7]

But, in fact, gingerbread moulds occur across a huge geographical spectrum, from the Urals to Potters Bar. Wherever woodcarvers exercised their craft, on furniture, textile printing blocks, farm carts and so forth, the skill to produce these decorative objects would have flourished. The subjects on the moulds vary, but a pattern seems to emerge of images from folklore, religious cults, ancient pre-Christian fertility symbols and contemporary commercial or patriotic subjects: the first steam engine to arrive in Budapest or the exploits of Kossuth.[8]

In the eighteenth century, the city of Haarlem celebrated the three-hundredth anniversary of Laurens Janszoon Koster's alleged invention of printing with a celebratory edition of gingerbread showing the first proof being pulled on an elegant wooden printing press. '*Spiegel der behoudenis*' – the mirror of salvation – it proclaims, 'Koster's first proof, and Haarlem's Glory'.[9] The mould for this was still around in the pre-war years, but attempts to trace both the mould and the printer of the book have been fruitless, perhaps because of the virtual destruction of Scheveningen during World War II. Haarlem was here celebrating its native son with a popular sweetmeat, as ephemeral as the power of the printed word is eternal.

But Haarlem was also famous for certain 'red cookies', some of them alphabetic, and we catch a glimpse of them in still-life paintings of the early seventeenth century by Pieter Claesz.[10]

The *speculaas* biscuits which bakers sell in the Netherlands, around the time that Sinterklaas is filling his bags with chocolate letters, are a delicious, friable biscuit mixture, flavoured with lemon peel and cinnamon, rather than a cakey dough. They are made in shallow moulds, with the patterns of windmills, animals, ships and so forth cut in shallow relief. A domestic version of these moulds is still in use in the home, a convenient strip of wood, to use and hang up afterwards. In the past these would have been two inches thick, with a carved impression on both sides. The biscuit mixture is pressed into the mould and carefully tipped out onto a baking sheet and cooked at a low heat until crisp and a pale gold colour. The logistics of doing this with some of the surviving historic moulds is terrifying, and posterity is grateful for ceramic casts, themselves 'cooked' to achieve a more durable result.

The idea of eating a symbol or sign is ancient. As babies try to grab the world and cram it into their mouths, so grownups ingest spiritual and corporeal aspects of divinity in communion wafers or food prepared for special religious occasions. Pagan Nordic deities were placated with baked grain cakes in the form of runes, we are told, and it is not hard to imagine the effect of these potent signs, often associated with magic, on both the bleak, cruel gods and their primitive worshippers.[11]

What began as propitiatory offerings evolved, over centuries, into mere harmless pleasures, and by the time Tuer and Pinto were collecting their pretty bygones, the horn-book and the gingerbread alphabet were amusing reminders of picturesque olden days, when our social inferiors picked up what little learning they needed in quaint village schools.

But gingerbread letters went on being eaten as treats for young and old away from the schoolroom. They were sold at fairs and made in quantities by confectioners. It has been suggested that the expression 'taking the gilt off the gingerbread' originated in the practice of selling off broken or defective pieces cheaply, presumably without the decoration of gold leaf that was often applied to the superior kinds of gingerbread. The use of gold and silver leaf on food is ancient; it was known in Moghul cuisine and is still used in the expensive and sophisticated cuisines of India and Asia. Roy Shipperbottom investigated its uses in English cuisine and pointed out that the gilt on cheap popular gingerbread would probably have been an alloy of copper and zinc, a cheerful thought for health freaks wishing to top up their intake of trendy trace elements.[12]

Gold leaf can be seen on a surviving piece of alphabetic gingerbread now in the Museum of London.[13] This unprepossessing (to some) object has recently been scrupulously restored. It was purchased by the Museum in 1912 and, thanks to some serendipitous worm-holes, can be matched exactly to one discussed by Tuer, illustrated together with a photograph of the mould and an impression from it.[14] This mould, signed 'Chadwick', had been given to Tuer by a Mr R.H.

Woodruff, who had got it from Mr Edward Jeboult of Taunton, whose grandfather had been a carver of moulds in the eighteenth century. The indefatigable Tuer tracked down Edward Jeboult and discovered that the mould in question had been used by a Mr Stagg of East Street, Taunton, whose family had been in the gingerbread business for generations. Already a 'collectable' way back in 1896, it was inevitable that someone in Tuer's circle might have fed this object to a gullible museum curator, even though the mould had already been mutilated by cutting the two-inch plank on which it was carved into half its width, ready to be nailed or pinned up as mere decoration.

Matthew Prior comments on the possible problems involved in gingerbread versions of non-Latin alphabets:[15]

> I mention'd diff'rent Ways of Breeding:
> Begin We in our Children's Reading.
> To Master John the English maid
> A Horn-book gives of Ginger-bread:
> And that the Child may learn the better,
> As he can name, he eats the Letter:
> Proceeding thus with vast Delight,
> He spells, and gnaws from Left to Right
> But shew a Hebrew's hopeful Son,
> Where We suppose the Book begun;
> The Child would thank you for your kindness,
> And read quite backward from our Finis:
> Devour the Learning ne'er so fast:
> Great A would be reserv'd the last.

A refreshing honesty about the function of alphabetic gingerbread is found in Poems by a Bard at Bromsgrove:[16]

> The bakers to increase their trade
> Made alphabets of gingerbread,
> That folks might swallow what they read.
> All the letters were digested,
> Hateful ignorance detested.

The thought of the apt and quick-witted chomping their way to dental crippledom is almost too painful to contemplate.

The horn-book might have a respectable pedigree, but by the time it was becoming obsolete the gingerbread alphabet, too, was on its way out. An illustration in volume two of Tuer's work says it all: a bawling child, with horn-book dangling from a clenched fist, is being led to the village school by an elegant mother, watched with concern by a group of villagers dressed in the charming high-waisted frocks and straw bonnets of the last age. This is the disingenuous rural idyll perpetuated in genre paintings of the late nineteenth century, where rosy-cheeked peasants who know their place live in sun-kissed settings, light years away from the rick-burnings, transportation, urban sprawl and industrial blight that were already eroding Tuer's green and pleasant land. In this context it is hard to see the gingerbread alphabet as a serious educational tool; a reward for effort, an incentive to persevere, a treat after a tough day at the chalk face perhaps, but a learning aid? Hardly. But, however irritating, antiquarianism and nostalgia, fuelling an instinct to collect, have, in this case, succeeded in documenting an aspect of food history that might otherwise have gone unrecorded.

Individual letters of the alphabet have been eaten for centuries. Beautiful, ornate, pastry letters in still-life paintings in the Netherlands suggest speculations about the significance of eating one's words.[17] We do not know why early seventeenth-century artists painted edible letters, or what was behind their choices, their own initials or some deeper symbolic meaning, but it does not seem to have been educational. Literacy mattered in the Dutch Republic, a rich trading nation whose citizens deployed figures and words to commercial, rather than cultural, ends and diligently read their bibles, but I found no evidence of children being taught to read with the letter cookies that were made in profusion by bakers and pastrycooks. They may have got some among the special goodies given to goody-goody children by Sint Nicolaas as rewards for exemplary behaviour during the year. This endearing and hard-working saint is portrayed in gingerbread moulds, his faithful horse weighed down with a huge pack of presents and cookies, but none of these look alphabetic. However, by the early years of this century these gifts had evolved into the chocolate letters that still arrive on 5 December, down every chimney in the land, when each child expects its initials in parity of weight, Johannes demanding precisely the same amount of chocolate as Willem, a headache for the manufacturers and a pain in the eye for typographers.[18]

There are many recipes in Dutch and English cookery books of the seventeenth and eighteenth centuries showing how to make banket-letters; usually in red or white versions of a paste of ground almonds, flour, sugar and egg, flavoured with lemon peel and spices; this could be rolled up in an outer crust of short pastry and made into letters, with the surface slashed in a decorative pattern to show the coloured filling within. We read of a 'white gingerbread' as a speciality of Ashbourne and a dark one from Ormskirk, which must have affinities with these coloured honeycakes, common in both manuscript and published texts in many countries from the seventeenth century onwards.[19]

This obsessive concern with alphabetic cookies can only be justified if it makes us more aware of the complexities of the gastronomic traditions within which they flourished, and recognizes that food history has to extend beyond the pots and pans and moulds and collectables of the 'heritage' country house kitchen, to the social and cultural context of food and the art of its preparation. We continue to toil away with the hope that, thanks to this beguiling contemplation of a small, mouth-watering microcosm, we shall emerge, like young Milo, from our burrowings and munchings, with a sense of wider horizons, an enhanced zest for life and a sceptical respect for the strange byways of scholarship.

REFERENCES

[1] Juster, Norton (1962) *The Phantom Tollbooth*, London: William Collins & Sons, pp. 40–44 and pp. 216–217.

[2] Andree, Richard (1905) 'ABC-Kuchen', in *Zeitschrift des Vereins für Volkskunde*, Bb. 15, p. 178.

[3] Funke, Fritz (1959) *Kleines Abcd erium*, Leipzig: Deutsches Buch- und Schriftmuseum der Deutschen Bucherei.

[4] Tuer p. 459. A typical passage of Antiques Road Show verbiage: 'The Raban horn-book sheet mentioned on p. 130, until recently belonging to Mr. N.Q. Pope of Brooklyn NY has been purchased by Messrs. Dodd, Mead, and Co., of New York who are asking two hundred dollars for it. It will be remembered that an exactly similar horn-book was sold at auction in 1878 for three shillings.'

[5] Tuer, Andrew W. (1896) *History of the Horn-Book*, London: The Leadenhall Press.

[6] Weiner, Piroska (1981) *Carved Honeycake Moulds*, Gyoma: Corvina Kiadó, p. 10.

[7] Piroska Weiner, op cit.

[8] Tuer, vol. 1, p. 27.

[9] Nannings, J.H. *Brood en Gebakformen en hunne Beteekenis in de Folklore*, Uitgeversbedrijf 'Eigen Volk', Scheveningen, nd. pp. 46 and 49.

[10] Riley, Gillian (Spring 2001) 'Eat your Words! Seventeenth-Century Edible Letterforms', in *Gastronomica*, vol. 1, no. 1.

[11] Verbal communication from Gerard Unger, who first drew my attention to the history of Dutch chocolate letters; the printed reference to this possibility is no doubt waiting to be unearthed in antiquarian studies of runes, but I have been unable to locate this so far.

[12] Davidson, Alan *The Oxford Companion to Food*, p. 343.

[13] Purchased by the Museum of London in 1912, acc. no. A 6802. I am grateful to Hazel Forsyth for spotting this treasure and ensuring its preservation.

[14] Tuer, vol. 2, pp. 265–266.

[15] Tuer, vol. 2, p. 263.

[16] ibid.

[17] Riley, *Gastronomica*.

[18] Ovink, G.W. (Winter 1985) 'Dutch Chocolate Letters', in *Typographica* [old series], 15; and Montijn, Ileen (1991) *Wat je Eet ben je Zelf*, Utrecht/Amsterdam: Uitgeverij Kosmos.

[19] Davidson, p. 338.

Food and Forgetfulness at Socratic Symposia

Luciana Romeri

I dislike a drinking-companion with a good memory (μισέω μνάμονα συμπόταν).[1]

This is the opening anonymous fragment of Plutarch's *Table Talk* (*Quaestiones conviviales*) (*Moralia*, tr. Clement, P.A. and Hoffleit, H.B., William Heinemann, 1969, I, 612cI) which is stated as a sort of slogan for the reader of this convivial text. Nevertheless, announced at the beginning, the phrase commits Plutarch to an explanation, an explanation which is in fact more of a distinction between what one should forget if one is a well-behaved guest – and not a hateful one – and what one should, on the other hand, remember, go over in one's mind (ἀναθεώρησις, cf. VI, 686cI), even impress on one's memory, simply by writing it down (ἀναγράψασθαι, cf. I, 612e). Thus, among everything that takes place at the table, there are things which it is appropriate to remember and those which should be forgotten. There are, therefore, two questions here, which are not of course mutually exclusive. Among things that happen at table and when one is a guest at a symposium of the kind referred to by Plutarch, what should one retain in one's memory and what on the other hand should one try to forget?

However, to answer this question one must first establish what kind of symposium Plutarch is talking about that could be described as a 'Socratic symposium'.

This expression designates, in the Περὶ μεθόδου δεινότητος of the orator Hermogenes,[2] a well defined rhetorical genre. Hermogenes defines, in the same group, συμπόσια Σωκρατικά, δημηγορία, διάλογος, κωμῳδία and τραγῳδία. All these examples are characterized by a double process. In this way the συμπόσια Σωκρατικά have a scheme which is serious and ridiculous at the same time, both concerning people and happenings. As examples of συμπόσια Σωκρατικά Hermogenes puts forward, obviously, the symposia of Plato and Xenophon and also, more surprisingly, the *Cyropaedia* of Xenophon. Hermogenes explains, in effect, that: 'Cyrus always took care that, when they [i.e. he and his soldiers] were eating together (συσκηνοῖεν), they only discussed agreeable matters and those which would encourage virtue (εἰς ἀρετήν).'[3]

In other words, a symposium can be Socratic even without Socrates.[4] The term 'Socratic' designates less the presence of Socrates at the symposium – or rather at this common meal – than the presence, during the meal, of an educative conversation encouraging virtue, such as the words of Socrates during the symposia of Callias and of Agathon. It is a question of speaking in the manner of Socrates, to educate and to guide those taking part towards the acquisition of virtue, even soldiers in a tent. It is the talk rather than the sympotic elements, and rather than the presence of Socrates himself, that characterizes a συμπόσια Σωκρατικά in that it is both a meeting of virtuous men and a literary form. The Platonic Symposium is the paradigm of this kind of symposium specifically because of the presence of Socrates, the only companion of Agathon who, by his philosophical conversation, is totally asympotic from the beginning to the end of the occasion. Thus, a symposium is 'Socratic' to the extent that it is philosophical; and that it is philosophical also makes it, according to Plutarch and following Plato, the only symposium that is legitimate and worthy of being remembered.

So I come back to my original question, or rather the double question: what is worthy of being remembered at a philosophical symposium and, on the other hand, what should be forgotten?

An initial response is found in the first dedication of Book I of the *Table Talk* of Plutarch (I 612d5–e7):

> Since you too believe that forgetfulness of folly (τῶν μὲν ἀτόπων ἡ λήθη) is in truth 'wise', as Euripides says,[5] yet to consign to utter oblivion all that occurs at a drinking-party (τὸ δ' ὅλως ἀμνημονεῖν τῶν ἐν οἴνῳ) is not only opposed to what we call the friend-making character of the dining table, but also has the most famous of the philosophers to bear witness against it, – Plato, Xenophon, Aristotle, Speusippus, Epicurus, Prytanis, Hieronymus, and Dio of the Academy,[6] who all considered the recording of conversations held at table (ἀναγράψασθαι λόγους παρὰ πότον γενομέςους) a task worth some effort – and since, moreover, you thought that I ought to collect such talk as suits our purpose from among the learned discussions in which I have often participated in various places both at Rome in your company and among us in Greece, with table and goblet before us, I have applied myself to the task and now send you three of the books, each containing ten questions...

Here Plutarch gives the theoretical justification of the composition of his *Table Talk*; in referring to Plato, and also Xenophon, Aristotle, Speusippus, Epicurus and other illustrious philosophers who have written about *Symposia*. Plutarch confirms the legitimacy of his report to his friend Sossius Senecio of the 'learned discussions', made during the course of several symposia. The evidence of Plato, who was the first to put in writing the discussions at a Socratic symposium, is for Plutarch the model to be followed in all descriptions of convivial talk. One must not forget 'all that occurs at a drinking-party', specifically because 'all that occurs' is, in the particular cases that Plutarch is thinking about, a conversation between learned men. As the discussions at symposia described by numerous philosophers, particularly Plato, bear witness, it is while drinking wine that one says memorable things which should be recorded and transmitted to posterity. In other words, since Plato has recorded the philosophical discussions held παρὰ πότον by Socrates and his friends, everything that happens παρὰ πότον is worthy of being remembered – as long as it takes place under the same conditions as the symposium of Agathon, that is to say, at a philosophical symposium of sober guests.

If that which should be remembered, that is to say recorded in writing, is not in doubt, it is not yet clear what kind of things are unsuitable, inappropriate, ἄτοπα, which it would be wise, on the other hand, to let fall into oblivion. These could include, of course, things said in drunkenness, where too much wine risks changing a symposium into a battle, a λόγος, into chit-chat, into a λάλη, as in the case of the *Symposium* of Lucian, a parody of the Platonic symposium. But there are other things that Plutarch wants to forget, and to be forgotten, in a symposium, a forgetting that he advocates to help the remembrance of the learned discussions. This is made clear in the dedication to Book VI of the *Table Talk* (VI, 686c10–d9):

> Yet if pleasure were purely physical, the proper thing would have been for both Plato and Xenophon to leave us a record, not of the conversation, but of the relishes, cakes, and sweets served at Callias's house and Agathon's. As it is, they never deign to mention such matters, for all the expense and effort these presumably involved; but they preserve in writing only the philosophical discussions, combining fun with serious effort. Thus they have left precedents to be followed not only in meeting together for good conversation over wine (παρὰ πότον), but in recording the conversation afterward (μεμνῆσθαι τῶν λαληθέτων).

Once again Plato, and with him Xenophon, is for Plutarch the undoubted paradigm on these questions. Once again the Socratic symposia are the legitimate symposia in the eyes of Plutarch. However, Plutarch makes explicit here something that Plato leaves implicit: that which one does not talk about at a philosophic symposium, which Plato and his followers allow to fall into oblivion – whether by simply forgetting[7] or by a deliberate choice – is the food; 'the relishes, cakes, and sweets' that Plato and Xenophon do not consider worthy of the slightest mention. Nothing is said during the *Symposia* of Plato and of Xenophon about the dishes served to the guests respectively of Agathon and Callias, as nothing is said in the *Table Talk* about the dishes prepared for the innumerable meetings to which Plutarch refers. As he says, in the dedication to book I, all the 'Talk' recounted here was pronounced παρὰ πότον, that is to say, during a true symposium; of the meal itself, which apparently preceded these symposia, only silence and oblivion.

One will notice that this silence, this culinary oblivion which characterizes Socratic symposia, beginning with those of Plato and Xenophon and continuing with those of Plutarch, brings out not so much the simplicity of the meal or a lack of pleasure at table, but rather a philosophic desire to emphasize the memory of the learned discussion. In other words, the lack of memory of the food is, in the Platonic philosophical symposium, the direct consequence of stressing the philosophy. The symposia offered by Plato, the symposia of the Academy, are explicitly taken as witness to this commemoration, this source of philosophical pleasure (*Table Talk*, VI, 686b9–c10):

> Another and not less valuable privilege guaranteed to Plato's guests was that of recalling afterwards what had been said over the drinks (ἡ τῶν λαληθέντων παρὰ πότον ἀναθεώρησις). Remembering past delights in food and drink is an ignoble kind of pleasure and one that is, besides, as insubstantial as yesterday's perfume or the lingering smell of cooking. On the other hand, the topics of philosophical inquiry and discussion not only give pleasure by remaining ever present and fresh to those who actually recall them (τοὺς μεμνημένους), but they also provide just as good a feast on the same food to those who, having been left out, partake of them through oral report. In this way, it is even today open to men of literary taste to enjoy and share in the Socratic banquets as much as did the original diners.

The pleasure of the table is not only volatile, since it disappears as soon as it is experienced, but it is equally a pleasure of which the memory only provokes the disgust of the guests. Only serious philosophical questions are the source of a pleasure which, because it persists in memory, also guarantees a pleasure the next day (cf. VI, 686b5–6). On the one hand, gastronomic pleasure brings with it disgust and forgetfulness; on the other hand, the pleasure of philosophical discussion is retained in memory and persists through time. The Socratic symposium can surpass the restricted framework of the symposium itself because the pleasure which it creates can be pursued in memory, in 'recalling afterwards what had been said over the drinks'. And the pleasure persists in the memory of 'what had been said', because these things 'said' do not describe the symposium itself, do not say anything about what a real symposium or meal should consist of, about 'the relishes, cakes, and sweets served'. The only and unique 'nourishment', admitted at the table of the philosophers by Plutarch, is talk, a nourishment that never disgusts and which, on the contrary, continues to give pleasure both to those that describe it (such as Apollodorus, Xenophon and Plutarch himself) and to those that listen.

Thus, forgetting the food and remembering the convivial conversation are merely two sides of the same coin, two faces of the Socratic symposium. The final proof of this is that caricature of a symposium which is the *Symposium* of Lucian. Here, the symposium of 'illustrious philosophers' is transformed into a battle of the Lapiths precisely because food takes pride of place in the description, and so in the memories of the guests, while the words are reduced to pure chat destined to be forgotten. In other words, in reversing comically the elements of the symposium, Lucian illustrates the same opposition between words and food, where the food is 'worthy of memory' exactly to the extent that the words are not.

In relation to this tradition, the only exception that one can find in the Greek convivial literature, both classical and late, is the *Deipnosophists* of Athenaeus. Athenaeus is, to my knowledge, the only author for whom learning and food are, at the same time and to the same extent, objects of memory and of a convivial text – and thus he puts himself outside the tradition of Platonic conviviality, in describing something other than a Socratic symposium. As the *epitomator* of the *Deipnosophists* says, in speaking of Athenaeus (tr. Yonge, C.D., Henry G. Bohn, 1853, I, 1a5–b5):

> ...there is no sort of gentlemanly knowledge which he does not mention (ἐμνημόνευσεν) in the conversation which he attributes to them; for he has put down in his book, fish, and their uses, and the meaning of their names; and he has described divers kinds of vegetables, and animals of all sorts. He has introduced also men who have written histories, and poets, and, in short, clever men of all sorts; and he discusses musical instruments, and quotes ten thousand jokes: he talks of the different kinds of drinking vessels, and of the riches of kings, and the size of ships, and numbers of other things which I cannot easily enumerate (ἀπομνημονεύσαιμι), and the day would fail me if I endeavoured to go through them separately.

There is no doubt that Athenaeus is setting up and differentiating his own symposium in comparison with the symposium of Agathon. For, in contrast and almost in opposition to what Plutarch proclaims, correctly following Plato, Athenaeus finds worthy of 'mention' and of remembering not only the learned *quaestiones* about 'musical instruments, drinking vessels, the riches of kings and ships', but also the range of 'fish', of 'vegetables' and of 'animals of all sorts', that is to say, 'the relishes, cakes, and sweets' for which Plutarch specifies oblivion. And it is these 'purely physical' things which, at the same time as philosophical questions, offer and compose the pleasure of the sages invited to Athenaeus' symposium; a symposium which one must take here as both a dialogue that he wrote and at the same time a symposium that he attended. This text is the only symposium where the talk of the learned men does not interfere with the description of a gastronomic occasion and where, on the other hand, the progress of a gastronomic occasion, the succession of dishes, does not prevent the exchange and the transmission of learned discourse.

Athenaeus rejects the opposition and separation between the discursive part and the eating part of a meal, an antagonism implicitly illustrated in the symposium of Plato and explicitly pointed out in the symposia of Plutarch. At the banquet of Larensis not only do the discussions of the guests continue from beginning to end – and here Athenaeus denies the concept of a 'silence', or a 'forgetfulness' of what they ate – but these same discussions arise from the dishes served – or are about them or their accessories – and here Athenaeus denies the concept of learned discussions, which are privileged by being the only convivial elements to be remembered. Talking and eating continue all the time and at the same time, in Athenaeus, and are both subjects to be remembered by the deipnosophists and Athenaeus himself. Thus, in the manner of a Plato and a Plutarch, Athenaeus reports the talk at the banquet of Larensis, thereby preserving the memory of the λόγος συμποτικός to demonstrate its erudition; but, using the same learned phrase, he specifically celebrates the nourishment of the body, the memory of which the most illustrious philosophers never considered worth retaining.

REFERENCES

[1] Page, P.M.G., p. 530. After Lucian (cf. *Symposium*, § 3). It referred to a ποιητικὸς λόγος.

[2] cf. Spengel, L. (ed.) (1854) *Rhetores Graeci*, vol. II, Lipsiae: Teubner, ch. 36, pp. 455–456.

[3] Xenophon, *Cyropaedia*, (II, 2, 1); cf. also III, 2, 25, where the verb συσκηνέω refers explicitly to a συνδεῖπνον. The verb συσκηνέω signifies more correctly 'to be under the same tent' and, only by extension, does Liddell-Scott-Jones translate it as 'mess together' in reference to these passages of Xenophon. It is true, though, that in military campaigns, living with someone under the same tent implies eating together. Elsewhere, in *The Constitution of the Lacedemonians*, Xenophon describes as συσκηνουντες those who participate in common meals (τὰ συσκηνία) established by Lycurgus (cf. V 2–4).

[4] Jacques Bompaire also speaks of the *Socratic symposium*, in referring to a literary genre which harks back to two traditions; he calls the first *de tendance érudite* and the second *de tendance divertissante* (*Lucien écrivain. Imitation et création*, Paris: De Boccard, 1958, p. 314).

[5] cf. *Orestes*, v. 213, though in this passage forgetfulness is the forgetfulness of sleep.

[6] Apart from Plato and Xenophon, no convivial text by these authors has come down to us. Nevertheless, we have some indirect information about a *Symposium* of Epicurus (in particular in Plutarch and in Athenaeus), a *Symposium* of Aristotle (in Athenaeus and in a scholion of Theocrites 3.21), and a Περι μέθησ by Aristotle (also in Athenaeus). For the other authors, cf. Fuhrmann, F. (1972) *Plutarque. Oeuvres morales. Propos de table*, vol. IX–l, Paris: Les Belles Lettres, note *ad locum*.

[7] As Socrates attests in the *Republic*, II, 372c4.

The Memory Factor in American Breakfast Joints

Robert Rubright

Memory, including nostalgia, one of its key components, is a main cog in the operation of successful breakfast restaurants in America. A restaurant proprietor with a sharp memory and a respect for the power and the rewards of a good memory may well succeed in a competitive bacon-and-eggs market place, where other restaurateurs may fall behind or fail completely.

A fine memory can help a breakfast-joint waitress secure her job and endear herself to owners, managers and customers. An owner or manager with a steel memory will develop close rapport with breakfast regulars, who often comprise up to 60 per cent of the morning business.

A chef or a cook must have a quick memory, that pictures breakfast time's most-ordered ten or twenty entrées, even when a cook or kitchen helper can neither read nor write. This is especially true when the orders fly into the kitchen during America's busiest breakfast hours, between seven and eleven a.m. on Saturdays and Sundays. A cashier or head-counter-waitress must maintain a memory bank crammed with the eccentricities and habits of customers who routinely sit at the counter for their meals. Are these people nocturnal animals? Insomniacs? Compulsory talkers? Loners? Picky eaters? Given to violent outbursts? And must such customers occupy the same stools at the breakfast counter every day? (The answer is, invariably, yes; more often than not, restaurant personnel endeavour to protect a stool until the rightful customer comes in to claim it. The choicest stools are always nearest the cashier, the person who quite frequently controls the flow, and even the theme, of conversation up and down the counter.)

In a very small percentage of American breakfast joints, the verbal ordering system is in effect. In one busy Kansas City restaurant, this system of transmitting customer orders to the kitchen has been in use for more than 75 years. The waitress takes a breakfast order, writes it down, then on her way to the kitchen or to its pass-through window memorizes the total order and conveys it verbally to the cook. If her memory pauses, the order surely will be botched and the customer will know the difference. Wait staffers who cannot learn the verbal system will not serve breakfast for long.

Some restaurants stipulate that orders should never be written down, not even at the customer's table or booth. At the O.T. Hodge Chile Parlor in St Louis, Missouri, Kay, an eighteen-year veteran of breakfast service, says, 'We're the only restaurant I've ever seen that doesn't write down orders. We don't write nothing down. We memorize them and call them over to the grill in shorthand. There have been times when we let a new waitress write down orders for short periods of time and then we say we better not catch you doing it again. And that's it.'

At the Goody Goody Restaurant deep in the heart of St Louis, owner Richard Connelly owes a great debt to Dale Carnegie, who wrote a book in the 1930s called *How to Win Friends and Influence People*. In the book, Carnegie underscored the importance of a good memory to social and business achievement. He also started Dale Carnegie Institutes which featured memory drills. Connelly took a Carnegie memory course and rattled off the first and last names of all 37 of his classmates the first time around. So effective was Connelly that the Institute's manager appointed him a graduate assistant to help succeeding classes groom their memories. Connelly's graduating plaque from the Institute hangs in a coveted spot in his office, next to a framed restaurant licence from the state of Missouri.

In his restaurant, Connelly has memorized the names of at least 1,000 customers, many of them regulars. 'I know their names, their faces, where they prefer to sit, their favorite waitress, and what they like to eat,' he says. He maintains a 'cheat' under glass, on his desk, with names of 50 or so newcomers whose names or faces he is not quite sure of. On it are quick notes to himself, such as: 'Cornelius, tall friend of Ron's'; 'Harold Owens–tireman'; or 'Virgil, business partner of Cecil'. As insurance, Connelly also carries a battery-driven electronic notemaker.

'I make it a point to call all my customers – 60 per cent of them who eat breakfast here are regulars – by their first names,' says Connelly. 'I really do know my 60-per-cent customers! If they can't get the table they want, I diplomatically hold them in the foyer until it's available. This gives me more opportunities to address them by their first names and to exercise my memory.'

Breakfast time – it spans at least five hours in many places: six a.m. to eleven a.m. – is a time of lazing, socializing, bonding and high calorie ingesting. Regular customers who share biscuits-and-gravy or pancakes or waffles recognize who the other regulars are. And when there is a noticeable absence, all the memories of that customer's habits, shortcomings and peculiarities come into play. Around the table in the morning, the collective memory of regular diners is strong and acute. As a consequence, many breakfast joints maintain informal policies for dealing with absentees as a way of stating: 'We remember you and want you back.'

At a barn-sized restaurant in rural Jerseyville, Illinois, a breakfast regular was in the hospital one day. 'He's a heavy smoker, but his wife doesn't know it,' said a fellow regular. 'During breakfast, he has one coffee and four cigarettes. Before going home he sprays himself with cologne right here at the table so his wife won't detect anything. Now he's on oxygen. Let's send him a card.' Farther south in Illinois, the exclusively-widows Cackle Club meets around a corner table at the Cedars Restaurant in Lebanon. 'There's always a greeting card circulating around our table for the sick, for birthdays and for deaths,' a member states. 'We all sign the cards and print little messages.' One card is stockpiled by the restaurant's owner in case of hospital stays by Cackle Club members. Its inscription: 'Don't stay in bed too long, you'll ruin your reputation.'

That card, signed by the members, invariably draws cackles. In addition to notes, the club will send flowers and perhaps 'put together a meat tray'. No member ever strays long from the coffee club's aggregate memory.

Ironically, many of the ten million Americans who say they eat breakfast out at least once a month are pestered by a memory lapse. For those who are not breakfast place regulars, there is uncanny indecision. 'More than 70 per cent of all suburban diners do not know where they are going to eat when they leave the driveway at home. That decision is made on the way to the restaurant and is heavily influenced by traffic, lines in front of the establishment, and not infrequently, intense last-minute interpersonal negotiation,' says Richard Pillsbury in his data-rich book, *No Foreign Food*. It is my observation that this culinary breakfast-hour memory slip carries into the restaurant itself. For instance, at Uncle Bill's Pancake and Dinner House in south St Louis, the pancake–waffle parade that marches through the dining room on the arms of skilled waitresses attracts the notice of the entrée-undecided. 'When a Chocolate Alaska Waffle topped with vanilla ice cream and our pure fudge sauce comes out of the kitchen and the waitress brings it into the dining area, people see her walking past and you immediately get a landslide of orders from newcomers for the same waffle,' says an Uncle Bill's manager. 'People ask the waitress, "What is that you're carrying?", then say, "I'll have that, too." Some days you'd think we were having Chocolate Alaska Waffle Day from Hell around here.'

If there is memory regression among customers at Uncle Bill's, there must be little hint of it among the waitress corps. Uncle Bill's waitresses not only must be able to carry plates of showy food though the dining area, but they must learn to balance a fixed number of loaded plates on their left arms, walk unassailed from the kitchen and reach their target tables without spillage. 'My cooks used to call me She-Man,' says another Uncle Bill's manager. 'I learned to balance eight full plates on my left arm. It has to be the left because you serve on the right. Orders like plates of diced ham and eggs or bacon and eggs are usually the bottom plates on your arm; the Chocolate Alaska Waffle or pancakes, the blueberries or strawberries or whipped cream orders are on the upper levels of your arm. It's like a platform that you build with your plates and then you go up your arm. You want to be sure you have the flat foods on the bottom and the fluffier foods on top. Eight full plates will take care of a table of four or five. If the waitress has had prior experience with arm service (as opposed to tray service) it takes about a week to refresh her memory and learn our version of arm service. If she can't remember this procedure in two weeks, then we'll have to replace her.'

A flagship restaurant of America's most distinguished pancake chain, the Oregon-based Original Pancake House Franchising Co., is Walker Brothers Original Pancake House in Wilmette, an affluent Chicago suburb. General manager Beth Perez says she is in charge of waitress 'plate carrying sessions' to demonstrate left arm plate stacking. 'I personally can do ten plates myself but I have to be very careful where I'm walking and I have a loud voice to warn people to stay out of my way,' she says.

There are other ways that memory plays a crucial part in breakfast restaurant operations; one of them is evident at the Hy Ho 24-hour restaurant in Belleville, Illinois. This is one of America's few restaurants that bans customers for specific infringements and sentences them to life or for as little as two months (automatic life for biting a waitress on her breast while she's serving your scrambled eggs; short time for hiding the toilet lid in the acoustic tile ceiling of the men's room after a dispute over a bill). The managers' memories must come to the fore, especially in the wee small hours, when banned customers tend to sneak into the restaurant for a cup of coffee, trusting that they will not be recognized. Because of so many midnight-hour incursions, the Hy Ho is considering publishing a 'rogue's gallery' of its banned list, so overnight managers can more easily identify them and bounce them anew. Incidentally, our painstaking research indicates that most Hy Ho perpetrators serve their sentences at the Hardee's fast-food outlet across the street.

If memory is a form of lodestar to breakfast nook functions, there is always the antithesis of memory. That honour is accorded Julie's Breakfast Club, a large endeavour in Menasha, a few miles south of Green Bay, Wisconsin. Julie's is 'home of the Big One', a one-pound Italian sausage; the 'Ultimate' buttermilk pancake, a seven-pound, 24-inch-in-diameter monster, brought to the table on a pizza pan and which serves 25 people and lasts for fifteens months in a freezer; and the much smaller 'Baby' pancake, twelve inches around and still large enough to permit youngsters to cut out the middle, stick their heads through the pancake and pretend it's a picture frame. 'I take their photographs when they do this,' says Julie, the owner.

On Saturdays and Sundays, when it appears as if half of Wisconsin's adult population is downloading cinnamon rolls or attacking a more than life-sized pancake, Julie stops dead centre in the middle of her expansive dining room to feign serious memory problems. She shouts loudly across the room to her second-in-command, an off-duty weekday Tupperware salesman named Uncle Stan: 'Do we have any coffee in the restaurant or do we have to send out?' Stan invariably shouts back: 'I'll see if the neighbors have some.' Then Julie and Uncle Stan trudge off to the kitchen, their put-on act about the owner's poor memory being the stunt that gives this bustling, one-time Chinese restaurant, its undeniably folksy character.

It's axiomatic, in my view, that a good, fertile memory is useful on the part of everyone in the breakfast restaurant cast: customers, who remember just why they choose to return to the same eatery day after day; owners, who have imprinted customer faces and whims firmly in their grey matter; managers, who have mentally recorded the mannerisms and eccentricities of customers, and wait-persons, who know, often to an infinite degree, just how well their regulars respond to the best hours of the morning.

Devouring the City

Alice Wooledge Salmon

> It is the place where a child is brought to lunch in the shadow of a great stone skyscraper, to be awed at the technology of the little boxes that take his nickels and dimes. That is the substitute for the awe he would feel at the skyscraper and the city itself, were he able to express it; the Automat takes its place.
> *Paul Goldberger, New York architecture connoisseur and critic.*

Manhattan inhabits our London living room, a full-on view down Wall Street across the East River from Brooklyn, that Street manifest as the narrowest of canyons between modulated layers of skyscraper greys and fawns. The towers seem to materialize from a troubled grey sky, piling forward in flattened perspective which emerges with the billowing smoke and dark shapes of shipping traffic on the restless green river below. A tugboat smokestack contributes the single note of red to a scene both Whistlerian and Modernist.

This arresting picture, a colour aquatint and etching dated 1936, is by Luigi Kasimir, an Austrian *émigré* who got caught up, like many of his contemporaries, in recording the drama of early twentieth-century New York. I've known the picture all my life, and was born into that view in the 1940s, living for my first ten years on the breezy bluffs of Brooklyn Heights among handsome tree-lined streets of nineteenth-century brownstone, brick, and wooden row houses spiced with twentieth-century interruptions.

If this early and compact New York 'suburb' – given breath and shape thanks to decades of steam ferries which formerly shuttled commuters between Brooklyn and lower Manhattan – seemed securely underwhelming, the right size and height for someone being carried around by her father, or wheeled by her mother in a funny wicker buggy, or skipping her stick along apartment house railings, I had only to look to the nearby end of our street (Clark or Pierrepont, depending on when), maybe twist and turn a little, to see – that view. That startling, oversized, living prospect, behind where our street intersected with the one called Columbia Heights; the view which hung on our Brooklyn living room wall, the reality barely changed since the 1930s: the pinnacle-packed island, the harbour filled with movement and the sound of boat horns, the Statue of Liberty away off to the left, Brooklyn Bridge to the right.

And every summer, 'ting-a-ling, ting-a-ling', the little white truck of the Good Humor Man would drive slowly around the neighbourhood. I particularly remember his stopping at the junction of Clark Street and Columbia Heights, with the river and skyscrapers heat-hazed beyond. The bells jangled and we all came running to the natty white van with a chocolate-covered vanilla ice-cream-on-a-stick – the Good Humor Bar! – emblazoned on the side.

The Bar was portrayed horizontally, extended towards us with stick distant and a huge bite gobbled out of the nearest corner. I was tantalized; *all* of us were tantalized, each of us holding our dime, thinking how good it would be when *we* were biting through the thin chocolate coating into the ice-cream. The Good Humor Man was dressed in white, he was cheerful and I'm sure he smiled as he reached through the door at the back of his van and pulled Good Humor Bars (and other things I don't remember) from the icy depths. I imagine I can still hear the 'clunk' of the freezer door as he slammed it shut to secure those treasures until next time.

Brooklyn was relatively skyscraper poor, though the Heights had some tallish buildings, including our own giddily embellished, stab-at-the-Renaissance, 35 Pierrepont. Along Montague, the Heights' 'Main Street', people lived above the stores and restaurants of converted brownstones, and in some of these, the future Miss Rheingold and maidens held court. Brooklyn at that time brewed oceans of lager, and each year, Rheingold, one of its famous marques, ran a greater-New York competition to choose their new 'Miss'. During contest season, each can of Rheingold Extra Dry sported a picture of one of that year's finalists, and in every beer-selling delicatessen and grocery, the six animated faces were displayed at eye level beside a ballot box. The girl who got the most votes was the next Miss Rheingold.

The contest was wildly successful, and the faces seemed to be everywhere. I stared at them, intently – wholesomely glamorous, and highly-groomed in the way of the 1950s; which one, which one, was the prettiest? *That* one. Or *that* one, I decided. Would 'my' Miss Rheingold be chosen? Needless to say, I never tasted the beer.

For more than routine shopping, my mother and I went east, on foot, or by bus, beyond Montague Street, the river behind us, past squat and sober Borough Hall on Joralemon, to Fulton Street in downtown Brooklyn. The small-scale Heights, though by then past its prime and not yet into its late twentieth-century renaissance, was attractive and leafy, interesting; it was fun to live there. Downtown Brooklyn, by contrast, was blowsy. My greatest memory is of glaring light and heat; there were no trees lending hot-weather shade, few tall towers to cast shadows and encourage cooling winds. The buildings were stolid commercial efforts mainly constructed over the previous 70 years, and I found them mostly boring – as I did going to A&S while my mother bought bedding or saucepans or anything else that people unearthed at Brooklyn's famous department store. Still, we might go to the movies at one of the strapping theatres – or better yet, eat at Chock full o'Nuts or the automat.

Chock full o'Nuts was a big luncheonette, one link of a New York chain, on raffish Court Street near Borough Hall, its name proclaimed in instantly recognizable cheery checked lettering. There were no tables, so you sat at the counter on high swivel stools, feeling quite mature and about to be party to special happenings; to this day, sitting at the counter almost anywhere fills me with expectation.

A large, fixed menu board, resembling a gingerbread house, detailed the restrained possibilities of coffee, doughnuts, a few chilled drinks, pies and cake, soup and sandwiches. The place was always crowded, which I liked. Most people, I think, drank the celebrated 'Heavenly Coffee' out of sturdy white cups with Chock's trademark small checks in a black and yellow band around the rim; I had 'Homogenized Vitamin D Milk' and always ate, as my mother did, a cream cheese and chopped walnut sandwich on whole wheat raisin bread. I thought these were wonderful, and the wonder was increased because everything was made before your eyes, by 'counter girls', mainly black, dressed in perky uniforms – pale green, I believe – with checked trim. A few feet opposite, the 'girls' *gloved* hands deftly prepared every item, wrapped each sandwich loosely in paper, and served. The company byword was food 'never touched by human hands'. *Really?* I pondered, watching the fast-moving fingers. *Never?* I marvelled, enduringly impressed.

Hands featured differently at Horn & Hardart, the automat, not far away. Part of an even larger low-priced chain than Chock full o'Nuts, the automat at 427 Fulton was 'Modern American throughout', and its mesmerizing charm was an ambitious variation on the competition's overtly hygienic approach.

Food at the automat came from compartments behind rectangular glass doors, row upon row of small windows set into the wall above a ledge where you passed along with your tray. Beside each door was the name of the dish, with the number of nickels required to get it; you put the nickels into a slot, turned a knob sharply clockwise, and as the door popped open, reached in to remove your macaroni and cheese, beef casserole, tapioca pudding, or cinnamon bun.

What happened next was truly bizarre: the door closed as the emptied shelf simultaneously revolved away. Seconds later, it reappeared, displaying a replacement. Sometimes, for a brief moment, you could see a disembodied (ungloved) hand inserting the new item. I did not know the word 'surreal', but I recognized the experience.

Being taken to the automat was a treat of treats. It was busy and clattery; someone might share your table. You could watch people going for change, inserting their nickels, raising the doors, collecting their food. I never got tired of seeing or doing it. The vending walls were in opaque white glass, enamel, and chrome, and around the tops, stripped-down capital letters announced HOT DISHES and CAKES. What I liked best was creamed spinach followed by huckleberry pie. Just as with the ritual, I couldn't get enough of either. Horn & Hardart's cafeteria section didn't interest me, but its retail shop – 'Less Work for Mother' – sold *my* mother the lemon meringue pies which brought the automat home to our kitchen.

Manhattan, arraying its powers just across the river, abounded in further links of both chains and was where we went for clothes, ice skating, visits to friends, museums, the circus, one special toy store, the occasional genuine restaurant. From Clark Street or Borough Hall my mother and I took the subway, or my father drove the three of us up beneath the cables and arches of Brooklyn Bridge, that Kasimir view in the living room shuss-shussing closer over our left shoulders and then moving out of sight when Daddy turned the car north past City Hall, through Chinatown and a succession of intriguing, low-rising, workaday neighbourhoods, across broad, teeming thoroughfares and on into the canyons of Park Avenue or Madison or some numbered Avenue to wherever we were going in mid- or uptown Manhattan.

Shopping at Altman's or Lord & Taylor, we were constantly involved with the Empire State Building, the piers of its base modulating a whole block of 5th Avenue, its silvery tower pencilling inexorably skyward through cloud, mist, or the New York blue as it guarded and dominated everything. Further north on 5th were Saks' perfumes and blouses from Best's flanking St. Patrick's Cathedral opposite the soaring slabs, plazas, and gold leaf of Rockefeller Center where we ice skated in winter beneath snap-flapping flags and the statue of Prometheus, and went probably more than once for the whole Rockettes-and-Disney extravaganza at Radio City Music Hall.

A stone's thrown distant was the Museum of Modern Art, and up around 57th Street, Bonwit Teller smelled as good as Saks and had paper shopping bags strewn with bunches of violets. Then, approaching ever-hallowed FAO Schwarz, world's most sublime toy store, we entered the great stage called Grand Army Plaza. Here the stretched-tall château of the Plaza Hotel was Edwardian backdrop to a whirl of yellow cabs, spray from a fountain, tourists riding in horse-drawn carriages, an inviting corner of Central Park, and three peaked and mansarded high-roofed hotels where people we knew would sometimes stay.

Nowhere seemed far from a Horn & Hardart or Chock full o'Nuts. Some of the former were heavily characterized, outside or in, by the sort of details I noticed on façades and in lobbies of midtown skyscrapers; this would later be called Art Deco, and acclaimed. All Chock full o'Nuts looked the same. There was one, I think, on Madison Avenue in the mid 1950s, nearly opposite the New York Exchange for Woman's Work, familiarly known as the Woman's Exchange.

This philanthropic body, part of a multi-state federation, sells handicrafts and edibles consigned to them by needy suppliers working at home, and for 60 years occupied 541 Madison where the Exchange volunteers ran a ground-floor restaurant. Upstairs, my mother bought clothes for me, a sewing bag or some Christmas ornaments, take-away cookies, presents for friends and their infants – all of them exquisite. Occasionally, we would drop in for lunch, surrounded by a much more homogeneous crowd than the mixture of ages, sexes, and types who frequented Chock full o'Nuts or the automat.

The Woman's Exchange restaurant was a bastion of WASP womanhood, charm bracelets, and correct dressing, with demeanour and voices to match. The waitresses were Irish and the decoration anonymous. The food? Well, I remember only the most delicious coconut layer cake and strawberry shortcake. Surely we had something else?

My friend Daphne Astor, impeccably clad in hand-smocked, Exchange-bought dresses which felt 'scratchy on the inside', was taken there by her Belfast Catholic nanny on Nanny's day off, and always ate 'the same thing, more or less': shrimp cocktail in Russian dressing; meat loaf with carrots and peas or succotash (lima beans and corn), or fillet of sole on Friday; caramel custard or rice pudding. Not allowed gravy with her meat loaf, lest she soil the hand-smocking, Daphne wiped the corners of her mouth with the white linen napkins and nervously cleaved to her best behaviour. She remembers the food, in detail, as bland and not moreish. I, recalling few particulars, have a general impression of home-made quality, the sort of meals we might have had at the high-up apartment of one or the other of my parents' Park Avenue-dwelling friends where the advancing tread of an able black cook, always female, made the parquet floors tremble.

Eating out in the evening happened much less often, for me, than at lunch or the late afternoon. In Manhattan, there were rare dinnertime visits to small French restaurants like Pierre au Tunnel and Charles à la Pomme Soufflée. After the circus at Madison Square Garden, we might go – oh, joy! – to Hamburg Heaven in the East 50s: a long cramped space where you sat in bliss at the counter savouring thick, rare, condiment-spread hamburgers followed – if you dared – by a hunk of devil's food cake. But my favourite special-occasion 6 o'clock restaurant was Schrafft's.

Like Chock and the automat, there were lots of Schrafft's in New York City, and the ones I knew blend together in my mind. A large example on Fulton

Street in Brooklyn near the automat; another in the heart of 5th Avenue; a couple in the high 50s, east and west of 5th; a big one my father liked on West 51st near Rockefeller Center because the design was more masculine than what I recall as the typical Austrian-curtains-with-prints (or murals) decor.

The entrance to Schrafft's usually revolved through plate glass windows embellished with the well known, vaguely Art Nouveau lettering of a name which promised staple good eating to three or four generations of northeastern Americans. Just inside were display cases offering Schrafft's' famous candies, and then there was a counter, or soda fountain, surrounded by high, probably leather-upholstered, low-backed stools.

If you wanted a table, you waited behind a fat and impressive-looking dip of rope which the hostess unhooked before leading you to the chair or banquette from which you could order, depending on the hour, breakfast, luncheon, tea, dinner, or some of Schrafft's' celebrated desserts and ice-cream. In the 1950s and 1960s, my friend Libba Robinson frequented Schrafft's on Madison at 76th for cinnamon toast with her chums after school, then sometimes dined with her parents further east, at Schrafft's 79th Street, where Libba's parents would begin with martinis or Scotch, and then somebody or everyone would tuck into 'chicken pot pie or broiled lamb chops or filet mignon with peas. Tasty but not fancy. Like country club food.'

I loved the buzz of these roomy, animated, warmly lit, austerely comfortable restaurants. I liked the crisp hiss of saying 'Schrafft's'. I thought that the people around us, men and women, were doing things worth doing, and felt terribly grown up to be sitting among them.

I didn't eat any of the sober-sided lamb chop/pot pie offerings, nor the home-style ham loaf, chicken à la king, or tomato stuffed with tuna fish salad-type menu 'suggestions' alternatively available at my 'home', other homes, country clubs, and for all I don't remember, the Woman's Exchange. What I wanted, and was allowed to have, after the circus or ballet or whatever else preceded, was a double-decker club sandwich: the layers of mayonnaise-spread toast interleaved with bacon, tomato, and dark meat or breast of chicken, the finished sandwich sliced on the bias and rushed to our table.

Remembering Schrafft's always brings to mind an ace club sandwich, just as savouring those layers invariably recalls the grown-up sentiments, the proximity of my parents, the substance and spread of the pinnacled metropolis which I took vividly for granted while it sank its impression. No matter that New York has changed and all of these kitchens been swept away – along with the Good Humor Man and Miss Rheingold – to be replaced by others. The city, the food, and the time are deeply connected within me and in anyone else who remembers.

From Pharmacy to Fast Food: the Evolution of the Persian Kitchen

Margaret Shaida

Introduction

When I heard that 'Memory' was to be the theme of this year's Symposium, I decided to interview my mother-in-law. Her memories would cover the greater part of the twentieth century, and would reveal the many changes that had taken place in the methods, equipment and even ingredients used in the kitchens of Iran in the past hundred years.

Her recollections of the kitchen of her childhood were indeed fascinating. In the days just after the First World War, she had cooked on charcoal, outside in the courtyard. She had made flour, pounding the grain and sifting the flour. She had pounded rock sugar to make granulated sugar or chipped it into small cubes. She had dried pulses, as well as fruits, nuts and herbs, and preserved meat and vegetables. Everything had been a lot of work in those days, she recalled: simply lighting the charcoal fire and keeping up an even heat was a hot and tiring task, and cleaning the blackened pots afterwards was one of the dirtiest jobs.

Having been brought up in a modern society, I was shocked and amazed in equal measures, at the amount of time spent on the preparation of basic ingredients, those items that I have always bought in shops. But much of what my mother-in-law told me about preserving and storing foods did not surprise me so much – I was, after all, brought up in the war years in England, and was very used to thrift, jams and preserves! But, as we chatted on, I gradually became aware of something very different. It was quite clear that my mother-in-law had spent a large amount of her time in the preparation of medical cures and beauty aids.

This, of course, would certainly have been true of every society in the world in earlier times. The two cuisines that I know (British and Iranian) both catered for sickness, health and beauty. When I was young, my mother would prepare her special dishes to help ease minor ailments such as colds, sore throats and tummy upsets. She also had some home remedies for sore eyes and sties, earache, tooth ache, spots and so on.

But progress in modern medicine in the twentieth century and the easy availability of ready-prepared basic ingredients have considerably reduced the work of the domestic kitchen. We tend to forget that throughout history, the kitchen was traditionally used not only as a place for preparing food and meals, but also as the pharmacy and the beauty salon for the entire family.

In this paper, I look at this aspect of cooking for health and beauty in Iran and the evolution of the Iranian kitchen, from a place of preparation of basic foodstuffs, meals, remedies and beauty aids to a place of simply preparing dishes.

Prevention is better than…

From the earliest times, the preservation of health has always had the highest priority in Iran. In the days before modern medicine and miracle cures, it was perceived to be wiser to attempt to prevent ill health, rather than to try to cure it.

To this end, more than 2,600 years ago, Zoroaster developed the doctrine of *Sard-o Garm*. Some of you will recall the paper concerning this diet given at the Oxford Symposium by Jill Tilsley-Benham some years ago,[1] which looked in some detail at this common Iranian belief.

Briefly, Zoroaster believed that the balance of life depended on the struggle for supremacy between the god of good and the god of evil. This conflict was reflected in the good and evil within every human being, as revealed by good moods and bad, by sickness and health. Everyone aspires to good health and cheerfulness over disease and despair. Good health and godliness went hand in hand with good food. 'You are what you eat' is a very ancient belief in Iran.

All food was thus classified as either 'hot' or 'cold', definitions that related to the inherent properties of the foods rather than to the temperature. It was believed that the heat of temper or fever could be alleviated by the consumption of 'cold' foods, while the coldness of melancholy or sickness could be eased by eating 'hot' foods. Having defined the symptoms, it was simply a matter of prescribing the correct foods.

While these definitions may today seem quite arbitrary, it has since been shown that most 'hot' foods are generally rich in calories and carbohydrates, whilst 'cold' foods are rather light and insubstantial. In any case, every Iranian housewife will know which items of food are defined as 'hot' and 'cold' and she will ensure that her catering is properly balanced at all times, and particularly in times of sickness, and in the care of her children. Hot-tempered or hyperactive children are given 'cold' foods to calm them, while docile or dull-witted children will be given 'hot' foods to pep them up.

Until as recently as the early part of the twentieth century, modern doctors were hard to find in Iran. In any case, it appears that the local doctors (or *hakims*) also complied with the same doctrine of *Sard-o Garm*. According to Dr Wills, an English medical officer posted to Iran in the late nineteenth century, the Persian system of medicine was 'delightful in its simplicity'. In the 1870s, he wrote:

> All diseases are cold or hot. All remedies are hot or cold. A hot disease requires a cold remedy, and vice-versa.

He went on:

> If the Persian doctor is called in, and has any doubt as to the nature of the disease, he prescribes a hot remedy, let us say; if the patient gets better, he was right; if worse, then he prescribes a cold remedy, and he sticks to it.[2]

It is quite clear that the local doctor had little to add to the knowledge of an experienced housewife.

Old habits die hard and, even today, the modern doctor in Iran will first ask what the patient has eaten before he will make a diagnosis. And he will certainly recommend a sensible diet along with the medication. I repeat here a joke that relates to this practice:

> A man went to the doctor complaining of a weak stomach and a touch of indigestion. The doctor asked him what he had eaten that day. The man said, 'Nothing much. I just had three kilos of melons for breakfast and two kilos of bread with three bowls of *harriseh* and a kilo or two of pomegranates. And then I had several glasses of fruit syrup and two kilos of sweetmeats to finish. Otherwise I've had nothing.'
>
> The doctor wrote out a prescription, recommending the man take two kilos of plums, two kilos of damsons, three glasses of rosewater, two kilos of tamarinds and one kilo of *taranjebeen* (a medicinal seed). 'It's the only thing that'll work for a "weak" stomach like yours,' said the doctor.

Despite the introduction of modern medicine in Iran during the twentieth century, the housewife still conforms to the *Sard-o Garm* diet. In a way, she has little choice, because all the most traditional and tasty Persian dishes conform, rather naturally, to the *Sard-o Garm* definitions. For instance, the so-called 'national dish' of Iran – *chellow kabab* – complies with the 'hot' and 'cold' system. This dish consists of hot steamed white rice with butter and raw egg yolk, accompanied by succulent lamb kebab garnished with *sumac*. The 'cold' rice is balanced with the 'hot' eggs, while the 'cold' *sumac* balances the 'hot' lamb. *Sumac* is also considered an aid to digestion, no bad thing after such a splendid meal.

Another, perhaps more famous, dish of Iran is *fesenjan*, which consists of hot steamed rice accompanied by duck in a sauce of ground walnuts and pomegranates. The 'hot' duck and 'hot' walnuts balance the 'cold' rice and 'cold' pomegranates.

...the cure

However, despite the best attempts to prevent illness with a careful diet, the fact remains that people still fall ill. At such times, an Iranian housewife will again turn to the *Sard-o Garm* diet to cater for the invalid. For example, anyone suffering with a cold will be given mung bean soup (to name but one dish). This consists of mung beans, turnips, onions, cinnamon, ginger and pepper, which are all 'hot'.

A hundred years ago, in the absence of doctors and chemists, for minor ailments people were obliged to supply their own remedies, which were usually prepared in the kitchen. My mother-in-law recalled that, as a child, she learned to make many balms, potions and tisanes for the care of her future family. She would gather (or buy) the herbs and spices used in these preparations, for drying and storage, to alleviate the aches and pains of daily living.

As an indication of the work of the kitchen in Iran in the early years of the last century, I give below a tiny selection of some of the remedies my mother-in-law used to prepare.

> COLDS AND SORE THROATS could be eased with a warm drink made by boiling quince seeds until they become soft, then adding honey; or by boiling wheat starch until thick, with added honey. But a sore throat from talking too much or from lack of sleep could be eased with a comforting drink of a tisane of dried fleawort (*Cineraria*).
>
> SLEEPLESSNESS could be overcome by inhaling powdered saffron, a remedy that could also be used to stop NOSEBLEED. To ALLEVIATE DEPRESSION, bring between half a gram and two grams of saffron to the boil in a litre of water, then take the cooled drink three times a day (morning, lunchtime and early evening); it would also STIMULATE THE APPETITE. WOMEN IN LABOUR were assisted with this saffron drink to speed up contractions, but my mother-in-law stressed that only a little should be given (a mere quarter of a teaspoon) because too much could abort the baby.

A FEVER could be brought down with a brew of dried violet flower petals, while oil of violets was taken to induce sleep, and indeed was considered an efficacious remedy for many ailments.

EARACHE: placing the central core of an onion, boiled, strained and cooled, into the infected ear would draw out the poison. Onion cores could also be boiled up and sugar added, to make a LAXATIVE drink.

For FRAYED NERVES, a tranquillizer could be made of a tisane of dried borage leaves, flavoured with powdered dried lime. Apparently, the dried lime improved the colour and flavour of the drink.

And if you arrived HOT AND THIRSTY, a cooling drink of well-washed *Tokhme-sharbati* (seeds of London rocket [*Iodanthus pinnatifida*]) mixed with water, rosewater and ice would rapidly cool the body and prevent the possibility of heat stroke. It is also good for DIARRHOEA due to heat.

INDIGESTION AND FLATULENCE could be eased with mint tea and crystallized sugar; and for babies with wind/colic, a drink of crystallized sugar dissolved in boiled water is excellent.

Opium, of course, was used as a last resort, to ease SEVERE PAIN. Opium could be bought in tiny round bars, like small cigars. These were be cut up into small pieces and dissolved in water. The resulting thick liquid would then be smeared on the source of pain.

Beauty aids

The borderline between health and beauty was less clearly defined in earlier societies. Even today, skin care can be the responsibility of the doctor as well as the beautician.

ACNE AND PIMPLES could be cleared up with a mixture of yoghurt and henna. Yoghurt is even today used to cleanse the skin as well as to soothe sunburn, while the skin of cucumber was always rubbed over the face to keep the skin healthy. Parsley stalks were boiled up and the water used for washing the face.

HAIR DYES could be made with henna, coffee, or rhubarb. A blend of one cup of henna, one spoonful of ground coffee and an egg yolk mixed with a little water would be massaged into the hair. After half an hour, it was washed out. If you wanted to go blonde, then you would have to use henna mixed with camomile.

A SHAMPOO could be made of boiled soapwort (*Saponaria*) and dried orange peel.

Conclusion

Clearly, I have only touched upon the vast store of home cures and beauty aids from Persia. Interestingly, after I had talked to my mother-in-law, I came across a book written by a student of herbal medicine in Iran in 1998.[3] Reza Aqiqi, a researcher in herbal medicine in Hamadan, Iran, confirmed many of the above remedies. Clearly there is not room in this paper to expand further on the matter of herbal remedies in Iran, a subject worthy of study in its own right.

But it is clear that with the introduction of modern medicine in the twentieth century and also the mass production of remedies and beauty care, the work of the Iranian kitchen is now much reduced. Added to this the commercial production of flour, sugar, pulses and other basic ingredients, and the increasing availability of shop-made bread, pastries and cakes, it can be seen that today's kitchen is no longer used for the preparation of basic foods either. Now, it has become simply a place for preparing meals. In 50 years' time, with the increasing popularity of ready-made meals, shall we see the kitchen become just an area for heating up meals, snacks and drinks?

REFERENCES

[1] Tilsley-Benham, Jill (1986) 'Is that Hippocrates in the Kitchen?', in *Oxford Symposium on Food and Cookery, 1984 & 1985, Cookery: Science, Lore & Books*, ed. Jaine, Tom, London: Prospect Books, 102.

[2] Wills, C.J. (1891) *The Land of the Lion and the Sun*, London: Ward, Lock & Co, 34.

[3] Aqiqi, Reza (1998) *Traditional Medicine* (covering popular and well-known recipes in Iran), in Persian, Tehran: Students Publications.

Food pin-ups. Woodcut by Claire Henley, from Yasmé, *by Harold Goulding, 1988.*

A Slice of the Moon

Sue Shephard

In the years following the end of World War II, many men, particularly officers, who had spent much of the war as prisoners of war felt compelled to write about their experiences of imprisonment under the Germans or Japanese. Some were published; one or two became best-sellers. These books, letters and diaries conjure up vivid memories of life behind barbed wire, the humanity and the horrors of camp life and, in particular, an obsession with the quality and quantity of food – or rather, the lack of it. The authors' memories of food in camp life seem almost as intense as the very different memories and dreams of food that they experienced during their incarcerations. Harold Goulding, serving in a British Light Anti-Aircraft Regiment, was captured by the Japanese in Java, Indonesia, in 1942 and spent three and a half years in various camps, including the infamous Changi Gaol. He waited more than 37 years before writing his book *Yasmé*. But he found that his memories, like those of many other ex-POWs, were still as vivid as ever. Goulding described how he still remembered the food in prison and, as he was writing about it, he would start to salivate as he did in the camps:

> The Dutch prisoners made a little Scotch pancake type of thing in the Sumatran camps, it was very nice. At the time it was so marvellous and it is one of the very vivid memories I have. I remember what it looked like, and will always remember the glorious taste, though it looked like a sodden lump of dough. But memory is all, and beauty is in the eye of the beholder, and it certainly looked very wonderful to us!

The overriding concerns for every prisoner, indeed the most important features of POW life, were the problems of food and hunger. Food became so dominant that it was all they ever talked about. For every prisoner in camp, 'memories of food was absolutely all. Without food, nothing else matters at all very much.' As Goulding recalled, 'Somebody listening in may have heard us talking about politics or sport, or anything else, but I think really those were just symbols and we were really talking about food all the time.'

'For you the war is over,' was often said to new prisoners when they were first captured. In fact, they soon discovered that they faced a very different one – a war of waiting and fighting boredom, hunger, homesickness, deprivation and humiliation. They suffered guilt over capture, damaged self respect and a deep bitterness from the realization that they were 'in the bag' and 'out of the picture'. After his release, Major P.H. Newman,[1] a young surgeon who had been in a German camp, wrote an article for the *British Medical Journal* in 1944 describing how POWs had gradually to come to terms with life in camp, suffering 'acute mental stress' made worse by the lack of personal belongings and a vision of five or ten years as a POW, which 'combined to make him a truly wretched creature.' Captain Mustardé, another ex-POW, wrote a conference paper in 1944 describing how, after the initial shock of capture, the prisoner found himself forced into:

> ...an existence with some ten or twenty thousand others crammed within the confines of a barbed-wire cage, the complete impersonality of everything – the exposure to the elements, and to everyone's gaze, the lack of all order and organization, and the loss of friends, social status, clothing, and everything else one held as private and permanent – the sudden crushing weight of all these happenings produces a stupefaction and apathy which robs the mind temporarily of definite and deliberate thought.

Another doctor described it as the 'all-enveloping fog of shattered values.' All of which contributed to the classic condition known in camps as 'barbed-wire-itis'. One POW wrote home: 'No, I'm not lonely – there are 1,000 men in this camp and most of them live in my room.'

Major Newman then recalled how each prisoner slowly began to take an interest in his surroundings, his personal hygiene, his food and life around him:

> He grasps at the small things which give him pleasure and builds his life around them. He gathers together what little personal belongings remain to him. He searches the camp for a piece of wood and fixes it to the wall near the head of his bed. On this shelf he sets a photograph, a pipe, a favourite book and anything else which represents to him a home in miniature.

Mind and spirit began to recover from the shock of being made prisoner:

> One begins to get used to this way of life, the constant queuing for food, the lack of privacy and books, sitting on the bare ground, the sense of frustration that the sight of barbed-wire engenders.

One ex-POW, who wrote to the *BMJ* in response to Major Newman's article, remembered that:

> From my own observations there quickly develops, during a varying period of semi-starvation, the outstanding mental reaction of prisoner-

of-war life namely 'food consciousness'. He acquires a marked 'food complex', a manifestation of self-preservation which will persist throughout the POW days and probably for some time after his ultimate release. Food, usually favourite dishes, is the main topic of conversation and of thought; and, yea, even invades one's fitful slumbers... I well remember dreaming on two consecutive nights of omelettes and treacle pudding, alas, but a dream, and rude was the awakening. Either was as obtainable as a slice of the moon.

Russell Braddon was a 'cheeky young Australian gunner' who served more than three years in some of the most infamous Japanese POW camps. His bestselling book *The Naked Island* describes the appalling suffering of starving, disease-ravaged prisoners as well as their ingenuity, spirit and determination. All day they talked about hunger and at night they dreamed: 'Our nightly dreams about food – quaint fantasies of chocolate eclairs mixed with steak and served heavily garnished with egg,' were reminiscent of schoolboys' treats; lashings of 'our favourite things'; the kind of free, undisciplined, non-adult-regulated feasts of childhood. It doesn't seem so surprising that, in the camp at Pudu where Braddon was held, home was, for security reasons, known as 'Ice-Cream'.

In the concentration and work camps, where men were slave labour, food rations were only given to those who worked. Those who were sick as a result of lack of nutritious food got sicker. Those that did survive only did so because of the generosity of working prisoners who shared their rations. In 1962 Alexander Solzhenitsyn drew on memories of near starvation in a concentration camp in *One Day in the Life of Ivan Denisovich*:

> Shukhov had recalled the way they used to eat in his village: whole saucepans of potatoes, pots of porridge, and, in the early days, big chunks of meat. And milk enough to split their guts. That wasn't the way to eat, he learned in camp. You had to eat with all your mind on the food – like now, nibbling the bread bit by bit, working the crumbs up into a paste with your tongue and sucking it into your cheeks. And how good it tasted, that soggy black bread!

A Holocaust survivor had similar acute memories, Primo Levi wrote in his book, *If This Is A Man*, about his incarceration in a work camp called Buna near Auschwitz. The different camps housed over ten thousand prisoners: politicals and criminals, Jews, POWs, internees, Poles, Greeks, Hungarians, Italians, English, Dutch, French, Slovak – a Babel of different languages, cultures and foods. He remembered the distribution of bread, 'of bread-Brot-

Broid-chlebpain-lechem-keynér, of the holy grey slab which seems gigantic in your neighbour's hand and in your own hand so small as to make you cry,' and he recalled how the harsh realities of day gave way to pathetic dreams at night when prisoners were transported through memories of their different national foods to the kitchens of their homes far away:

> One can hear the sleepers breathing and snoring; some groan and speak. Many lick their lips and move their jaws. They are dreaming of eating; this is also a collective dream...you not only see the food, you feel it in your hands, distinct and concrete, you are aware of its rich and striking smell.

It was, as Levi wrote, a 'pitilous dream', the 'dream of Tantalus', offering memories of home; comforts and food of home mixed with nightmares too terrible to describe. Levi also recalled how prisoners, forced to do backbreaking work with broken, starving bodies, in their extreme hunger and suffering, hallucinated with food memories. Everything made them think of food – even the greedy jaws of a steam shovel gobbling mouthfuls of earth created fantasies of hunger and they thought of home, wherever it was:

> Sigi is seventeen years old and is hungrier than everybody... He had begun to speak of his home in Vienna and of his mother, but then he slipped on to the subject of food and now he talks endlessly about some marriage luncheon and remembers with genuine regret that he failed to finish his third plate of bean soup. And everyone tells him to keep quiet, but within ten minutes Béla is describing his Hungarian countryside and the fields of maize and a recipe to make meat-pies with corncobs and lard and spices and...and he is cursed, sworn at and a third one begins to describe...

Numerous books about prison camps in Germany describe memories of food which was both inadequate and monotonous. The quality and quantity of German rations was seriously poor early in the war and became more so with the passage of time. In 1941 the most common complaint was lack of variety in the German diet and this soon became part of a general dissatisfaction about the lack of food altogether. Lacking a decently balanced diet, without meat or fresh vegetables, POWs with bellies distended from hunger went down with stomach disorders, dysentery, boils and rashes. 'I'm literally starving,' wrote Sergeant Harcus in December 1942. POWs were given rations of thin, scum-covered turnip, cabbage or barley soup, rotten potatoes and coarse, stale, dry bread (in many camps the bread was stamped with the *year* it was baked), though some got ersatz coffee and even jam. Sergeant Kelly remembered being one of a group of POWs, in the summer of 1944, who gathered each day, about noon, outside the back window of the camp kitchens, when staff threw out rotten swedes or potatoes considered inedible, even in what passed for prison soup:

> We thereupon dived into this mess in the mud, stuffing what we could into our battledress and taking it back to our barracks to carefully pare off the edible pieces of swede or potato, which supplemented our rations. On one occasion the RSM in charge was walking past and in a loud voice said, 'Come on lads, remember you are British,' or words to that effect. From the melée of bodies a former Spitfire pilot emerged... His retort has always lived in my memory. He said, 'Sgt Major, I would have you know I am an officer and a gentleman,' and with that he returned to the fray.

Rations were collected by each hut's 'duty stooge' who was responsible for producing something like an edible meal for his mess mates. Prisoners hated this duty. Eating meals became a very private occasion. People would sit with their backs to each other or sit close to the wall of the hut or in their bed space so that no-one could see them eating. Eating ceased to be a social event; it was done totally privately without talking with other prisoners.

Prisoners adopted many kinds of survival techniques. With the growing shortage of fuel in POW camps, as Germany's position worsened, prisoners were forced to devise new means of cooking. Various contraptions were put together from old Red Cross 'Klim' tins (they contained powdered milk, hence the name) and wired directly into the camp's electricity system. Highly efficient 'blowers' were also constructed which, by inducing air through several metal chambers, driven by a hand-cranked wheel and utilizing only small scraps of materials, could boil a brew of tea in a few minutes. At night water could be heated indoors by the light of home-made lamps, using German margarine for oil and Red Cross string as a wick. But a general lack of food sometimes made even these primitive arrangements useless. 'Bowls up' was kriegie slang for food on the horizon though, as one POW put it, 'grub up' was a fallacy! Sergeant Bruce remembered how he could never quite stomach the 'stinking, fishy slime which passed for German regulation-issue cheese.' Some weird food concoctions were created over hut stoves from parcel rations – especially 'glop', a mixture of practically anything which could be turned into semi-solid form. 'Connie' (condensed milk) and 'Nutty' (bars of chocolate) were both remembered long after with 'drooling affection'.

But in the Japanese POW camps things were far worse. During the war, little was known about the very different circumstances of more than 130,000 prisoners and internees in Japanese camps. The Japanese did not sign the Geneva Convention, nor did they allow Red Cross delegates to visit camps. Of the few Red Cross parcels that got through, the Japanese stole up to a third of the food (except the cheese, which they thought was disgusting, smelly, white man's food). They held back letters from relatives, and allowed only 25-word cards at monthly intervals. What was not known then was how very much worse the 'food complex', which persisted throughout the POW days and after, was for prisoners in the Far East. (Even less was known about internees in concentration and work camps.)

J.E. Nardini, an American ex-POW medic, writing in the *American Journal of Psychiatry* in 1952, described how US military prisoners, captured by the Japanese between April and May 1942 in the Philippine Islands, suffered:

> ...the feeling of being deserted and abandoned by one's own people; the severe deprivation of food, warmth, clothes, living comforts, and sense of respectability; the constant intimidation and physical beatings from the captors; loss of self-respect and the respect for others; the day-to-day uncertainty of livelihood and the vague indeterminable unknown future date of deliverance.

Hungry, threatened, sick men found it difficult to think or plan beyond the next bowl of rice. Medical care and medicines were almost non-existent and living conditions were uniformly miserable. Young men living and working in an uncaring, hostile environment, were ill-prepared both physically and psychologically for incarceration in the Far East and many thousands died. David Piper, a POW in Formosa, wrote that it was the 'urgency of hunger' that was:

> ...the essential governor of survival, its insistent concentration surely the reason why so few prisoners went mad...only when it faded could despair overwhelm fatally; known in all Far Eastern prison camps was that stage in a prisoner's illness when hunger failed; then the man would turn his face to the wall, and simply surrender life and die – not necessarily for the pathological reasons, but because he had no longer any incentive to live.

While dreams and memories of food served to distance men from the cruel reality of their daily lives, they also helped to ease the last days of the dying; Braddon remembers one such case: 'Young Norm' was nineteen years old and dying of tuberculosis. As he drifted in and out of a coma, he dreamed his dreams:

> When he woke up the orderlies asked him where he'd been; he always replied 'Home'. He dreamt of food. Everyone in the camp tried to steal

some delicacies for him. Every day men would ask 'How's young Norm today?' and 'What's he done at home lately?'

Norm's dreams of home and home cooking always seemed better than theirs. He died in December, after dreaming of a Christmas party at home, a family feast with all the trimmings, and then drifted off into his last and final 'after-Christmas sleep'.

Harold Goulding never forgot how the Japanese showed cruel contempt for their prisoners. Their religion and culture made them abhor the whole concept of prisoners of war. Russell Braddon recalled the violent 'transition to gaol life' when each man was stripped of everything, including eating utensils.

> We ate out of the lids of gaol bed-pans, old hub-caps, battered kidney dishes. We ate with our fingers and bits of wood, and what we ate was not less violent a transition than anything else – rice, with no salt or flavouring or vegetable matter of any kind, and cooked as only Army cooks who do not know the habits of rice can cook it. We consumed a couple of pints of this glue a day.'

Some men could not tolerate rice and, without exception, none of them survived. Rice became a powerful weapon:

> The Japanese love their rice. To them rice was life itself; they believed it controlled history. There were guards who told the prisoners that the Japanese were winning the war by rice; the emperor's armies had captured all the rice on earth, and without rice the rest of the world would starve. There is no more rice in London!

But the POWs were meat-and-potatoes men; to them rice was miserable Asiatic 'glop'. Prison rice was the worst kind: dirty, maggot and weevil infested. Sometimes they were fed seaweed, strange roots, pastes and gelatinous substances made out of soybean, which they called 'snotty gobbles' and 'elephant semen'. Some were given a virulent green weed, like very tough spinach, called *kan-kong*: 'a gutter weed that grew in horrible places', but, as it was full of protein and vitamin C, the men forced themselves to eat it. They ate frogs and passing cats, but never rats. Fish heads sometimes appeared creating, for Goulding, memories of, 'the most beautiful tasting and filling food we ever received. We could even suck the eye for hours on end. It was a true luxury to have the head.'

Russell Braddon was determined that, in order to survive, he would eat everything he could lay his hands on, 'thus cats, dogs, frogs, snakes, bad fish, bad meat, blown tinned-food, snails, grubs, fungus, crude vegetable oil, green leaves from almost everything that grew, roots and rubber nuts all went the same remorseless route.' Braddon wrote a footnote in his book:

> For the information of the shrinking reader, snake tastes like gritty chicken mixed with fish: dog tastes like rather coarse beef: cat like rabbit, only better; and snails (Changi-style) like something cut off a tyre by Messrs Dunlop.

Some sources of food, however, were frowned on. A prisoner 'who trapped sparrows with a Heath-Robinson-like contraption of bricks, strings and grains of rice was flatly forbidden to convert the feathery bones into a soup.' In both Japanese and German camps the divisions between officers and men sometimes interfered with their efforts to feed themselves. In one camp, the men were forbidden to catch snails for eating because they were meant to feed the chickens in the officers' poultry farm. In another, a 'mad Englishman' spent days stalking a frilly-necked lizard. He eventually captured it and was just about to pop it into the pot when he received an urgent order from a senior officer: 'Officers will not eat lizards,' it said. But, in the main, prisoners of war in the Far East ate anything that was not actually poisonous. 'It was a sign of the times that man's main preoccupations in those days were the inhalation into his lungs of smoke, the filling of his stomach and the evacuation of his bowels;' extreme constipation or diarrhoea being the only conditions the bowels knew.

Red Cross parcels sent to the majority of POW camps in Europe prevented men from suffering severe malnourishment. Parcels containing clothes and food were sent via Switzerland to all prisoners of war from their families and friends. Prisoners in Germany received parcels and personal letters fairly frequently. Parcel days were special:

> There was always something extra for lunch on parcel day. An extra biscuit each, spread with liver paste, a half a quarter pound slab of chocolate.

Red Cross parcels for British POWs included tins of dried milk, margarine and sardines, boxes of prunes and cheese, malted milk, tins of condensed milk, bully beef and fruit, dried fruit, chocolate and coffee, with Benger's food, Horlicks and Bemax wheat germ for the hospitals. Later came a 'new kind of canned meat called Spam that the prisoners had never seen before, wonderfully fatty.' Eric Williams remembers, in his book *The Wooden Horse*, that Red Cross parcels could almost make life civilized:

> Peter sat at the table waiting for John to finish his breakfast.
>   'Parcels tomorrow.'

'Good show,' John spoke through a mouthful of bread-and-jam.

'We can have the last tin of salmon for dinner. What about rissoles?'

'No,' Peter said, 'you have to fry those. Better make a shepherd's pie and stick it in the oven.'

'Don't burn it this time,' Bennett said. 'If you'd only do it the way I told you. You want to cover the tip with greased paper.'

Peter ignored him. 'If we can get any raisins we'll swap them for biscuits. Then we can make a cake tomorrow.'

'We'll bake it in the afternoon,' John agreed. 'Then if it turns out to be a pudding we can have it for dinner.'

'And if it turns out to be porridge we'll have it for breakfast.' Bennett said.

As soon as they received their food parcels, some men tore off the wrappings and wolfed down all the contents. This habit of 'bashing' parcels convinced Warrant Officer Deans and the Medical Officer at Stalag Luft III of the need to pool them and this was started in a number of camps. The keen, almost pathetic anticipation with which the prisoner awaited the life-saving Red Cross food parcel vied with his eagerness to receive mail from home. Letters, when they did arrive, might be short and late but said everything. Russell Braddon received a sixteen-months-old, Japanese regulation 25-word card from his sister through the Red Cross:

'Dear Russ, Mum's puddings are still as lumpy as ever. Oodles of love from us all. Pat.' If twenty-five words was all the Japanese would allow our folk to write then that letter told me all I wanted to know – that the family did not accept that I was 'killed', as posted: that the old household jokes about my mother's rather abandoned cooking still flourished: that home was still home.

Parcels sent from home were particularly hard, bringing memories of family and loved ones. The little touches of home: 'the hand-knitted pullover, the familiar English tooth-paste and the razor blades fastened together with an elastic band'; the familiar home-made cakes and biscuits, chocolate and sweets, a jar of Marmite or anchovy paste, special, tasty little favourites that were heart- and gut-wrenchingly painful triggers to men's memories:

Had two biscuits and cheese and tea at 3pm today. Miraculous...Maybe we'll get out of here sometime and be able to say 'Biscuits and cheese? No, not just now thank you.'

Many POWs in Japanese camps heard nothing from home for months, even years. Time almost ceased to have any significance. The seasons came and went. Birthdays and Christmas were the only events worth trying to remember. Those 'little anniversary memorials of the old days,' wrote Solzhenitsyn, 'reviving family customs and the memory of departed friends and remind us that we once lived well and what's more were hospitable to others.' In one Japanese camp David Piper remembers celebrating his birthday with his friend:

> Jack's version of cottage pie – sweet potatoes (smuggled into camp) mixed with a tin of Red Cross tomatoes, and a tin of bully from last year's Red Cross. Baked surreptitiously at the sterilization boiler. Heaven.

In return, Piper created for Jack's birthday:

> Hash supreme – sweet potatoes, chillies, can tomatoes, onions and the last tin of bully. And a tin of steak pudding. And Honey (First in four years!) in the tea.

At Christmas time, however, it was considered more important to get blind drunk with specially prepared, home-brewed hooch: 'Christmas was an opportunity to make a deadly brew, to eat some extra food, three slices of bread for breakfast instead of two.' Jack Nopp's apricot brandy, for example, 'tasted of petrol mixed with creosote and hair oil. Jack took one gulp and said "Lovely stuff,"' while all around, 'in the soft snow-lit darkness, people were systematically sicking up the food which they had saved for so long.'

Gradually prisoners began to pull themselves together and build some sort of life, and to find different ways to fill their days and avoid the mind-dumbing boredom and depression of camp life. As they slowly came to terms with the present they also started to create their own memories and fantasies with which to get in touch with their past. Most men regressed to a childish state of dependency, indulging in childish games and fantasies and a longing for home and mum's cooking. They lived just to taste again, 'a cool beer, hot dogs, a steak dinner, home cooking, a new car, a clean bed with a mattress, the home town, the mountains, or just plain freedom.' Sometimes homesickness and nostalgia for home became overpowering. The sight of a flower or a tree rustling in the breeze beyond the perimeter fence, a bird singing, the smell of chocolate or even a newly opened tin of bully beef could set them off. 'At home they are having breakfast. I wish I had their sausages; a bellyful.' For many prisoners, thinking about food became much more about a longing for home than a battle for survival. Even the most active and positive minded indulged in daydreaming and fantasizing.

They dreamed and remembered all kinds of sensory things from their past: the smell of damp leaves, the splash of bodies leaping into a pool, the smell of new mown hay, snatches of music, a sister's laugh and a mother's warm, enveloping hug, while all of them talked, dreamed and remembered food: good, simple, home-cooked food; the warm, homely smell of the kitchen: fresh roast coffee, frying bacon, newly baked bread; mother or the cook, roasting meat with thick gravy and generous dumplings or Yorkshire puddings; eating steaming roly-poly puddings, pouring on thick, golden-yellow custard, dribbling syrup into rice pudding; plates piled with bread and golden-yellow butter, and mugs of warm, milky, sweet tea. Few tried to recall the elegant meals, in restaurants, of scallops and oyster, Dover soles, pheasant or Chateaubriand steaks. That wasn't the food they wanted to remember; it was home food of childhood which represented unconditional love, without cares or responsibilities.

Cleverness, a sense of humour and a strong fantasy life were certainly helpful attributes while, for others, an obsessive interest in escape and escape plans kept them occupied. For many of the middle class youths, who were now officers in the army and RAF, it was rather like school days again: playing japes, planning extravagant escapades and arrogant piss-taking of the staff – only now they were German guards or, much worse, Japanese. Robert Kee, a young bomber pilot shot down and captured, wrote in *A Crowd is Not Company* that, 'Commercial travellers began to paint, stockbrokers to act and footballers to write poetry.'

The criminally inclined set up lucrative black markets in cigarettes and food. A few took pleasure in cooking up imaginative and ingenious dishes with food from Red Cross parcels and produce from the camp gardens: 'small patches of cultivated ground fertilized by primitive means – each bearing its sparse crop of lettuces, of tomato plants.' Many played cards or chess with home-made pieces, took up wood carving or joined in impromptu study courses learning languages:

> For my own part I was most fortunate, as I was given the job of messing officer and spent my time evolving appetizing dishes from a handful of rice and a small roll per man per day!

Food was often stolen wherever possible, but never from other POWs. Russell Braddon recalls a blissful day in a work party, clearing out the Japanese barracks and finding a store of Japanese Army biscuits: 'little round biscuits like marbles and hard as iron;' they stole and munched biscuits all day. The theft was discovered next day when a party of Dutch native troops had replaced them and were terribly beaten for the Aussies' crimes. In one camp a prisoner remembered how he created menus for the restaurant he planned to open when he returned home, and one New Zealander typically recalled how, 'I used to lie on my bed all day thinking about every bloody meal I'd ever had in my life. At the end of each day my pillow was so soaked in saliva that I had to wring it out on the floor.'

According to Eric Williams, a few even created a complete escapist fantasy life for themselves: 'Mark usually took more interest in his garden than in the war. Even in winter when the ground was hard under snow, he would spend much of his time looking at the onions he had stored in a box under his bed or planning where to put his tomato plants next year.' While David became a dedicated farmer, at least in his mind and on paper: 'At the right time of year he would sow his crops and in due course he would harvest them. If it rained on the day when he had decided to reap he would walk about with a face of doom...' There was one memorable occasion when:

> ...the lower meadows were flooding and David drove a flock of sheep to the safety of the hillside above the farm. The guards had been alarmed when the whole hut turned out to help him drive the sheep across the compound. They had reached for their tommy-guns when they saw the throng of hissing, whistling, shouting prisoners driving nothing towards the fence. But the upper meadow was inside the wire, and no shots were fired.

Officers and men had very different memories of home. Many officers recalled childhood memories of public school, servants in the home and even the culinary delights of foreign travel. Bernard Fergusson was not a POW, but the isolation and suffering he and his men experienced whilst on the Wingate expedition, deep into Japanese-occupied Burma, in 1943 were similar to those of many fighting men serving abroad in difficult and remote parts, where hunger and unfamiliar food left them with longing for some decent 'chow'. Lack of food gave them all a terrible craving for sugar:

> Everyone had hallucinations about sugar, differing only according to their background. Mine were based on memories, fifteen years old, of a patisserie in Tours, where I had spent two summer holidays from Eton, learning French in a 'family'. Every afternoon, when I was feeling rich enough, I used to bicycle down to Massie's, on the right-hand side of the Rue Nationale, and have chocolate to drink, and cakes to eat. One would equip oneself with a plate and a curious implement, like a pair of scissors, and wander along the glass shelves, helping oneself to whichever cakes took one's fancy.

The memory of one particular cake came to haunt him in the sweating, insect-infested, dangerous and barely penetrable jungle: 'a concoction of coffee cream, coated with chocolate, and so rich that a couple of them made one unwilling, and three would have made one unable, to bicycle home again.'

Many POWs experienced fears of forgetting their loved ones: 'we found it increasingly difficult to conjure up a picture of them as we had known them...they seemed more remote and outside our world than ever.' Sex ceased to be important in the camps, 'where even the desire to contemplate desire could not be evoked.' 'Belly empty think of food, belly full think of women,' summarized one soldier. 'Two years without beer or women or good food,' noted Gunnar Robinson; when full, which was not very often, he certainly missed 'the feel of a few silk-clad legs.' But dreams of a sexual nature were not, recalled the Reverend Naylor, any more common than in normal times: 'The most persistent dreams concerned lashings of food.' Food became a powerful substitute for sex: more interesting than sex and easier to create fantasies around. Goulding treasured his copy of Richard Llewellyn's *How Green Was My Valley* which he came to think of as the most erotic book he had ever read. It was about a village in Wales:

> As I remember it now, nearly every chapter seemed to have a very long, detailed description of a meal. I read this and I drooled; I could feel the saliva coming down in my mouth as I read it and I know my eyes sort of screwed up in an almost sexual type of enjoyment. But the two things were very similar, and I know, that in a prison camp hunger was much more powerful than the sex drive.

Goulding realized he had a gold mine with the book and hired it out, for others to read the 'dirty passages', for cigarettes. The look on their faces was as sensual an experience as sex:

> Their eyes would light up; they would get a fairly glazed intense look, and it was easy to see them dribbling and their tongues licking their lips, and in some cases, even their swallowing, as they read about somebody eating an English hot meal.

Goulding also described how the ubiquitous pin-ups of film stars or half naked girls on the walls and bunks were unknown, even photos of wives and sweethearts were kept folded up and concealed in pockets. Pin-ups certainly did, however, exist, but they were of food. American magazines, found in the camps, were cut up and colour pictures of food, 'lovely cakes, cream cakes, or succulent brown roast chicken,' were cut out and pinned up. Some prisoners would go round asking for recipes from the magazines which they would write in their little notebooks like 'dirty books'. People used to lie down on their own and read them, often out loud, and 'really get some sort of satisfaction, very sensual in nature, just by reading food out loud.'

Some POWs' memories of food were quite bizarre and crazier than any schoolboy's midnight feast. Russell Braddon was on a work party, in the docks of Singapore's Kepple Harbour, which was sent into a boat with a mixed cargo:

> For eight riotous hours, as we worked under the justifiably suspicious eyes of our guards, we ate chocolates and cough jubes, drank bay rhum, cough mixture, cod-liver oil and essence of vanilla – in equal and indiscriminate quantities: applied hair tonic to the hair, face cream to the face and iodex to almost everything: mixed handsful of sugar with handsful of herrings in tomato sauce and devoured the resulting mess...it couldn't last, of course, but by the time we were caught we had all of us stored vast quantities of patent medicines, concentrated foods and culinary flavourings where they could never be retrieved. Though severely thrashed, we were happy.

But not all post-war writers had such strong post-war memories of hunger. David Piper, a POW in Formosa, claimed in 1965 that he could no longer feel, or even remember, the state of being hungry, of living as hunger. Nevertheless, he wrote that, 'I still have my rice bowl, three and a half inches across, two and a half inches high; at bad times this, filled with boiled rice three times a day, was our total food ration. I use it as an ashtray.' What he most clearly remembered, however, was the suffering of the men around him and the many deaths while imprisoned on the island of Formosa for three years. Perhaps his most ironic memory was hearing American B-29s flying very low over the camp just after the Japanese had announced that the war was over. They were parachuting huge, shining metal cylinders packed with food. As he sat in his hut among starving fellow prisoners, bloated with oedema from beriberi, Piper heard loud crashing sounds. An orderly came into the hut and told them him that the parachutes on two of the food canisters had failed to open:

> 'Went thundering slap through the roof of a hut. Burst like a bloody bomb. Two men copped it, and several hurt...'
>
> The hulk on the next bed had closed his eyes and was resting.
>
> 'Silly,' he said without opening his eyes. 'Getting killed. Three and a half years you manage not to die, then get knocked off by a bloody great can of condensed milk dropped on you in loving kindness.'
>
> He breathed heavily, and the jelly of his stomach wobbled. 'Funny, really,' he said.

When cooking and distribution of starvation rations reduced men to such a desperate state, what they ate ceased to be food, but merely fuel: a matter of life and death in a grain of rice, a gob of fat or half a rotten potato. If food existed in these men's lives, it could only be in their fantasies, in their memories of plentiful, good, wholesome, delicious-looking, saliva-inducing aromas that were inextricably bound up in their memories of the world they left behind, of which they had been deprived and, most importantly, of Mother and of home.

ACKNOWLEDGEMENT

I would like to thank to my husband Ben Shephard for his help. His book *War Of Nerves*, on the history of military psychiatry, will be published in October 2000.

BIBLIOGRAPHY

Braddon, Russell (1951) *The Naked Island*, Penguin.
Daws, Gavan (1995) *Prisoners of the Japanese. POWs of World War II In the Pacific*, Robson Books.
Fergusson, Bernard (1962) *Beyond The Chindwin*, Collins.
Goulding, Harold (1988) *Yasmé*, People's Publications.
Kee, Robert *A Crowd is Not Company*.
Levi, Primo (1979) *If This Is A Man*, Penguin.
Newby, Eric (1971) *Love and War In the Apennines*, Hodder.
Piper, David (1998) *I am Well, Who Are You? Writings of a Japanese Prisoner of War*, Anne Piper.
Rolf, David (1958) *Prisoners of the Reich: Germany's Captives, 1939–1945*, Leo Cooper.
Solzhenitsyn, Alexander (1970) *One Day in the Life of Ivan Denisovich*, Sphere.
van der Post, Laurens (1966) *The Seed and the Sower*, Penguin.
Williams, Eric (1980) *The Wooden Horse*, Fontana.

Articles and Conference Papers
Cochrane, A.L. 'Notes on the Psychology of Prisoners of War', in *BMJ*, February 1946.
Dunlop, E.E. 'Medical Experiences In Japanese Captivity', in *BMJ*, October 1946.
Dearlove, A.R. 'Enforced Leisure – A study of the Activities of Officer Prisoners of War', in *BMJ*, March 1945.
Markowitz, Captain J. 'The RAMC in Thailand POW Camps', in *Journal of the Royal Army Medical Corps*, April 1946.
Mustarde, Captain, 'Adjustment and Mal-Adjustment within the Camp', in 'Minutes of a Conference of Military Psychiatrists', in *York Medical Society*, October 1944, Contemporary Medical Archives Centre, Wellcome Institute.
Nardini, J.E. 'Survival Factors in American Prisoners of War of the Japanese', in *American Journal of Psychiatry*, October 1952.
Newman, P.H. 'The Prisoner of War Mentality – Its effect After Repatriation', in *BMJ*, January 1944.
Pether, G.C. 'The Returned Prisoner-of-War', in *The Lancet*, May 1945.
Vaughan-Eley, A.W. 'Letter', in *BMJ*, 18 Mar 1944.

REFERENCES

[1] In 1943 there was an exchange between Germany and Britain of prisoners who had medical training.

The Bialy Eaters: the Story of a Bread and a Lost World

Mimi Sheraton

Just to be clear from the start, my subject is an onion-topped, yeast bread roll that is eaten as an alternative to the bagel, and that is known as a bialy in New York City and elsewhere in the United States, although it is a rarity in much of the rest of the country. The traditional name for this roll is the Bialystoker kuchen, honouring its place of origin, the city of Bialystok in northeast Poland. For those unfortunates who do not know the bialy, let me explain that the identifying feature of this flat, round roll is the depressed centre well, that is crisp, and a soft outer rim. That well differentiates the bialy from a larger, rounder, level-top forerunner known as the pletzel, made of the same dough (a mix of high-gluten flour, yeast, salt and water), and by the same bakers.

As I did research, during the past seven and a half years, for a small book about this bread and the people who remember it, I was confronted by doubters who insisted that the bialy was unknown in Bialystok and that it is a New York invention. I think the recollections of the many Bialystok emigrés I interviewed all over the world provide ample evidence of the roll's existence in Bialystok, where it was not known as a bialy, but rather as a Bialystoker kuchen. Besides the name, the big, and so far inexplicable, difference between the original Bialystoker kuchen and its American descendant is that the former always was liberally topped with poppy seeds, although it seems never to have been in the States.

There is visual proof of the bialy's existence in the documentary film *Jewish Life in Bialystok*, produced in 1939 and distributed by the National Center for Jewish Film. It clearly shows laughing children eating the kuchen, that look almost exactly like today's bialys, although a bit larger and with a wider well.

Furthermore, no less an authority than the Yiddishist, Leo Rosten, in his dictionary *The Joys of Yiddish*, describes the bialy's shape as being like a wading pool and adds, 'The name is taken from the bakers of Bialystok, where this exquisite product was presumably perfected.' Then, his illustrative story:

> 'Forty cents a dozen for bialies?' protested Mrs. Becker. 'The baker across the street is asking only twenty!'
> 'So buy them across the street.'

'Today, he happens to be sold out.'
'When I'm out of bialies, I charge only twenty cents a dozen, too.'

My guess is that the Bialystoker kuchen originated by accident as a variation on the pletzel. I firmly believe that one day a round of unbaked pletzel fell onto a bakery floor and was stepped on with the heel of a shoe. Not wanting to waste anything, the frugal baker topped it with onions and poppy seeds, baked it, tasted it, and proclaimed a *eureka* moment in bread history.

With that background, let me read you a brief memoir told to me by Samuel Pisar, a renowned international lawyer and diplomatic advisor who is a Holocaust survivor and the author of an autobiography, *Of Blood and Hope*.

> When I was an adolescent in Auschwitz lying on the hard shelf that was my bed and hallucinating from hunger, I would often try to recall the shape and savory aroma of the kuchen we used to eat at home in Bialystok. By then I had lost all of my family and schoolfriends. Years later, when I was in New York, I would often watch those street-corner wagons that sell coffee and bread in the morning. I marveled at the whites, blacks, Asians, and Latinos as they munched on their bialys. I felt as though I was from another planet. To each of them, it was simply a tasty snack. How could they know they were partaking of something sacred – a bread that evoked bittersweet memories of a cultured and tragic corner of eastern Poland? A bread that, in my psyche, summons up even today the mystical dream world of Marc Chagall and Isaac Bashevis Singer.

Pisar continues:

> Bialys or kuchen were invented in Bialystok by Jewish bakers and were a staple of our diet. They always had onions and poppy seeds and very crisp centers and it was very important to hear the crackle and feel the snap when you broke one... I can feel and smell them and I search for them with a passion everywhere I go. It's not the taste so much as the symbol. It reminds me of coming home safely from school in the late afternoons of Bialystok's long, dark season. I can still hear the women vendors carrying hot kuchen in big straw baskets as they went through the streets yelling at the top of their lungs, 'Kuchen, kuchen, heisse kuchen...' They had to be heisse, not cold. My grandmother would spread butter or cream cheese on the back of a kuchen without cutting it open, and I would munch it as I went out to play with friends. It was very important not to lose a single poppy seed. Every single one counted.

Here are a few more excerpts from the recollections I gathered. The first two are of early bialy baking days in New York that began roughly in 1920.

This is from Roy Mersky, a scholar at the University of Texas Law School and the son of one of the original partners in Kossar's Bialystoker Kuchen Bakery in New York, where the world's best bialys are still baked.

> I recall my father talking about delivering bialys with a horse and wagon before the 1930s in Manhattan. He always had a partner. One man handled the baking and the other, my father, was responsible for the deliveries. As a young boy in high school, I would go down to the Lower East Side on Sundays and help him deliver the bialys to restaurants and retail stores. I would sit in the truck backwards on a box, where the passenger seat would have been and the strong onion aroma was so pervasive that it frequently nauseated me, especially since I rode backwards.
>
> There were three people on the truck: one drove, one counted, and the third person stood on the running board, jumping off and dropping off the hot bialys. I was the counter. The bialys actually were hot, just out of the oven. They were in big wicker laundry baskets with two handles and I would put them into bags – two dozen, three dozen, or a dozen-and-a-half and hand them to the person riding the running board.

Then, Slim Schwartzberg, known as the fastest 'baller' in the business; this respondent who, in his heyday, could shape 90 dozen balls of yeast dough in an hour, once worked at Kossar's and, with his sons, went on to establish a chain of bagel and bialy bakeries in Florida and on Long Island:

> I began working in a bialy bakery – the one that became Mersky & Kossar – in 1929 when I was eleven. I wanted a warm place to sleep because our apartment was cold, even though we had big eiderdown coverlets that my parents brought with them from Lublin. The bosses at the bakery said that if I carried in the coal and wood for the ovens, I could sleep on top of the flour sacks where the ovens were always hot. I loved sleeping there with the smell of burning wood and yeast.
>
> I made extra money on Fridays, because the bakery closed at 7 a.m. and didn't open until Saturday at 5:30 p.m. I kept the ovens warm and on Friday Orthodox women in the neighborhood who were not allowed to cook over *shabbes* would bring their pots of cholent to be baked in the ovens and I charged them 25 cents each. I could do that because I was not so religious as they were.

Leo Melamed, a brilliant financier, who is chairman emeritus of the Chicago Mercantile Exchange and the founder of the International Money Market, left Bialystok when he was seven with this memory:

> What I remember most of the kuchen are feet. I would go to the kuchen bakeries with my Aunt Bobble and because I was so small, I could only see people's feet. But once in a while my aunt would lift me up so I could watch the hot kuchen coming out of the oven on big wooden paddles. No matter what else you had to eat, you could always use a kuchen.

A very sweet respondent, Hannah Sielecka, a Holocaust survivor who lived in Queens, told me the following:

> You know, I am really from Bialystok. Many people say they are, but are not. We used to buy kuchen on Urovetska Street. I liked the crisp center and my brother liked the soft rim, so we would break the kuchen and share. We used to have our big meal at two in the afternoon and we ate kuchen with everything because they are *pareve* [neutral foods that laws of *kashrut* permit with either meat or dairy products]. I have tried them here many times, but they never taste right.

Ben Halpern, another Bialystoker who made his life in Michigan and who was 102 when I last interviewed him, shortly before his death, said:

> Kuchen were our main meat, morning, noon and night. We loved to have them with smoked fish for *vechere* [Polish for evening or dinner]. When I went every day to *cheder* [Hebrew school], my mother always gave me a buttered kuchen to eat on the way. I held it in my hand, of course, and one day a street walker came along and she begged for money which I did not have to give her. So she grabbed my kuchen and ran away eating it. I still remember how hungry I was in school that day. Bialys in Detroit don't taste like the real ones so I'm still hungry.

Among others in Israel, I interviewed Yerachmiel Giladi, who wrote to me after reading about my search in the *Bialystoker Shtimme*, a magazine published by the Bialystoker Center in New York and sent to emigrés all over the world. Not only a champion of bialys, he was also a staunch speaker of Esperanto, the one-world language, that was created in Bialystok by an opthalmologist, Dr. Ludwig Zahmenhof. In his first letter he wrote:

> I don't know how the kuchen look or taste in New York, but as one who ate them every day in Bialystok, I cannot forget how they tasted

there even though I left in 1929. It was not for nothing that the Yidden [Jews] from the city were called Bialystoker kuchen fressers [prodigious eaters].

When I visited him with some bialys especially baked for me by a Yemenite baker in Gedera, Israel (a whole, wild story in itself), Mr. Giladi carefully put the bialys in his freezer, calling them *kukoi* in Esperanto: 'The scent reminds me of early morning in the small store where my mother sold kuchen to supplement my father's income. We ate the kuchen with butter that we spread in the center well and around the soft edges and we did not cut it,' he said.

As I left, Yerachmiel Giladi gave me the primer, *A Practical Course in Esperanto* by Dr Ferenc Szilágyi, assuring me it was an easy language to learn. As an example, he said, '*Dankon pro la kukoy*,' thanking me for the kuchen. Too bad I was unable to bid him farewell with '*Adiau. Gis revido*,' 'Good-bye, until we meet again.'

In Argentina I met with Velvl Matinsky, an 83-year-old who had been a bialy baker in Bialystok before World War II, during which he was a partisan, hiding in the woods around his native city.

Before the Germans arrived in Bialystok he baked kuchen in his family's bakery, getting up at 3:00 a.m. so that the first batch would come out of the oven around 5:00 or 5:30, when customers began to line up to buy kuchen for seven groschen. He recalled that women who sold kuchen in baskets in the street bought them for five and a half groschen and also sold them for seven. 'We made them with flour, water, salt and yeast – *nada mas*,' he said, confirming the use of the little rolling-pin I sketched for him:

> After I was in Argentina for a while working in a textile factory that belonged to my wife's family, I started to make kuchen for a baker who offered me a partnership, but my wife Mina said no, because bakers always lived over their stores and she didn't want to. So I continued to work in the textile mill. But to tell you the truth, I always would rather have made kuchen.

The last excerpt I will read to you came from Pesach Szmusz, who lived in Camberwell, Australia, close to Melbourne. When I asked my usual question, about there being bialys in Australia, he assured me that no Bialystok kuchen baker would have emigrated to Australia because, 'it was always considered the end of the world.' Then he continued:

> I am answering your questions about Bialystoker kuchen with great pleasure. This kuchen was specific to Bialystok. Nowhere else in Poland or old Russia did the Jewish bakers make that kuchen and other Jewish

people in Poland made fun of us, and called us 'Bialystoker kuchen fressers'. But when some of them visited our town, the first thing they did was to taste our kuchen and buy dozens to take back home.

The kuchen goes back many years. When I was about seven, my great-grandmother told me that when she was my age in the 1850s, she would come down in the afternoon to her father's bakery and watch her mother and her twelve-year-old sister roll out the kuchen dough and she would help by putting on the onions and the poppy seeds.

In the 1920s and 1930s, every little street in our Bialystok had its own small kuchen bakery. The owner was the baker with his sons, sons-in-law, wife and daughters working with him. Everything was done by hand. The men would finish baking about five or six in the morning, then go to sleep and let the women do the selling. About midday, the father-baker would come down and start mixing the kuchen dough from flour, water, yeast and salt and leave it to rise. Then the women would take over, rolling the dough into two sizes – a small one that sold for 5 groschen and a larger size for 10 groschen. The women rolled the dough with two rolling pins. One woman used a regular rolling pin to shape a round about six-inches across and one-inch thick. Then the other woman would take over with her special rolling pin that had a two-inch center that pressed down the center.

She would brush the top of each kuchen with water, put on finely cut onion rings and poppy-seeds and place four to six kuchen on a big wooden spade [a peel] and pass it to the baker at the oven. He would lay them flat on the right side of the oven floor against the flames of the fire that was always made with dry pine-wood. It let out a nice aroma that gave the crust a very special taste. The kuchen would bake in ten minutes and customers would already be waiting to grab them as soon as they came out of the oven. They were brown and crisp on top and the center was like a crisp matzoh but maybe a little thicker. Very tasty indeed.

Many bakeries were on streets where the Jewish working class lived. The rich people ate kuchen sometimes, but the poor would eat them everyday. There was Moishe-Griske the kuchen baker of Mazoiecka Street, and Piaskes the Long-Nose on Zelazna Street, and Sholem-Maike on Sosnova Street opposite the old Jewish cemetery. Berl-Amolek was on the Shul-hof and Yosl-the-Deaf-One was on the Fishmarkt. They are only a few of the many.

We also ate kuchen with halvah from a shop called the Macedonian. There were two such shops that were like coffeehouses where you could buy halvah to take with you or sit at a table and eat it with a drink made of rice that was called bouza, sold in very small bottles. Generally we ate kuchen with butter or cheese, always spreading them on top, over the onions. It was also very tasty with kosher sausage.

Another Bialystoker Aussie had different thoughts about halvah. Said Felix Flicker, 'I personally do not believe in eating halvah with kuchen or any other bread. Halvah is a meal in itself. But some people did eat the kuchen with halvah. Some people ate halvah with you name it...'

Now I'll let Pesach Mr Szmusz have the last word:

In June, 1941 the Nazis came to us and since then there are no more Bialystoker kuchen and no more kuchen bakeries and no more of our Bialystok Jews. The Nazis killed almost all of us. I was in Auschwitz and other concentration camps, and I was liberated in Dachau, then spent four months in a tuberculosis hospital... I don't forgive the Nazis, but I don't forgive the Poles either. When the Nazis came to Bialystok on June 27th, 1941, Poles showed them where the Jews lived and Poles robbed the Jewish houses. The Nazis did not build Auschwitz, Treblinka or Maidanek in France, Belgium or Holland. They built them in Poland because they knew the Poles would help them kill the Jews. The Poles were partners in our destruction.

And this is the story of the Bialystoker kuchen. I do not think that any Bialystoker can tell you more.

Passionate for the Pasty: the Cornish Pasty in Michigan's Upper Peninsula

Leslie Cory Shoemaker

I dearly luv a pasty
a 'ot 'n' leaky wun
Weth taties, mayt 'n' turmit
Purs'ly 'n' honyun
Un' crus be made with su't
'N' shaped like 'alf a moon,
 Weth crinkly h'edges, freshly baked.
'E always gone too soon!

Mining Journal, 25 March 1971.

On 20 March 1913, in the Marquette Iron Range of Michigan's Upper Peninsula, deep within the bowels of the earth, where darkness is eternal and ore dust penetrates every pore of his body, a Cornish miner shines a lantern on his pocket watch to confirm what his stomach already knows. It is twelve noon: time to break for lunch. He is too far underground to hear the noon whistle blow that the others above ground have been waiting to hear. He, unlike his co-workers above ground, will remain in darkness and eat his lunch by lamplight; probably still standing in the same spot he had been working when the clock struck twelve.

This miner, an immigrant from Cornwall, and known in America as a 'cousin Jack', leans against a wheelbarrow of ore, takes from his pocket a square package wrapped in newspaper, and places it on the same shovel he uses to fill his wheelbarrow full of ore twelve hours every day, six days a week. Underneath the shovel he firmly positions his lantern to warm the shovel and heat his lunch, contained within the neatly wrapped newspaper. It isn't long before the familiar aromas of lean meat, starchy white potatoes, vegetables and savoury pastry rise from the shovel and reach his sooty nose and, in anticipation of the first mouthful, his stomach rumbles.

The miner, like all other 'cousin Jacks', will be eating a Cornish pasty for his lunch. The pasty is a portable, well-balanced meal in one, wrapped in pastry, its crimped edge making a convenient 'handle', therefore requiring no utensils and little or no light in order to consume it – a perfect lunch for the miner in the bottom of the mine-shaft, almost overwhelmed by hunger and fatigue. What a comfort and delight: to sit down and unwrap your lunch and inhale the aroma of warm crust, wrapped around meat and vegetables, and savour the taste of a complete meal prepared by loving hands.

Deep ore mining was the work of Cornish miners who brought their skills, sledges, drills and blasting powder from the mining pits of Cornwall to the prospering shafts of Lake Superior, where copper and iron deposits were discovered in Michigan's Upper Peninsula in the late 1840s. Their families brought a way of life that included the pasty, a delectable potato and meat turnover that the miner carried with him and ate with a flask of tea (Stafford 1994; Lockwood 1998).

According to the Authentic Cornish Pasty Company's web site, 'to the Cornish Miners, the pasty represented an essential part of the daily diet. As they worked in the mines, at lunchtime the men would arrange for their pasties to be dropped down the mineshaft. Often the wives would make a complete meal of the pasty by structuring the pasty filling so that the men ate the vegetable end first, then as he ate through the pasty, he would come across the meat, and then finally to a fruit such as apple, blackberries or mango. It was from the miners that the classic Cornish pasty shape was formed. The crimped side edge of the Cornish pasty was not eaten, but used as a handle for the miner to hold while eating the rest of the pasty' (Hatcher 1999).

The cousin Jack's wife; usually an excellent cook was called a 'cousin Jenny' and pasty making was an ethnic art form passed on from one generation to the next, and still is to this day. The quality of the product was not dependent on the written instructions, but rather on the skills and talent of the producer. Unlike visual art, creative derivations and innovations were not to be tolerated, and the criteria for the perfect pasty were standard among its judges. To date, the only derivation from my own Cornish great-grandmother's recipe has been to substitute the cholesterol-laden beef suet in the pastry recipe for vegetable shortening.

Anyone who has grown up in the Upper Peninsula of Michigan, or has spent a reasonable amount of time there at all, knows very well what a delight a pasty is to consume. One doesn't have to be of Cornish descent to recognize the signs for pasty shops that exist in every small town, and dot almost every scenic highway along the Lake Michigan and Lake Superior coastlines. Once you have eaten your first pasty you instantly know it will not be your last. Pasties have become so much a part of the culture of the Upper Peninsula of Michigan, and the pasty's fame had spread so far that, in 1968, Michigan

Governor George Romney officially designated May 24 as 'Michigan Pasty Day' (Magnaghi 1997).

It is said that there are as many pasty recipes as there are individuals in the County of Cornwall, but my family has produced the same recipe for generations. The perfect blend of tender, juicy steak and pork, layered with thinly sliced potatoes, rutabagas (known as swedes in England), onions, seasoned with fresh parsley, salt, pepper and a pat of butter, wrapped securely together in a savoury pastry crust, is a taste sensation like no other. As the great-granddaughter of Cornish immigrants, pasties are a part of my ethnic heritage and I have vivid memories of my Nana making pasties in her small kitchen. By this time my family was no longer involved in the mining industry, but when my grandfather, the son of the captain of the Rolling Mills Mine in Marquette County, married my Nana, along with the exchange of marriage vows came the coveted family pasty recipe. Pasties were not made in the household on a weekly basis any more but, when they were made, the whole family was told in advance and no one was ever late for dinner. Pasty dinners are as much an event as the American Thanksgiving turkey in modern Cornish-American homes, however, they happen much more often than once a year!

Whenever one mentions the pasty in conversation with a native of the Upper Peninsula, a 'pasty story' usually follows. It seems everyone has something to say about the pasty. No other food evokes such vivid memories, nostalgia, and intense debate, as the Cornish pasty, in the Upper Peninsula. The pasty speaks to us of home; of grandmothers and mothers in the comfort of their warm kitchens and of hard-working fathers off at the mine. It speaks to us of our youth and school lunches, of church bake-sales, of picnics, of college days (when many people who came to Upper Peninsula universities first experienced them), and of something that was carried with you no matter how far you might stray from the Upper Peninsula, or how many new foods you may have come to love.

The Cornish pasty is a beloved meal, the ultimate finger food and perhaps an original 'fast food', as it is so portable and easy to eat. According to John Owen of the *Seattle Post-Intelligencer*, 'You need only pronounce the words "Cornish pasty" and devotees around the world begin to sniff, salivate and generally behave as though they've been surviving on sunflower husks and vinegar water since the last millennium.'

In February of 2000, I started soliciting and collecting these so-called 'pasty memories'. I was overwhelmed with the response that followed. Within two hours of putting out a university-wide email, asking for pasty stories, I got 25 responses, one as far away as Arizona and, by the end of the next month, after a university press release announcing my research, I had 75 responses from all over the United States, including telephone calls, emails and personal letters. I even received a hand-written letter from a one hundred-year-old Cornish woman living in the Upper Peninsula who still made her own pasties from a recipe her mother had received from a Cornish woman in 1905. Not everyone I heard from was actually of Cornish heritage; however, roughly 75 per cent of my respondents were direct descendents of Cornish families.

The common threads that ran through all the memories that I received were that the Cornish pasty had deeply embedded itself in the very core of people's life stories, and that nobody had ever made pasties as tasty as their mothers had made them. No matter how far away from the Upper Peninsula people's lives had taken them, they took the pasty along with them in their hearts, memories, and taste buds. One person wrote to me saying, 'I never realized how much I loved pasties until I was no longer able to find them.' What follows are a few of the pasty memoirs taken from my research, some nostalgic, some humorous, some historical, but all in all – passionate for the pasty!

I received an email from a woman in Republic, Michigan (mailto: Ojmqt@aol.com), who told me that, while visiting her son and daughter-in-law at Travis Air Force Base in California, she succumbed to their persistent requests for her home-made pasties. She proceeded to make a huge batch and, while some were frozen for future consumption, they headed to Stinson Beach on the Pacific Ocean and had a picnic lunch of her genuine Cornish pasties. This has now become a ritual for the family whenever Mom comes from Michigan to California to visit. She even brings rutabaga with her from Michigan, as it is often hard to find in California. What makes this story really interesting is that, after hearing from this woman, I received an email from her son as well, who relayed the same story and much more.

Khris Kennedy, her son, is a flight engineer for the United States Air force and flies on the C-5 Galaxy, the Free World's largest airplane. One of the places he cooked up one of his mother's frozen pasties is actually aboard the C-5 Galaxy, while flying 37,000 feet over the Red Sea on the way to Dhahran, Saudi Arabia, during Operation Desert Storm. Khris said, 'the wonderful aroma coming from the galley oven made all the rest of the crew envious of my lunch!'

Kathleen Olivier of Marquette, Michigan, wrote, 'My favorite pasty memory is the time my mother was chatting with a group of women who were bragging about their pasty recipes. After listening to glorious exaggerations she calmly mentioned that her pasties were so good, the recipe had been requested from all over the world. Upon further inquisition from the ladies it was discovered that my uncle, who at the time was a chaplain in the Air Force and traveled all over the world, loved my mother's pasties and always gave the recipe to the air base's cook in fervent hopes they could duplicate them. Unfortunately, my uncle was fairly unorganized and managed to lose the recipe repeatedly, forcing him to re-request it whenever he got transferred to a new base. The requests literally came from cities across the U.S., Japan, England, etc.'

Dr Charles DeRidder wrote that he grew up with the pasty in Norway, Michigan, and cannot recall a time, growing up, when he couldn't find a pasty if he tried hard enough. He goes on to say that while attending Michigan State University in downstate Lansing, Michigan, he only found a few students who had ever heard of the pasty, however, each time he returned home he got his 'fix':

> After my military time and graduate work at Oregon State University, I took to making my own. Ha, the crust was my downfall! However, I had to introduce my bride (a native Oregonian) to pasties other than mine. On one of our earlier trips back to Northern Michigan I took to purchasing an ice cooler along with twelve pasties and put them in the trunk of the car and departed for Oregon. Yes, I eat them cold, however my wife and daughter didn't think much of this idea. They wanted them warm – IDEA – I wrapped one in foil and placed it on the engine manifold for about 20 miles of driving and it came out tasting good. No gasoline and piping hot.

Diane Vasquez, an administrative associate at The University of Michigan in Ann Arbor, Michigan writes:

> I grew up in Iron River, Michigan, with a Mom in the house who was the best cook in the whole world – as evidenced by the fantastic pasties she'd make once a week. My brothers, sisters, and I were spoiled; didn't children everywhere get pasties for supper?
>
> I had a rude awakening when I got married to a Marine Corps officer and left the U.P. forever (except for bi-annual visits home). Pasties were no longer part of my existence. We could only indulge our pasty-tooth when visiting the U.P. After Mom died, we were fortunate that Dad remarried another great pasty-maker and often were given a supply of frozen pasties to take us through until the next visit. But these had to be rationed carefully. Finally, in self-preservation, my sister began to make pasties, perfecting her attempts until I could finally say that they are just like Mom's.

The deeply rooted tradition of pasty making and eating in Michigan's Upper Peninsula runs like a strong current among most all the memoirs I have collected. Jeff Kleinschmidt tells the story of his grandmother's immigration from Cornwall to the Upper Peninsula:

Pasties have always been a part of my family history. My grandmother emigrated to the U.S. from Cornwall, England when she was eight years old. She remembers that her handicapped mother was on Ellis Island trying to get in the country when the judge asked her where she was going and what skills she had to support herself. She said that she was going to Calumet, Michigan, and that she could bake pasties. The judge was very familiar with Calumet and agreed that she could make a living selling pasties there and let her in.

Mary Allwin Tuisku and Jeanne Allwin Lantto also wrote of their grandmother:

Our grandma Prideaux, whose family came from Cornwall, was the best pasty maker in the world. She died when I was 8 and my sister was 6. One of our fondest memories was climbing the steps to her upstairs apartment and being greeted with the smell of fresh baked pasties. She would store the pasties in a cabinet and the first thing we did was run to it and search for those pasties. We'd sit on the floor where she couldn't see us and eat the pasty as fast as we could before we got caught. As we grew older, we realized the pasties were placed there for us to find and the whole thing was a type of game she played with us. To this day we have not tasted a pasty as good as hers!

Mrs. Yorkhouse from Colorado wrote to me last May about a recent family gathering:

Last week my sister from Upper Michigan and her family were here in Colorado to visit us. One morning we gals made 42 pasties, while the guys planned our travel route for the day. It should be noted that my sister hauls her rolling pin wherever she travels, because she likes to use her own pin to roll pasty crust – and she also hauls rutabaga (Swedes) in her suitcase to go in the pasty... We then ate pasties on the Shelf Rd. and the Gold Camp Rd. and on the Phantom Canyon Rd. – all back roads of Colorado with beautiful scenery and innumerable wild animals – and wonderful food! This is a family tradition wherever we get together. We have fun making them, they transport well and are a no fuss meal and always make the tours special.

Sue Hewitt recalls her days of eating pasties in the car when she was a college student at Northern Michigan University:

My favorite pasty memory occurred when I was a student at NMU in the late 1960s. A group of us students used to car pool home on the weekends. Our journey lead us through Chatam, Michigan. The time was usually around suppertime and we were usually hungry and always rather poor. Our favorite place to stop on cold winter Fridays was a gas station store for the purpose of picking up pasties. On many occasions, there would be no clerk present to sell the pasties. There was a warming box in the entry filled with fresh, warm pasties. The aroma in there was wonderful. You could pick out your own and put what you owed in a tin box. I believe the price of each was $2.00, maybe less. I thank the cook for providing us with a satisfying 'home-like' meal that could be eaten in the car.

Family tradition, days of youth, college days and journeys beyond the Upper Peninsula are not the only places people's memories of the pasty have taken them. They also include the time-honoured tales of love and marriage. Joe Holman of Marquette, Michigan, recalls his parent's courtship:

My parents started dating in 1929 when my mom was fourteen. The first dish my mom ever made for my father was a pasty as it was the favorite meal my Grandmother, who came from Cornwall, made. My mom proudly sat the pasty down in front of my dad; my dad said it looked like a crumpled boxcar. She cried. He ate the whole thing. I'm not sure she ever forgave him but they were married for 51 years.

Gail Anthony of Marquette wrote about her 'romance' with the pasty:

My husband's first career was a pasty maker in the Copper Country. He left for work every day for almost 10 years at 2:30 a.m. so the pasties would be ready for the noon rush. He also proposed to me 21 years ago after an intimate dinner of (you guessed it) pasties!

Kurt Granroth, who lives in Arizona, was one of the first people who contacted me with his pasty story. His brother, who lives in Marquette, forwarded him my original email calling for pasty stories because he knew that Kurt had a good one to tell:

When my wife and I got married four years ago, we debated for quite some time as to what main dish we should serve at our wedding reception. We had very different tastes in food back then so it was not an easy job...until, that is, I suggested we serve pasties. My wife-to-be had fallen in love with pasties while going to school at Michigan Technological University in Houghton, Michigan, and we agreed instantly. I scarcely need to say it but the pasties were a big hit!

It is evident that the Cornish pasty holds a very special place in the hearts and memories of the people who love it. Whether or not they are of Cornish descent, the people of the Upper Peninsula of Michigan have claimed the Cornish Pasty as 'the number one U.P. food'. There are many people whose lives take them far away from the Upper Peninsula, but they never forget what the pasty means to them, their lives and their families and either search for a reasonable facsimile when not available, try to make their own if possible, or just wait until they visit the Upper Peninsula again – and head straight for the nearest pasty shop!

It seems only fitting to conclude with the following poem that expresses our passion for the pasty, written by Henry Rogers. Mr Rogers came from Cornwall to work as a Methodist pastor in the Upper Peninsula in 1896, and his only living descendent, Mrs Marilyn Frank of Ironwood, Michigan, sent this poem to me:

> How dear to my lip is a hot Cornish pasty,
> When fondly my missus presents it to view;
> It makes my mouth water to see it there steaming,
> The most delicious that I ever knew.
> The twist on its edges, the hole in the middle,
> The sight of it gives me an appetite keen;
> Someday they may find out a meal that is better,
> But up to this time it has never been seen.
> A good Cornish pasty, a hot Cornish pasty,
> A big Cornish pasty, it's praises I'll tell...'

BIBLIOGRAPHY

Bartelli, Ingrid (25 March 1971) 'Food Buy-Ways: Pasty – U.P.'s Family Crest', in *The Mining Journal*, pp. 12–13.

Frank, Marilyn (27 April 2000) personal letter to the author.

Grimes, William (4 August 1999) 'Critic's Notebook; No Fury Like the Pasty Scorned', in *The New York Times*.

Hatcher, Robert (1999) *The Authentic Cornish Pasty Company: History of the Cornish Pasty*, (online) http://authenticcornishpasty.co.uk/History.htm.

Lockwood, Yvonne R. and Lockwood, William G. (1998) 'Pasties in Michigan's Upper Peninsula: Foodways, Interethnic Relations, and Regionalism', in Shortridge, B. (ed.), *The Taste of American Place*, Latham, Maryland: Rowman & Littlefield, pp. 21–36.

Magnaghi, Russell T. (1997) 'The Cornish Pasty: Its History and Lore', in Magnaghi, R. (ed.) *A Sense of Place: Michigan's Upper Peninsula*, Marquette, Michigan: Northern Michigan University Press, pp.119–132.

Owen, John (21 April 1999) 'Love of Pasties Brings Trays of Contacts', in *Seattle Post-Intelligencer*, p. C2.

Stafford, Daniel J. (1994) *The Cornish Oven*, (online) http://tcoinc.com/tco/tco3.html.

Anecdotal Sources: all sent by email to the author, lshoe@nmu.edu.

Anthony, Gail (10 April 2000) mailto: ganthony@nmu.edu.
De Ridder, Charles (25 April 2000) mailto: deridder@mail.europa.com.
Granroth, Kurt (17 February 2000) mailto: kurt@granroth.org.
Hewitt, Sue (17 February 2000) mailto: shewitt@nmu.edu.
Holman, Joe (17 February 2000) mailto: jholman@nmu.edu.
Kennedy, Khris (7 May 2000) mailto: toolsvaca@aol.com.
Kleinschmidt, Jeff (18 February 2000) mailto: jkleinsc@nmu.edu.
Olivier, Kathleen (12 May 2000) mailto: kolivier@nmu.edu.
Tuisku, Mary (10 June 2000) mailto: mtuisku@up,net.
Vasquez, Diane (2 May 2000 mailto: dvasquez@d.imap.itd.umich.edu.
Yorkhouse, M. (30 May 2000) mailto: yorkhouse@aol,com.

False Memories: the Invention of Culinary Fakelore[1] and Food Fallacies

Andrew F. Smith

When I began exploring the history-specific culinary products, years ago, I quickly discovered that some foods had been researched extensively, while others seemed to have been overlooked. Surprisingly, the tomato was one commonly consumed food whose history had not been examined. But what was written about the tomato's history was intriguing: many writers claimed that the tomato had been considered poisonous and was an aphrodisiac. Other writers offered stories about how the tomato entered into the American diet. One such story was pre-eminent: Robert Gibbon Johnson, claimed many writers, ate the first tomato in the United States on the court-house steps of Salem, New Jersey, on 26 September 1820. Thousands of people watched him in horrified expectation that he would drop dead with his first bite into the poisonous love-apple, or so the story goes. However, the authors who recounted this story offered no primary evidence and various versions of the story differed dramatically.

I found the story intriguing enough to visit Salem, where I examined newspapers from the period, books written about Salem in the nineteenth century, hundreds of articles in magazines and agricultural journals, memoirs and other primary source material. Robert Gibbon Johnson was a prominent Salemite and much was written about him. Unfortunately, I found no evidence connecting him to the tomato. The first version of the story appeared in print 86 years after the purported event. All it said was that Johnson ate a tomato in 1820.[2] Subsequent authors embellished the story, adding extraneous information, and the purported event was dramatized on national radio in 1949. Subsequently, versions have appeared in numerous professional and scholarly journals, newspapers and popular magazines.[3]

While it is impossible to say that something did not happen, based on all the evidence uncovered about Johnson and Salem in the nineteenth century, it is extremely unlikely that any such event occurred. I wrote up an article debunking the myth. However, the story acquired a life of its own and writers have continued to perpetuate it – even those who are well aware that it was not likely true. The 'Johnson and the tomato' story has graduated to a national legend, not unlike the tale of Johnny Appleseed planting apple trees throughout the Midwest, dramatized by Walt Disney in cartoon format, and believed by most Americans.[4]

The Johnson story suggests several characteristics of how fakelore becomes enshrined as legend. Firstly, the story rings true and is presented in such a way as to be difficult or impossible to disprove.[5] Secondly, the story explains a real problem. Everyone knew that Salemites did not eat tomatoes during their early years, so a story that explained why they shifted from not eating tomatoes provided locals with the solution to a puzzling mystery. Thirdly, simple stories are more enjoyable than complex reality. Fourthly, some Salemites believed the story gave their community visibility, and therefore promoted the story to magazine, newspaper and book writers. Finally, writers found the story attractive. As there was no primary source evidence, writers could – and did – embellish the story to give punch to their writing.

Towards a typology of culinary fakelore and logical fallacies
Since uncovering the Johnson fakelore, I've located hundreds of other food stories and I suspect that they are inherent in all culinary histories. Some contain statements that are easily disproved; others that are likely false; and still others that are possibly true, but undocumented. Part of the reason for accepting undocumented stories is the fact that historically food preparation has largely been based on oral traditions: cooks orally passed on techniques, recipes and lore to successor generations. This is particularly true in non-literate cultures but, even in literate societies, methods, traditions and rituals of food preparation and consumption were rarely recorded until the twentieth century. And much of what was written down in cookery manuscripts or diaries has been lost, hence oral traditions may be the only sources available. Yet, undocumented culinary folklore cannot be accepted at face value without qualification: oral traditions change over time, with information dropped and other aspects added. While culinary folklore and oral traditions are important dimensions of food history and need further exploration, it is clear that many stories that purport to be folklore in fact have been invented in modern times, for reasons other than historical accuracy, such as promotion of people, places and products.

Fakelore is not the same as mistakes made by authors. All authors make mistakes. However, factual or other mistakes are usually easily fixed. Neither are we concerned with genuine oral traditions, which may be not be documented with primary print sources. Culinary fakelore specifically refers to invented stories that serve purposes other than historical accuracy. While stories that serve other purposes are not necessarily false, other motives coupled without documentation should arouse suspicions. The usual motivations that underlie culinary fakelore are:

JOURNALISTIC ENRICHMENT: undocumented accounts repeated by writers who want to spice up their stories with 'exciting tales'. Journalists usually do not invent basic information, but they do frequently add facts, dialogue and drama. The reasons for this are several. They frequently rely on interviews and often fail to check the information given to them with primary sources. Most newspaper and magazine writers are not historians; they are usually on a deadline and need a story quickly, which usually precludes their examination of primary sources. Finally, journalists adore pithy quotes or sound bites with unusual twists.

Logical fallacies: undocumented connections that are logical but not supported by fact. For example, in the Johnson story, one writer noted correctly that Johnson had supported the local agricultural society and logically concluded that Johnson had used the agricultural society to promote tomato growing and consumption. However, many records of the Salem Agricultural Society have survived and there is no mention of tomatoes during the first half of the nineteenth century.

Presentism fallacies: undocumented belief that because something is true in the present it has always been so. Today, ketchup is closely associated with Americans, and many writers assume that Americans invented it. However, Americans neither created ketchup nor, in its origin, was it thick, sweet or tomato-based.[6]

CULINARY JINGOISM: undocumented stories about cuisines intended to improperly attribute origins of particular dishes to a specific location, group or nationality.

Local boosterism: undocumented stories fostering a community's claim to have invented a particular dish; this technique is often used to attract tourists. Salemites pushed the tomato-eating myth long after tomato growing ceased to be a commercial crop in the area.

Negative stereotypes: undocumented, negative stories attributing particular foods/dishes to people in other nations, cultures, races, religions or groups. Numerous sources report that Catherine de Medici brought her cooks to France and introduced the French to good cookery, yet no evidence has been uncovered to support this, according to culinary historian Barbara Wheaton.[7]

Temporal jingoism: the belief that food and cookery in the present are better than food and cookery in previous times. An example is the frequently repeated myth that meat was highly spiced in the Middle Ages because spices killed the taste of the rotten meat.

GREAT (USUALLY WHITE) MEN STORIES: undocumented attribution of origins of dishes to specific individuals. The Johnson story is but one example of this tendency to identify great men as the inventors, introducers or originators of food, recipes and other culinary matters. Thomas Jefferson is frequently credited, for instance, with introducing Carolina Gold rice, which, according to culinary historian Karen Hess, was grown in South Carolina well before Jefferson was born.[8]

Individual puffery: undocumented personal claims by individuals to have invented a specific dish when they did not do so. Many individuals claim to have invented a particular dish. John Harvey Kellogg, for instance, claimed to have invented peanut butter, even though ground peanuts had been used for centuries in South America, Africa and, in the American South, by African-Americans. In this case, however, Kellogg was responsible for the term *peanut butter* and he certainly did popularize it.[9]

'Founding fathers' or other famous personage dishes: undocumented stories attributing a food/dish to a particular famous person. In addition to the above example of Thomas Jefferson, many other 'great' men have been associated with particular dishes. For instance, Napoleon has been the subject of several associations, such as Chicken Marengo, purportedly created after the battle of Marengo by Napoleon's chef, who only had a few ingredients, including chicken and tomatoes. In fact, the earliest recipes for Chicken Marengo did not contain tomatoes and the first mention of tomatoes as an ingredient did not appear until almost 40 years after the battle. Alternatively, many chicken recipes with tomatoes as an ingredient were published prior to the date of the chicken Marengo recipes.[10] Another example is the association of popcorn with the Pilgrims at the 'first Thanksgiving' in 1621, when there is no evidence that popcorn was grown or consumed in North America until the beginning of the nineteenth century.[11]

Political correctness or historical revisionism: undocumented attribution of foods to non-white males. African-American scientist George Washington Carver is frequently credited with inventing peanut butter, even though he made no such claim himself and peanut butter had been a commercial product for twenty years before Carver became interested in peanuts.

Alternatively, numerous sources have claimed that Native Americans introduced popcorn to colonial Americans, yet no evidence has surfaced indicating that Native Americans possessed popcorn prior to the nineteenth century.[12]

Invented culinary traditions: undocumented statements that particular groups consumed food in previous historical periods.[13] The 'Soul Food' tradition of African-Americans appears to fall into this category. While it is true that some African-Americans may have consumed the foods identified as 'soul food', it is not likely that these dishes were commonly eaten by large numbers of African-Americans in any historical period. Likewise, many of those who make historical statements about the foods of Native Americans, usually without documentation, are inaccurate. Finally, many foods identified as 'Mexican' or other such identification have been altered so much in their translation into mainstream food products that they now have little in common with their mother cuisines.[14]

COMMERCIAL PROMOTION: undocumented stories repeated by corporations in their advertising intended to sell commercial products. Almost all food advertising that makes reference to historical events is inaccurate. In this case, advertisers are interested in promoting sales, not in accurately telling history.

HEALTH MYTHS: medicinal claims for specific foods/products frequently repeated without solid scientific basis.

Vegetarian/anti-vegetarian myths: undocumented health claims by vegetarians or anti-vegetarians about the healthy effects of eating meat or non-meat diets.

Aphrodisiac claims: undocumented claims about the aphrodisiac qualities of specific foods/dishes. Aphrodisiac claims for numerous foods have been made, but fakelorists take this one step further. For instance, pseudo-historians report that the early interest in obtaining spices was because of the supposed aphrodisiac effects of spices. While some people in the sixteenth century may have believed that spices were aphrodisiacs, not everyone did, and the main interest in spices appears to be related to their culinary uses rather than as aphrodisiacs. Likewise, in the case of the tomato, many modern writers have assumed that people in times past considered them aphrodisiacs because of their name 'love-apple'. Despite the term, there is little evidence for this claim except in modern literature.

Conclusion

George Lang wrote in 1980 that, 'Culinary history is a collection of questionable happenings, recorded by persons of dubious credibility, about events no one cares about and people of no consequence.'[15] Lang went on to prove this point by presenting many culinary stories as fact while offering no evidence for them. In fact, much of what has been written under the rubric 'culinary history' has been collections of twice-told myths.

Food fakelore is frequently repeated because there are few easily accessible, accurate culinary histories. This general lack of serious work depends, in large part, upon the failure of academics to take culinary history seriously. Academic course offerings in culinary history are haphazard and sporadic. Partly at fault is the rigid departmental structure of modern universities. Since no departments of culinary history exist, courses must be tacked onto history or culinary arts departments. Most mainstream historians – even social historians – have little interest in food except as it relates to war, mass starvation, malnutrition or an economic ingredient to trade. Few historians consider the cookbook an important primary source for information about people or about the times in which they live. Other academics in the arts and humanities do not consider food to be an art form, or certainly not 'high art', like painting, poetry or music. Hence, food history is usually segregated into culinary schools or nutrition departments. Still, despite its shallow toe-holds in academia, culinary history enjoys wide popular appeal, permitting amateurs, dilettantes and popularizers to jump on the chuck wagon without any need to consult an established canon of knowledge.

Hence, anything goes in the culinary history field – particularly the telling of undocumented food stories, which become the grist for newspapers, magazines, cookbooks and even serious works that purport to be well researched. Myths gain reality through repetition and, unfortunately, almost all modern food writers are guilty of repetition at one time or another. However, if the field of culinary history is to thrive, it must promote higher evidentiary standards. Failure to do so will result in culinary history's relegation to the arena of fiction and trivia.

REFERENCES

[1] The term *fakelore* was borrowed from Dorson, Richard M. (1976) *Folklore and Fakelore*, Cambridge, Massachusetts: Harvard University Press, p. 5.

[2] Sickler, Joseph S. (1946) *The Old Houses of Salem County*, Salem, New Jersey: Sunbeam Publishing, p. 40; Holbrook, Steward H. (1946) *Lost Men of American History*, London: Macmillan, p. 131; *Salem Sunbeam*, 1 February 1949.

[3] Longone, Jan (Autumn–Winter 1987–88) 'From the Kitchen', in *American Magazine*, 3, 1; *Salem Sunbeam*, 22 July 1988; 24 July 1988.

[4] Smith, Andrew F. (Fall–Winter 1990) 'The Making of the Legend of Robert Gibbon Johnson and the Tomato', in *New Jersey History*, 108, 59–74; Smith, Andrew F. (1994) *The Tomato in America: Early History, Culture and Cookery*, Columbia: University of South Carolina Press.

[5] For more information about the introduction of the tomato into America, see Smith, 1994.

[6] Smith, Andrew F. (December 1991) 'The History of Home-made Anglo-American Tomato Ketchup', in *Petits Propos Culinaires*, 39, 35.

[7] Wheaton, Barbara Ketcham (1983) *Savoring the Past; The French Kitchen and Table from 1300 to 1789*, Philadelphia: University of Pennsylvania, pp. 42–48.

[8] Hess, Karen (1992) *The Carolina Rice Kitchen; The African Connection*, Columbia: University of South Carolina Press, pp. 19–20.

[9] Smith, Andrew F. (forthcoming) *Just Peanuts: A Culinary History*, Urbana: University of Illinois Press, p. 1.

[10] For instance, see L.E.A. [Louis-Eustache Audot] (1841) *La Cuisinière de la Campagne et de la Ville*, 25th ed., Paris: Audot, p. 215, in which no tomatoes are mentioned in the recipe; Viart, A. (1842) *Le Cuisinier Royal*, 18e éd., augmentée de douze cents articles nouveaux par MM. Fouret et Délan, Paris: Gustave Barba, p. 298, which uses tomatoes as an ingredient and mentions the Napoleon story.

[11] Smith, Andrew F. (1999) *Popped Culture: A Social History of Popcorn in America*, Columbia: University of South Carolina Press, pp. 3–5.

[12] Smith (forthcoming), p. 1.

[13] For a broader discussion of invented traditions, see Hobsbawm, Eric and Ranger, Terence (eds.) (1983) *The Invention of Tradition*, New York: Cambridge University Press.

[14] Smith, Andrew F. (1999) 'Tacos, Enchiladas and Refried Beans: The Invention of Mexican-American Cookery', in Kelsey, Mary Wallace and Holmes, ZoeAnn (eds.) (1999) *Cultural and Historical Aspects of Foods*, Corvallis: Oregon State University, pp. 183–203; Smith, Andrew F. (forthcoming) 'Tomatoes, Peanuts and Okra: African-American Influence on Early American Cookery', p. 2.

[15] Lang, George (1980) *Lang's Compendium of Culinary Nonsense and Trivia*, New York: Clarkson N. Potter, Inc., p. 11.

Memories of a Vanishing Eskimo Cuisine

Zona Spray

Introduction

Alaska's Arctic is a harsh land, where long winters plummet to 70°F below freezing and temperatures can soar to 65°F above zero during summers. Lacking a climate to support an agrarian society, Eskimos migrated to available food resources, seemingly limited at first glance but immensely rich upon close inspection. By the late 1800s, small villages were established and food preparation had developed into a unique style of cooking, albeit misunderstood and considered primitive by Western standards.

Having lived above the Arctic Circle in an Alaskan Eskimo village as a child, I returned a half-century later, hoping to understand subsistence cooking before White Man introduced refined foods. Elders took me fishing, berry picking and up-river to gather greens for preserving in seal oil, and they shared memories of living in a subsistence and fur-trading culture which no longer exists.

Their stories revealed a remarkably ingenious cuisine, though undocumented in a systematic fashion. Without pen or paper, methods to prepare food for long dark winters passed verbally from generation to generation. Women carefully cut, chopped, sliced and mashed to prepare dishes utilizing cooking methods as varied as those used in our Western world. However, Eskimo subsistence cuisine differs from Alaskan cooking, which is primarily a Western cuisine using regional products. This paper presents the Alaskan Arctic cuisine during its most developed state, and is limited to an area approximately one hundred miles north and south of Alaska's Arctic Circle, between 1880 and World War II.

By the time World War II was brewing, Arctic villages had ventured from subsistence, defined as 'customary and traditional, non-commercial uses of wild resources',[1] to a mixed-economy lifestyle. It was a time when Eskimos coupled hunting and gathering food with trading furs to acquire guns and some clothing, plus sugar, flour and tea.[2] My memories and the stories presented here reflect the early mixed-economy period, when skins became kayaks, furs and hides were sewn into intricately patterned parkas and mukluks, and nearly all food was hunted or gathered.

Gaining access into the Eskimo[3] culture is relatively easy. Gaining the trust to document subsistence ways and work side by side with Eskimos is more difficult. My entry into the community was aided by being born in Shungnak, Alaska, prior to World War II. A small native village, inhabited by 200 Eskimos, it lies 30 miles above the Arctic Circle and 150 miles inland from the Bering Strait. Travelling to remote Eskimo villages in 1929, my parents taught grades one through eight for the United States Government Indian Service. Since teachers are esteemed in villages, their name was remembered 50 years later. However, being related to a well-known and respected Eskimo family was even more important.

When my aunt Pauline died, five years ago, a vast knowledge of Alaska's Arctic subsistence foods, gleaned over her 84 years, went with her. Remembering the statement, 'Eskimo subsistence will be gone within ten years,'[4] I was haunted by how to document traditional foods. With only a few young women learning subsistence food preparations, Eskimo elders were the best resource.

Sharing, especially sharing food, is an important value in Eskimo life. Taking stock of what I could share with elders, lending strong hands and being trained as a chef seemed my most valuable assets. So, after days of helping fish, pick, clean and put up food for the winter, I frequently created dinners and comfortable settings conducive to telling stories. In return, a kind and generous people offered its time and shared tales of fishing, hunting, gathering herbs and berries, drying, smoking and fermenting; all the old subsistence ways practised by elders and a handful of young people who opt for subsistence. By day, we worked and laughed together. At night, I recorded their memories.

Once Eskimo food preparation techniques and cooking methods were analysed, a cleverly fashioned cuisine took shape. The food preparations presented here were prevalent prior to 1942 and World War II, before the culture was forced into the twentieth century. Today, Eskimo food has blurred into Western, or white man's food. Dubbed Alaskan food by many, dishes made by oven roasting, frying with onions or baking have no relationship to Eskimo cuisine in a mixed economy prior to the 1940s.

The Arctic cuisine

Using food historian and cookbook author Giuliano Bugialli's definition of cuisine, an Arctic cuisine is clearly evident. His five distinct criteria are: indigenous foodstuffs; unique cooking methods and preserving techniques; specialized cooking implements and preserving equipment; a specific heat source; a distinctive flavouring or seasoning base giving all foods a unified taste.[5]

Arctic cuisine is not a variation of Western or Eastern cuisines, but is composed of a high-fat, high-protein diet without grains, supplemented with wild greens, roots and berries. Dieticians consider the diet nutritious and balanced with abundant vitamins, minerals, proteins and valuable unsaturated fats[6] derived from a vast array of sea and land mammals, fish, fowl, wild plants and berries.

Arctic dishes were cooked and preserved by moist heat (boiling, poaching, simmering, blanching) and dry heat (roasting over an open fire), plus altering cellular structure by fermenting, drying, half-drying and rendering. Food for winter consumption was nearly always prepared, in large quantities, during summertime, and eventually frozen. While wood was summer's heat source, seal oil or another fat was primarily used during winter months to warm previously prepared, frozen food. Handmade cooking implements and large cooking equipment were designed specifically for picking, digging, cooking and food preparation, plus the inevitable long storage when frozen. Seal oil unified the cuisine's flavour.[7] It touched nearly every food, either in its preparation, as a preserver during storage, or as a final seasoning.

The heat source

Food was cooked with flames made from wood or fat, while the sun rendered and the wind dried. Along the barren Arctic coast, trees were and are still almost non-existent, so small bits of driftwood were sparingly burned. Abundant wood was available from inland forests, but since small sod igloos were vulnerable to open flames, cooking was delegated to an area adjacent to the living quarters. As late as 1900, winter's light and heat source was seal oil or another fat, placed in a shallow stone dish carved from jade, flint or other indigenous material. Oil fuelled a tiny wick, made from twisted arctic wild cotton, which burned continuously. Women used the dish's contents to warm uncooked frozen fish or meat, and heat previously cooked food, frozen for winter consumption during long hours of darkness and a few hours of twilight.

Seal oil, the basic flavouring

Without a doubt, seal oil was the cuisine's salt and pepper. It bound the culture with a common flavour. Not only was all food stored in seal oil, most of the food chain hints of seal oil or, at the very least, a delicate fish flavour. Because virtually everything feeds on the sea, a fish flavour permeates all sea mammals and many land animals. Even the flesh of fish-eating fowl suggests the sea's contents. The most telling example of the pervasive fish taste is the low growing tundra salmonberry, which differs from the tall bushy salmonberry found along the north-west coast of the United States. Salmonberries neither grow in the sea nor on the seashore. Rather, their raspberry shaped, salmon-coloured fruit grows over miles and miles of tundra, as far as 150 miles inland from the Chukchi Sea. The colour is true to its name and, even more cogent, the flavour is definitely salmon.

Preparing seal oil is an arduous task demanding numerous hands. Sealskins with blubber attached can weigh 200 pounds. The blubber is removed with an *ulu*, which is the woman's knife, into two-inch wide blood- and meat-free strips. Rendering temperatures must be about 50°F. Too hot and the oil turns cloudy and tastes fishy. If too cold, the rendering process slows and rancidity develops. Meticulous care is necessary from beginning to end. As elder Esther Bourdon says, 'The finest cooks prepare the best seal oil.'

Small cooking and gathering implements
Women use the *ulu* for everything, from sewing and fashioning caribou sinews into thread to cutting blubber from sealskins and cleaning fish for drying. The most common size is seven inches wide, shaped into a half circle, with an ivory or wood handle at the top. For sewing, women productive enough to make one, use a tiny *ulu* no larger than two inches wide. Originally carved from stone or jade during the 1920s, the prized *ulu* was, and still is, shaped from a carbon steel sawmill blade. It takes a deadly sharp edge with two or three swipes across a rock, unlike the stainless steel *ulu* sold as a souvenir at every store and airport in Alaska.

Another imperative implement, especially for coastal Eskimo women, is the skinning board. It is used to support heavy, blubber-laden sealskins as women cut fat from skins, and offers vertical rigidity to awkward sealskins, which facilitates cleaning. About fifteen by eighteen inches, the skinning board is a traditional coastal wedding gift, though inland woman often work without such luxury.

For centuries Eskimo women carved digging trowels and picks from local jade and flint, for uprooting willow stems or robbing roots from a mouse nest. Poke blowers, for blowing air into skins to make containers, were fashioned from ivory or small hollow bones. For stirring and mashing, they carved wooden tools. One resembled a meat-pounder without a handle. Another looked like a long-handled wooden spoon, but had a wide grooved foot rather than the concave bowl. At the turn of the twentieth century, furs were swapped for small, metal digging tools, but few women owned them.

Early cooking pots were made of clay from the Kotzebue lagoons, a 150 mile trip by dog sled or kayak from Shungnak. Soft, short ptarmigan leg feathers were mixed with the clay to hold it intact. Since clay pots were dried, not fired, they were nestled next to the fire to prevent cracking. Hot rocks were added until liquid and meat boiled. The fourth rock usually did the job.[8] By 1900, Eskimos had traded furs for brass pots that could withstand the heat of an open fire. During summertime, when most cooking and preserving was done, the brass pot was continuously suspended over an outdoor fire. The vessel simmered, boiled and braised a remarkable array of fish, fowl, meats and plants. Even today, the brass pot works diligently in the fish camps along the riverbanks.

Containers of all sizes and shapes were woven from reeds and grasses. Beautiful black baskets were woven from whale baleen, and birch bark was constructed into rectangular baskets with handles. One clever berry-picking basket had straight twigs, six inches long and half an inch apart, projecting from one side. When swiped through low berry bushes, a bountiful harvest was quick; it was especially helpful for finding cranberries after light snows, saving fingers from long hours of exposure.

Large cooking equipment for food preparation and storage
Cooking equipment for preparing and storing food was large. Dishes were prepared in huge quantities during the short summer months and frozen in permafrost cellars for eating during the bitter cold winter months ahead. Food had to last a family of six to ten persons throughout the winter, when no one could predict the availability of wildlife, or whether frozen berries would still cling to stems under the snow.

Gathering and preparing food, whenever available, was important to survival. Famine, a common theme when telling stories, occurred primarily before village living, when families migrated in search of food or men hunted for months at a time. However, an abundant food source was responsible for developing a new village close to Shungnak after World War II.[9]

Elder Caroline Penayak reminisced about gathering abundant greens on a camping trip when she was a child. Sourdock was everywhere and the family picked for three days, only to realize they had no way to transport the huge volume of greens home. Rather than waste their bounty, they cooked the greens on the spot and buried them in the permafrost. Once fall coloured the ground white, they returned by dog sled and retrieved their cache of greens. Without knowing what the future holds, Eskimos learn to take what is offered, when it is offered.

Drying racks for hanging fish and black seal, called *ugruk* in the Eskimo Inupiaq language, resembled skeletons of a frame house, long clothes lines or lean-tos. They were constructed from sturdy limbs or skinny, gnarled tree trunks, stunted from years of bitter, cold winters. During a plentiful fish run, hundreds of pounds of gutted fish hung from the horizontal bars as breezes airdried the fish within a few days.

Cold cellars were dug into the permafrost, or icy ground, to keep food-filled pokes and baskets cold during the summer or frozen during cold winter months. Some of the old-style caches were six feet deep and six foot square, laboriously carved into the ground with walls as straight and smooth as any modern house.

Sourdock, mixed with oil or dried salmon eggs, was frequently buried for over a year, and wonderfully fresh when retrieved. Though few, if any, cellars have been made within the last 40 years, due to village modernization after Alaska's 1957 statehood, they still chill summer's bounty at fish camp.

In the interior, large birch baskets were constructed to fit one into another. When filled with berries and stacked on top of each other, only the top basket needed a cover. Not only were they waterproof, they repelled mice, which would not eat birch bark. Like pokes, they held berries, fish, meat or a combination of cooked meats with berries or greens and were stored in cold cellars to freeze.

When storage containers were filled, women cleverly fashioned mini-cold cellars or simple shallow holes in the icy ground, ingeniously lined with grass. A layer of large, highly acidic leaves,[10] either wilted or dipped in boiling water, were carefully pressed to the sides and bottom to make it waterproof. Without leaking, thick purées of fermenting berries could be poured into the hole. Yet another cleverly-devised lining technique was to mash boiled, acidic leaves into a purée, which was drained and smeared directly onto the sides and bottom of the dirt cellar. Their covers were additional acidic leaves, topped with grasses, skins or wood and dirt. Anything and everything was used to keep the contents clean, out of the sun and away from flies, which laid dreaded maggot-bearing eggs. There was nothing more abhorrent to Eskimos than flies and their potential damage to food.

Pokes were made from skins or animal parts, fashioned into storage vessels for food or rendering blubber into oil. Along the coast, spotted sealskins were ideal because the fur adhered to the skin after it was turned fur-side in, stuffed with meat and plants plus fat for rendering, then stored for months. For medicinal purposes, pokes held young willow shoots covered with water, for birthing mothers, to relieve pain, or for mild maladies.[11] In the interior, caribou or moose stomachs frequently sufficed as vessels and were made airtight and waterproof to withstand long storage. Duck skins, plucked clean, were also used to store fish eggs and oil.[12] Occasionally, a large fish skin served as a storage vessel, but few women knew how to prepare them.[13]

Cooking/food-preparation methods
Women dried abundant amounts of meats and fish, or half-dried and cooked them later. They also rendered, boiled, braised, steamed or simmered, fermented[14] and roasted over an open fire. For winter consumption, everything was frozen. While interior peoples frequently cool-smoked their drying fish under a cover of branches or skins to prevent flies laying eggs in the moist flesh, smoking was unknown among coastal elders. Perhaps the constant gusty ocean winds made containing smoke impracticable.

Dried and half-dried fish

Hanging fish from poles to dry in the cool breezes was a common summer sight. In my little village of Shungnak, women and children seined every day with 30-foot-long nets during fish runs. Women elders, unable to lift and pull the weighty fish-laden nets, deftly gutted and filleted large salmon and sheefish for drying or half-drying as they sat amidst hundreds of fish strewn over the ground.

Drying appears to be a simple regimen, and it is, if each step is carefully executed. First, the fish must be carefully prepared. Heads are removed and saved for stink-heads, a fermented delicacy aptly described by the name. Frames and guts are lifted and returned to the sea; the eggs are saved and cured for fish bait, fermented or turned into numerous dishes. The livers and milt are for special simmered fare. To facilitate hanging, the fillets are carefully left attached at the tail. To aid drying, the oily fins and heavy fat deposits are removed along the belly. The final gesture is to carefully cut deep incisions slanted toward the head, two inches apart and almost to the skin. With skin side out and tails pointed toward the sky, the hanging fish dry on racks under the bright sun. Their silvery skins shimmer and sparkle in the Arctic breezes like a Christmas tree and everyone hopes for continued cool breezes without rain.

When I was a child, a cover of branches or hides was used to protect drying fish from summer's misty rain. Wet fillets do not dry. The result is spoiled fish and days of wasted work. Then, too, without breezes, flies lay eggs on the hanging fish and horrible maggots develop. The only recourse to small, white fly eggs is hours and hours of painstaking scraping; a spirit-dampening task for everyone involved. To prevent flies in Shungnak, slow-burning embers efficiently smoke the flies away, while the coastal people rely on breezes.

For half-dried fish, the fillets hang about two days until barely moist inside; only experience and knowing fingers can decipher the exact time. Half dried fish are always cooked before eaten or stored in seal oil to prevent possible sickness. Longer drying eliminates all moisture and can take as long as five or six days. Once dried, the thinly-sliced fish are eaten without further preparation, except for a dousing in seal oil, or are stored in seal oil for the winter. Dried salmon, finely sliced and wrapped in young willow leaves dressed with seal oil, has been a favoured dish for centuries. It is still enjoyed today by those lucky enough to have it on their tables.

Moist heat: boil, poach, simmer, blanch

Boiling, when a heat source was plentiful, was the most often-used technique to prepare food. My mother always said, 'Everything is boiled.' As a cooking technique, it was consistent and bland, but women had little time to devise recipes. Boiling was common knowledge, easy and reliable; there were no decisions and no creative mistakes. However, the term 'boil' could very well be a misnomer. Not once did I see a bubbling pot. Rather, the liquid gently shimmered, or poached, on the surface. With a limited heat source, if a pot did boil, it was for a short time. In addition, elders stressed putting meats or fish in cold water before cooking, which produced a broth with more flavour than when putting proteins into hot water.

In contrast, sourdock and many greens were blanched, or quickly boiled in water, to preserve colour and flavour. At other times, only a tiny amount of water was needed to braise or steam and timing was important, lest coveted foodstuffs overcooked. Nonetheless, the descriptive term was always 'boiled', and the resulting broth was either drunk, saved for another dish or given to the dogs. They, too, needed nourishment since they provided an important mode of travel. A sampling of recipes using moist heat includes:

DUCK OR SEAGULL EGGS Take from nests in early spring; boil, cool in cold water.

TOMCOD (an Interior fish thought to make one sick unless cooked) Boil.

TOMCOD LIVERS Use lots; they are small. Cook gently to render out oil, remove oil and cook until livers are tiny, add sugar and berries.

WHITEFISH Cut in three pieces of even length (head, body, tail), boil, serve.

SMELT Clean, cover with water, boil a few minutes only.

BULLHEADS (similar to small monkfish) Same as above but cook fifteen minutes, cut into three pieces and serve.

SOURDOCK (also called Arctic Chard) Boil in one-third its volume of water for one hour, stir, add more leaves, cook until thick and saucy. Serve with sugar or seal oil. Or boil in a little water, cool, mash with small pieces of blubber, cool, store in poke until blackberries are in season and add berries to sourdock-filled poke.

BABY BIRDS, OWL, DUCKS, LOON, RABBIT, SQUIRRELS AND PTARMIGAN Clean, cut, boil.

BEAR MEAT Boil, cool, add seal oil to flavour.

UGRUK OR SEAL Boil only a few minutes, or cook half-dried ugruk a few minutes, put in poke layered with dried ugruk pieces on bottom, then blubber, then cooked meat.

SEAL INTESTINES Boil a few minutes just until they turn white, eat or put in poke.

COOKED BLUBBER Take pieces from poke, pour hot water over, cook until oil comes out, eat.

SEAL HEAD Remove head, cut into pieces as small as possible, cook for a long time. Eat meat, breaking the skull open and eating everything.

WHITE WHALE Boil until done, add fat from inside small intestines and cook.
WALRUS Boil skin and fat to make soup.
WALRUS LIVER BROTH Cook walrus liver in water until full-flavoured, remove liver and cook broth slowly until reduced and thick like a sauce. Set aside for two weeks, or until a little sour; use as a dipping sauce for seal.[15]

Roasting

During the summer, someone was always cooking over an open fire. But spit roasting, or dry heat, was a method used more on hunting trips or at fish camp, for immediate consumption. Since preserving food entailed freezing, the charred exterior would certainly have imparted a bitter taste to poke contents.[16] Occasionally, fish were spit-roasted but this was a tricky business. When overcooked, fish flesh separates and dinner would plunge into the ashes. Elders rarely mentioned roasting meat.

Fermenting

Where and when Eskimos learned to ferment is unknown. Some theories suggest they carried the Asian fermenting process eastward into Alaska via the Aleutians or the Bering Strait. However, there are also anthropologists who believe Eskimos travelled around the Arctic westward, going to Iceland, Greenland, Canada and eventually to Alaska.[17] Regardless, fermentation is a centuries-old process and, according to Dr Albert Sonnenfield, was originally devised to extend a food's life and then became a preferred taste.[18] Two methods produced fermented foods: (a) controlled fermenting and (b) hunting.

The controlled process, which sometimes eluded controlling, was conducted in holes dug into the ground, or in waterproof baskets or pokes. Every step was carefully executed to create an adequate pH environment. When the acidic balance tipped too far, the dish could become a deadly killer. Eskimo women knew that fermenting required an acidic environment, or at least that sour plants were a necessary factor in the process, but they didn't know why. They also knew that cool temperatures and minimal fat played an important role. In addition, valuable time and work were wasted if mould developed, leaving the food unfit to eat. Over years of preserving, and a verbal history of health and sickness, safe fermenting rules were passed from generation to generation. For centuries women prepared combinations of berries, meats, fish, greens, fish eggs or animal parts in an acidic environment that turned them into favoured delicacies.

When berries ferment, their sugars turn acidic, developing yeast and carbon dioxide. The sweet liquid centres expand, the skin breaks and eventually the container's contents bubble over the top. Women learned that restricting air would slow fermentation so they cleverly devised lids to keep the contents sealed. They briefly blanched and wilted acidic, sour-tasting leaves and carefully spread them over the fermenting surface. Sometimes, a hard fat from caribou, moose or bear was melted, poured over the top of the berries and left to harden. Pouring seal oil or fish oil over the contents was a last resort since, as they were not hydrogenated, they failed to congeal. Another problem with unsaturated oils was their propensity for rancidity, which was never pleasant.

To make fermented stink heads along the Arctic seashore, a hole was dug in the sand and lined with acidic leaves. It was filled with fish heads and salmon eggs, preferably from humpies or pinks caught going up-river. They were individually wrapped, or simply layered, with wild celery leaves and/or dried eelgrass. After covering with more acidic leaves and topping with wood or dirt, the contents were left to ripen either for two weeks or two months.[19] Women from my village made the same dish, substituting sheefish and salmon heads.

Similarly, fermented ugruk flippers, a dish favoured by elders, was made by putting seal flippers in a shallow hole lined with grasses, and covered with blubber to lend a special unctuousness to the dish. Once covered with more grasses, it remained for six weeks until the fur peeled off easily. After the meat and bones were picked free of fur, hot water was poured over them; they were poached for a few minutes, then cut into small pieces for eating or to use in soup.[20] Fermented ugruk intestines and soured seal liver take far less time, as the 'sour' name implies. Each was stored in a warm spot out of the sun, in a basket or enamelled pan, covered with seal oil or blubber for five to ten days.

Young Arctic natives no longer eat fermented foods such as stink heads and eggs, or fermented seal flippers. When plastic buckets became available, women thought they would be perfect fermenting vessels. Unfortunately the plastic, unlike the sand and earth and grasses, failed to impart the micro-organisms necessary for an antiseptic environment. The contents decayed, causing extreme sickness and often death. Since fermented foods are an acquired taste and sickness is a threat, it is not surprising that young people hesitate to eat fermented foods.

The alternative method for procuring fermented food products was second-hand; from the stomach contents of freshly-killed moose and caribou, or ptarmigan intestines. Herbivorous animals frequently ate lichens and grasses toxic to humans, but, once decomposed or fermented with the aid of the animal's digestive juices, the stomach contents were perfectly safe for human consumption.

Rendering
While rendering in Western cooking involves heat, Eskimos use no heat to extract gallons and gallons of seal oil from mounds of blubber. The process

takes about two weeks for oil to ooze from the blubber and is more the result of gravity than anything else. Performed from spring to fall, the ritual of rendering seal oil is imperative; seal oil is the flavour base of the Arctic. It touches nearly every food put into one's mouth and cooks are judged by the quality of their seal oil. Sheltering blubber from the sun's heat and keeping temperatures around 50°F is the best rendering situation for mild, clear oil. Then, too, blubber must be free of meat to achieve a light yellow colour. Clarity depends upon the absence of blood.

Pokes were used for rendering until guns became the main hunting weapons, which often left skins riddled with holes. Eventually, wooden barrels replaced pokes, though remote villages still proudly acknowledge women skilled in the art of making pokes. In the interior, bear or another solid fat was rendered over an open fire to satisfy hunger during hunting trips or when food was scarce.

Freezing/Preserving

All food for winter consumption was frozen, either in cold cellars or mini-cellars dug into the permafrost. Like our grandmothers, who canned to preserve their harvest, Eskimo women did the same but without heat or jars. Women stuffed pokes or baskets with meats, fish, greens and/or berries and filled the air spaces with seal oil to hermetically seal the contents with fat, similar to the French technique of preserving *confit* in duck, goose or pork fat. The airtight poke's skin also helped preserve the frozen contents, especially when stored longer than a year in a permafrost cellar amidst leafy branches.

Conclusion

By analysing and systematizing methods of food preparation depicted in stories and memories, a definitive Alaskan Arctic Eskimo cuisine clearly emerges according to Giuliano Bugialli's five criteria. Women designed implements to pick, prepare and cook indigenous foodstuffs according to rules verbally transferred from generation to generation, and bound their dishes with a distinctive flavouring base. Though little has been written about the cuisine's methodology, existing literature refers to scattered dishes without putting them into perspective. Hopefully, by viewing the food as a systematic entity, Eskimo cuisine will be more understood. Though the time frame and geographic area presented here are limited, perhaps similar principles could define the cuisines of all Arctic peoples.

BIBLIOGRAPHY

Bugialli, Giuliano (April 1989), personal interview, Kent, Ohio.
Subsistence in Alaska (1994) 1994 update, Division of Subsistence, Alaska Department of Fish and Game, Juneau, Alaska.
Evans, Dyfed (ed.) (1917) *The Eskimo*, Nome, Alaska: Nome Nugget.
Jones, Anore (1983) *Nauriat Niginqtuat, Plants That We Eat*, Traditional Nutrition Project. Kotzebue, Alaska: Maniilaq Association.
Lee, Linda, Sampson, Ruthie, Tennant, Ed and Mendenhall, Hannah (eds.) (1990) *Lore of The Inupiat; The Elders Speak*, vol. II, Kotzebue, Alaska: Northwest Arctic Borough School District.
––––––– (1992) *Lore of The Inupiat: The Elders Speak*, vol. III, Kotzebue, Alaska: Northwest Arctic Borough School District.
Mendenhall, Hannah, Sampson, Ruthie and Tennant, Edward (eds.) (1989) *Lore of The Inupiat: The Elders Speak*, vol. I. Kotzebue, Alaska: Northwest Arctic Borough School District.
Miller, Hannah (10 April 1996) personal interview, Nome, Alaska.
Nobmann, Elizabeth, MPH, RD (1993) *Nutrient Value of Alaska Native Foods*, U.S. Department of Health and Human Services, Indian Health Service, Anchorage, Alaska.
Penayak, Caroline (August 1994) personal interview, Anchorage, Alaska.
Sonnenfield, Albert (ed.) (1999) *Food, A Culinary History From Antiquity to the Present*, New York Columbia University Press.
Stapleton, Rob (Arctic scholar) (April 1995) personal interview, Nome, Alaska.

REFERENCES

[1] *Subsistence in Alaska*, p. 1.
[2] These three products were available before WWII though minimally used because they were costly and women did not understand how to employ them in dishes.
[3] The word Eskimo will refer to Alaska's Arctic Eskimo and is the term they prefer.
[4] Stapleton.
[5] Bugialli.
[6] Nobmann.
[7] There were some regional and seasonal differences. Seal oil was traded between villages, but when in short supply, fish or whale oil substituted whenever possible. Fat from caribou, bear or mountain sheep was used when nothing else was available.
[8] 'Interview with Blanche Lincoln', in *Lore of The Inupiat*, III, p. 239.
[9] Because food sources were declining, soon after 1942 a small group from Shungnak migrated thirty miles north up the Kobuk and started another tiny village called Ambler.
[10] Coltsfoot, sourdock or rhubarb leaves are the most acidic leaves in the Arctic and were used most frequently for fermenting.
[11] Personal interview with Caroline Penayak, 6 August 1994.
[12] 'Interview with Elmer Ballot', in *Lore of The Inupiat*, I, p. 27.
[13] ibid. p. 31.
[14] Fermenting is not really a cooking technique, however, it does alter the product chemically.
[15] Collected from personal interviews with elders Polly Kuwolak, Esther Bourdon, Ardeth Esau and Hannah Miller in Shungnak, Shishmaref and Nome (1993–1997).
[16] As a consultant for a major frozen food corporation, I soon learned grilled meats impart an unpalatable dirty flavour to frozen food.
[17] Evans, p. 3.
[18] Sonenfield, p. 17.
[19] Miller.
[20] 'Interview with Bessie Anausuk', in *Lore of the Inupiat*, II, p. 70.

Prisoners of the Rising Sun: Food Memories of American POWs in the Far East During World War II

Jan Thompson

O God, O somber God in sunset dust –
Now I come Home
But I am nothing like
The green and hopeful thing that went away.
From Glory For Me *by MacKinley Kantor, Coward-McCann, Inc., 1945.*

Prologue

While growing up, my brothers and I knew that my father had been a prisoner under the Imperial Japanese Army for three and a half years during World War II. He was reluctant to talk about his experiences and we rarely had the courage to ask. We understood how terrible his experiences had been and did not want to stir up memories of horrors. This was a common experience among children of former prisoners of war.

My father remained in the service after the war and made a career of it, so my brothers and I experienced 'the military way of doing things', as filtered through his wartime experiences. It was only lately that I discovered the orders that he would bark out, '*Waka-roo! Waka-roo!*' weren't Tagalog, the Filipino language, but a rude form of Japanese, meaning 'Understand! Understand!'

As the years passed, my father mellowed, and my interest in understanding his life grew. When my father's father died his belongings were sent to his only child. Going through them at my parents' house I found a large suitcase filled with family archives. The majority of the suitcase's contents were wartime letters to and from my father and his parents. Amidst them there was a small wooden badge with Japanese lettering and numbers. It was his POW badge. It and other artefacts quickened my interest in the story of American and Allied 'Prisoners of the Sun'.

Only then did I finally get the nerve to start asking questions of my father and his peers. I began to attend POW reunions around the United States and to interview many of the men and women who themselves had been prisoners. My goal is to produce a documentary on the subject – and I have been collecting information now for more than eight years. As I attended these reunions, I found other children of POWs who, during their childhood, had also walked wide circles around their fathers. Now they also are trying to learn more.

One of the unexpected aspects of my research has to do with food. Occasionally during the interview process the men would discuss something many of them did while prisoners: engaging in food fantasies and recipe collecting. While doing research at several archives, I was surprised to find menus and recipes in the men's diaries. Not all men collected these; my father didn't. Many men avoided the discussion of food because for them it was another form of torture. But many men, whether as a form of defiance or out of boredom, did discuss food, recipes and menus – sometimes to the point of mania.

Today, thinking back, they remember how they starved. Maynard Booth, a former first lieutenant of the Philippine Army, opened the doors to the extra two freezers in his garage, packed with frozen foods, and told me, 'I'll never go hungry again.'

Sixty years ago, while prisoners of war, they did go hungry. And their thoughts often turned to home, usually to their families, and of the meals they had eaten. 'I wanted a meal from my maternal grandmother. I dreamed of her cooking all the time' (Gene Boyt, Army). 'I dreamed of the steaks at the Cattleman's Restaurant in Fort Worth,' remarked Jack Heinzal, a pilot with the Army Air Corps.

> Let's set the record straight, we didn't dream, we flat *fantasized* day and night…Mom's home cooking of Beef Roasts, Stews, Pork Roasts, Pork Chops, Swiss Steak, Roast Goose (on holidays)…M's desserts always shared the spotlight at Fantasy-Time. Most memorable were Pumpkin Pie, Hot Mince Pie, Apple Pie Marble Cake and Bread Pudding. Strangely, though, one thing in particular always stood out (and still does) in my mind. At the butcher shop my mother used to buy economical Jowl Bacon, which came in squares and, when prepared, yielded copious amounts of hot fat. It was a pleasure of my father's, and later, mine, to pour the hot, deliciously bacon-flavored, sizzling liquid onto buckwheat pancakes.
>
> *4th Marine Jorg Jergenson remembers growing up in rural Iowa.*

The story of the POW has many layers: hunger and starvation, disease and brutality. But the strongest layer was that of food and memory. In the end, their means of survival would be their memories of family life and home cooking.

The camps

The majority of the men started captivity in weakened condition: they were already malnourished due to their rations having been cut to one third within the first two weeks of war. Many suffered from dysentery or malaria when they entered the prison camps scattered throughout the Philippine Islands.

The rule was: if you didn't work you would receive half rations. Even if the men were sick and in the camp hospital, their rations were cut in half. There were three rations: 'a working man's ration, a non-working man ration and a sick person ration, so if you were sick and couldn't work your chances of dying were 100 per cent,' said Gene Boyt. It depended on the camp commander as to how the rule would be enforced.

The men were generally fed three times a day: rice and *lugao*. *Lugao*, a Filipino word, was typically served for breakfast. It was a watery rice gruel made with some kind of green vegetable. The ration was about 8 ounces, or a mess kit, and it contained about 160 calories. The noon meal was served to working men only.

Usually each man received 24 ounces. of cooked rice in his mess kit – only twelve grams of protein were supplied by this rice. Normally a man needs one gram of protein for each kilo of body weight, or about 70 grams a day. If the body does not get this it will utilize the stored protein in the muscles.[1]

John M. Cook, an Army Medical Corpsman, remembered a time when a Japanese officer allowed a detail to go to a Manila warehouse that had been bombed. There had been sacks of flour damaged and the detail would be permitted to sweep it up and bring it back to the camp to use. So the idea was to make good old fashioned doughnuts for breakfast:

> ...so we take rice and water into a five-gallon stainless pot to soak and ferment but had no sugar, but we had pralines that were fed to the Philippine Calesa horses. But they contained horse manure and straw so we put some in a pot with some water and made syrup and then had to strain this through a cloth so it could be used...we then mixed our items in a large mixing bowl for the project. All went well we had smell and the taste of donut batter...we started the next morning and used a can to cut the donuts and used a clean Proctoscope for the center hole, we had to improvise as you know since we were prisoners of war.

The doughnuts never made it to the chow line because the cooks were soon informed that the flour had been contaminated with plaster of Paris that had also been stored at the warehouse.

When the Japanese got some flour off of an American ship that had been sunk in the bay, I volunteered to make bread. We did not have any ingredients to really make bread... We did the best with what we had and the men were contented to have some nourishment. Two of us who were bakers worked a shift to feed about two hundred men a slice of bread. There were approximately one thousand or so men being given a slice of bread every fourth or fifth day. This flour lasted for about two months. To bake this bread we made an oven out of mud brick and all the scrap iron and metal we could find. It took about three weeks to build the oven. Our bread pans were made from sheet metal roofing. So many of the men worked on this project. The excitement of making an oven to have bread was a great incentive to keep many of the men going. Can you imagine the effort to complete this project? Bread was to the Americans as rice was to the Japanese. A staple of life.

Morris Lewis, Army Mess Sergeant.

It wasn't long before the men began smuggling and eating anything that happened to crawl or fly into the camp. And with that came '*quanning*'.

Quan is a Filipino word meaning 'what you call it or thingumajig'. Some time early in the internment, someone applied the word to something edible that was not part of the ration. The word not only gained acceptance, its application was broadened to refer to the act of preparing any concoction that was a mixture of non-rationed foodstuffs or non-rationed and rice.[2] As Jorge Jergenson defines *quanning*: 'It pertains to preparing a makeshift meal over a makeshift fire, using makeshift utensils, much the same as hoboes did in the '30s.'

Quanning was an act of supreme pleasure in O'Donnell and later camps. No sensation was as thrilling. The joyful anticipation that was experienced as one mixed and, if appropriate, cooked a private melange of rice and a tasty smuggled ingredient cannot be expressed. The men often said that perhaps the greatest virtue of rice is that anything will improve it.[3]

The meals were cooked by prisoners inside the camps. Under intense scrutiny from those waiting in line these cooks were responsible for serving out the portions. Though some thought the best job in camp would be the job of cooking the food and distributing the rice, some men didn't, as Wilbur Marrs related: 'That was a hard job. That was the worst job you could get, because everybody wanted to get an equal amount and it was hard to do. You couldn't make everybody equal.'

What I did is everybody had their number on the bowl where it couldn't be seen underneath, then we'd line up all the bowls, fill the bowls...nobody was suppose to know who the hell's bowl it was...it was a trust job. If you were chosen for that, you were considered to be pretty good.

Bob Ehrhart, Marine Corps.

Army Medical Corpsman John M. Cook recalls a time when his assignment was the mess hall in Zero Ward, which was the staging area for those who were dying at the Camp Cabanatuan Hospital:

> [I] was asked to come in early and help cook the Lugao. It would still be dark and only a 40 watt bulb at a distance and I could not see too well when we put the rice into the water. At about day break there were ten or twelve scrawny patients watching us work to see that we did not eat or steal anything, when I noticed something in the water or should I say Lugao, and it was a rat. I called the first cook over and he told me to flip the rat out the back window opening of the mess hall when he lifted the cover off the opening. He opened the cover and out went the rat cooked and tender. And you should have seen the fight over the darn rat. Those sick patients would have all made the skeleton in any Doctor's office. In five minutes there was not a trace of the varmint.

It was said the first meat or protein issued in Camp O'Donnell were the knit worms found in the *Lugao*.

At the civilian camps, the internees were organized into cooking squads and took turns preparing the meals each day. Jane Fredrickson, a seventeen-year-old American, remembers her early days of internment on Cebu Island:

> We cooked over open fires and we often used native foods where they were available, we had to buy all our food. In the Cebu Camps, not once in the months that we were interned there, did the Japanese give us a single centavo with which to buy food nor did they give us any food. Their policy was 'the internees are responsible for feeding themselves.' We relied upon our friends, Filipino and Spanish, for food. We pooled our money, most had no money. We gave money to our buyers, two young Filipino men, to buy food for us. And we formed a committee to oversee the expenditures for food. We pooled the food. We wrote IOUs...and some IOUs were written for money borrowed from the outside. Many friends came to the gate bringing us food and expecting nothing in return for what they gave. It was a fine example of concern and human compassion...we never knew from day to day whether we would have enough food, but what we did have we tried to prepare in appetizing ways. Our squad of women cooks (and the men,

also) were creative cooks. None of us gained weight, but we were not starving then.

The rice was cooked in a variety of containers depending on the camp. On the Tabayas road work detail it was in wheel barrels. At Camp O'Donnell it was in oil drums; in other camps, especially those in Japan, there were woks:

> ...the type of pot your grandmother used to make soap or apple sauce. When you cooked rice in these containers it ends up with a half-inch layer of burnt rice on the bottom. They would scrape it out and parcel it out in a coffee can. It tasted like pop corn and it filled our belly.'
>
> *Gene Boyt, Army Air Corps.*

We Americans had to learn to cook rice. Often we would burn the rice while cooking and we placed the burnt rice out as scraps available for anyone. Soon we had many men fighting over the burned rice and we later started issuing it out to a different barracks each day to share what was available. Through the course of time it was discovered eating the burned rice cured dysentery. Burned rice soon became the treatment for men with dysentery.

Mess-sergeant Morris Lewis.

Work details outside the camps provided opportunities for men to steal and smuggle food back into camp. John Hildebrand recalls a time, when out on a work detail, when he found a family of mice, a mother and four babies. 'You know, that mother wouldn't leave those babies,' he recalled, teary eyed, 60 years later at a recent prisoner reunion. 'I had to take them all, and I shared them with my buddies. We skinned them and then boiled them.'

Life in camp was monotonous. Some camps started classes of whatever subject could be taught. The civilian camps had children, so schools were set up. Men played cards, cribbage, chess and checkers. A portion of the library from the United States Embassy made its way to the Zentsugi camp (Japan), but not all camps had libraries.

Paper and writing utensils were scarce. But those that had them had a mental advantage. It was on paper that they could plan the rest of their lives. It was on paper they could write down where to go and what to buy, once liberated and back in the States. And it was on paper they could write their favourite foods, recipes or menus:

> 'During the forty three months that I was a POW I spent a lot of time just writing out food and holiday menus to keep myself somewhat sane and focused. I don't know if I did this because I was craving food or to

keep myself up to the task of being the Mess Sergeant... Imagine being asked by your soldiers to tell them what was going to be on the Christmas menu, all knowing that there would never be such a meal. But here we were with each soldier coming to me and asking if they could put their dish on menu. It did give us all a sense of what we were remembering most and the will to go on another day. We were planning more than meals, we were providing a sense of hope for what should be or would be again someday.

Mess-sergeant Morris Lewis.

Morris Lewis wrote out a Thanksgiving menu in camp, saved these 60 years:

Thanksgiving Dinner Menu

Roast Turkey
Creamed tomato soup ◆ Oyster soup
Virgina Baked Ham ◆ Fried Rabbit
Fresh Ass. Fruit & Grapes
Cramberry [sic] Sauce ◆ Apple Sauce
Raisin Dressing ◆ Gibblet Gravy
Snowflake Potatoes ◆ Candied Sweet Potatoes
Buttered Sweet Corn ◆ French Peas
Green String Beans ◆ Fried Egg Plant
Buttered Asparagus Tip ◆ Green Stuffed Olives
Sweet Mix Pickles ◆ Sliced Tomatoes
Lettuce ◆ Mayonaise [sic] Dressing
Pineapple & cottage salad
Bread, whole wheat bread, Graham bread, raisin bread, Hot Rolls
Assorted Cookies ◆ Fresh butter & Ass. Jams
Fruit Cake ◆ Devil Food Cake
Coconut Layer Cake ◆ Strawberry Short Cake ◆ Whipped cream
Mince Meat Cake ◆ Pumpkin Pie
Fresh Apple Pie ◆ Chocolate Merangue [sic] Pie
Assorted Nuts ◆ Assorted Candies
Assorted Ice Cream ◆ Malted Milk ◆ Fresh Milk
Fruit Punch ◆ Coffee
Cigarettes ◆ Iced Cold Beer ◆ Cigars

Many of the men would spend entire days chasing down recipes and compiling recipes on every scrap of paper they could find...to an extreme... I never allowed myself to do it, I wanted to keep my mind off it...towards the end I tried to find the BEST recipes by the gourmet experts so to speak...from different nationalities...

Gene Boyt, Army Air Corps.

I never wrote out recipes or menus but we had a number of POWs in our barracks that held conferences about concocting food, which would drive me crazy!!!

Jim Hildebrand, Navy.

The men could not stop thinking about food. Gene Boyt used to fantasize:

> I went to sleep many nights and use to go to bed dreaming about a sandwhich with two Hershey bars with crisp bacon in between. I couldn't understand why nobody had manufactured this years before and sold it, because it would be a world beater. Must have been because of the two things we were lacking in our diet: fat and sugar. But, ohooo, that sounded to me best possible thing you could conjure up. I never did try it.

> Food-fantasizing was a group act only. I don't remember ever, solitarily, fantasizing about it; only with other 'buddies'. In any case, the recipes that I can recall, were oral and started with someone wishfully thinking about, say, Swiss Steak swimming in dark brown gravy with chunks of onion, etc. Someone else would add another ingredient or dimension, etc., until, were it physically possible, we would had salivated or climaxed or both... Afterthought: perhaps it was just our rundown physical conditioning, but, after the first year and a half or so, in general, girls and femininity did not, any longer, enter into the POW's thought process.

Jorg Jergenson.

> Then there was Frenchy, The Rock...he was always dreaming of blueberry pie. And he used to diddle with his food. A lot of guys did. They didn't want to eat it all right a way, and they'd mix tea leaves in with it and they'd pat it down...well a lot of us, we were not all there any more. After eating nothing but rice and then getting your brains beat, you weren't in good shape.

Bob Ehrhart, Marine.

Jane Fredrickson wrote in her diary:

> In Spanish class we held a conversation about food. One lady, explaining a favorite dish, suddenly broke out in enthusiastic English, 'You put the meat on top of the potatoes so the juice runs down and through them!', she said.

On New Year's Eve 1943 the men in Lt. Colonel Jones's barracks composed a song describing each of its members.

I.	VII.
An earnest room leader called Scottie	An American Welshman called Jones
Developed a tongue that was spotty	Would speak in the loudest of tones
When asked to explain	He grew a long beard
He replied, 'it's the strain,	And the use soon appeared
Of controlling a room that's gone dotty.'	Was to filter the stew from the stones.

As our conversations grew around the holiday menu planning we would always turn toward remembering home and what we would do when we got back home. We always seem to try and sort out the next Thanksgiving, Christmas or birthday with our families. It seems to me the conversation would always be 'if I'm free by next...this what I want to do.'

Mess-sergeant Morris Lewis.

They were the memories of home. These memories of home, with their loved ones gathered at the dinner table during the holidays. The menus were memories of childhood holiday gatherings. The recipes were from their mothers' kitchens. These memories helped the men survive their ordeal. The family fabric was strong back home because they had endured a similar situation during the depression. The family may not have had enough food but they had each other for comfort.

The Red Cross Parcel

Eventually Red Cross Parcels were distributed to the camps. Each camp's distribution of parcels would be based on location and the individual camp's commandant. At some camps men received their own individual parcels but this rarely happened. At camps such as Zentsugi, a model camp used for propaganda purposes, and the camps that held the senior officers, such as Generals Wainwright, King and Percival, packages were regularly received.

John Hildebrand remembers: 'There was enough food for seven days if eaten normally. I used my tooth powder to sweeten the rice.'

> I remember it was an 11 pound box, they were all alike, with a few important distinctions... We would take it back to the bunk area and would open it excitedly to see what the few differences were... The box contained a big box of cubed sugar, a can about a pound of powdered

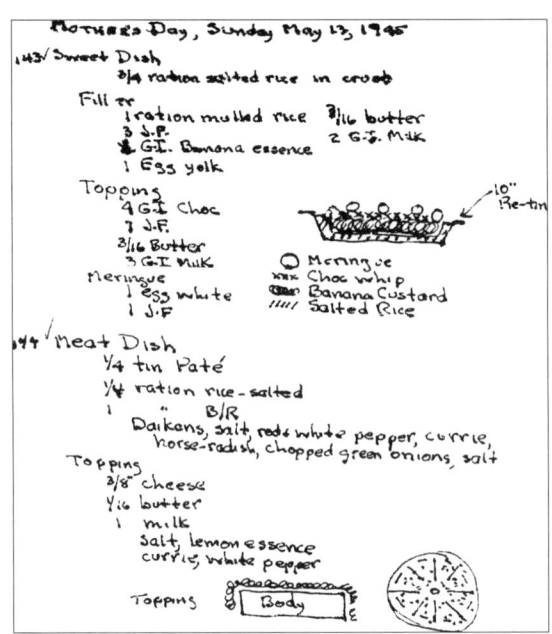

A page from Colonel Jones' prison-camp journal, featuring his Mother's Day cake.

milk, a small can of powdered coffee, 1–2 cans of jam or jelly, strawberry, apricot various kinds. Once you opened those, there was trading market and fellows began to trade…the Camel cigarettes traded at 20 while the others, Chesterfields or Lucky Strikes were worth 22, because the Camel had more tobacco in it…it contained a one pound box either dried raisin or prunes. And HERE was the discrepancy; oh you wanted the raisins you didn't want the prunes. Because they had seeds in them…there was a D ration chocolate bar. I saved that and would make it last days and days and days. And just break off a small chunk after lights out and I was in bed, and your heart would begin to pound because of the rich sugar in your system.

Gene Boyt, Army Air Corps.

The men became very creative with their Red Cross parcel contents. Colonel Richard Jones kept several journals while a POW. Of ten separate journals, five were collections of recipes in very precise detail. He wrote down over 800 recipes, of which 64 were original masterpieces using the contents of their Red Cross Parcels. Often these dishes were augmented by drawings showing how each layer of filling should be applied. The majority of the recipes were for cakes or pies, and during the last year of captivity thoughts of sweets kept them in a frenzy of creation. John Cook remembers:

In 1944 I cooked a Chocolate-Prune pie with rice flour crust. Tasted good at the time, but when I came home and made one, it tasted like, you know what! We made rice pudding and got oil of cloves from the Dentist to season it...

Gene Boyt remembers how he and a buddy saved their rations of rice to make a cake:

...we saved sugar, chocolate, milk and butter. We built a cake. When the people found out that butter, sugar and milk if you beat it would be whip crème. So there were many inventions of beaters in prison, to gain a mechanical advantage to make whip cream with. The whip crème wouldn't win any prizes back home but it was considered the nectar of the Gods. So we designed out of rice a big castle with the engineers insigna on it... Of course the rice was cold. But we finished a real work of art. A couple of months ahead of that, we got hold of a glass pop bottle and took some raisins and prunes and made a mixture with water. From the kitchen we got a start of yeast, the kitchen had this because the Japanese had our cooks baking sweet rolls for them, so they had bread facilities. We got the riser and corked it. We made a hydrometer, a vial that we put air in. We put the bottle in the sunshine and it would bubble and work and if the vial sunk too much, we had too much pressure, we'd take it out of the sun. We were in the process of making champagne. On the day of March 17 we built the cake, sat there in front of 28 men and gorged ourselves. No sharing. Washed it down with the sorriest champagne, but it was a glorious celebration.
Gene Boyt, Army Air Corps.

There was always trading going on, never more prevalent than when a new shipment of Red Cross packages were distributed:

It was a madhouse, like an oriental fish market trying to trade jellies and jams and prunes and raisins. Also five sticks of gum was in there – I have hated gum ever since. I thought that was ridiculous but all in all a wonderful package, and Red Cross did a super job of designing it, it was the best thing to send to starving men.
Gene Boyt, Army Air Corps.

During the last year of the war the food supplies getting to the camps began to dwindle, especially to the civilian internees in the Philippine Islands:

Oct. 13, 1944: we are so hungry – so desperately hungry. 'How long?' we asked fifty times a day. We are starving... I feel so weak and depressed – I weighed myself – 92 lbs, and I'm still losing. My insides are practically ruined. Besides, I don't have an appetite anymore...when I go to sleep at 9:30, I can't sleep on my back since my vertebrae ache. I usually waken in the middle of the night – usually from a bad dream.

Jane Fredrickson, diary.

Liberation

If food was the number one subject on the men's minds, then number two subject was liberation, and then what to eat when they got back home. Colonel Jones also wrote in his journal what he wanted to eat once he returned to the United States. He wrote it menu-style:

DESIRED MEAL FOR FIRST DAY BACK IN THE STATES
Dinner

Dry Martinis • Canapes
-o-
Green Olives • Ripe Olives • Small Onions
Celery • Gherkins
Radishes
-o-
Hard Rolls • Napkin Rolls • Orange Rolls • Poppy Seed Rolls
Rye Bread • Dark Bread
Bread Sticks
-o-
Crab-Avocado Cocktail
-o-
Split Pea Soup
Au
Croutons
-o-
Top Sirloin (Large) Medium Rare
French Fried Spanish Onions • French Fried Shoestring Potatoes
Sliced Tomatoes
Baked Idaho Potato, Hollandaise
Garden Peas
Corn on the Cob
Creamed Carrots

Lime Sherbert
Burgundy
-o-
Heart of Young Imperial Lettuce
Roquefort Dressing
-o-
Large Serving Fresh Green Apple Pie
Wisconsin Sharp Cheese
-o-
Camembert Cheese • Hard Crackers
Madeira
-o-
Santa Fe Biltmores • (Gran Marniere)
Coffee

As much as the men had been warned by their officers, they did gorge. And many paid the price:

So our Commander had told us before that when supplies did come, to gather it up and bring it to the kitchen so the doctors could prepare quantities that our stomachs could handle. Well, there were hundreds of drums and in front of every drum the prisoners built a fire and started cooking a meal. Well, my buddies and I did so too. Everyone had a fire going frying spam or corn beef, it was delicious and it was great, and it made us very sick. So we'd get sick and come back and cook and eat and this went on for several days.

Gene Boyt, Army Engineers.

I have been like a mad dog in a meat house, not knowing what to bite first, the past week with so much good food; which we haven't had under the Japs. To eat and so little capacity. Peaches, fruit cocktail, meat, cocoa, gum, cigarettes, etc... Things we use to take for granted before the war and which no one fully appreciated until forced to do with out.

Medical Corpsman Robert E. Thompson: letter to his parents, September 1945, Mukden, Manchuria.

Jane Fredrickson, now age twenty, weighed herself the week before she was liberated and weighed in at 78 pounds. Most of the men lost an average of 40–60 pounds during their imprisonment. It was usually more evident on the taller men. It was not unheard of that some men weighed 80 pounds or less. The average weight gain was about one and a half pounds per day once the camps received the food drops.

Conclusion

Studies of POWs reveals that while one per cent of American prisoners of war in Europe died, 57 per cent of those imprisoned in Asia died.[4]

When the men were asked why they were able to survive, they all mentioned they had family waiting for them at home. Those thoughts of home often focused on family meals and dishes made at special times: holidays and mother's pies and cakes. There seems to be another factor almost all survivors had in common: the majority were farm boys who had had to cope with hard scrabble farming during the tough years of the 1920s, and especially the Great Depression. Their rigorous childhoods, with diets often of rice, red beans, corn and pork fat, fitted them to cope with even harder times. And when the family cooked for the holidays or harvest time, many watched and helped the womenfolk in their work. That is why so many could reconstruct dishes in their minds when they thought of home and dreamed of feasts.

REFERENCES

[1] Olson, John E. (1985) *O'Donnell, Andersonville of the Pacific*, self-published.

[2] Curtis, Colonel Donald, *Let's eat*, unpublished document in the collection of Brigadier General Donald Curtis USMC, Personal Papers, Archives Branch Marine Corps Research Center, Quantico, VA.

[3] Keene, R.R. (April 1992) 'Murder on Bataan', in *Leatherneck* magazine.

[4] Permission from Mrs Lillian Jones and family for all information and excerpts from Lietenant Colonel Richard Jones' unpublished journals.

The other quotations are either from personal interviews or are answers to a questionnaire that I had given out or mailed. They are all from men and women who are alive today.

Between their Memories and Mine: Confit Revisited

Renée Valeri

The incarnation – if one may say so – of a food turning into memory is, for many literati (and more recently maybe even for some others), a small madeleine cake soaked in an infusion of lime-flowers. The memory it triggered in Marcel Proust led him to slowly unfold a world of memories from his life among the bourgeoisie in Paris (and their visits to Normandy) one hundred years ago. In his eight volumes of *A la recherche du temps perdu*, hundreds of people and thousands of details compose a rich tapestry of the kinds of character and behaviour peculiar to that particular class.

A century later, the madeleine cake is offered to the masses in the 1,600 outlets of Starbucks, the coffee-shops that have so rapidly spread over North America, and now also to Europe. The American coffee, which in the United States used to be a comparatively pale and watery (albeit hot), thirst-quenching beverage, is, in the Starbucks version, more often than not espresso-based. This is consumed as a stimulant, in dozens of varieties, combined with sweet additives borrowed from tastes reminiscent of an ice-cream parlour. At the counter, where the customer stands brooding over whether to accompany the coffee with one of the giant croissants or muffins, he can forgo these for a madeleine.

Here this confection is strangely out of context. Not only is Proust's lime-flower infusion lacking, but also one wonders how many customers are able to recall it to any previous experience at all.

However, this is also a typical contemporary phenomenon: an element that has been removed from a specific geographical context is now becoming part of the cultural baggage of people today, independent of where they live. In our example, a cookie with references to France is nibbled together with coffee that hails from Italy, but both are consumed in the United States and with flavours that are definitely American. Still, the matter of authenticity – originality and belonging to a specific place – is not really an issue, since it is not authenticity that is asked for.

This breaking down of the geography of many foods also has some implications for our perceptions of taste. Taste is only partly olfactory and gustatory. To a large extent it is connected with memory and thinking, since we transform our perceptions into memory and thinking. When foods are moved out of context and offered to people who have no memories to relate them to, not even the knowledge that would help them to assess the value of these foods, they lose their meanings.

It has been suggested that we travel in order to have things to tell when we get back. Even the foods encountered in travelling offer many good subjects for storytelling.[1] But food out of context is a treacherous subject. One of the simplest examples, the word 'bread', refers to innumerable different realities. The same food will change character as it moves from one country to another. But it will also change over time.

As changes are occurring more rapidly today, more attention is necessarily given to the authentic. But what is authentic? Haven't changes always been going on, even in the field of food and drink? Reaching an age that makes comparisons over time possible, I thought it would be interesting to make a small case study on food change in south-western France.

Thirty years ago, when food research was still a very small field, I did an extensive study of the ethnography of 'traditional food' in south-western France. What started out as a study of the cultural history and geography of common foods in this region – interesting because of Gascony's reputation for the 'good life', and because it had been left relatively untouched by the centralizing efforts in the early nineteenth century – eventually ended up by focusing on the role of *confit*. This preparation, which in the late 1960s was still little known outside the region where it was made, is a preserve made of fattened goose (or duck, or pork), salted pieces, which were cooked and kept until needed, sealed by its own fat from the deteriorating effects of air. So *confit* conveniently turned out to embody various characteristics of the region, such as the cultivation of millet or maize (made into bread or a polenta-like dish, but also used to feed the animals), and the keeping of geese (since the sizes of the farms usually did not allow larger animals). The geese were fattened by means of force-feeding with millet/maize, and the oversized livers (*foies gras*) were given to the landowner by contract.[2] The tenant farmers got to keep the meat and preserved it in its own fat as *confit*. This fat was greatly appreciated for cooking, or for flavouring the ubiquitous soup.

I recently went back to visit to see if and how things had changed. Having lived elsewhere in the meantime, I had not been back in the 30 years that had passed. To me, the food in this region was therefore frozen in time. The reference-frames of many of the individuals I now encountered were different from mine and, since even those that I had met and talked to 30 years earlier had lived a slow change, I was reminded that there are many versions of history.

During this time some important changes have taken place in the practices linked to the production of *confit* and *foie gras*. In the late 1960s geese and ducks were raised and fattened during the winter on most farms in the area, most intensively in the eastern part of the Landes. The fattened, force-fed geese or ducks – be it the whole animals with the liver inside, only the livers, or the fat-laden carcasses without the liver – were sold (slaughtered) at lively, specialized markets, *marchés au gras*, in the area. Buyers would come from other parts of France, especially the Périgord, where there were many *confit* and *foie gras* factories, but where there was little domestic production.

What at that time was, at most, a side income for the families is now carried out on a more industrial scale, and today, when much of this commerce is instead channelled through cooperatives, the *marchés au gras* are much smaller, and their geographical focus has shifted. Thirty years ago the Landes was clearly the centre for the production of *gras* and, judging from the prizes awarded at the agricultural fair in Paris, it still seems to be. However, the biggest *marchés au gras* are now found in the department of Gers, which also markets itself as the home of the *foie gras* – made into 'the royal product'[3] of its farmers.[4]

In the whole area, production is now on a more industrial scale. Here, European Union regulations and the emergence of technicians and inspectors determine how the animals are to be raised, slaughtered and made into preserves for sale. The investment in machinery and new buildings is forcing people to professionalize the activities involved in the production of the force-fed animals and the resulting canned foods.

While the *marchés au gras* in some places are disappearing because people use cooperatives instead, they flourish in other localities by attracting tourists, such as in Gimont (Gers). People will travel from all of southern France to the Sunday *marché au gras* in this small town to get their own provisions of fattened ducks and geese. One of the biggest *marchés au gras* today is the Monday one in Samatan (Gers), where, for instance, at the end of February 1999, in the hour allotted to the sale of *foie gras*, roughly 1,300 kilos were sold, 1,200 of duck (at 190FF/kg) and 100 of goose (at 300FF/kg). The ideal size of a duck liver is around 600–700 grams, whereas the liver of a goose can be considerably bigger.

Most of the *marchés au gras* are, of course, combined with sales of other products (not in the same area, though – the sale of the *gras* is always in a hall of its own) such as live birds, rabbits, garlic, various produce, honey, nuts, cheese, *charcuterie*, even brooms. Outside is a regular farmers' market with anything from umbrellas to seeds and cheese to clothing, wine by the litre, and produce.

Others, such as the one in Pomarez (Landes) which used to be very big in *gras*, are now about to completely disappear in this sector, as is Aire-sur-Adour, a little further north in the same area. Still, families will come there to buy a couple of dozen ducks to make confit for their own consumption. They will thus be able to offer this dish to friends or relatives visiting from other regions of France.

Observing the changes in the character of these markets is not just a matter of the visitor's nostalgia for a colourful and rather spectacular event. These changes reflect bigger, structural changes affecting both agriculture and society at large, such as European Union regulations and the expansion of tourism, and lead, in the end, to changes in taste. People living in the area today explain the situation:

> Buying the machines to force-feed the ducks (and make *foie gras* and *confit*) is a big investment – if you are to follow all the rules: different things must be at the right temperature, the hygiene right, and so on. Separate rooms are required for each phase in the process – there are even rules for the electricity – and technicians are constantly coming by to check that the regulations are being followed.[5] If they aren't, you are not allowed to sell – and you can be subject to control at any time. The farmers need to get their investment back. As their margins are becoming ever smaller, it's harder to make ends meet. It is true that people nowadays fatten the animals all year round (as opposed to the past, when this was done only in the winter) but it is also done in a different way. It gets harder to manage the labour-intensive part, so people have to use machines.

> Many people now sell the animals directly to the factories (*les conserveries*). It is more convenient – but also easier when the quality is not high (private customers can be difficult!). That happens when the ducks are stuffed with maize gruel instead of whole kernels, the way it used to be done. Also, the animals can be force-fed at a younger age by using maize gruel which the young ducklings assimilate better. With the new technique one can fatten a larger number of ducks and do it in a shorter time (16 days instead of 3 weeks). However, the meat is less tasty, less '*fait*' – a difference as between a broiler and a hen. It is not suitable for *confit*, and does not yield that much fat. The goal now is really to obtain *foie* and *magret* (the fillet), in contrast to the situation thirty years ago when one wanted a lot of fat and big livers. Obviously, this also leads to different foodways.

> In the 1960s the farmers would explain the increase in the numbers of ducks (instead of geese) by saying that the taste of duck was '*plus fin*'.

Then and now, though, they also admit that geese are more difficult to stuff, requiring force-feeding three times per day instead of two, and for a longer period. To this one should add that the kilo price of a goose liver is nearly double that of duck liver, and admittedly tastier. And it is still not uncommon to see a goose liver of 1.3 kg – although the record from the 1970s was way above that.

There also appears another advantage with geese: they are a mark of quality in the sense that people with geese have control over the whole process: breeding, feeding and production of *confit/foie gras*, whereas with ducks, many farmers now specialize in just one phase. Some will only produce ducklings, ready to be fattened, others only do the force-feeding, and still others buy the animals to make the preserves. It is a true industry, with numbers unheard of thirty years ago.

Still, the goose is traditionally the animal primarily associated with force-feeding, and with *foie gras*. (Abroad, *foie gras* is often called 'goose-liver paté', although it might not be.) Along with the expansion of this trade, the movement of protests against the cruel treatment of animals has been more vociferous against force-feeding practices in the last few years. For instance, a recent action (July 2000) led to removal of all *foie gras* from supermarket shelves in Denmark.

People who have the opportunity will buy their slaughtered ducks from people they know, so they know how the animals have been raised.[6]

Nostalgia

As one drives through the countryside, memories from what it was like 'then' will superimpose themselves on the landscape/environment. One of the most obvious differences is the numerous billboards scattered along the roads: *Foie Gras Confit, Confit Foie Gras, Vente directe de la Ferme, Table Paysanne, Bienvenu à la Ferme, Conserves à la ferme, Ail du pays*. And, as an ironic comment in the heart of this land of delicious fats, at Eugénie-les-Bains, where Michel Guérard resides, a billboard at the entrance of the town reads: *Eugénie-les-Bains, 1er village minceur de la France*.

On the whole, the marketing of regional foods – both in Paris and locally – has increased manifold. It would today be difficult to ignore what *confit* is. Specialized chains, such as 'La Duchesse de Barry', or 'Les Ducs de Gascogne', sell it as well as farms that promote their wares on the billboards along the roadside (something that was never seen thirty years ago). At that period, *confit* was rarely offered in restaurants or hotels. Now many small villages have their own restaurants with local twists to the theme. Tourists in search of even more local flavour can get lists of farmers who will offer lunches with regional specialities, such as preparations with *confit, foie gras*, etc.

In the study of *confit* mentioned earlier, one important conclusion, at least to the author, was the hierarchy of different foods encountered that revealed itself through the collected material. The value attributed to a specific food would vary over time, in different areas and in different social contexts.

It was not only a matter of the raw product (such as the relative value of beef, chicken, geese, etc.), but of how it was prepared, how common, and other parameters. Ultimately, however, and in the light of the changes that have taken place, one must also add a further point, the quality of the product – which is no longer what it used to be – or is it just our memory playing tricks?

In France, food is very much part of the national heritage. As recently as 1977, a survey revealed that 84 per cent of the French thought that French cooking was the best in the world.[7] However, French cooking tended not to be equated with a number of regional dishes, but with 'haute cuisine', i.e. the cooking of various chefs, or with 'cuisine bourgeoise'. Although certain local products were still part of the national treasure (certain cheeses, oysters, or the *foie gras*) it is only during the last 25 years that attention has begun to focus on regional foods. The *Conseil National des Arts Culinaires* started publishing their series on the French regions in 1992,[8] and has now compiled a very extensive inventory of what can be found, with history, recipes, etc.

The consumption of ethnic or regional foods is said to provide an opportunity to enter another culture, and establish closeness to the foreign. This is an important aspect of tourism, but one should add that instead of just travelling to another geographical environment, we can now travel in time, and even socially, through food and drink. Taste and smell are senses that are well suited to assist this transfer. In memory we can transcend the separate spheres of time and space, making our own sensory history and geography, parallel to or different from the official one. The expansion of modern tourism bears witness to people's eagerness to make new experiences but, even for those preferring armchair travel, the focus is the pursuit of pleasure.

Nostalgia was originally the term for an illness, homesickness in its most severe form. Today it is often used as a means to identify and reinforce, if not create, belonging. This widespread, vague longing to belong has become part of modern life in general, since playing with other identities is an interesting and widespread phenomenon in contemporary society. In earlier times it was done through literature and through theatre. Film and television made it easier to imagine other people's lives, and enter another identity. With the spread of leisure travel to the middle classes and the profusion of know-how publications on entertaining, gardening, and travelling, open to anyone interested, food and drink belonging to life-styles in other places (as we noted at the beginning of this paper) and other social contexts are now open to almost anyone.

What seems to be happening today is that we assume the nostalgia of others. Nostalgia, which used to be the longing for home, and all the memories connected with home, is now transferred to pleasures and sensory experiences that belong to places, times or social groupings with which we have no connections, other than imagined ones. In modern patchwork identities, however, it makes perfect sense.

At the same time, there is another phenomenon (or ailment) emerging alongside the nostalgia: its counterpart, the apodemialgia, the longing to go away, which can also be expressed in terms of food and drink.[9] So we have our espresso, with a madeleine, sitting in a place that has no memories of either.

BIBLIOGRAPHY

Köstlin, Konrad (1998) 'Tourism, Ethnic Food and Symbolic Values', in *Food and the Traveller – Migration, Immigration, Tourism and Ethnic Food*, ed. Lysaght, P., Cyprus.
Le Confit et son role dans l'alimentation traditionelle du Sud-Ouest de la France (1997) Lund.
Pitte, Jean-Robert (1991) *Gastronomie française – Historie et géographie d'une passion*, Paris.
Rodaway, Paul (1994) *Sensuous Geographies – body, sense and place*, London.
Tiger, Lionel (1992) *The Pursuit of Pleasure*, London and New York.
Valeri, Renée (1998) 'A Different Taste', in *Food and the Traveller – Migration, Immigration, Tourism and Ethnic Food*, ed. Lysaght, P., Cyprus.

REFERENCES

[1] Köstlin 1998.
[2] In a region with small acreages and a prevalence of land tenure, most farms were not owned but farmed by tenants on contracts. Conveniently enough, the climate was well suited to the culture of millet /maize but, generally, each farm grew a little bit of everything for the family's own needs.
[3] cf. pamphlets at the local tourist agencies.
[4] Two reasons for the current differences in Landes and Gers might be, respectively: the creation of farmers' cooperatives in the 1970s and 1980s, and the focus on food for attracting tourists; matters that can be handled differently in different *départements*.
[5] The emergence of technicians and inspectors plays a determining role in how the animals shall be raised, force-fed, slaughtered and made into preserves for sale. The investment in machinery and new buildings forces people to professionalize the activities involved in producing the force-fed animals as well as the resulting canned foods.
[6] Discrimination is not uncommon among the customers, like two elderly ladies who were complaining over the taste of the *magret* (fillet) and the hearts sold in the supermarkets: 'Completely inedible!'
[7] Jean-Robert Pitte 1991.
[8] See for instance *L'inventaire du patrimoine culinaire de la France, Aquitaine, Produits du terroir et recettes traditionelles* (1997) eds. Hyman, Philip and Hyman, Mary.
[9] Tourism can of course be seen as an oscillation between the two (cf. Valeri 1998).

The Velveeta Chronicles: a Food Memoir

Phyllis Weaver

Eating, cooking, family feeding, menu planning, recipe testing and cookbook reading. These activities don't just punctuate my life story, they tell it. Making and eating food together binds three generations of my family like bread crumbs and eggs bind the different ingredients in a meatloaf. I can still recall, with equal enthusiasm and precision, the best fried-egg sandwich I ever ate and the first time I ate white truffles shaved over fresh pasta. I remember vividly my childhood favourite foods, their colours, tastes and smells, and the long-ago table around which I ate them. But are the memories accurate? Distinguished Co-Chair, Theodore Zeldin, concluded the opening session of the 2000 Symposium noting that all memory is inaccurate. When we consider memory – whether of food or family or war or flowers – we necessarily consider it in the context of psychology. Food memories are shaped and reshaped by our individual and collective psyches, to serve the needs of our psyches. In memoir form I explore and interpret the significance of my childhood food memories, inaccuracies and all.

Ingredients: take two sisters

They were sisters, my mother, Ida, and my aunt Evelyn, born to Rumanian-Jewish immigrant parents, Bubby and Zady (grandmother and grandfather) to me. Both girls were smart but neither went to college after high school. Beyond their intelligence Ida and Evelyn bore little resemblance to one another: not in appearance, disposition, or life style. Although I loved them both dearly, as a child, I sometimes wished for a part-time family transplant, where Evelyn was my mother and Ida was my aunt. Family background reveals the reason.

My mother was an attractive, often stout, strawberry blonde. Although she moved away from Bubby and Zady, she never expanded her horizon. She married my father, the vagabond lover, Frank Sinatra look-alike, who blew into town and swept her off her feet, literally. (He was a dancer.) He had many 'careers'. He worked for Zady peddling cigars, cigarettes and candy. He owned saloons, one with a craps game upstairs. He drove a taxi. He was a furrier. He sold cars and aluminium siding, and he fixed televisions and re-modelled kitchens. He kept company with low-level gangsters, when they weren't in jail. He adored us but he didn't offer much day-to-day emotional or financial stability.

Ida tried to keep house and raise us, her two daughters. But she wrapped herself in a protective fantasy world so the banality of her everyday life could only disappoint her. She suffered from bouts of depression before the condition became a household word. So our home was chaotic and our lives unscheduled. My sister and I were governed more by whim than by rules; we were often left to find and make our own way. But sometimes when our mother was in the kitchen she shined like the colour of her hair. When she cooked her dishes were seldom ready at the same time, and some never even made it out of the kitchen. But there were stretches when the recipes worked and arrived at the table about the same time we did.

Aunt Evelyn, six years younger, was long-legged and lean with coarse black hair. She effervesced like the bottles of seltzer water delivered to the back door of our house. She always lived with or near her parents, but her spirit propelled her out of the small first-generation world she was raised in. Evie married well: the young doctor she met while working at the local veterans' hospital. She set her sights on him, attracted to his future as much as to his refinement and intellectual brilliance. He became an allergist, and she became a homemaker. She painted and sculpted; she gave dinner parties with themes. She tap-danced and wrote musical parodies for charity events. She raised four children and then educated herself. Evelyn embraced the role of traditional homemaker as much as Ida was overwhelmed by it. Her house was clean and orderly and her meals were served like clockwork. The food from her kitchen was as reliable and consistent as she was. I thought it was delicious.

Ingredients: stir in the grandparents
Bubby and Zady's house was my home for the first five years of my life. We lived with them (and Aunt Evie, until she married) in the three-family house they owned. They were Orthodox Jews, kept kosher and spoke Yiddish.

Zady was a practical man. He smoked his cigar from a pipe to free up his hands, cut holes in his leather shoes to make room for his bunions and recommended *Briosci* after dinner for heartburn and indigestion. It stood tall in its cobalt-blue glass jar, right next to the seltzer bottle on the kitchen table, both at attention guarding against digestive angst. He would hold court at that same table for anyone who would listen: 'I know fowl,' he might command. 'I know chicken; I know capon; I know turkey,' expounding on the culinary advantages of each. He treasured his grandchildren: '*meine kinderlach*,' he called us, and we worshipped him.

Bubby was a quiet, simple woman. She kept house and cooked peasant food. She dressed early every morning, corsetted in a 'house dress', wearing gartered stockings and sensible shoes. Her flower-printed apron held hard candies in its big front pocket for us grandchildren to help ourselves. She rarely smiled and she was not gentle-handed. When she bathed us we were scoured clean – like her pots and pans. But we never doubted her unconditional love.

Zady spoke a little English, Bubby spoke virtually none, and she never learned to drive. So Zady did the food shopping according to her instructions. He was the driving force in their small empire; but he let Bubby believe she was empress of the kitchen. Their kitchen conjures up food memories with faraway names like *helzel, prakas, essig fleisch* and *lukchen* and *kay*. To me *helzel* could be a cousin, *prakas* a river, *essig fleisch* an industrial city and *lukchen* and *kay* a couple. Except for *helzel*, stuffed chicken neck, I loved these strange sounding foods. (The remaining three are stuffed cabbage, sweet and sour beef, and noodles with farmers' cheese, respectively.)

Bubby did the everyday cooking. On Friday mornings she made egg noodles for the chicken soup she'd ladle out at Shabbat dinner. She would knead and then roll out the dough, paper thin, dust it with flour, and roll it tight, jelly-roll fashion. After she had cut thin slices across the roll my sister and I got to uncoil the velvety noodles between our up-turned, floured fingers. Under Bubby's watchful eye we'd transfer them to a bed to dry, laid out on clean linen towels.

Zady commandeered the kitchen for the preparation of special dishes. He was in charge of making gefilte fish on Passover, starting with the white fish swimming laps in the bathtub. Live chickens spent their last hours pacing in our cellar, soon to become our Jewish holiday main attraction. On those Sunday mornings that Zady declared special he made *mamaliga*, a corn meal mush of Rumanian descent. Long before polenta went mainstream we knew about cornmeal. Zady would boil it up, stirring with a giant dowel, and then he'd ceremoniously turn the steaming yellow mound onto a wooden cutting board. Just a second ago it was a viscous liquid; now it was a brick he sliced with a string held taut between his hands. We ate it dripping with butter, farmers' cheese and sour cream; comfort food without equal.

Meals at Bubby and Zady's were heavy, delicious and memorable. These two were born of peasant stock. Their food reflected their culture, and their hefty bodies reflected their food. The dishes contained few ingredients, lacked subtlety and were prepared without much magic. They stuck to my ribs like the names stick in my memory. Every dish was made from scratch with none of the canned or frozen conveniences of the next generation. The recipes for Evie and Ida's specialities were often from the backs of boxes or from labels on cans. They beckoned more for their names than their tastes. These names could be exciting, using words like 'soufflé' or 'surprise' in the titles. Or they could be alliterative names like 'cheesy tuna chowder', 'cold curried rice salad' or 'chocolate super speeder'. The sisters clipped, saved and traded recipes, Evie's modified for her kosher kitchen.

Sea(food) change

When I was five years old there was a sea change in our kitchen and in our lives. We moved away to another house in another city and state, leaving behind the security of our warm and steady home. It was scary and exciting at the same time to be on our own. I remember the thrill my parents expressed over their decision to stop keeping kosher. They were giddy as they integrated the separate milk and meat flatware and dishes into the same cabinets and drawers. They wasted no time bringing forbidden pork products to the table. Now we could have bacon and eggs for breakfast, with butter on the biscuits that came from a cardboard tube. We were free to add ham to a cheese sandwich or cheese to a hamburger.

When our turbulent financial circumstances were calm and steady I remember my mother managing the housework and cooking. Then we might have the all-American shrimp cocktail, filet mignon and twice-baked potatoes for celebratory suppers; but such extravagances were rare. Apart from these special meals, her cooking didn't vary regardless of our financial security. Because my father had more financial downs than ups my mother preferred to steel herself for the inevitable tough times ahead. So she embraced recipes that called for lesser cuts of meat and ones where ground beef was stretched with fillers. Our kitchen, our meals and our whole house were only loosely organized, and then only some of the time. There were no strictly scheduled mealtimes. We ate when Ida got the food ready, or we snacked when we got hungry; often the latter came first. I am ashamed to remember that my sister and I spent more time ridiculing our mother's culinary efforts than we did supporting them. The balance in our family was delicate, and it was easily and often upset. Accordingly, if we minimized the importance of her cooking when she could do it, then we could deny its impact when she couldn't.

Yellow: the colour of my dream food

I was always hungry and could satisfy my hunger best at my aunt's table. I longed, not so much for her food, but what her food signified: the order and predictability of her kind of mothering. If Aunt Evie was the sometimes mother of my fantasies, then her house was my dream house and being with her in the kitchen was my dream come true. Evelyn was bigger than life, a

Technicolor screen shielding me from the burdensome circumstances of my own family.

Breakfast, lunch and dinner were at the same time every day. I can still picture Aunt Evie: 8.00 a.m. and she was in the kitchen with her apron on, ready to fix breakfast. Cereal boxes were on the table, and Wonderbread was near the toaster. While my cousins and I ate we could watch her do her prep work for future meals. On Friday she might be readying a brisket for Shabbat dinner or making blintzes to freeze for Sunday brunch. When we finished eating we were ready to help her.

When I was too young for serious kitchen work I would play on the floor with my younger cousins. The bottom cabinets held treasures just for us: plastic bowls and wooden spoons, measuring cups and cookie cutters. We were her shadow chefs, ready to do in thin air what she did with the raw ingredients of my dream food. In time we had real jobs suited to our age and skill: spooning flour into measuring cups, spinning just-washed lettuce in a mesh metal basket.

Lunch was at noon. One cousin only ate Kraft macaroni and cheese, sliced hard-boiled eggs, baked potatoes – a carbo-loader before the days of marathons. Another cousin ate only grilled cheese sandwiches. He wouldn't eat them unless Evie made them according to a formula so precise it would have challenged future rocket scientists. She could only use one thin slice of Velveeta, cut with a certain cheese slicer. And she had to render it virtually two-dimensional as it cooked, squeezing the marigold yellow guts out of it with the pancake turner. If my cousins ate few things, I would eat anything Evie prepared.

Dinner was at six. Keeping a kosher kitchen meant that meals were either dairy or meat. Her dairy meals form my most vivid memories: three cheesy, starchy dishes in particular. Although we had tuna burger surprise regularly, it remained a mystery. Cubes of Velveeta, 'hidden' in tuna salad, held the surprise position of honour, but not for me. Every time Evie fixed it, I'd marvel: 'How can you bake sandwiches in waxed paper bags without them catching fire? Why doesn't the wax melt onto the buns?' Evie never revealed how the waxed paper baked without pyrotechnics, so her kitchen magic, not Velveeta, held the surprise for me.

I loved Evie's tuna noodle casserole. Helping her make it was child's play: boiling, draining, chopping, dicing, stirring, layering, sprinkling, baking. It emerged from the oven in its glass vessel. Bubbling up through the cracks in the buttered bread-crumb topping, the molten cream of mushroom soup erupted. It rose through the volcanic layers of spaghetti alternating with flaked tuna and diced Velveeta, onion and green pepper. Once it settled down we could excavate the layers. I studied the second day's chilled remains, the layers visible now, each in cross-section.

There is a world of difference between a cheese sandwich and The Cheese Sandwich Soufflé. They start out the same, white bread and slices of yellow American cheese. There the similarities end. The cheese sandwich soufflé works its magic overnight; assembled in a buttered baking dish, it hibernates in a milk and custard bath, refrigerated until ready for the oven. Before it is baked, melted butter is poured over the top. Up it puffs, the butter forming a rich, crusty, protective cover. After an hour under fire it is ready to eat for whichever meal you crave it.

So it was that Aunt Evie could perform miracles with milk and eggs and bread and cheese. She was the queen of canned tuna fish. Her leftovers were legendary, her casseroles fit for royalty. Yellow was the predominant colour of her dairy meals. And it is the colour of my dream food. At the warm centre of the colour spectrum it seems to illuminate and bring warmth to every other colour. My Aunt Evelyn must have known instinctively how to translate the warmth of her soul to the palate of her kitchen.

My dream food: a nightmare in yellow
And then I tested the recipes. I prepared the three yellow cheese dishes I so fondly remember. That I hadn't had tuna burger surprise or cheese sandwich soufflé in over 25 years should have been a hint. During my pregnancy, thirteen years ago, I craved and indulged in the tuna noodle casserole. It was delicious. My tastes and eating habits are different now – dare I say more sophisticated and worldly? Nevertheless, I was fully convinced these homey provincial dishes would be tasty and satisfying. I was unprepared for the results. Firstly, the tuna noodle casserole was only edible, the crumb topping good, but not rich and delicious as I remembered it. Overall runny and bland, it simply was not worth the time it took to make and eat it. Thinning the condensed cream of mushroom soup recalled the colour, smell and consistency of the flour and water paste we concocted in grade school for making papier mâché.

Secondly, the cheese sandwich soufflé was notably ghastly. The spongy bread turns to mush from the long soak in custard, and the American cheese within is oily and too tangy. The prescribed one-hour cooking time dries out the edges. I could not eat a full portion. My son, Chaz, and I have been making a contemporary version of this dish for about two years now. We use a good, store-bought bread and fresh mozzarella cheese. Sometimes we bake the sandwiches, sometimes we pan-grill them French toast style. My son calls our dish French-toast *Arepas*, a take on the Columbian street food we buy in Miami Beach. We think they are delicious. I hope Chaz still does when he remakes them as an adult.

Thirdly, tuna surprise was the biggest surprise of all. It was inedible. The bun was papery dry and tasted of melted wax; the filling looked and tasted pre-digested, and there was no cheesy surprise. I could not eat it. Neither would my West Highland Terrier. 'No matter,' I mused, 'with its onion and celery filler the tuna salad would make a tasty cold sandwich tomorrow.' Tomorrow came but the Velveeta vanished. The package features a slogan, 'The magic is in the melt.' It sure is! This processed cheese food can melt even without being heated.

If American cheese is no longer to my liking, millions of others apparently do not agree. I learned from Kraft Foods that their cheese slices sold in the United States, placed end on end, would circle the world fifteen times. And across my country approximately 24 sandwiches with Kraft cheese are eaten every second. These are just one company's sales. Velveeta was developed in 1928 by Kraft scientists to prevent the loss of milk nutrients removed during cheese making. They perfected a means to incorporate the whey components into the processed cheese food. It's ironic that such an unlikely source of nutrition in fact was developed to meet a nutritional need.

These taste-testing disasters did not tarnish my food memories in the least. Instead, they strengthen a theory that, in memory, the food is far less important than the maker. Remembering my aunt and her food in a halo of perfection is suspect, suggesting that her exaggerated image served to defend against a far less sanguine reality at home. My preference, in memory, for yellow food is significant. Yellow is the colour of butter, cream and eggs that associate to mother's milk, both literally and figuratively.

Meatloaf revisited

If my aunt and her food were not as perfect as my memories are, then was my mother and her food necessarily as flawed as I remember them? Yes and no. My sister, six years my senior, confirms the loss of stability when we moved away from our grandparents and aunt. She recalls the same disorder and lack of regularity in our household and our meals. But we put our heads together and could remember our favourite foods from our mother's kitchen. Sometimes, from the chaos, dishes emerged that were brown and orange and reliable. And, unlike my aunt's yellow cheese recipes that I so fondly remember but do not use, I realize some of my mother's staples are my family's favourites to this day.

Ida and Evie used the same recipe for sweet and sour brisket, but my mother's rendition was tastier. Being more budget conscious and less health conscious she used the fatty second cut of meat for this treat. A top layer of fat-laden meat moistened and protected the lean meat below. I include this recipe here but I have renamed it 'Sweet and Sour Ida's Brisket' to acknowledge her travails. Please try this at home.

Glazed corned beef was a kosher stand-in for baked ham. At our house we could have either. But we begged for the corned beef version because Ida used the dreaded pre-shaped ham from a can. My sister and I would gag as the metal top was rolled back to reveal the gelatinous pink and white mess inside the tin. Like the ham version, glazed corned beef had canned pineapple rings that caramelized as they baked on top of the meat.

The sisters made the same meatloaf, but ours was topped with bacon. It was an ugly pinkish orange in the mixing bowl but I defend it, nonetheless, with its fillers of ketchup, canned evaporated milk and cornflake crumbs, because the end result was so delicious. At dinner my sister and I would fight over the slices with the most bacon. There was none left to fight over by the time we had it cold in sandwiches the next day.

I didn't cook with my mother very often, although there is one dish I remember making with her. I enjoyed preparing it more than eating it. She called it porcupine meatballs. I got to mix the ground beef with uncooked rice then roll the combination golf-ball size. As I lowered them into the pot, they would sink and then disappear into the canned cream-of-tomato soup sauce. I remember peeking into the steaming pot, watching the sauce bubble, hoping to witness the moment when the rice would expand into porcupine needles, enlarging the meatballs to their end-game size. When I tested this dish recently it wasn't good, though I found it comforting and edible. It is the meatball magic and the shared food experience that give me a taste of the mother I longed for and the mother I try to remember.

Conclusions

Jewish tradition and 1950s post-war America form the tableau against which my childhood food memories are set. Traditional Jewish food strengthened the spiritual bond of the dispersed Hebrews of the Diaspora (Dolader 1999), and it tied me to the family we moved away from. But more prominent in my memory were the convenience foods of the post-war era prepared by my aunt in her Betty Crocker inspired kitchen. As an adult, remembering her food was far more satisfying than eating it. Shremp (1991) notes, 'reminiscences...make the food sound so special...but nostalgia gives it more status than it deserves.' If my aunt embodied Betty Crocker, then my mother was the Anti-Crocker. Anna Freud (1965) explains how, in the 'food-equals-mother' equation, the mother-child relationship is played out over feeding and eating, but conflicts can be circumvented by mother substitutes, in my case grandparents and aunt.

We all respond to the appearance of food in forming our preferences, and colour is among the first attributes we perceive. In fact, the evolution of colour in flowers and fruit arose from the co-evolution of vision and food colour. In the jungle, red and yellow fruit evolved to help animals distinguish it from foliage:

> Zoologists are satisfied that the mechanism of color vision can develop or diminish in various species according to the requirements of survival.
> *Hutchings, 1999.*

It is no coincidence that yellow is a favoured food colour. According to Kaufman and Dahl (1992), noted colour designers, yellow appears to pervade our surroundings like sunshine. We associate yellow with light, so it is both illuminating and compelling. Our eyes are always drawn to a source of light. When we moved my aunt was my sunshine; her yellow food was my source of light.

There is, in psychoanalytic theory, reference to the screen memory, which I think is particularly relevant. Dreams or memories that are bathed in very bright light sometimes serve to cover, or screen, true memories. The more troublesome the actual circumstances are, the more unnaturally bright the screen light needs to be to shield reality. This mechanism accounts for the hyper-importance of my aunt and her yellow food. I remembered her and her 'perfect' cooking in uncommon detail, cast in a sunlit-like glow. Like the halo effect, everything associated with her was as good as gold.

Sweet and Sour Ida's Brisket

2 large onions, coarsely chopped • ½ cup unsulphured molasses
10 garlic cloves, peeled, left whole • Juice of 1 large lemon
3½ pound whole beef brisket, first or second cut • ¾ cup ketchup
Salt and pepper to taste

1. Pre-heat oven to 350°F.
2. Spread onions and garlic on the bottom of a shallow lidded baking dish.
3. Rub salt and pepper onto brisket and place in pan.
4. Mix molasses, lemon juice, and ketchup and spread over the meat.
5. Cover tightly or seal with heavy-duty aluminium foil. No steam must escape.
6. Bake 2½ to 3 hours or until very tender.
7. Slice across the grain and serve with pan juices.
Serves 4–6.

BIBLIOGRAPHY

Bordo, Susan (1988) 'Hunger as Ideology', in Schapp, Ron and Seitz, Brian (eds.) *Eating Culture*, Albany, NY: State University of New York Press.
Brenner, Leslie (1999) *American Appetite*, New York, NY: Avon Books, Inc.
Butterfield, Suzanne (1998) *Color Palettes*, New York, NY: Clarkson N. Potter, Inc,.
Capaldi, Elizabeth (ed.) (1996) *Why We Eat What We Eat*, Washington, DC: APA. 1996.
Dolader, Miguel-Angel Motis (1999) 'Mediterranean Jewish Diet and Traditions in the Middle Ages', in, Sonnenfeld, Albert, *Food*, New York, NY: Columbia University Press.
Freud, Anna (1965) *Normality and Pathology in Childhood*, Madison, CT: International Universities Press.
Griffiths, Sian and Wallace, Jennifer (eds.) (1998) *Consuming Passions*, Manchester: Mandolin.
Hutchings, John B. (1999) *Food Color and Appearance*, second edition, Gaithersburg, MD: Aspen Publishers, Inc.
Kaufman, Donald and Dahl, Taffy (1992) *Color*, New York, NY: Clarkson N. Potter.
Klepper, Nicolae (1997) *Taste of Romania*, New York, NY: Hippocrene Books, Inc.
Roth, Geneen (1982) *Feeding the Hungry Heart*, New York, NY: New American Library.
Schapp, Ron and Seitz, Brian (eds.) (1998) *Eating Culture*, Albany, NY: State University of New York Press.
Shremp, Gerry (1991) *Kitchen Culture. Fifty Years of Food Fads*, New York, NY: Pharos Books.
Sonnenfeld, Albert (1999) *Food*, New York, NY: Columbia University Press.
Steinberg, Stephen (1998) 'Bubbie's Challah', in Schapp, Ron and Seitz, Brian (eds.) *Eating Culture*, Albany, NY: State University of New York Press.
Stern, Jane and Stern, Michael (1991) *American Gourmet*, New York, NY: HarperCollins.
Tisdale, Sallie (2000) *The Best Thing I Ever Tasted*, New York, NY: Riverhead Books.

Memories of a Time, Place and People where Food Nurtured Intimate Social Community Values: Thai Street Vendors, a Vanishing Human Connection

Su-Mei Yu

My fondest memory of growing up in Bangkok, Thailand, during the late 1940s and 1950s, was the parade of street vendors who sold their wares in our neighbourhood; a bustling, narrow alley, cramped and overcrowded with box-like wooden shop-houses.

From the crack of dawn, to the late hours in the evening, the vendors came, balancing their goods on the ends of long bamboo poles hoisted over their shoulders. Some travelled on tricycles with the front fitted with wooden cabinets. Like a troupe of colourful street performers they came, like clockwork, announcing their presence with a melodic cry, the clacking of bamboo sticks, bells chiming or horns blaring, always to the delight of neighbourhood children and relief of the adults.

In those days, we depended on street vendors for nearly every necessity of life. And they provided everything we needed, right at the doorsteps of our homes. For our small neighbourhood and others all over the city, street vendors were links that bound us together.

Everyday at dawn, when the sky was barely visible, a clear song of a *bel canto* resonated and echoed through our quiet, sleepy alley. '*Yew ja keuy*,' he sang, welcoming us to a new morning. The neighbourhood stirred with the sound of doors being unbolted, followed by the rustling of unfolding oilcloth and liquid being ladled into metal pots.

This young boy with the sweet voice was the first street vendor to arrive. His basket was filled with warm fried bread or '*yew ja keuy*' and steaming hot soymilk. Shortly after, a man with '*kao tomm moo*' or rice porridge with pork came, clanging brass sticks together to announce his presence. Not only did this pair make for a lovely sunrise symphony, but their offerings made the perfect combination for a Thai breakfast.

By mid-day, a vegetable vendor sauntered into the alley. Her perpetual bad mood was only an act to discourage any bargaining from the neighbouring women. She brooded about the endless drought plaguing the countryside as well as other gloomy prospects – this, despite the pristine colour of her vegetables.

After her, it was a relief to see the fruit vendor bouncing into our neighbourhood! With her peculiar laugh, she was believed to be slightly mad – or, as the local women put it, 'nutty as a fruit herself'. Her bamboo baskets, overflowing with a bountiful harvest, assured that all was indeed well in the countryside.

But the most-awaited vendor of the day was the meat seller. As he cycled into our alley, the women abandoned chores and other vendors, rushing toward his greasy, filthy tricycle as if he were the Pied Piper. It was not his merchandise they were awaiting, but his latest news of the other neighbourhoods. He was a notorious gossip, who spread juicy stories from one neighbourhood to the next. While his excited audience huddled close, chewing on the latest pieces of news, the weight and price of the meat dangling from his scale would inch up an extra notch. This slimy little man could only be set straight by the sight of our servant, Ah Sum, whose no-nonsense way drove a spear of holy terror through him. She silenced him immediately.

Her steely glare equally terrorized the live chicken and duck salesman who entered our alley with great reluctance. Other women were content to let him choose for them the live birds trapped in two large bamboo cages. But Ah Sum was different. She circled the cages: one, then the other, quietly and slowly, eyeing the squawking chickens like a hawk. Before the salesman could protest, she would reach in and grab the victim, turn it upside down; then pluck the feathers clean off its rear end to inspect its health. If it looked unfit, she would throw the poor creature back into the cage and repeat the procedure until she found one she liked. It was not surprising that the salesman readily accepted her offered price.

For the rest of the day, streams of vendors came and went selling noodles, curries, Thai and Chinese desserts, candies, sweet meats, snacks and pickles. My mother's and my personal favourites, however, were the satay vendor and a woman selling a Thai snack called *miang khum*. They came in the afternoon when the houses heated up like ovens and the streets baked in the unbearably hot sun. We wallowed in the suffocating air until the smell of cooked, marinated pork jolted us back to our senses. The satay man set his charcoal grill down right in front of our shop-house. The tiny pork skewers sizzled and crackled as he fanned the smoke away from our house. He toasted tiny squares of bread along with the pork. Then he lined the perfectly cooked skewers and the toasted bread on our plate, with bowls of creamy, rich peanut sauce and pickling sweet-sour cucumber relish, speckled with red bird chillies and shallots.

The *miang khum* lady inspired my fanciful imagination. I remember her as a pretty, middle-aged Thai woman darkened by the sun. As she entered our alley, she swayed her bamboo baskets gracefully back and forth. Instead of singing out her sales, she stopped at each house and politely asked if we would like to buy *miang khum*. Mother invited her inside our home as if she were a guest.

She sat her baskets down in the centre of our living room, then proceeded to fill a large enamel tray with fresh *cha plu*, or betel leaves, as though making a floral arrangement. On top of each heart-shaped leaf, she carefully arranged nuggets of fresh, sliced lime, young ginger, shallots, bird chillies, roasted peanuts, dried shrimp and thinly-sliced, roasted coconut flakes. In the centre of the tray, she set a bowl of dark, syrupy sauce made with palm sugar, ginger, shrimp paste and grated coconut. With a graceful motion, she beckoned us to follow suit by carefully picking up each filled leaf and folding it into a pouch, before drizzling tiny drops of sauce into it. One bite of her *miang khum* seemed to turn everything fresh and alive once again.

At suppertime came my father's favourite vendor – the roasted duck and pork man. By the time he got to our home, he was at the end of his route, with just a duck or two left and a thin sliver of the roasted pork, dangling on the hooks inside his dirty glass cases. Mother claimed the man never cleaned either himself or his cases. He was a sight to behold, dressed in dirty rags soaked through and through with grease. His presence always ignited fierce arguments between my parents. As Mother hurled insults at the man, Father would be smacking his lips in anticipation of a great supper. He always bought everything this vendor had left, ignoring my mother's loud objections.

There were other vendors who came on regular intervals to our neighbourhood. I especially remember a scruffy-looking bottle and newspaper collector along with a charcoal vendor, so covered with soot that only the whites of his eyes could be seen. Then there was a pots and pans repairman, who delighted the children as he worked, spilling hot, liquid mercury on the ground. A stately fortune teller with wispy white hair and a long beard came occasionally, carrying a cage filled with tame finches, as well as a man who pierced ears and opened cabinets filled with beautiful gold and silver trinkets. A Chinese Ah Mah came every month to beautify the Chinese women in our neighbourhood with facials, using only a cake of rice powder and a spool of ordinary white thread. The eclectic personalities and fascinating skills of each character remain imprinted in my memory.

Today, Thai people, with their modern Western lifestyles, have no need for street vendors, an ancient and historical fixture of Thai traditional life styles since the time of king Narai and the Ayuthiya kingdom in 1656. Once, their presence demonstrated how simple know-how such as cooking, mending shoes or collecting discarded goods could provide a decent living and good life with so little income.

For Thailand, as a nation, there was once no need for modern technology such as automobiles, radio, television or even newspapers. Street vendors not only sold goods and services at one's doorstep, but also connected the neighbourhoods with the rest of the cities and provinces. The intimate human relationships provided by street vendors enriched the quality of existence in ways which the new generation of Thai, weaned on technology, will sadly never experience.

The disappearance of the street vendors is a symbol, signifying the end of an era that nurtured a way of life which was simpler, gentler and uniquely Thai.

Breakfast in Memory

Sami Zubaida

Breakfast is the stuff of embellished memory and nostalgia. The twilight hour between sleep and consciousness, to the sounds and smells (especially smells) of food being prepared, close but out of sight. Then the hazy actions of rising, ablutions, then the table and the food, the aromas, the drinks, revival of spirit and the opening of a new day. How many memoirs, stories and reminiscences feature the smell of bacon, the sound of sizzling in the fry, the aroma of coffee and a thousand subtle food cues signalling the start of the day?

Breakfasts of days past

The nostalgia is especially poignant in the contrast of the banality of modern breakfasts to those of some golden past. The pressures of modern life, work, health preoccupations and sedentary styles all are seen to have contributed to the brevity, the paucity, even the omission of breakfast: the fruit juice, the bowl of cereal or smeared toast, and dare you drink coffee, or even real breakfast tea (as against the pallid concoctions in current favour)? Gone are the multi-course breakfasts of history and memory: bring porridge enriched with butter and cream, bring devilled kidneys, bring black pudding, bangers and partridge legs, but 'please,' pleaded the poet (whose name I forget), 'make the foundation bacon and eggs!'

Within the days past, travellers longed for the favoured meals of their native lands. Witness Mark Twain, travelling in Europe, contemptuous of the table offerings there, and salivating in nostalgia for his American breakfast:

> ...a mighty porterhouse steak an inch and a half thick, hot and sputtering from the griddle; dusted with fragrant pepper; enriched with little melting bits of butter of the most unimpeachable freshness and genuineness; the precious juices of the meat trickling out and joining the gravy, archipelagoed with mushrooms; a township or two of tender yellowish fat gracing an outlying district of this ample county of beefsteak; the long white bone which divides the sirloin from the tenderloin still in its place; and...a great cup of American home-made coffee, with cream a-froth on top, some real butter, firm and yellow

and fresh, some smoking-hot biscuits, a plate of hot buckwheat cakes, with transparent syrup.

P.P. Bober, Art, Culture and Cuisine, *Chicago 1999, 524.*

[Fancy drinking coffee with steak of this magnitude, and not some deep Burgundy! The anaemic filet mignon, nowadays served in East Coast brunch joints, washed down with coffee *and* Chardonnay, doesn't quite measure up. And butter!]

But from this despised Europe, many other kinds of breakfast are the stuff of nostalgia. An academic colleague who grew up in rural south-west France reminisced once, with longing, for the crusty loaf rubbed on the outside with garlic, stuffed with onions, copious oil poured over, eaten as a breakfast sandwich; its ultimate rationale: 'it made the coffee taste so good!' I bet it did.

From the other side of the world, a Baghdadi diplomat, posted in the gastronomic wasteland of post-WWII London, records in his memoirs a list of breakfast items from his native land:

KAHI Millefeuille-like pancake, layered with butter and sugar, bought from the cook shops of Mustansiriyya (in the old market area of the city, indicating that such items were not prepared at home, but sent for from specialist vendors).
HARISSA Pounded meat and wheat, from Maulakhana (another market district), dressed with butter-fat, sugar and cinnamon.
PACHA Tripe, heads and feet stew, from Maulakhana.
TASHRIB Broth of lamb knuckles in tomato.
Another MEAT BROTH with pomegranate seeds or tamarind, with a sprinkle of penny-royal.
BROTH OF FAVA BEANS, dressed in butter fat and penny-royal, topped with fried eggs.
AL-MARIS Hot, fresh bread (naan type flat bread), broken up, with butter and sugar.
PASTURMA Slices fried with egg.
EGGS Cooked in hot ashes.
GAYMER Iraqi pronunciation of the Turkish *kaymak*, thick cream from buffalo milk, with apple jam.
DATES Fried in butter fat and topped with fried eggs.
A variety of SOUPS Made with various pulses, with the addition of the said *gaymer* or *kishk/kashk*. [He has special praise for a soup made from *hurtuman*, a kind of yellow split pea, topped with onions fried in butter.]
KEBABS of meat (*tikka*), liver, kidney and lungs (*fashafish*).

And, finally, a special breakfast item is yesterday's BAMIA (okra) stew, with broken bread. [This last item is one I recall fondly: *bamia* cooked with meat and rice dumplings in a sweet/sour tomato sauce with garlic and mint for Friday lunch, remains left to cool overnight on the roof, where people slept in the summer, and eaten for breakfast on Saturday morning. *Bamia* doesn't taste like that any more!]

Amin al-Mumayyiz, Baghdad kama araftuha, *[Baghdad as I knew it]*, Baghdad 1983, 135–136.

Al-Mumayyiz goes on to tell us that tea was little known in Baghdad (only from travellers' tales and samples from Iran and Central Asia), until introduced by the British occupation after World War I. So, it does not feature in the accounts of old breakfasts. Strange to think how such a recent introduction has become such an intimate part of the life and lore of the whole region.

Of course, most ordinary Baghdadis breakfasted on bread and dates, and in winter a hot breakfast from street vendors: boiled fava beans dressed in lemon and pennyroyal, with yesterday's bread dipped into the broth. It is related that workmen carried their own stale bread marked with coloured thread, which they gave to the vendor to dip in the pot, and reclaimed by shouting the colour of their thread.

Feast-day breakfasts
Without the rush of the working day, leisurely and extensive breakfasts may be prepared. Feast-day breakfasts in our home often featured meat, otherwise unknown at the start of the day. A lazy morning in bed, without the threat of the rigours of the school day, waking up to the sounds and smells of the *manqal* (coal brazier) being prepared for the grills, followed by the aroma of roasting mutton and burning onion – enough to drive you out of bed with a consuming hunger. And the breakfast specific to particular feasts: the Jewish feast of *shebu'oth* always featured *kahi*, the millefeuille-like pastry described above, but cooked at home like a folded pancake with butter in the folds, sprinkled with sugar, honey or date-syrup. The aromas were even more compelling than grilled meats and onion.

For Muslims, Ramadan breakfasts are a different affair: eaten before daybreak, in preparation for the day-long fast. The more leisured individuals stay awake with entertainment and feasting all night (and sleep during the fasting day), culminating in the *suhur* meal before daybreak. But the majority of working people were woken in the old days by street criers with drums, or the firing of the citadel cannon, in order to fortify themselves for the rigours of the day ahead. Again, modern sensibilities dictate light dishes of bread and jam and maybe cheese. The *suhur* of old was altogether a more substantial affair. For 'real' men, it was stews and broths of tripe, heads and feet, variously, in addition to grills, beans and lentils, always with copious quantities of bread. A mere memory and wonder for most now: grandparents telling the tale to youngsters, like those of bravery in war.

Another kind of feasting is that of the party-goers and the clientele of bars and night-clubs. There is an ubiquitous lore, which is featured in many places and cultures, from Afghanistan to France, spanning the Middle East and the Balkans, of these revellers ending up in the early hours of the morning at market stalls catering for the workers, and partaking in a hearty broth of tripe, head and feet. The *tripes à la mode de Caen*, of Les Halles in Paris, the *kalla pacha* of Iran, Turkey and Central Asia, the *patcha* of Iraq, *patsas* of Greece and the *kawari* of Egypt and Syria: all these were originally dispensed in the central market areas in cities, in which early-rising market workers and late-to-bed revellers mingled. Now that central markets have left many cities, the smart leisure areas which replaced them, typically Les Halles in Paris, have retained eateries, now up-market tourist attractions, which serve versions of the old specialities. In Istanbul, *Iskembe salonu*, tripe and offal parlours, have sprung up all over the city, many of them open all night, often catering to clientele hailing from the bars and cabarets (they themselves, however, don't, as a rule, serve alcohol).

Breakfast as a literary device: Najib Mahfuz's Bain al-Qasrain *(Palace Walk)*

An early chapter in the book (set in Cairo in the opening decades of the twentieth century) introduces the family which is to be at its centre, through an account of the household waking up to the sounds of the dough being kneaded in the oven room. Amina, the mother, rises at daybreak and wakes up the servant, Um Hanafi; they light the oven, then start on the dough. It is the sound of kneading and pounding which rises to the upper rooms, slowly waking each member of the household. The narrative introduces each character as they awake, their temperament and dispositions revealed through the manner of their sleep and ease or difficulty of waking, and the thoughts with which they face the day. There are two daughters: Khadija, twenty years of age, with a sharp tongue and cruel humour, mostly directed against the younger Aysha, much prettier, dreamy and sweet. Aysha sets a problem and a challenge to the mother and the servant, because no matter how much they feed her (their main duty to the girls) she does not gain the desirable and pleasing flesh and fat to make her more marriageable.

The men of the family, tyrannical and feared father and the three sons, seat themselves around the *sofra*; the mother enters, carrying the food on a tray which she sets before the men, then withdraws; the women will eat at a more leisurely pace after the men have departed for their daily occupations or studies. At the centre of the table is an oval dish filled with *foul medammes* fried in butter fat and eggs; around it are distributed smaller plates, some of hot food (unspecified), others containing cheese, pickled peppers and lemons, *shatta* (a chilli sauce) and condiments. At the muttered command of the father they all start eating, attacking the plates in turn, in the order of age and seniority. The narrative then elaborates the characters in relation to their manner of eating, and their thoughts at that silent meal.

Breakfast, here, serves as a literary device, which, in starting the day, defines the characters and relationships, which go on to unfold in the subsequent narrative.

Memories, memoirs and literary forms may record for us the foods and foodways of past times and elsewhere. Valuable as these are, it is the embellishment of memory, nostalgia and indirect comment on the present which makes them even more fascinating. Breakfast, in particular, because of its intimate domestic context and association with the world of sleep and gradual consciousness, lends itself particularly well to the mytho-poetic world of memory.

Other Papers Given at the Symposium

As in previous years, it has not been possible to include all the papers presented in this volume. This in no way implies that the papers excluded are of inferior quality; several of them will be or have been published elsewhere.

Michael Abdalla
Perpetuated in Tradition: The Role of Wheat Products in the Narratives of the Contemporary Assyrians
Proverbs, aphorisms, maxims and metaphors about food and particularly about bread.

Gwen Barclay
The Taste and Flavour of Memory
The role of flavourings and seasonings in the enjoyment and recognition of memorable foods.

Carol A Déry
Memories in Stone – Pompeii and the Archeology of Eating
The importance of Pompeii in the field of food history.

James G Ferguson Jnr.
'Do This in Remembrance': Ritual Observance as the 'Rough Ground' of Memory
The transmission, preservation and authentication of food practices derived from ritual religious observances.

Doreen G Fernandez
Sulipan Cuisine: Food in Active Memory
A description of the feasts and parties held in Sulipan at the end of the nineteenth century. Sulipan no longer exists, but its memory and influence remain.

Lyons Filmer
In My Mother's Kitchen
The author, a producer and speaker on radio in the United States, describes his experience with this programme as narrator and interviewer. He stresses the spiritual value in the sensual pleasure of satisfying our hunger.

Dr Annie Hauck-Lawson
When Memories Stir the 'Food Voice'
A study of our personal foodways that the author calls food voices. She focuses on people's memories and their food meanings and practices.

Karen Karp
Memory: A Living Procession Through Time
The author describes the importance of memory for both owners and customers in restaurants. She goes on to consider recent practices in agriculture and the isolation that this has caused between producers and consumers and the breakdown brought about in this valuable memory.

Carolyn Nadeau
Of Weddings and Funerals: Dining in Tirso de Molina's 'The Trickster of Seville'
A consideration of the themes of honour, loyalty and justice and also social values in the first Don Juan play, written in early seventeenth-century Spain.

Ambeth R Ocampo
The Malolos Banquet: Food as Historical Document
A description of the luncheon and dinner given on 29 September 1898 on the occasion of the Solemne Reatificacion de la Independencia of the Philippines. Both meals demonstrated a 'tasteless display of wealth...even in the midst of war.'

Ann Rycraft
'They know it well enough': The Medieval English Cook's Memory
A consideration of how cooks learned their trade studied from the very scanty records of the twelfth to the fifteenth century.

Shlomith Samish
Early Memories of Feeding and Eating Experiences: A Powerful Tool for Exploring Interactions
The study of these memories and experiences can be helpful in such areas as parenting classes, overweight classes, working with feeding and eating problems, psychological sessions, early childhood seminars, etc.

Colin Spencer
A Collective Memory?
Is our evolutionary diet still remembered in our genes?

David Sutton
Global Food: Memory Destroyer?
The availability of foods irrespective of season and from anywhere in the world challenges local knowledge and memories. This question is studied in the island of Kalymnos.

Barbara A West
Our Grandmothers Said, 'If There's Sugar, Flour and Lard in the Pantry, Then There's No Problem': Food, Nostalgic Discourse and the Construction of Memory in Postsocialist Hungary
The effect in Hungary of the collapse of socialism on the way of life of women. The role of women's magazines is particularly studied.

Carolin C Young
Le Songe de Vaux
The magnificent entertainment given by Nicolas Fouquet at Vaux-le-Vicomte in 1661 not only caused Fouquet's downfall but also demonstrated the use that can be made of such lavish entertainment as a tool of state.

List of those attending the Symposium

Dr Michael Abdalla, Poznan, Poland.
Joy Adapon, London.
Dr Joan P. Alcock, London.
Antonia Allegra, St Helena, CA, USA.
Brigid Allen, Charlbury.
Maria Teresa Arida, London.
Noga Arikha, London.
Alice Arndt, Austin, TX, USA.
Rose Arnold, Glasgow.
Jeanne Jacob-Ashkenazi, Leamington Spa.
Dr Michael Ashkenazi, Leamington Spa.
Monica Askay, Ely.
Anne Bamborough, Oxford.
Chitrita Banerji, Cambridge.
Debby Banham, University of Cambridge.
Gwen Barclay, Round Top, TX, USA.
Ann Barr, London.
Rosemary Barron, Cheddar.
Michael Bateman, London.
Harriet Bell, New York, USA.
Dr A. Blake, Geneva, Switzerland.
A. P. Bradshaw, Wirral.
Lynne Bradshaw, Wirral.
Marilyn Bright, Dublin, Ireland.
François Brocard, London.
Catherine Brown, Glasgow.
Deirdre Bryan-Brown, Wallingford.
Professor R. J. Buswell, Cowbridge.
Gloria Capel, Pellegrue, France.
John F. Carafoli, Sagamore Beach, MA, USA.
Robert Chenciner, London.
Janet Clarke, Bath.
Claire Clifton, Winchelsea.
Albert Coenders, Oss, Netherlands.
Caroline Conran, London.
Merryl Cook, Cheshire.
Joanna Cowan, London.
Zia K. Cromer, Chapel Hill, NC, USA.
Fred Czarra, St Mary's City, MD.
Andrew Dalby, Saint-Coutant, France.
Alan Davidson, London.
Caroline Davidson, London.
Jane Davidson, London.
Silvija Davidson, London.
Joy Davies, London.
Daphne L. Derven, Napa, CA, USA.
Mrs Carol Déry, University of Wales.
Cara De Silva, New York, USA.
Hugo Dunn-Meynell, London.
Michael Erben, Oxford.
Ferda Erdinç, Istanbul, Turkey.
Rianna S. Erker, Atlanta, GA, USA.
Elizabeth Erraught, Dublin, Ireland.
Rachael Evans, Abingdon.
Sarah Jane Evans, London.
Patrick Faas, Amsterdam, Netherlands.
James G. Ferguson Jr, Chapel Hill, NC, USA.
Fred Ferretti, Montclair, NJ, USA.
Elizabeth Field, Sandy Cove, Ireland.
Lyons Filmer, Fairfax, CA, USA.
Wendy Fogarty, Thame.
Ove Fosså, Sandnes, Norway.
Svein Fosså, Grimstad, Norway.
Sarah Freeman, London.
Mrs Jean Freemantle, Waddesdon.
Susan Friedland, New York, USA.
Elizabeth Gabay MW, London.
Brenda Garza Sada, and Silvia Garza Sada, San Pedro Garza Garcia, Mexico.

Hanne Goldschmidt, Virum, Denmark.
Sally Grainger, Hindhead.
Sophie Grigson, Daventry.
Nevin Halici, Konya, Turkey.
Dr Annie Hauck-Lawson RD, Brooklyn, NY, USA.
Vicky Hayward, Madrid, Spain.
Mrs Jane A. D. Hedges, Didcot.
Andrea Heinzinger, Muenchen, Germany.
Anissa Helou, London.
Madalene Hill, Round Top, TX, USA.
Ruth Hingley, Oxford.
Vicki Hingley, Norwich.
Ethel G. Hofman, Merion Station, PA, USA.
Geraldene Holt, Oxford.
Nina Horta, London.
Jeffrey Hyman, London.
Patsy Iddison, Abu Dhabi, UAE.
Phil Iddison, Abu Dhabi, UAE.
Jan Krag Jacobsen, Farum, Denmark.
Heather Jarman, Cambridge.
Rosemary Joekes, Bath.
Andrew Jones, London, David Natt, London.
Gareth Spencer Jones, London.
Karen Karp, Southold, NY, USA.
Cathy Kaufman, New York, USA.
Aynsley Kelly, Darling Pr, Australia.
David T. Kelly, Darling Pr, Australia.
Kate Kinnimont, London, David Natt, London.
Lidia Kitrikalis, Tessaloniki, Greece.
Sotiris Kitrikalis, Tessaloniki, Greece.
Bruce Kraig, Chicago, IL, USA.
Vasiliki Kravva, London.
Mark P. Lake, Sandford Saint Martin.
Professor Tim Lang, Thames Valley University.
Deborah Lansley, Bellville, TX, USA.
Janet Laurence, Somerton.
Jane Levi, London.
Audrey Levy, Kingston-upon-Thames.
Paul Levy, Witney.
Regina M Lim, Oxford.
Pia Lim-Castillo, Makati City, Philippines.
Dr R. E. Lister, Beaconsfield.
William Lockwood, Michigan State University Museum, USA.
Susan H. Loomis, Louviers, France.
Fiona Lucas, Toronto, Canada.
Fiona Lucraft, Ely.
Dr Jeremy MacClancy, Eynsham.
Martin Mac Con Iomaire, Dublin Institute of Technology, Ireland.
Russell Magnaghi, Northern Michigan University, USA.
J. Mardon, Leatherhead.
Mrs G. Marden, Leatherhead.
Professor Gerald Mars, London.
Dr Valerie Mars, London.
Laura Mason, York.
Stephen W. Massil, London.
Tessa McKirdy, Rottingdean.
Patricia Michelson, London. UK.
Janny de Moor, Harde, Netherlands.
Araminta Morris, Frilford.
Mrs Freda Morrow Brown, Derby.
Dr Harry Morrow Brown, Derby.
Carolyn Nadeau, Bloomington, IL, USA.
David Natt, London.
Lizabeth Nicol, Saint Augustin, France.
Shirley Olivier, Hove.
Roger Owen, London.
Sri Owen, London.
Gaitri Pagrach-Chandra, Tricht, Netherlands.

Helen Peacocke, Eynsham.
Marcia L. Pelchat, Philadelphia, PA, USA.
Dorothea A. Pelham, Oxford.
Elia Petridou, London.
Gae Pincus, Glebe, Australia.
Hawys Pritchard, Cowbridge.
Gillian Riley, Rottingdean.
Alicia Rios Ivars, Madrid, Spain.
Luciana Romeri, Santo Antônio, Brazil.
Dr Barry S. Rose, Davenham.
Mrs Brenda S. Rose, Davenham.
Judith Pierce Rosenberg, Palo Alto, CA, USA.
Lynn Rubright, St Louis, MO, USA.
Robert Rubright, St Louis, MO, USA.
Ann Rycraft, York.
Alison Ryley, Huntingdon, NY, USA.
Helen J. Saberi, London.
Rena Salaman, London.
Alice Wooledge Salmon, London.
Shlomith Samish, Hebrew University of Jerusalem, Israel.
Dan M. Schickentanz, Witney.
David E. Schoonover, The University of Iowa, USA.
Liz Seeber, Barcombe.
Maria José Sevilla, London.
Margaret Shaida, Engordany, Andorra.
Marjorie Shaw, London.
Colin Spencer, Winchelsea.
Zona Spray, Hudson, OH, USA.
Rosemary Stark, London.
Grant Starks, Hudson, OH, USA.
Jeffrey L. Steingarten, New York, USA.
David Sutton, S. Illinois University, USA.
Dr Layinka M. Swinburne, Leeds.
Anne Tait, Sherborne.
Malcolm Thick, Didcot.
Sue Shephard, Bristol.
Mimi Sheraton, New York, USA.
Leslie Cory Shoemaker, Marquette, MI, USA.
Birgit Siesby, Virum, Denmark.
Helen J. Simpson, Eardisland.
Anne Skillion, New York, USA.
Andrew F. Smith, New York, USA.
Raymond Sokolov, New York, USA.
Jan Thompson, Chicago, IL, USA.
Dr Renée Valeri, Lund, Switzerland.
Pat Van Den Wall Bake-Thompson, Amsterdam, Netherlands.
Alex Veness, London.
Jennifer Walker, Reading.
Harlan Walker, Birmingham.
Phyllis Weaver, Englewood, NJ, USA.
Robin Weir, London.
Barbara A. West, University of the Pacific, USA.
Barbara Ketcham Wheaton, Concord, MA, USA.
Faith Heller Willinger, Florence, Italy.
Bee Wilson, Cambridge.
Mary Wondrausch OBE, Guildford.
Caroline Yeldham, Stevenage.
Carolin C. Young, New York, USA.
Sue Young, Paris, France.
Su-Mei Yu, La Jolla, CA, USA.
Dr Theodore Zeldin, Oxford.
Sami Zubaida, London.